PHILIP'S · **OS Ordnance Survey®**

ST LAS
Warwickshire

First published 1995 by

Philip's, a division of
Octopus Publishing Group Ltd
2–4 Heron Quays, London E14 4JP

Second colour edition 2002
First impression 2002

ISBN 0-540-08126-4

© Philip's 2002

OS Ordnance Survey®

This product includes mapping data licensed from Ordnance Survey® with the permission of the Controller of Her Majesty's Stationery Office. © Crown copyright 2002. All rights reserved. Licence number 100011710

Printed and bound in Spain
by Cayfosa-Quebecor

Contents

III	**Key to map symbols**
IV	**Key to map pages**
VI	**Route planning**
VIII	**Administrative and Postcode boundaries**
1	**Street maps** at 2½ inches to 1 mile
112	**Street maps** at 1¼ inches to 1 mile
143	**Street maps** at 2½ inches to 1 mile
151	**Street map of Coventry city centre** at 5 inches to 1 mile
152	**Town maps** of Banbury and Tamworth
153	**Index** of towns and villages
154	**Index** of streets, hospitals, industrial estates, railway stations, schools, shopping centres, universities and places of interest

Digital Data

The exceptionally high-quality mapping found in this atlas is available as digital data in TIFF format, which is easily convertible to other bit mapped (raster) image formats.

The index is also available in digital form as a standard database table. It contains all the details found in the printed index together with the National Grid reference for the map square in which each entry is named.

For further information and to discuss your requirements, please contact Philip's on 020 7531 8439 or george.philip@philips-maps.co.uk

	Motorway with junction number
	Primary route – dual/single carriageway
	A road – dual/single carriageway
	B road – dual/single carriageway
	Minor road – dual/single carriageway
	Other minor road – dual/single carriageway
	Road under construction
	Pedestrianised area
DY7	**Postcode boundaries**
	County and unitary authority boundaries
	Railway, railway under construction
	Tramway, tramway under construction
	Miniature railway
	Rural track, private road or narrow road in urban area
	Gate or obstruction to traffic (restrictions may not apply at all times or to all vehicles)
	Path, bridleway, byway open to all traffic, road used as a public path
	The representation in this atlas of a road, track or path is no evidence of the existence of a right of way
231 84	**Adjoining page indicators** (The colour of the arrow indicates the scale of the adjoining page - see scales below)
173 165 246 203	**Adjoining page indicator** showing the pages adjoining the top and bottom halves of the current page
	The map areas within the pink/blue bands are shown at a larger scale on the page, indicated by the red/blue blocks and arrows

Walsall	**Railway station**
	Private railway station
West Bromwich Central	**Metro station**
	Tram stop
	Bus, coach station
	Ambulance station
	Coastguard station
	Fire station
	Police station
+	**Accident and Emergency entrance to hospital**
H	**Hospital**
+	**Place of worship**
i	**Information Centre** (open all year)
P	**Parking**
P&R	**Park and Ride**
PO	**Post Office**
	Camping site
	Caravan site
	Golf course
	Picnic site
Prim Sch	**Important buildings, schools, colleges, universities and hospitals**
River Medway	**Water name**
	River, stream
	Lock, weir
	Water
	Tidal water
	Woods
	Built up area
Church	**Non-Roman antiquity**
ROMAN FORT	**Roman antiquity**

Acad	**Academy**	Inst	**Institute**	Recn Gd	**Recreation Ground**
Allot Gdns	**Allotments**	Ct	**Law Court**		
Cemy	**Cemetery**	L Ctr	**Leisure Centre**	Resr	**Reservoir**
C Ctr	**Civic Centre**	LC	**Level Crossing**	Ret Pk	**Retail Park**
CH	**Club House**	Liby	**Library**	Sch	**School**
Coll	**College**	Mkt	**Market**	Sh Ctr	**Shopping Centre**
Crem	**Crematorium**	Meml	**Memorial**	TH	**Town Hall/House**
Ent	**Enterprise**	Mon	**Monument**	Trad Est	**Trading Estate**
Ex H	**Exhibition Hall**	Mus	**Museum**	Univ	**University**
Ind Est	**Industrial Estate**	Obsy	**Observatory**	Wks	**Works**
IRB Sta	**Inshore Rescue**	Pal	**Royal Palace**	YH	**Youth Hostel**
	Boat Station	PH	**Public House**		

■ The small numbers around the edges of the maps identify the 1 kilometre National Grid lines ■ The dark grey border on the inside edge of some pages indicates that the mapping does not continue onto the adjacent page

The scale of the maps on the pages numbered in blue is 3.92 cm to 1 km • 2½ inches to 1 mile • 1: 25344	0 ¼ ½ ¾ 1 mile / 0 250m 500m 750m 1 kilometre
The scale of the maps on pages numbered in green is 1.96 cm to 1 km • 1¼ inches to 1 mile • 1: 50688	0 ¼ ½ ¾ 1 mile / 0 250m 500m 750m 1kilometre
The scale of the maps on pages numbered in red is 7.84 cm to 1 km • 5 inches to 1 mile • 1: 12672	0 220 yards 440 yards 660 yards ½ mile / 0 125m 250m 375m ½ kilometre

IV

Key to map pages

Map pages at 5 inches to 1 mile
151

Map pages at 2½ inches to 1 mile
150

Map pages at 1¼ inches to 1 mile
142

Leicestershire STREET ATLAS

Derbyshire STREET ATLAS

Staffordshire STREET ATLAS

Birmingham & West Midlands STREET ATLAS

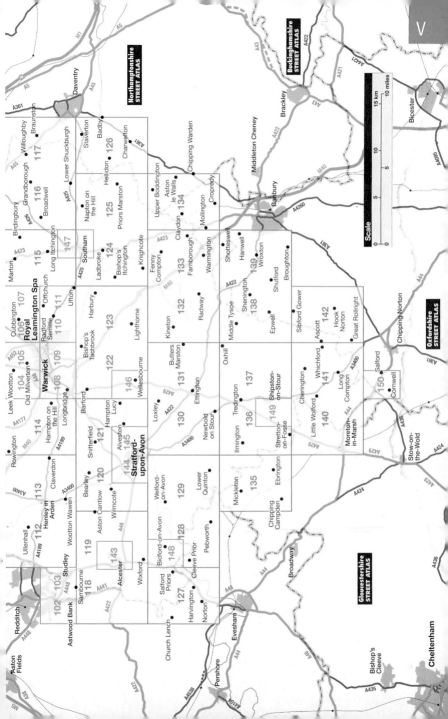

Route planning

Scale

0 1 2 3 4 5 6 7 8 km
0 1 2 3 4 5 miles

Major administrative and
Postcode boundaries

County and unitary
authority boundaries
District boundaries
.... Postcode boundaries
Area covered by this atlas

Scale
0   5   10   15 km
0   5   10 miles

Staffordshire

Walsall
SK
SP

Birmingham

Solihull

Worcestershire

Gloucestershire

Leicestershire

Northamptonshire

Oxfordshire

B79
DE12
Newton
Regis
Warton
Orton-on-
the-Hill
B77
B75
B78
Kingsbury
Atherstone
CV13
Stoke
Golding
B76
Curdworth
North
Warwickshire
Hinckley
LE9
B35
B46
Ansley
Nuneaton
CV10
CV11
LE10
B36
Coleshill
Nuneaton and
Bedworth
Wolvey
B37
Fillongley
CV12
Bedworth
Shilton
LE17
B26
B40
CV7
Hampton in
Arden
CV5
CV6
CV2
Monks
Kirby
B91
B92
Allesley
CV1
Coventry
Coventry
Brinklow
B47
B90
Cheswick Green
Balsall
Common
CV4
CV3
Binley
Woods
Wolston
CV21
Rugby
B93
Rugby
B48
Tanworth-in-
Arden
B94
Kingswood
Kenilworth
CV8
Frankton
CV22
Dunchurch
B98
CV23
Grandborough
Henley-in-
Arden
Warwickshire
Braunston
B97
B80
Studley
B95
Norton
Lindsey
Warwick
CV32
CV34
Royal
Leamington Spa
Long
Itchington
Flecknoe
B96
Wootton
Wawen
Whitnash
CV31
Southam
Staverton
B49
Alcester
Wilmcote
Barford
Harbury
CV33
Bishop's
Itchington
Priors
Marston
NN11
WR7
Stratford-
upon-Avon
CV35
Wellesbourne
CV47
Bidford-on-
Avon
Welford-
on-Avon
Fenny
Compton
B50
CV37
Stratford-on-
Avon
Kineton
WR11
Lower
Quinton
Ettington
Warmington
OX17
Middle
Tysoe
Ilmington
Shipston-on-
Stour
OX16
GL55
CV36
OX15
Stourton
Moreton-in-
Marsh
Long
Compton
Hook
Norton
GL56
OX7

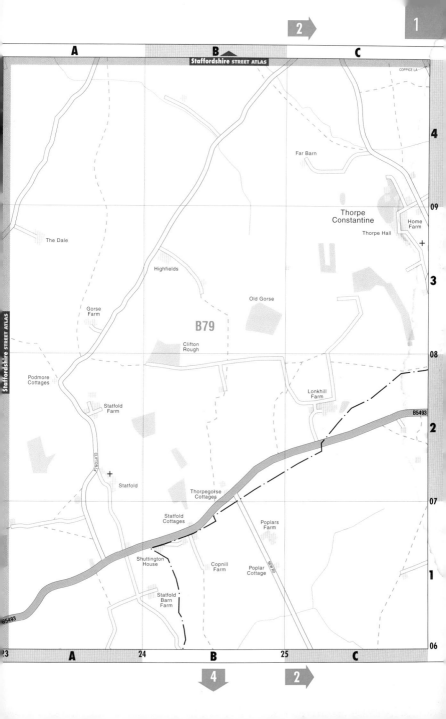

COPPICE LA

4

Far Barn

09

Thorpe
Constantine

Home
Farm

The Dale

Thorpe Hall

+

Highfields

3

Old Gorse

Gorse
Farm

B79

Clifton
Rough

08

Podmore
Cottages

Lonkhill
Farm

Statfold
Farm

B5493

2

CLIFTON LA

Statfold

+

Thorpegorse
Cottages

07

Statfold
Cottages

Poplars
Farm

Shuttington
House

Copnill
Farm

Poplar
Cottage

B5493

1

B5493

Statfold
Barn
Farm

06

A

B

C

Leicestershire STREET ATLAS

QUARRY BERRY LA
Honeyhill
Farm

DE12

Campville
House

Newton
Field

Highfield
Farm

4

Big Meadow
Hovel

B5493
 AUSTREY LA

09

Sandy Lane
Barn

No Man's
Heath

Leys Field
Hovel

SANDY LA

Sandy Lane
Spinney

3

Newton Moor
Cottages

The
Grange

B79

Newton
Gorse

08

ANKER LA

Newton
Regis

TOWNEND CL

B5493

2

Newton
Farm

HAREL LA

PH

HAREL DRI

Newton Regis
CE Prim Sch

AUSTREY LA

+

NEWTON LA

A442

CV9

NEWTON LA

SECKINGTON LA

OLD HALL CT

THE GREEN

Seckington

07

MAIN RD

HARKNELL LA

1

A442

06

26

A

27

B

28

C

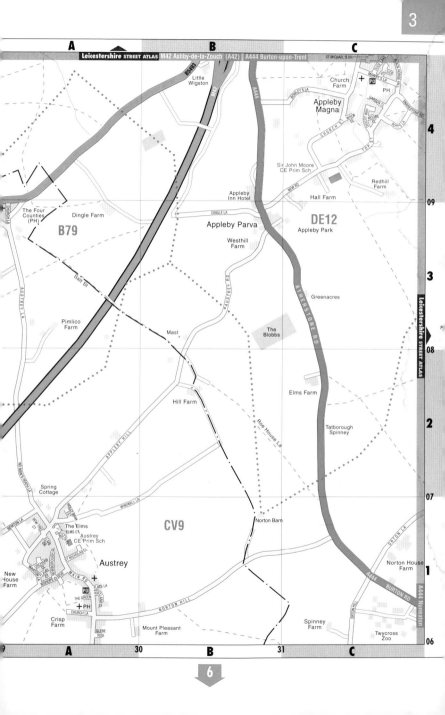

1

A   B   C

Amington Hall

Decoy Barn

Cow Barn

The Decoy

4

Amington
Old Hall

Shuttington
Bridge

Wolferstan Arms
(PH)

Shuttington

Church Farm

05

The Pretty Pigs
(PH)

SHUTTINGTON RD

B79

Alvecote

ALVECOTE
COTTS

Nature
Reserve

Askew
Bridge

Greenacres
Prim Sch

Cemy

Hodge La

Coventry Canal

River Anker

3

Marina

Alvecote
Priory

04

1 SUNNINGDALE
2 MUIRFIELD

Amington

B77

CH

Alvecote
Wood

B78

2

Amington Heath
Com Prim Sch

Quince
Tree Sch

Amber
Bsns
Village

Tamworth
Bshs Pk

Priory
Farm

Works

Pooley
Fields
Heritage
Ctr

Lodge
Farm

B5000

Amington
Ind Est

Mercian
Pk

Tamworth
Bsns Ctr

TAMWORTH

War Meml

Pooley Hall
and remains of
Hall

03

Sch

GLASCOTE RD

B5000

Darwell
Pk

ABBERLEY

Priory
Farm

B42

B50

1

FARINGTON

PENNINE WAY

B5000

Stoneydelph
La

Sports
Gd

TAMWORTH RD

The
Hermitage

Playing
Field
Stoneydelph
Prim Sch

02

23   A   24   B   25   C

10

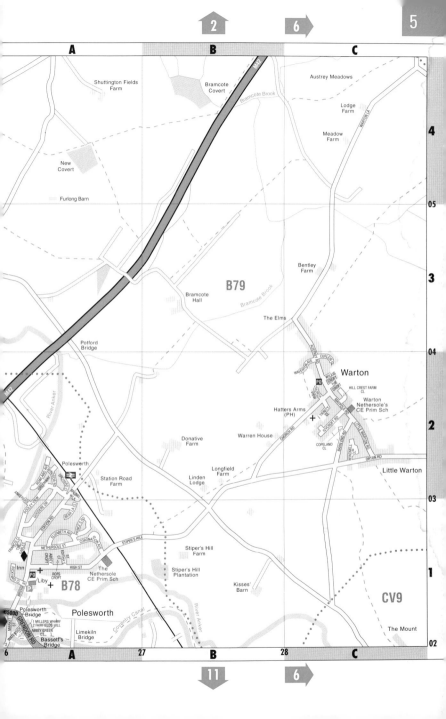

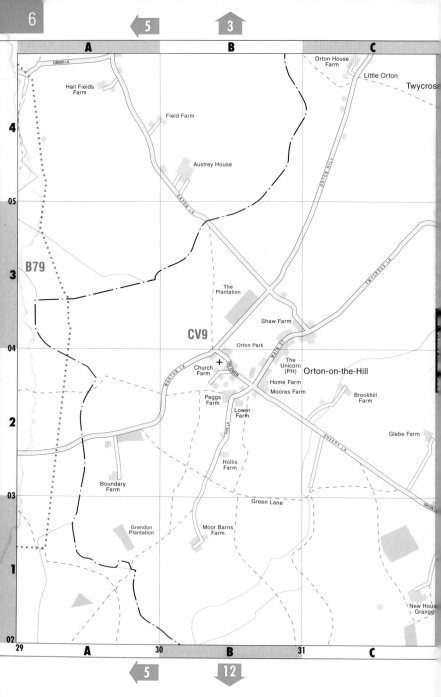

A
B
C

CINDER LA

Hall Fields
Farm

Field Farm

4

Austrey House

ORTON LA

05

Orton House
Farm

Little Orton

Twycross

ORTON HILL

TWYCROSS LA

B79

3

The
Plantation

Shaw Farm

CV9

Orton Park

The Unicorn
(PH)

Orton-on-the-Hill

Church
Farm

MANOR LA

THE GREEN

Home Farm

MAIN ST

Moores Farm

Brookhill
Farm

Peggs
Farm

Lower
Farm

2

PIPE LA

SHEEPY LA

Glebe Farm

ORTON L

Hollis
Farm

Boundary
Farm

03

Green Lane

Grendon
Plantation

Moor Barns
Farm

1

New Hous
Grange

02

29
A
30
B
31
C

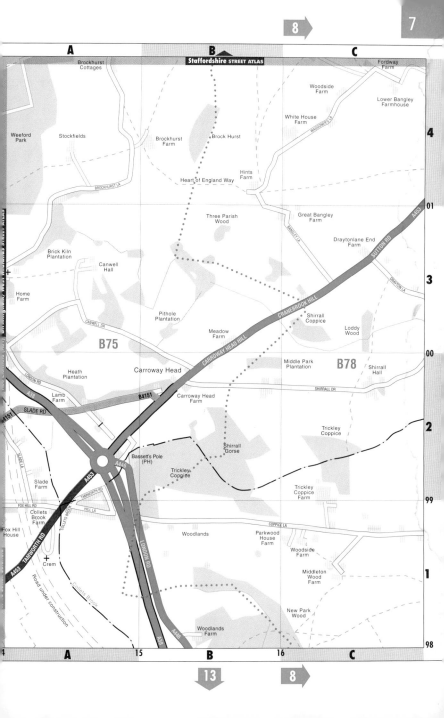

Staffordshire STREET ATLAS

Brockhurst
Cottages

Fordway
Farm

Woodside
Farm

Lower Bangley
Farmhouse

White House
Farm

WAGGONER'S LA

Weeford
Park

Stockfields

Brockhurst
Farm

Brock Hurst

4

BROCKHURST LA

Hints
Farm

Heart of England Way

Great Bangley
Farm

01

Three Parish
Wood

BANGLEY LA

Draytonlane End
Farm

SUTTON RD

A453

Brick Kiln
Plantation

Canwell
Hall

DRAYTON LA

3

Home
Farm

CANWELL DR

Pithole
Plantation

CRANEBROOK HILL

Shirrall
Coppice

Loddy
Wood

Meadow
Farm

B75

CARROWAY HEAD HILL

Middle Park
Plantation

B78

Shirrall
Hall

00

Heath
Plantation

Carroway Head

LONDON RD

SHIRRALL DR

Lamb
Farm

A38

SLADE RD

B4151

Carroway Head
Farm

Trickley
Coppice

2

A4151

SLADE LA

Bassett's Pole
(PH)

A446

Shirrall
Gorse

Trickley
Coppice

Slade
Farm

TAMWORTH RD

Trickley
Coppice

Trickley
Coppice
Farm

FOX HILL RD

HILL LA

99

COLLETS BRIDGE

Collets
Brook
Farm

COPPICE LA

Fox Hill
House

Woodlands

Parkwood
House
Farm

Woodside
Farm

A453 TAMWORTH RD

Crem

LONDON RD

Middleton
Wood
Farm

1

Road under construction

Collets Brook

New Park
Wood

A446

Woodlands
Farm

98

A453 Tamworth

New House
Farm

BANGLEY LA

SUTTON RD

A453

Mile Oak

KIRKLAND WAY

GAINSBOROUGH HILL

CRANWELL RISE

Bourne
Bridge

Alder
Wood

Bourne Brook

Bourne Brook Cut

Seventeen Acre
Wood

Duck
Decoy

Lodge Farm

Hill Farm

Fazeley

YORKSAND RD
REINDEER RD

DAMA RD

MAYAMA RD

DRAYTON MANOR DR

SHELLDUCK DR

Longwood
House

Works

Drayton Manor
Park

CH

Drayton
Park

COLESHILL RD

A4091

Longwood
Stables

Heathley
Farm

HENNETTA

Bullocks End
Farm

Edden's
Wood

Drayton
Bassett

Oak Farm
Craft Ctr

Heart of England Way

DRAYTON LA

IMPERIAL DR

Stone House

Ashdene Farm

B78

OLD MANOR CL

MALT DR

CHURCH CL

PD

PEEL CL

NEW RD

RECTORY CL

SALTS LA

EDENS WOOD CL

Manor
Prim Sch
Sewage
Works

Drayton
Brick
Bridge

PORTLEYS LA

Brook Farm

Brook End
Farm

Birmingham and Fazeley Canal

Heart of Engla

Upper House
Farm

Gallows Brook

COPPICE LA

Quarry

Mill
Plantation

Middleton

Middleton
Park

Newhouse
Farm

DOSTHILL

The Green Man
(PH)

PD

VICARAGE HILL

CHURCH LA

Highfields
Farm

Walker's
Spinney

Sewage
Works

Langley Brook

CROXHILL LA

Park-gate
Farm

A4091

Middleton
Pool

Middleton
Hall

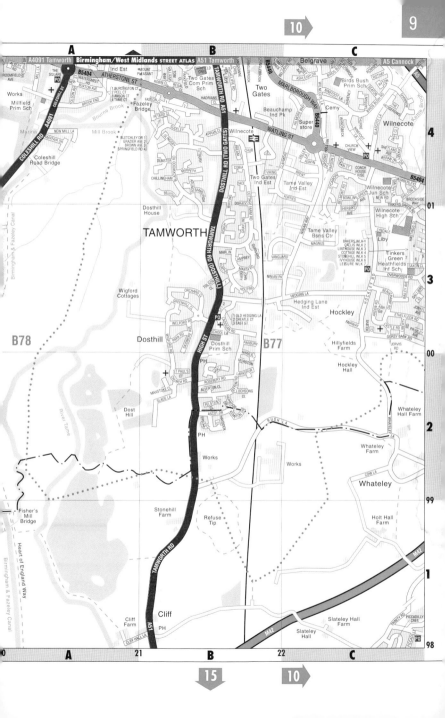

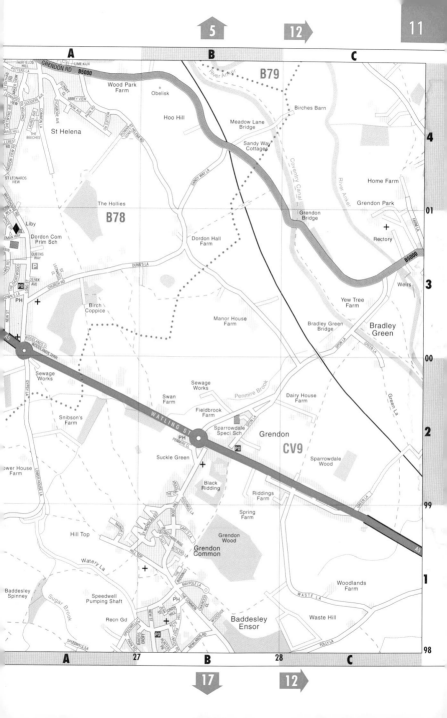

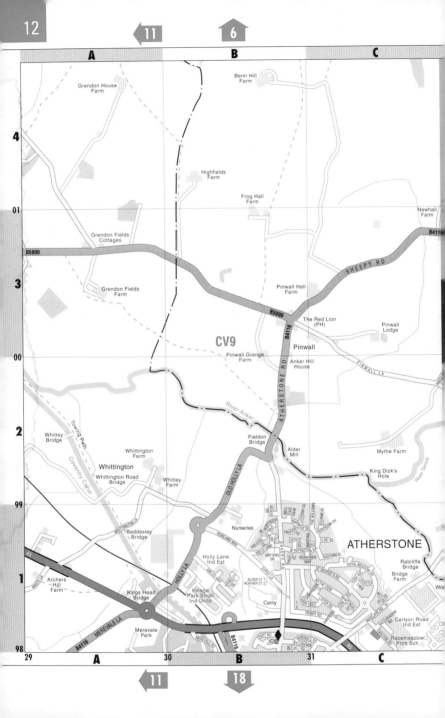

A   **B**   **C**

Grendon House Farm

Benn Hill Farm

4

Highfields Farm

Frog Hall Farm

01

Newhall Farm

B4116

Grendon Fields Cottages

B5000

SHEEPY RD

3

Grendon Fields Farm

Pinwall Hall Farm

B5000

The Red Lion (PH)

Pinwall Lodge

CV9

B4116

ATHERSTONE RD

Pinwall

00

Pinwall Grange Farm

Anker Hill House

PINWALL LA

River Anker

Whitley Bridge

Towing Path

Whittington Farm

Fieldon Bridge

Alder Mill

Mythe Farm

River Sence

2

Coventry Canal

Whittington

Whittington Road Bridge

Whitley Farm

OLD POLLY LA

King Dick's Hole

99

Whittington La

Baddesley Bridge

ROWLAND WAY

Nurseries

ATHERSTONE

Ratcliffe Bridge

A5

Holly Lane Ind Est

HATTERS DR

SHEEPY RD

Bridge Farm

1

Archers Hill Farm

HOLLY LA

Innage Pack Small Ind Units

ALDER CT 1
HEATHER CT 2

GYPSY LA

Cemy

Carlyon Road Ind Est

Kings Head Bridge

B4116

MEREVALE LA

Merevale Park

MEREVALE RD

B4116

SOFT RD

A5

Racemeadow Prim Sch

98

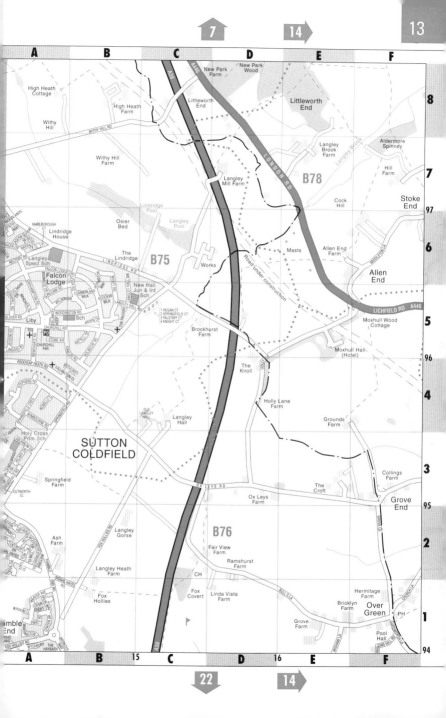

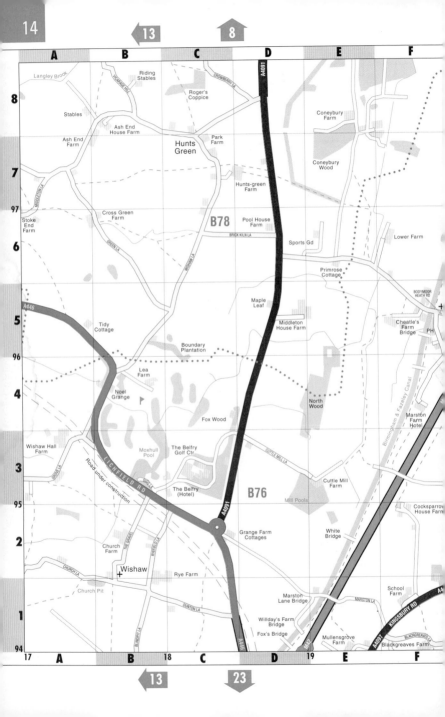

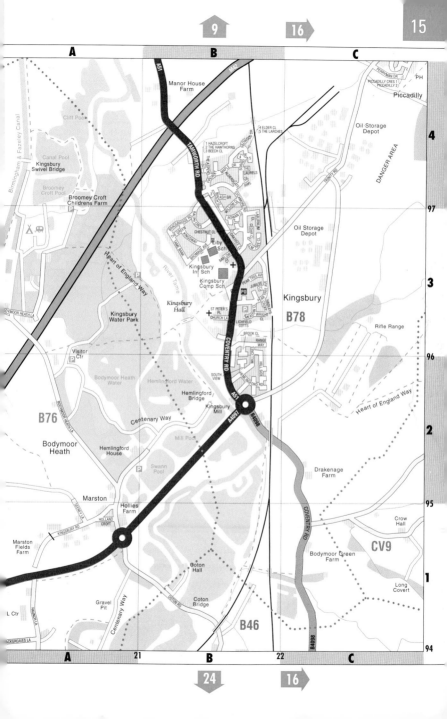

A B C

A 21 B 22 C

4

97

3

96

2

95

1

94

Birmingham & Fazeley Canal

A51

Manor House Farm

Cliff Pool

Canal Pool
Kingsbury Swivel Bridge

Broomey Croft Pool

Broomey Croft Childrens Farm

TAMWORTH RD

1 HAZELCROFT
2 THE HAWTHORNS
3 BEECH CL

4 ELDER CL
5 THE LARCHES

THE LAURELS

ASH GR

CHESTNUT CL

Liby Sch

ROWAN

Kingsbury Inf Sch

Kingsbury Comp Sch

PEAR TREE AVE

JUBILEE

PO

Kingsbury

B78

Oil Storage Depot

DANGER AREA

PERRYMAN DR
PICCADILLY CRES 1
PICCADILLY 2

PH

Piccadilly

Oil Storage Depot

TRINITY RD

Heart of England Way

River Tame

Kingsbury Water Park

Kingsbury Hall

St PETER'S PL
CHURCH LA

LICHFIELD COTTS

GLASS WRIGHT CL

Rifle Range

BROOK CL

RANGE WAY

Visitor Ctr

P

Bodymoor Heath Water

Hemlingford Water

SOUTH VIEW

Heart of England Way

B76

Bodymoor Heath

Hemlingford House

Hemlingford Bridge

Kingsbury Mill

Centenary Way

A51

A4097

B4098

Mill Pool

Swann Pool

Drakenage Farm

COVENTRY RD

Marston

Hollies Farm

HOLLAND CROFT

KINGSBURY RD

Marston Fields Farm

Coton Hall

Coton Bridge

Gravel Pit

Centenary Way

COTON RD

B46

Bodymoor Green Farm

COVENTRY RD

B4098

CV9

Crow Hall

Long Covert

L Ctr

BACKGREAVES LA

HURLEY LA

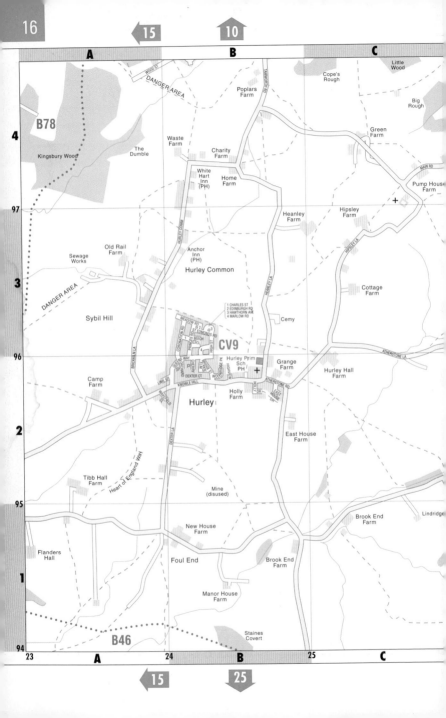

A
B
C

Coopers Grove

SPEEDWELL LA

NEWLANDS RD
BEAZLEY RD
ALLENS CL

1 ROTHERHAMS HILL
2 WALNUT CROFT

Grendon Wood

FOLLY LA

Baddesley Common

White's Farm

Long Wood

Colliery Farm

Rose Farm

Baxterley Hall Farm

Baddesley Colliery (dis)

The Alders

B4116

MEREVALE LA

4

MAIN RD

THE ORCHARD
THE ORCHARD

Swans Wood Farm

97

Charity Farm

Kiddle's Farm

Baxterley

The Rose Inn (PH)

Holly Park Spinney

SMYTHE RD

Malt House Farm

WINDMILL LA

TWENTY ONE OAKS

Drybrooks Wood

Drybrookes Farm

WIGSTON HILL

3

Bentley Common

Old Hall Farm

CV9

Wheatleys Wood

School Farm

Bentley Common

ATHERSTONE LA

Boult Bee's Farm

Monks Park Wood

96

Captains Wood

Crawshaws

Horse & Jockey (PH)

Bentley

Kimberley Hall Farm

Simon de Blyth's Wood

Square Wood

Epps Farm

2

Lloyds Coppice

Bentley Park Wood

Nightingale's Wood

95

Cottage Farm

Nightingale's Farm

Bentley Hall Farm

Broomfield Farm

Birchley Heath

THE BOOKERY

PO

Centenary Way

CV10

1

Malthouse Farm

Bentley Bar

BRICHLEY HEATH

Birchley Farm

Chapel Farm

B4116

Butler's Wood

BREACH LA

Batefield Wood

94

A
27
B
28
C

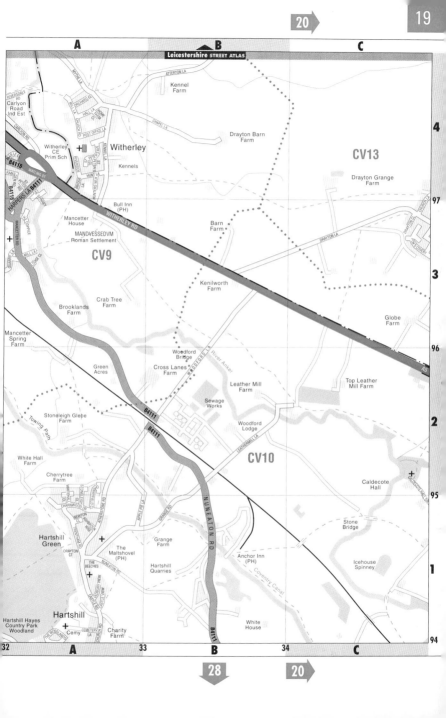

4

RIVERSDALE RD
Carlyon Road Ind Est
CARLYON RD
MITRE LA
ATTERTON LA
ORCHARD CL
HALL LA
POST OFFICE LA
CHAPEL LA

Kennel Farm

Drayton Barn Farm

CV13

B4110
B4110 HARPERS LA B4111
RAMAR
WATLING ST
Witherley CE Prim Sch
Witherley
PETERS LA
HUNT LA
Kennels

Drayton Grange Farm

97

Bull Inn (PH)
WITHERLEY RD
MANCETTER RD
COPPICE
MILL LA
OLDE CL
Mancetter House
MANDVESSEDVM Roman Settlement
CV9

Barn Farm

DRAYTON LA

3

Kenilworth Farm

Crab Tree Farm

Brooklands Farm

Globe Farm

Mancetter Spring Farm

96

Green Acres
Woodford Bridge
Cross Lanes Farm
River Anker
WADDOFT LA

Leather Mill Farm

Top Leather Mill Farm

A5

2

B4111
Stoneleigh Glebe Farm
Towing Path

Sewage Works

Woodford Lodge

LEATHERMILL LA

CV10

B4111
White Hall Farm
Cherrytree Farm
WHITACRE DELL
STONE LEIGH
CHARNWOOD
NEWTON CL
DRAYTON CT
Hartshill Green
The Maltshovel (PH)
THE BEECHES
NUNEATON RD
BIRKDALE RD
NEW RD
CASTLE CROFT

Grange Farm

Caldecote Hall
CALDECOTE LA

95

NUNEATON RD

Anchor Inn (PH)

Stone Bridge

Icehouse Spinney

1

Hartshill Quarries

Hartshill Hayes Country Park Woodland
Hartshill
Cemy
CEMETERY LA
THE HIGHLANDS
Charity Farm

B4111

White House

Coventry Canal

94

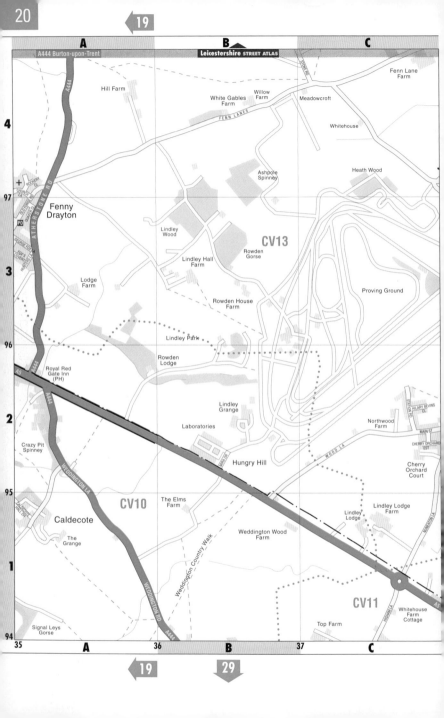

19

A444 Burton-upon-Trent

Leicestershire STREET ATLAS

A444

Fenn Lane Farm

Hill Farm

White Gables Farm

Willow Farm

Meadowcroft

STOKE RD

Whitehouse

4

FENN LANES

Heath Wood

Ashpole Spinney

97

Fenny Drayton

ATHERSTONE RD

Lindley Wood

Rowden Gorse

CV13

Lindley Hall Farm

Proving Ground

3

Lodge Farm

Rowden House Farm

Lindley Park

96

Rowden Lodge

A5

Royal Red Gate Inn (PH)

Lindley Grange

STATION RD

HILARY BEVINS CL

Northwood Farm

MAIN ST

A444

2

Laboratories

BENS DR

CHERRY ORCHARD EST

Crazy Pit Spinney

Hungry Hill

WOOD LA

Cherry Orchard Court

95

WEDDINGTON LA

CV10

The Elms Farm

Lindley Lodge Farm

WINDMILL LA

Caldecote

Lindley Lodge

The Grange

Weddington Wood Farm

Weddington Country Walk

1

A5

WEDDINGTON RD

CV11

Whitehouse Farm Cottage

Signal Leys Gorse

A444

Top Farm

94

35   A   **36**   B   **37**   C

19   29

A B C

STAPLETON LA

THE GREEN

STOKE LA

TODOLINGTON LA

Fox Covert Farm

Grange Farm

Marina

Ivy House Farm

Lodge Farm

UPTON LA

Willow Park Ind Est

Crown Hill

Crown Hill Farm

CHURCH

ROSE WAY

WHITEMOORS CL

St Martin's Convent

St Martin's RC High Sch

4

Brook Farm

STATION RD

BLACKWATERFIELD

CHURCH WLK

PO

ST MAGRET'S

SHERWOOD RD

GREENWOOD

HINCKLEY RD

Higham Fields Court

Stoke Golding

CEMY

TITHE CL

STONEY RD

PH

St Margaret's CE Prim Sch

FINE CL

OAKS

Stoke Fields Farm

STOKE LA

97

Willow Farm

Brook House

Brook Farm

CV13

Millfield Farm

Highfield Farm

3

Cuckoos Nest Farm

Compass Fields Farm

Oaklands

Oak Tree Farm

Basin Bridge Farm

Ashby-de-la-Zouch Canal

Basin Bridge

Wykin Fields

96

STOKE LA

Vale Farm

BASIN BRIDGE LA

The Hollows

Spring Hill Farm

Manor Farm

HIGHAM LA

Leicestershire STREET ATLAS

Higham on the Hill CE Prim Sch

Church Farm

PH

MAIN ST

Hall Farm

HINCKLEY LA

Higham on the Hill

Higham Hall

Towing Path

Wykin House Farm

HIGHAM LA

Wykin

Wykin Hall

2

PO

BASIL LA

LE10

A47 Leicester

95

Grange Farm

Harper's Hill

Higham Grange

Higham Thorns

NORMANDY WAY

OUTLANDS DR

1

Change Brook

Higham Gorse

Hijaz Coll

FLORIAN WAY

MARYWELL CL 1
LOSSIEMOUTH RD 2
BRASCOTE RD 3
LOVETTS CL 4

Hollow Farm

CV11

A5

Works

A47

94

A 39 B 40 C

SUTTON
COLDFIELD

Peddimore
Hall

The
Cottage

Vine
Cottage

Wiggins Hill
Cottages

B76

Wiggins Hill
Farm

Hurst Green
Farm

Wiggins Hill
Road Bridge

Birmingham & Fazeley Canal

A4097

Hypermarket

Minworth
Greaves

Kingsbury
Bsns Pk

THE
GREAVES

Minworth
Ind Pk

Liby
Ind Pk

SUTTON
RD

Castle Vale
Ind Est

Metalloys
Ind Est

KINGSBURY RD

Nature Park

B24

Midpoint Park
Ind Est

Minworth

CONEYBURY WLK 1
ARBURY WLK 2

WATER ORTON RD

Minworth Jun
& Inf Sch

ROBINSON'S
WAY

Sewage Works

KINGSBURY RD

Sch

Northolt
Dr Liby

Prim
Sch

Sec
Sch

Castle
Vale

Sch

CRANWELL
WAY

BROOK PIECE WLK

HERCULES
HO

PIONEER
HO

VULCAN
HO

JAVELIN
HO

KESTRAL
HO

B35

Works

1 RYE GRASS WLK
2 ANDOVER HO
3 ORCHARD MEADOW WLK
4 WORTHY DOWN WLK

Castle Vale
Sports Ctr

Parkhall
Wood

B46

BIRMINGHAM RD   B41

Sch

River Tame

Parkhill
Wood

BIRMINGHAM

Langley Hill
Wood

Park Hall
Sch

Lanchester
Park

Forest Oak
Specl Sch

B36

Castle Bromwich
Bsns Pk

M6

M6 5

A452 Brownhills

A452

KYTER

TIDDINGTON

Park Hall
GdNS

HILL HURST GR 1
REDLIFF AVE 2
DELAMERE CL 3

WATER ORTON RD

B118

Bosworth Wood
Prim Sch

AUSTIN CROFT

A2
1 CHIVENOR HO
2 DE HAVILLAND DR
3 HURRICANE WAY
4 KENRICK CROFT
5 SPITFIRE WAY

A3
1 LONG CLOSE WLK
2 WELLINGTON WAY
3 SQUIRES GATE WLK
4 TERNHILL HO

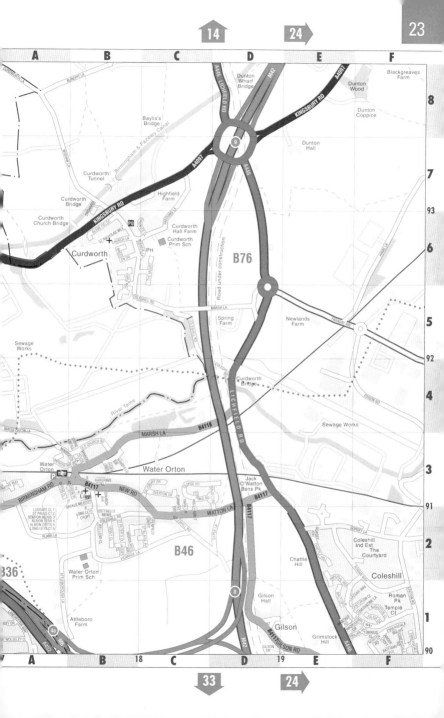

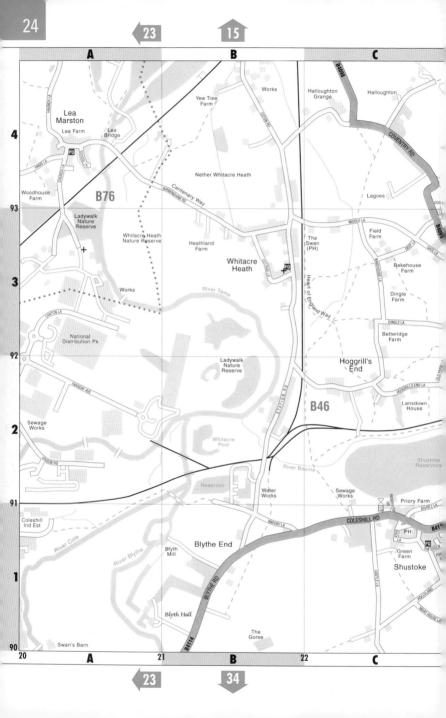

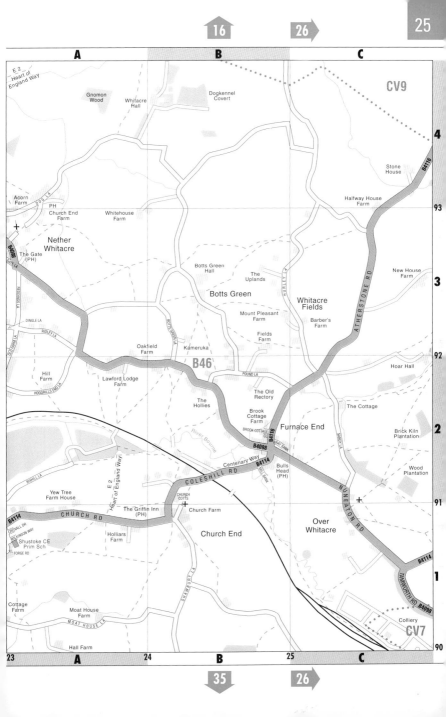

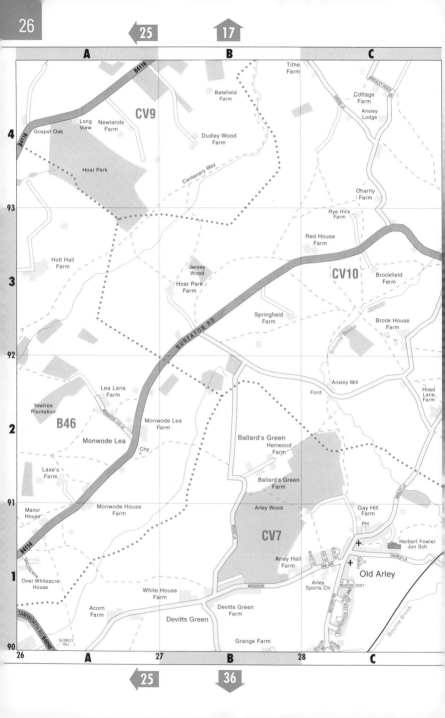

A B C

4

93

3

92

2

91

1

90

B4116

CV9

Gospel Oak

Long View

Newlands Farm

Hoar Park

B4114

Batefield Farm

Dudley Wood Farm

Centenary Way

Tithe Farm

BRICKLEY HEATH RD

GREEN LA

Cottage Farm

Ansley Lodge

Charity Farm

Rye Hills Farm

Red House Farm

CV10

Brookfield Farm

Holt Hall Farm

Jersey Wood

Hoar Park Farm

Springfield Farm

NUNEATON RD

Brook House Farm

Bourne Brook

Yewtree Plantation

B46

Lea Lane Farm

MONWODE LEA LA

Monwode Lea Farm

Monwode Lea

Chy

Ansley Mill

Ford

Hood Lane Farm

Ballard's Green

Henwood Farm

Laxe's Farm

Ballard's Green Farm

Arley Wood

Gay Hill Farm

PH

GREEN LA

Manor House

Monwode House Farm

CV7

Arley Hall Farm

Herbert Fowler Jun Sch

Old Arley

CHURCH LA

BISCO LA

OAK AVE

CHURCH

Arley Sports Ctr

MEADOW CROFT

B4114

SACKLERS WOOD

Over Whiteacre House

Acorn Farm

White House Farm

Devitts Green Farm

Devitts Green

WOODSIDE

BRACEBRIDGE CL

SPRINGS CRES

STATION RD

SPRING HILL

Bourne Brook

TAMWORTH RD

SLOWLEY HILL

Grange Farm

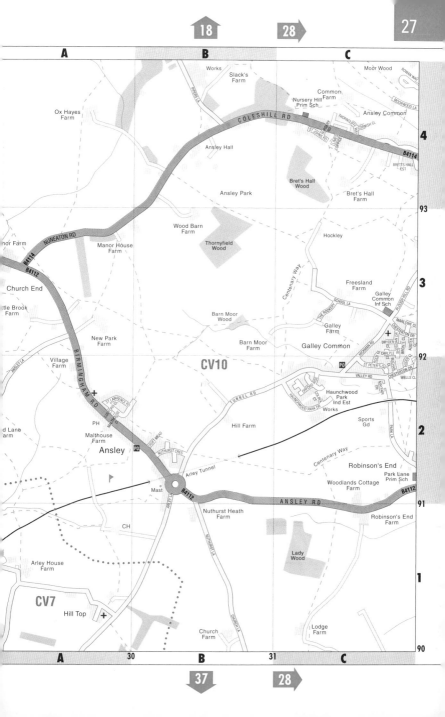

4

93

3

92

2

91

1

90

Works
Slack's Farm
Moor Wood
ROWAN WAY

Common Farm
Nursery Hill Prim Sch
Ansley Common
MOORWOOD LA

Ox Hayes Farm

COLESHILL RD
THORNCLIFFE RD
CUBBISH CL
ST JOHNS RD
B4114

Ansley Hall
BRETTS HALL EST

Ansley Park
Bret's Hall Wood
Bret's Hall Farm

or Farm
NUNEATON RD
Wood Barn Farm
Hockley

B4114
Manor House Farm
Thornyfield Wood
Centenary Way
Freesland Farm
Galley Common Inf Sch

B4112
Church End
THE BOUNDRY
SCHOOL LA
MARLOWE CL

tle Brook Farm
Barn Moor Wood
Galley Farm
CHESTERTON DR
AUSTEN CL
DRYDEN CL
CARLYLE

New Park Farm
Barn Moor Farm
Galley Common
NEWMAN RD
ST PETER'S CL

ANSLEY LA
CV10
VALLEY RD
WELLS CL

Village Farm
PO
CHESTERTON DR

BIRMINGHAM RD
ST LAWRENCE RD
LUNNEL RD
Hill Farm
HAUNCHWOOD PARK DR
CHERRY
Haunchwood Park Ind Est
Works
Sports Gd
PARK LA

d Lane arm
PH
Malthouse Farm
Ansley
PO
NUTHURST CRES
STONE MEAD
Centenary Way
Robinson's End

ARLEY LA
Mast
Arley Tunnel
B4112
Woodlands Cottage Farm
Park Lane Prim Sch
B4112

ANSLEY RD
Robinson's End Farm

CH
Nuthurst Heath Farm
NUTHURST LA
Lady Wood

Arley House Farm

CV7
Church Farm
CHURCH LA
Lodge Farm

Hill Top

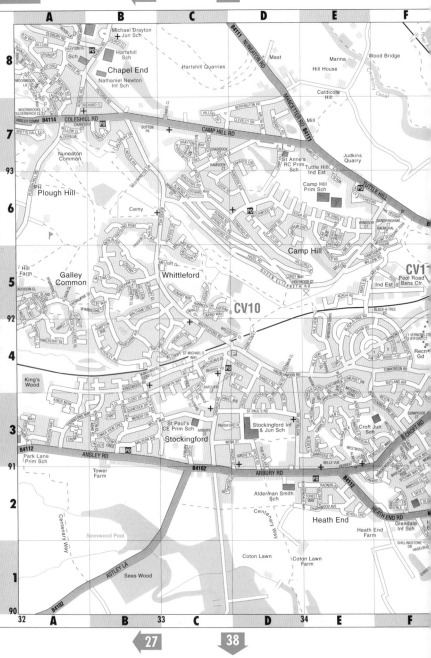

8

7

93

6

5

92

4

3

91

2

1

90

Michael Drayton
Jun Sch

Hartshill
Sch

Chapel End

Nathaniel Newton
Inf Sch

Hartshill Quarries

Mast

Marina

Hill House

Wood Bridge

Caldicote
Hill

COLESHILL RD

CAMP HILL RD

Nuneaton
Common

Plough Hill

Cemy

St Anne's
RC Prim
Sch

Camp Hill
Prim Sch

Judkins
Quarry

Tuttle Hill
Ind Est

TUTTLE HILL

Camp Hill

CV1

Pool Road
Bsns Ctr

Hill
Farm

Galley
Common

Whittleford

CV10

Ind Est

King's
Wood

St Michael's
Way

St Paul's
CE Prim Sch

Stockingford

Stockingford Inf
& Jun Sch

Croft Jun
Sch

Recn
Gd

Park Lane
Prim Sch

ANSLEY RD

ARBURY RD

Tower
Farm

Alderman Smith
Sch

Heath End

Glendale
Inf Sch

Heath End
Farm

Centenary Way

Seeswood Pool

Coton Lawn

Coton Lawn
Farm

ASTLEY LA

Sees Wood

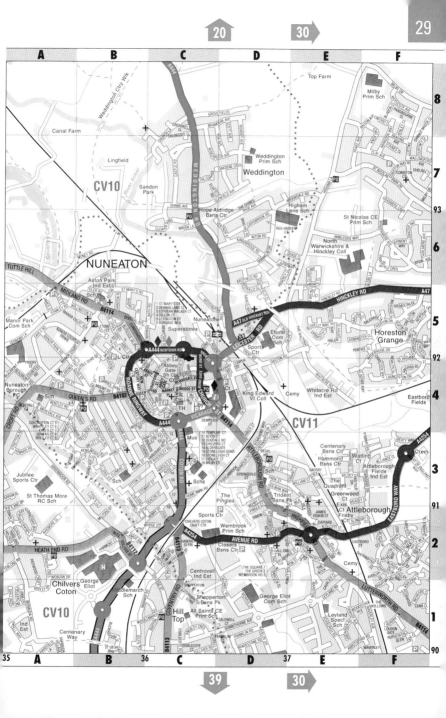

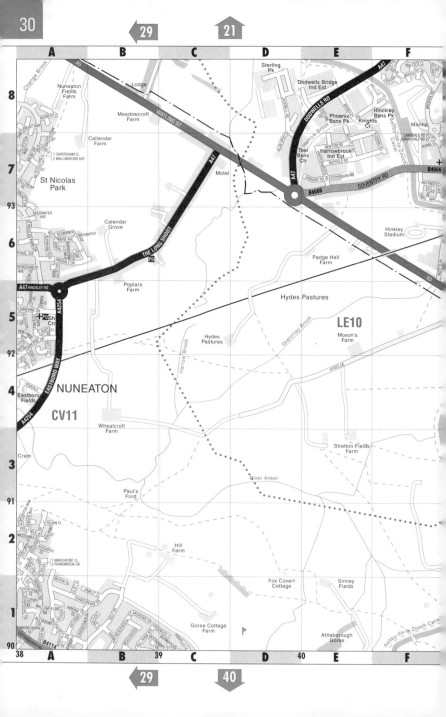

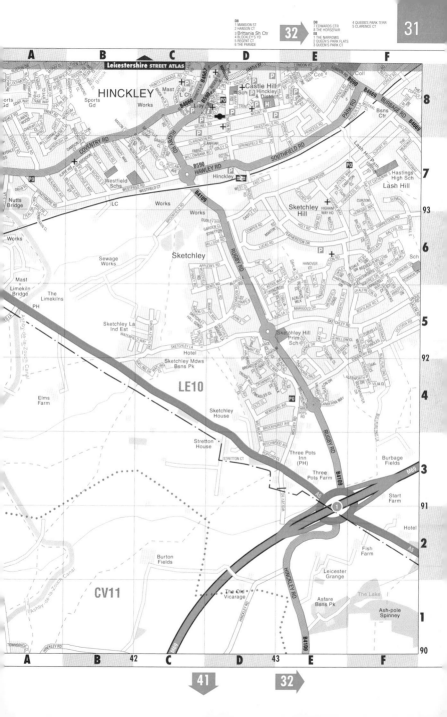

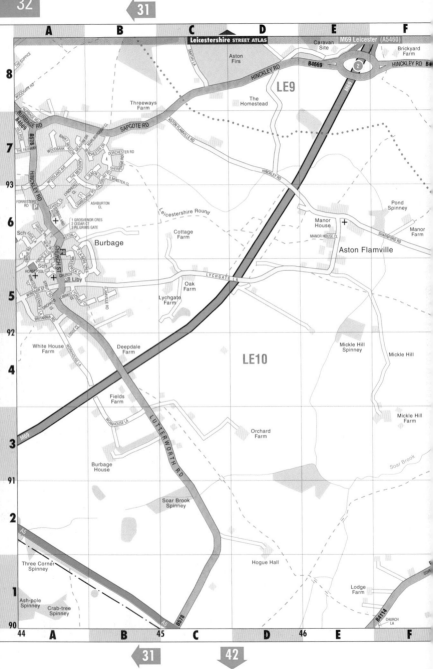

A   B   C   D   E   F

Leicestershire STREET ATLAS

Caravan Site

M69 Leicester (A5460)

Brickyard Farm

Aston Firs

HINCKLEY RD

B4669

HINCKLEY RD B4*

8

LE9

The Homestead

Threeways Farm

SAPCOTE RD

HINCKLEY RD

7

THE FAIRWAY

WOODBANK

DORCHESTER RD

SHERIFF

B578

BURBAGE RD

B4669

HINCKLEY RD

Pond Spinney

93

FORRESTERS RD

ASHBURTON CL

Leicestershire Round

Manor House

Manor Farm

SHARNFORD RD

6

1 GROSVENOR CRES
2 CEDAR CT
3 PILGRIMS GATE

Burbage

Cottage Farm

MANOR HOUSE CL

Aston Flamville

Sch

Sch

HORSEPOOL

CHURCH ST

Liby

Oak Farm

LYCHGATE LA

PO

FLAMVILLE RD

Lychgate Farm

5

WINDSOR RD

BRITANNIA

LONG CL

White House Farm

Deepdale Farm

Mickle Hill Spinney

Mickle Hill

92

LE10

4

Fields Farm

MOORHOUSE LA

Mickle Hill Farm

3

M69

LUTTERWORTH RD

Burbage House

Orchard Farm

Soar Brook

91

Soar Brook Spinney

2

A5

Three Corner Spinney

Hogue Hall

1

Ash-pole Spinney

Crab-tree Spinney

B578

A5

Lodge Farm

B4114

CHURCH LA

COV

90

44   A   B   45   C   D   46   E   F

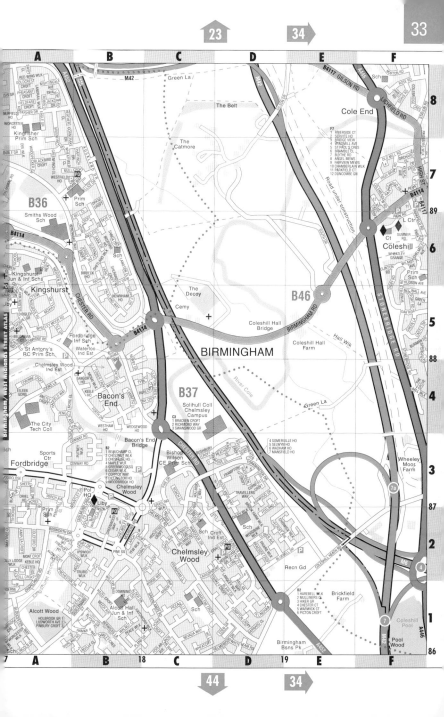

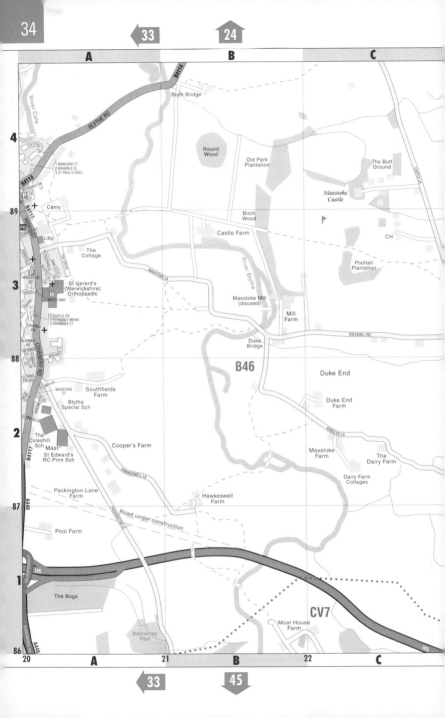

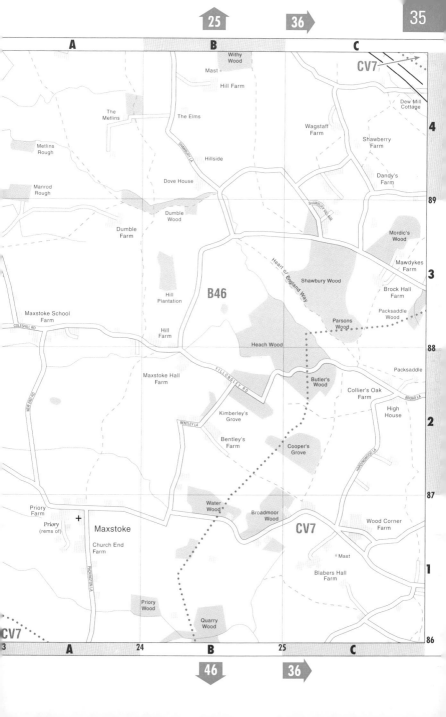

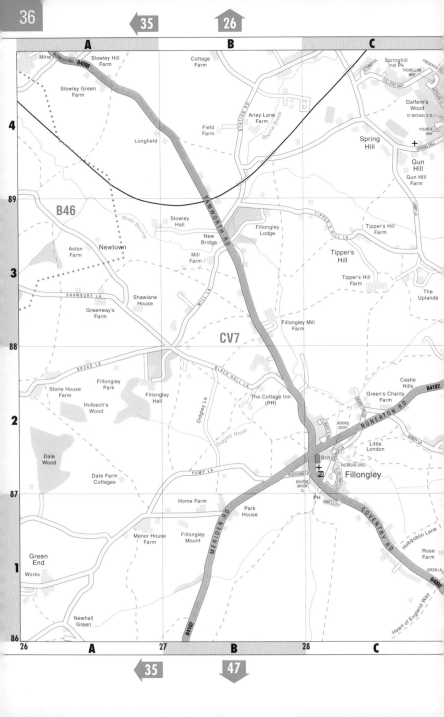

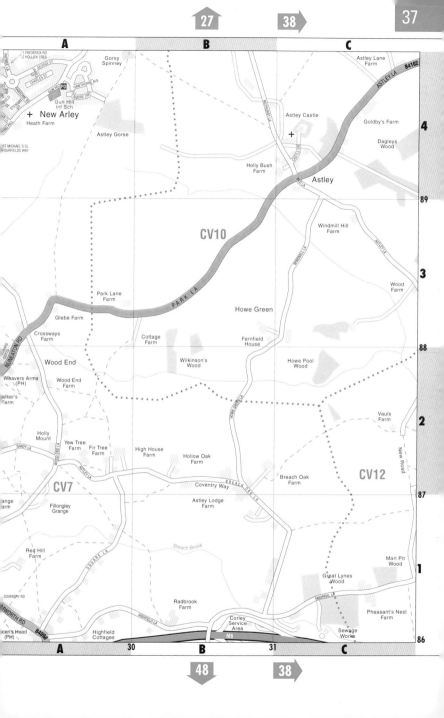

A   B   C

Gorsy Spinney

(1 FREDERICK RD
2 HOLLICK CRES

ST GEORGE ST
CHARLES ST
HAWTHORNE AVE
ELMORE CLO

PO

Gun Hill
Inf Sch

+ New Arley

Heath Farm

ST MICHAEL'S CL
FOURFIELDS WAY

Astley Gorse

Astley Lane Farm

ASTLEY LA   B4102

Astley Castle

+

Holly Bush Farm

Astley

CASTLE DRIVE

Goldby's Farm

Dagleys Wood

4

89

CV10

Windmill Hill Farm

WINDMILL LA

ASTLEY LA

Wood Farm

3

PARK LA

Park Lane Farm

Glebe Farm

Crossways Farm

NUNEATON RD

COTON

Wood End

Weavers Arms (PH)

Wood End Farm

Walker's Farm

Howe Green

Cottage Farm

Fernfield House

Wilkinson's Wood

Howe Pool Wood

88

HOME GREEN LA

Vauls Farm

2

New Road

Holly Mount

SANDY LA

WOOD RD LA

ASTLEY LA

Yew Tree Farm

Fir Tree Farm

High House Farm

Hollow Oak Farm

BREACH OAK LA

Breach Oak Farm

CV12

CV7

range Farm

Fillongley Grange

Coventry Way

Astley Lodge Farm

87

Red Hill Farm

SQUIRE LA

Breach Brook

Great Lynes Wood

Marl Pit Wood

1

COVENTRY RD

NTWORTH RD

en's Head (PH)

B4098

Highfield Cottages

HIGHFIELD LA

Radbrook Farm

Corley Service Area

M6

SMORDAL LA

Sewage Works

Pheasant's Nest Farm

86

A   30   B   31   C

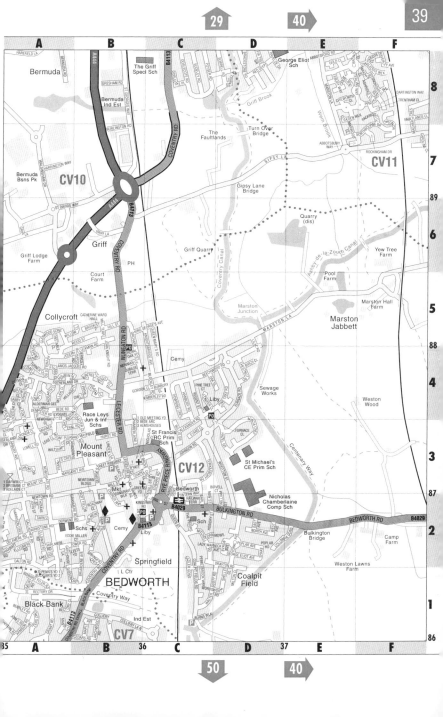

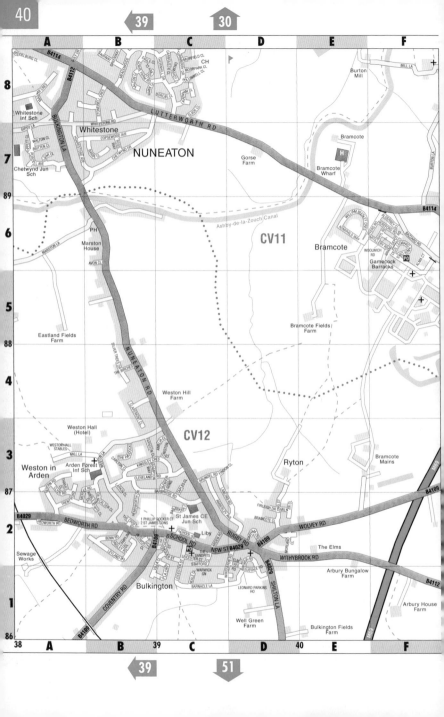

A   B   C

Burton Hastings

Manor Farm

TOWNSENDS CL

HINCKLEY RD

Cottage Farm

Dents Farm

Crossways Farm

Cicey Lane

Burton Fields

B4109

HINCKLEY RD

Abbey Farm

Heath Farm

CV11

Shelford House Farm

Shelford Farm

Shelford Cottage Farm

Anker Bridge

Shelford

Shelford Farm

PH

BISSY LA

B4114

CHADDINGTON LA

FIVE LANE ENDS

FLUDGEX BURGLA

LUTTERWORTH RD

MOAT LA

Wolvey Heath

TEMPLE HILL

LEICESTER RD

MILL LA

HALL ROW

Wolvershill Hall Farm

CH

Mast

BOXGRE RD

River Anker

Wolvey Grange

CHURCH HILL

Hall

PH

HALL LA

HALL RD

CHURCH CL

SCHOOL LA

BULKINGTON RD

B4109

THE SQUARE

Wolvey CE Prim Sch

Wolvey

Hollick Way

KEN DR

ORCHARD CL

MEADOW CL

EW

OX EN DR

BRIDGE LD

B4065

COVENTRY RD

Cemy

WOLDS LA

White House

LE10

Ridgway Farm

Bradley House Farm

CV12

Cottage Farm

Wolvey Villa Farm

Wolvey Fields Farm

Bayton Lodge

Cross Roads

Home Pastures

CV7

B4065

B4112

COAL PIT LA

Breach Cottage

A   42   B   43   C

4

89

3

88

2

87

1

86

A   B   C

4

89

3

88

2

87

1

86

44   A   45   B   46   C

SMOCKINGTON LA

A5

Red Lion Farm

Watling Street Farm

B4114

Smockington Pear Tree Farm

Smockington Farm

B4114

B4114

CHURCH LA

Wigston
+ Parva

A5

High Cross Quarry

Orchard Farm

Copston Lodge Farm

Copston Spinney

MILL LA

CLOUDESLEY BUSH LA

Grange Farm
The Hollies Farm

+

MERE LA

COPSTON LA

Copston Magna

LE10

LE17

Copston Spinney

Copston Fields Farm

Wolvey Lodge Farm

Fosse Way Cottage

WOLDS LA

MERE LA

Grove Farm

CV23

FOSSE WAY

B4455

Wolvey Wolds

Cloudesley Bush

Coal Pit Lane

COAL PIT LA

MONKS LA

CV7

Withybrook Spinney

B4455

Birmingham/West Midlands STREET ATLAS

8

1 EXETER DR
2 WELLS WLK

Marston Green

Marston Green
Jun & Inf Schs

Liby

ELMDON CT

Coleshill Heath

Sports Ctr

TULIP WLK

WHITE BEAM RD

1 NEWINGTON RD
2 FULWELL MEWS

COLESHILL RD

Heath Farm

THE CRESCENT

SOLIHULL PARKWAY

PARK RD

BISHOPS CT

Birmingham Bsns Pk

A452

CHESTER RD

M42

7

85

Bickenhill Rd

School Rough

1 ROTHERBY GR
2 WOLVERTON RD

B37

COLESHILL HEATH RD

Cemy

BLACKFIRS LA.

BICKENHILL PARKWAY

Hotel

B4438

6

Century Pk

STARLEY WAY

Hotel

Bickenhill Plantations

P

P

P

B46

5

84

Low Brook

Eldmon Trad Est

THE STATION RD

P

P
P

EXHIBITION WAY

P
P

NORTH WAY

EXHIBITION WAY

National Exhibition Ctr (The NEC)

B40

EAST CAR PARK RD

4

Birmingham International Airport

AMBASSADOR RD 1
VANGUARD RD 2
STATION LINK RD 3

PEARL RD

HMS RD

BICKENHILL LA

EXETER RD

PERIMETER RD

THE MAIN PASS

Birmingham International

Hotel

Pendigo Lake

PENDIGO WAY

PENDIGO WAY

ELM FIELD

3

83

P

HANGER RD

QUOMISARY RD

TIMBERLAKE RD

Mast

Hotels

B26

HERMES RD

AIRPORT WAY

VIKING RD

P

Depot

B4438

Trinity Pk

GROUND WAY

SOUTH WAY

SOUTH CAR PARK RD

P

P

P

Hotel

Wyckhams Close

A45

6

A45

2

A45 Birmingham

OLD TANNERS LA

CH

Dunston Farm

COVENTRY RD

CLOCK LA

P

The Clock Inn (PH)

CATHERINE DE BARNES LA

OLD TANNERS LA

1

82

The Jungle

Castle Hills

B92

Caravan Park

BICKENHILL GREEN CT

Grange Farm

Bickenhill

B4438

CHERRY LA

ST PETERS

17 A **B** **18** C **D** **19** E **F**

A B C D E F

8

7

85

6

5

84

4

3

83

2

1

82

B37
The Bogs Farm
Bannerley Rough
Depot
Todd's Rough
Mulliner's Rough
M6
B46
Nursery
Nursery Farm
Ford
Broadwater
Golf & Country Club
Refuse Tip
Little Packington
Brook Farm
Foxes Den
Fish Breeding Farm
The Ash Beds
DENBIGH CNR
STONEBRIDGE RD
A46
DRIVER'S LA
Denbigh Spinney
Church Farm
Butler's Moors
River Blythe
Packington Park
Park Meadow
Deer Park
CHESTER RD
MIDDLE BICKENHILL LA
PINFOLD LA
Garden Spinney
CV7
Packington Hall
Park Farm
Siding Wood
Hall Pool
Great Pool
The Wilderness
Beech Lodge
Middle Bickenhill
B92
Mill Shrubbery
The Mill Farm
Little Dayhouse Wood
P
EAST WAY
PH
COVENTRY RD
COVENTRY RD
Stonebridge
BIRMINGHAM RD
Dials Pool
A45
The National Motorcycle Mus
Works
Pasture Farm
Geary's Heath
Mills Gorse
Diddington Hill
DIDDINGTON LA
Diddington Hall
KENILWORTH RD
CH
OLD ELM LA
Shadow Brook
The Somers
THE GROVE
Mouldings Green Farm
Molands Bridge
A45
SOMERS RD
B4102

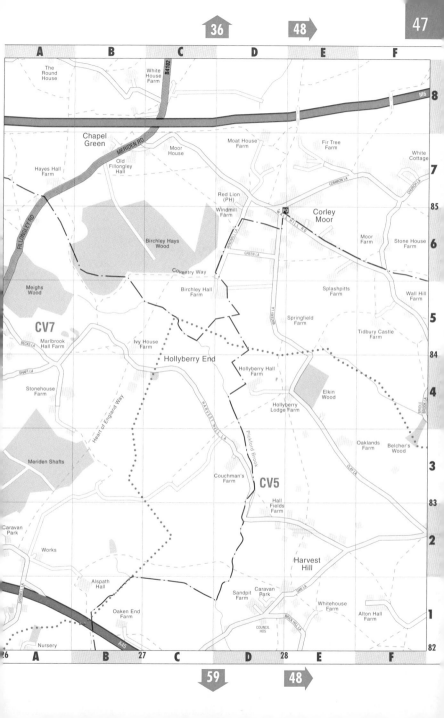

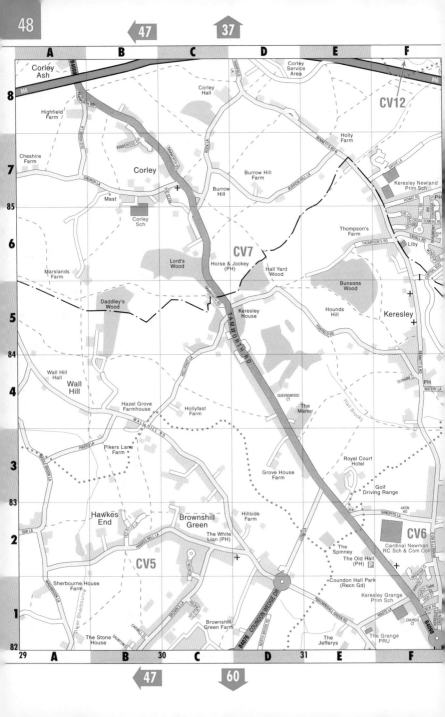

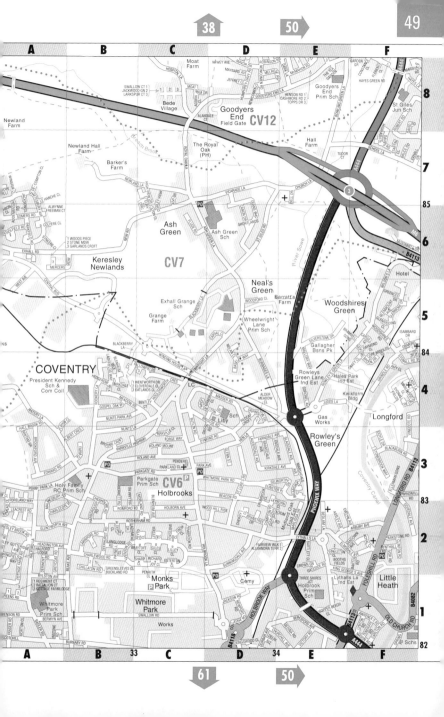

CV12

Hollyhurst
Farm

Hollyhurst

Coventry Way

Sweet Laud's
Wood

Weston Hayes
Farm

Mile Tree
Farm

CV7

Hawkesbury
Hall Farm

Mile Tree
Farm

Tolldish Hall
Farm

Trossachs
Farm

The Greyhound
Inn (PH)

Hawkesbury
Hall

Grove
Farm

Hawkesbury

Grange
Farm

Three Spires
Ind Est

Foxford

Foxford Sch
& Com Arts
Coll

PH

1 LONGFORD SQ
2 WRENBURY DR
3 KENDRICK CL
4 KESWORTH CL
5 ELMHURST RD

1 HURN WAY
2 LINSTOCK WAY
3 WORCESTER CT
4 LINGFIELD CT
5 SAPCOTE GR
6 FARMCOTE LODGE

Sowe Fields
Farm

CV2

Oxford Canal

Oxford Canal Wlk

Lenton's
Lane Farm

Allot
Gdns

Hawkesbury
Fields Sch

Alderman's
Green

Alderman's
Green Com
Prim Sch

Wyken
Pool

Sowe
Common

Hall Green

CV6

Longford
Park Prim
Sch

Manor
House

Sports
Gd

Cemy

Little
Heath
Ind Est

Foleshill
CE Prim
Sch

1 CELANDINE RD
2 BILBERRY RD
3 STRAWBERRY WLK
4 LOXLEY CT

Eburne
Prim
Sch

Cemy
Potters
Green
Prim Sch

Alpha
Bsns Pk

Woody
Park Sch
Com Sch

OLD CHURCH RD

Sch

Wood
End

St Patrick's
RC Prim
Sch

Wood End
Prim Sch

Potter's Green

Cardinal
Wiseman
RC Sch

B1
1 ALICE ARNOLD HO
2 EMILY SMITH HO
3 JOSEPH LATHAM HO
4 DEWIS HO
5 SAMUEL HAYWARD HO

B2
1 CAMELLIA RD
2 WISTARIA CL
3 FUCHSIA CL
4 PEAR TREE CL
5 SPRUCE RD

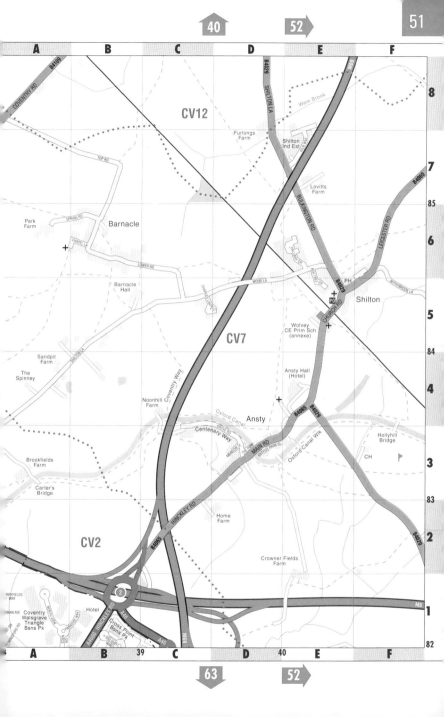

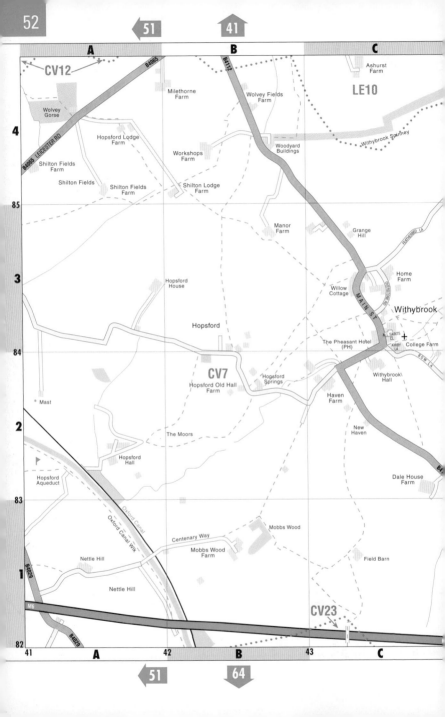

A
B
C

CV12

B4065

B4112

Ashurst
Farm

LE10

Milethorne
Farm

Wolvey Fields
Farm

Wolvey
Gorse

4

B4065 LEICESTER RD

Hopsford Lodge
Farm

Workshops
Farm

Woodyard
Buildings

Withybrook Spinney

Shilton Fields
Farm

Shilton Fields

Shilton Fields
Farm

Shilton Lodge
Farm

85

Manor
Farm

Grange
Hill

HARBERD LA

3

Hopsford
House

Willow
Cottage

Home
Farm

DERBY LANE END

MAIN ST

Withybrook

Hopsford

84

CV7

Hopsford Old Hall
Farm

Hopsford
Springs

The Pheasant Hotel
(PH)

ALL SAINTS
CL

KIRBY
LA

College Farm

Withybrook
Hall

BOW LA

Mast

Haven
Farm

The Moors

New
Haven

Hopsford
Hall

B4?

2

Hopsford
Aqueduct

Dale House
Farm

83

Oxford Canal

Oxford Canal Wlk

Centenary Way

Mobbs Wood

Nettle Hill

Mobbs Wood
Farm

Field Barn

1

B4029

Nettle Hill

M6

CV23

82

B4029

41
A
42
B
43
C

53
43

A **B** **C**

LE17

4

Wood Farm

Spring Farm

Willey Fields Farm

Cottons Furze

Norwood Farm

85

Newnham Lodge Farm

COAL PIT LA

The Sarah Mansfield (PH)

Church La

3

Larch Covert

The Old Kennels

Willey

Kennel Spinney

Long Spinney

The Nursery

CV23

Garden Spinney

84

The Grove

Burton Pool Wood

Newnham Fields Farm

Muswell Leys

The Pinetum

2

Park Cottage

Newnham Paddox

The Kennels

Railway Covert

Newnham Paddox Park

Pinch Furlong

Cabbage Clump

83

Folly Bridge Spinney

Little Walton

B40

1

Hillcrest Rose Cott

LUTTERWORTH RD

Pailton Fields Farm

Pailton Pastures Farm

NOBLE LA

A 48 **B** 49 **C**

B4027

Wood End Farm

WOODBY LA

Bittesby Cottages

Bittesby House

Airfield (disused)

4

HAWAL WAY

Field Farm

85

Mast

Blakenhall Farm

VULCAN WAY

Magna Pk

MAGNA PARK

Lutterworth

3

Woodbrig House Farm

COVENTRY RD

SHACKLETON WAY

WELLINGTON

COVENTRY RD

Wood Bridge

A4303

84

A4303

A4303 M1 Junction 20

Leicestershire STREET ATLAS

COAL PIT LA

Cross In Hand

LE17

Glebe Farm

Long Spinney

B4027

Padge Hall

Cross In Hand Farm

2

Moorbarns Farm

CV23

Moorbarns Motel

83

Streetfield Spinney

Moorbarns

Little Walton Lodge Farm

Streetfield Farm

Lodge Mill Spinneys

1

River Swift

Bransford Bridge

A5

Burrow Spinney

82

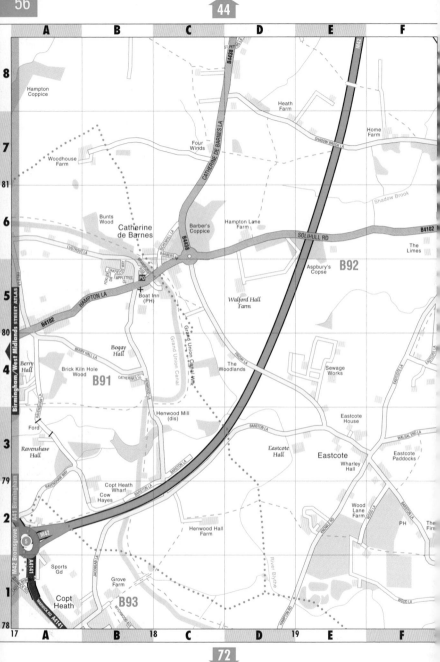

44

8

7

81

6

5

80

4

79

3

2

1

78

A   B   C   D   E   F

17   18   19

72

St Peter's La
B443B
Catherine de Barnes La
Heath Farm
Home Farm
Shadow Brook La
Shadow Brook
Four Winds
Hampton Coppice
Woodhouse Farm
Bunts Wood
Catherine de Barnes
Barber's Coppice
Hampton Lane Farm
SOLIHULL RD
B4102
The Limes
Lugtrout La
Bickenhill La
B443B
PO
Aspbury's Copse
B92
HAMPTON LA
B4102
Boat Inn (PH)
Oak Fld
Fox La
Appletree Cl
Walford Hall Farm
Priory La
M42
Bogay Hall
Berry Hall La
Grand Union Canal Wlk
Grand Union Canal
The Woodlands
Sewage Works
Cressdale La
Cressdale La
Berry Hall
Brick Kiln Hole Wood
B91
Catherine's Cl
Henwood La
Henwood Mill (dis)
Barston La
Eastcote House
Eastcote
Walsal End La
Ford
Ravenshaw Hall
Ravenshaw Way
Barston La
Barston La
Eastcote Hall
Eastcote
Wharley Hall
Eastcote Paddocks
Copt Heath Wharf
Cow Hayes
Henwood Hall Farm
Wood Lane Farm
Wood La
Barston La
PH
The Firs
M42
A41 Birmingham
A41 Bromsgrove
A4141
Sports Gd
Jacobean La
Grove Farm
B93
Copt Heath
Wychwood Ave
River Blythe
Hampton Rd
Wood La
WARWICK RD A4141

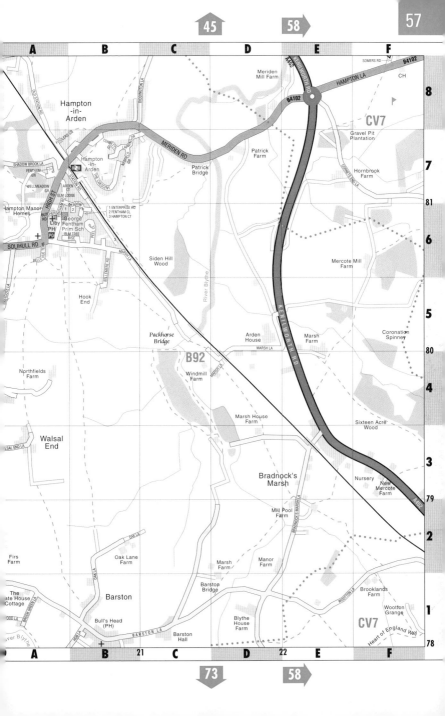

A **B** **C** **D** **E** **F**

8

Hampton
-in-
Arden

CV7

SOMERS RD
B4102
HAMPTON LA
CH
B4102

Meriden
Mill Farm

MERIDEN RD

Gravel Pit
Plantation

7

Hampton-in-Arden

Patrick
Bridge

Patrick
Farm

Hornbrook
Farm

81

SHADOW BROOK LA
FENTHAM
GR
WELLMEADOW
ARDEN
CT
ELM LODGE

1 ENTERPRISE RD
2 FENTHAM CL
3 HAMPTON CT

6

Hampton Manor
Homes

George
Fentham
Prim Sch

Liby
PH
PO

ELM TREE
RISE

SOLIHULL RD

Siden Hill
Wood

Mercote Mill
Farm

Hook
End

River Blythe

5

Packhorse
Bridge

Arden
House

Marsh
Farm

Coronation
Spinney

80

B92

MARSH LA

Northfields
Farm

Windmill
Farm

4

Walsal
End

WALSAL END LA

Marsh House
Farm

Sixteen Acre
Wood

3

Bradnock's
Marsh

Nursery

New
Mercote
Farm

79

BRADNOCK'S MARSHLA

Mill Pool
Farm

2

Firs
Farm

Oak Lane
Farm

OAK LA

Marsh
Farm

Manor
Farm

Brooklands
Farm

WOOTTON RD

Wootton
Grange

The
Gate House
Cottage

Barston

Bull's Head
(PH)

Barston
Bridge

BARSTON LA

Barston
Hall

Blythe
House
Farm

CV7

Heart of England Way

1

River Blythe

78

A **B** 21 **C** **D** 22 **E** **F**

8

Heath Farm

Sewage Works

Meriden Hall

MAIN RD

B4102

OLD RD

DARLASTON CT

MERIDEN HILL

BIRMINGHAM RD

Meriden House

Church Farm

CHURCH LA

Alspath House

Moat House Farm

B41

7

Works

Berry Fields Farm

Heart of England Way

CV

Crow Wood

Keeper's Cottage

BROWNELL RD

81

Cornets End Farm

Cornets End

Wad Barn Farm

Jack Pit

6

Four Oaks

Greenways Farm

CORNET'S END LA

Holloway Farm

BACK LA

Rock Farm

Back Lane Farm

5

Park Farm

Four Oaks Farm

MERIDEN RD

80

Park Pool

Home Farm

CV7

Blind Hall Farm

BLIND LA

Coventry Way

Hill House Farm

4

The Bogs

THE STABLES

Garden Wood

Berkswell Hall

Berkswell

COVENTRY RD

Fir Tree Farm

B92

CHURCH LA

Berkswell CE Jun & Inf Sch

PO

PH

POUND RD

The Moat

Benton Green Lane Farm House

3

Mus

Benton Green

BLYTHE RD

Benton Lane Farm

KENILWORTH RD

Heart of England Way

Marlowes

79

Victoria Farm

A452

The Roughs

PARK LA

Priory Orchard

Lower Farm

SPENCER'S LA

2

Wootton Green Farm

LAVENDER HALL LA

Skew Bridge

Lodge Farm

GREEN LA

Fern Bank

1

Wootton Green

A452

Lavender Hall

Ram Hall

BRICK LA

Yew Tree House

Beechcote

HEZELOR LA

PH

78

23 | **A** | **B** | **24** | **C** | **D** | **25** | **E** | **F**

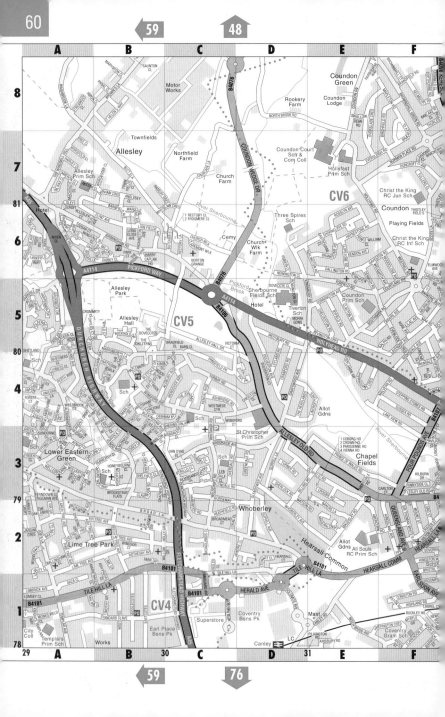

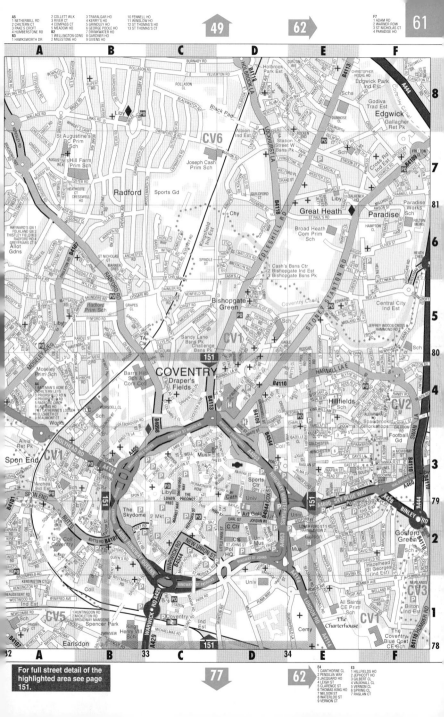

A5
1 NETHERMILL RD
2 CHILTERN CT
3 PIKE S CROFT
4 HAWKSWORTH RD
B3
1 HAWKSWORTH DR

2 COLLETT WLK
3 RIVER CT
4 COMPASS CT
5 MEADOW HO
B2
1 WELLINGTON GDNS
2 MILESTONE HO

3 TRAFALGAR HO
4 KERRY'S HO
5 GRINDLEY ST
6 GEORGE POOLE HO
7 DRINKWATER HO
8 GARDNER HO
9 GIVENS HO

10 FENNELL HO
11 WINSLOW HO
12 ST THOMAS'S HO
13 ST THOMAS'S CT

F7
1 ADAM RD
2 WARNER ROW
3 ST NICHOLAS CT
4 PARADISE HO

61

CV6

CV1

Radford

St Augustine's
RC Prim Sch

Hill Farm
Prim Sch

Joseph Cash
Prim Sch

Sports Gd

Radford
Prim Sch

Kingfield
Ind Est

Great Heath

Broad Heath
Com Prim
Sch

Edgwick Park
Ind Est

Godiva
Trad Est

Edgwick

Gallagher
Ret Pk

Paradise
Works

Paradise

Central City
Ind Est

1 Cash's Bsns Ctr
2 Bishopgate Ind Est
3 Bishopgate Bsns Pk

Bishopgate
Green

Sandy Lane
Bsns Pk Challenge
Bsns Pk

CV1

COVENTRY

Draper's
Fields

Moseley
Prim Sch

Barr's Hill
Sch

Hillfields
Sch

CV2

Alvis
Ret Pk

CV1

Sparkbrook
Workshops

Sparkbrook
Hazlehead
Football
Gd

Spon End

The
Arches
Ind Est

Spon End

Mus

Sports
Ctr

Skydome

Liby

City Coll
Coventry

Cath

Univ

Art Gall

Univ Mus

The
Skydome

Mkt

C Ctr

St Johns
Pol
HQ

Univ

Gosford
Green

Mus

CV5

1 HUNTINGDON RD
2 MICKLETON ST
3 BROADWAY MANSIONS

Spencer Park

King
Henry VIII
Sch

Coventry
Ind Est

Univ

All Saints
CE Prim
Sch

Bilton
Ind Est

CV3

CV1

The
Charterhouse

The
Coventry
Blue Coat
CE Sch

Earlsdon

Cemy

For full street detail of the
highlighted area see page
151.

77   62

E4
1 CAWTHORNE CL
2 PENSILIA WAY
3 JACQUARD HO
4 LEIGH ST
5 CLARENCE ST
6 THOMAS KING HO
7 NELSON ST
8 WATERLOO ST
9 VERNON CT

E3
1 HILLFIELDS HO
2 JEPHCOTT HO
3 GILBERT CL
4 VAUXHALL CL
5 VERNON CL
6 SPRING CL
7 RAGLAN CT

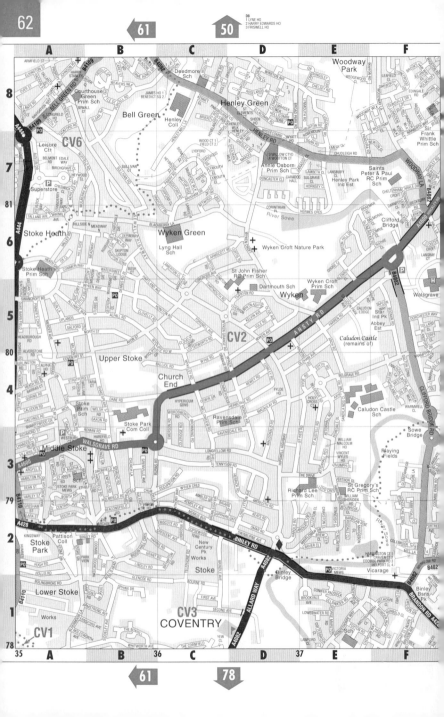

A   **B**   **C**

CV7

M6

Mast

B4455

B4027

Campbell Farm

Stretton under Fosse

Manor House

Malt Kiln Farm

4

Bloore's Spinney

Hill Crest

The Wharf Ind Est

Stretton Wharf

PH

Dog Kennel Spinney

FOSSE WAY

MAIN ST

Tower Cottages

Smite Brook

The Grove

81

NUNEATON LA

B4455

Keeper's Spinney

Newbold Revel Coll

M6

Conery Spinney

3

Black Hovel Spinney

Brick Kiln Spinney

Hare Spinney

Tumley Wood

Wood Way Spinney

CV23

Little Gorse

Tumley Hill

80

Welkin Farm

Apple Tree Farm

COAL LA

Bottom Barn

Slang Spinney

Town Thorns Wood

Larch Spinney

Manor Farm

FENNIS LA

BRINKLOW RD

MAIN ST

PH

The Hill

Easenhall

RUGBY RD

2

Oxford Canal Wlk

Adderley Spinney

Crabtree Spinney

Keeper's Lodge

79

Cathiron Spinneys

Town Thorns Farm

Oxford Canal

Brickyard Spinney

Hungerfield Bridge

Hungerfield

Cathiron Bridge

All Oaks Wood

CATHIRON LA

1

Cattles Covert

Cathiron Farm

Walton's Bridge

78

4   **A**   45   **B**   46   **C**

65
54

A **B** **C**

Pailton Pastures

COVENTRY RD
B4112

B4027 LUTTERWORTH RD

B4027

Yews Farm

PO

HOME FARM CL

CLDENIS VIEW

Tythe Farm

Pailton

POST HOUSE GDNS

PO

RUGBY RD B4112

4

Greenway Farm

Masts

81

Thwaite Farm

Montilo Farm

LORD LA

M6

Fieldgate Farm

3

Glebe Farm

MONTILO LA

CV23

80

Hospital Farm

M6

Harborough Magna

2

PAILTON RD

BACK LA

THE CRESCENT

PH

MARY

Cosford

Grange Farm

CHURCH ST

BARN ST

HARTHORN TERR

Spike Lane

Cosford Hall Farm

Church Farm

Manor Farm

79

LODGE FARM

FABENHALL RD

Sandercock Farm

Harborough Parva

Cosford Grounds

CV21

Lodge Farm

Chestnut Farm

RUGBY RD

CATHIRON LA

1

Tuckey's Farm

VALLEY D

Tuckey's Bridge

Oxford Canal

Oxford Canal Wlk.

Swift Valle Ind Est

SWIFT POINT

High Oaks

CATHIRON LA

B4112

78

47 **A** **48** **B** **49** **C**

65
82

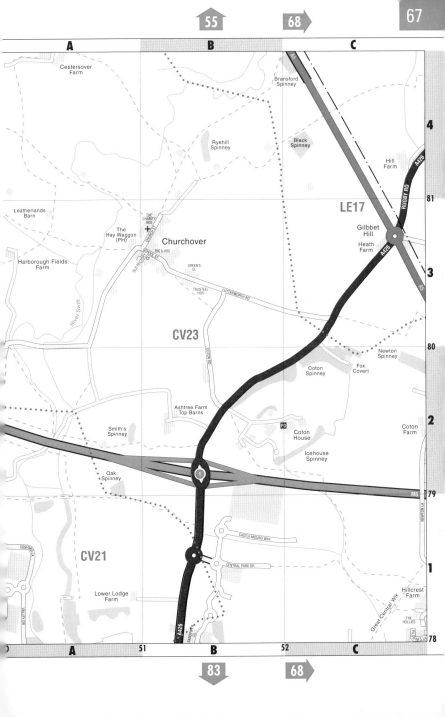

A
B
C

4

81

3

80

2

79

1

78

Cestersover
Farm

Bransford
Spinney

Ryehill
Spinney

Black
Spinney

Hill
Farm

LE17

Gilbbet
Hill

Leatherlands
Barn

The
Hay Waggon
(PH)

THE CHARITY
HOS

Churchover

Heath
Farm

Harborough Fields
Farm

THE S HOS

GREEN'S
CL

LUTTERWORTH RD

TRUSTEEL
HOS

River Swift

CV23

Newton
Spinney

Coton
Spinney

Fox
Covert

COTON RD

Ashtree Farm
Top Barns

Smith's
Spinney

PO

Coton
House

Coton
Farm

Icehouse
Spinney

Oak
Spinney

1

M6

NEWTON LA

CV21

CASTLE MOUND WAY

CENTRAL PARK DR

Lower Lodge
Farm

A426

Hillcrest
Farm

Great Central Wlk

THE
HOLLIES

COSFORD LA

VALLEY DR

OLD RECTORY CL

SCHOOL ST

CHURCH ST

RUGBY RD

A426

A5

A5

A426 Leicester
M1 Leicester (A5460)

A   **B**   **C**

Shawell Wood

Town End
Farm

Lodge
Plantations

Home
Farm

Hill Farm

Spinney
Farm

4

West Cottages

Hill Farm

Cotesbach Fields
Farm

Shawell Lodge
Farm

South
Lodge

81

Green Lane
Spinney

GIBBET LA

Barn
Farm

LE17

3

Works

Middle
Farm

THE
GREEN

The
White Swan
(PH)

PO

Rose
Farm

Shawell

Hill Top
Farm

80

Shawell
Manor

Stables

BILLACES LA

CATTHORPE RD

Hall
Farm

2

Grange
Farm

Tomley Hall
Farm

Depot

19

79   M6

M6

Great Central Wlk

Depots

CV23

Old Barn
Farm

1

THE
LEYES

Manor
Farm

Catthorpe

ELM LA

CATTHORPE
MANOR

PH

Newton

MAIN ST

WATLING
CRES

Works

HERMITAGE
CL

Cherry Tree
(PH)

78   53

1 THE PADDOCK
2 THE ORCHARDS
3 PILGRIMS LA
4 SILVER ST
5 NEWTON RD

A   54   **B**   55   **C**

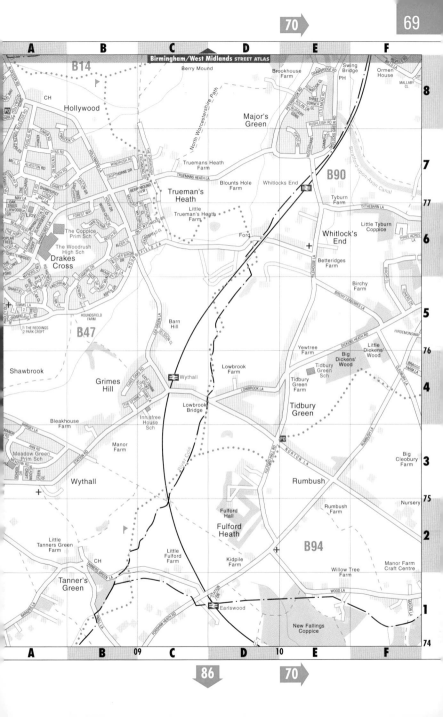

A   B   C   D   E   F

B14

Berry Mound

Hollywood

Brookhouse Farm

Swing Bridge PH

Ormen House

MALLABY CL

8

Major's Green

North Worcestershire Path

Truemans Heath Farm

THREE CORNER LA

7

Truemans Heath La

B90

Trueman's Heath

Blounts Hole Farm

Whitlocks End

Stratford-upon-Avon Canal

77

Little Trueman's Heath Farm

Tyburn Farm

TYTHEBARN LA

The Coppice Prim Sch

Ford

Whitlock's End

Little Tyburn Coppice

THREE ACRES LA

6

The Woodrush High Sch

Betteridges Farm

Birchy Farm

BIRCH CL

FISCHER CR

Drakes Cross

Birchy Leasowes La

5

SIMMS LA

HOUNDSFIELD FARM

Barn Hill

HIRDEMONSWAY

1 THE REDDINGS 2 PARK CROFT

B47

Yewtree Farm

Dickens Heath Rd

Little Dickens' Wood

76

BRAGGS FARM LA

Shawbrook

LEE GREEN LA

THREE OAKS RD

Wythall

Lowbrook Farm

Big Dickens' Wood

Tidbury Green Sch

Grimes Hill

LOWBROOK LA

Tidbury Green Farm

Tidbury Green

4

Innisfree House Sch

Lowbrook Bridge

Bleakhouse Farm

River Cole

Manor Farm

RUMBUSH LA

PO

NORTON LA

Big Cleobury Farm

3

Meadow Green Prim Sch

Wythall

Rumbush

Rumbush Farm

Nursery

75

Fulford Hall

Fulford Heath

B94

Manor Farm Craft Centre

2

Little Tanners Green Farm

CH

Little Fulford Farm

Kidpile Farm

Willow Tree Farm

EDGBASTON HEATH RD

WOOD LA

Tanner's Green

TANNERS GREEN LA

Earlswood

New Fallings Coppice

1

BARNES LA

74

A   B   09   C   D   10   E   F

69

C9
1 HARWOOD GR   7 YARNINGDALE
2 SHIRLEYDALE
3 CHELTONDALE
4 HENLEYDALE
5 QUINTONDALE
6 ARDENDALE

A34 Birmingham
Birmingham/West Midlands STREET ATLAS
B9
Paris Pole

Solihull
Ret Pk

Light Hall
Sch

Whitlock's End
Farm

Our Lady
of the
Wayside
RC Prim Sch

Shirley
Heath

The Swallows
Ind Est

Radway
Ind Est

Research
Ctr

Three
Maypoles

Light Hall
Farm

Monkspath
Bsns Pk

Hotel

Three
Maypoles
Farm

Three
Acres

Dickens
Heath

Baroda
Farm

Wharf
Farm

1 BROCKHURST LA
2 HARESFIELD
3 RUMBUSH LA
4 WADBURN
5 TRUNDALLS LA
6 OLD DICKENS HEATH RD
7 LEDWELL
8 BACK LA

Jerrings Hall
Farm

High Leas
Farm

B90

Monkspath
Street

MEERHILL AVE 1
SHERIMORE CROFT 2
STONEHILL CROFT 3
COLEHURST CROFT 4
SLATELEY CRES 5

The
Plough
(PH)

1 HENSBOROUGH
2 WILLOWHERB WAY
3 PRIMROSE
4 CAMPION WAY
5 DICKENS HEATH RD

Square Acre
Farm

WREN'S NEST CL

Chatsworth Cl
Cheswick
Green
Prim Sch

Cheswick Green
Farm

CH

Mount Dairy
Farm

Greenside

Cheswick
Green

Braggs
Farm

Lady Lane
Farm

River Blythe

Little Cleobury
Farm

Brook
House

Winterton
Farm

L Ctr

Blythe Valley
Park

Bedsworth
Farm

St Patrick's
CE Prim Sch

B94

Salter
Street

Lodge
Paddocks

Woodfield
Farm

Brook Farm
Ind Est

Model
Railway
Club

Illshaw
Heath

Manor Farm
Craft Centre

Earlswood

Engine
Pool

Earlswood Lakes

Blue Bell
Cider House
(PH)

Waring's
Green

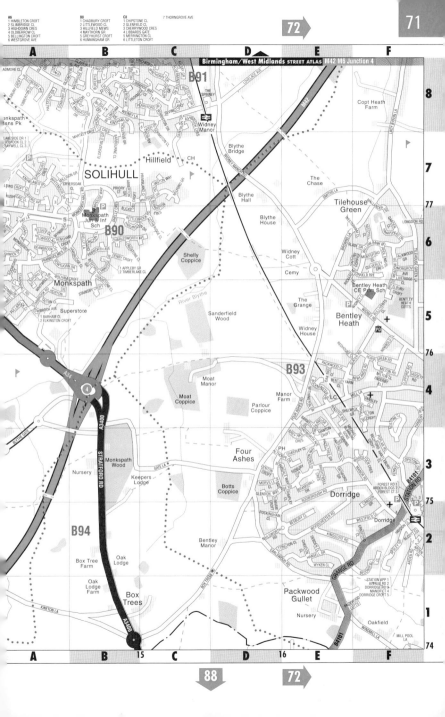

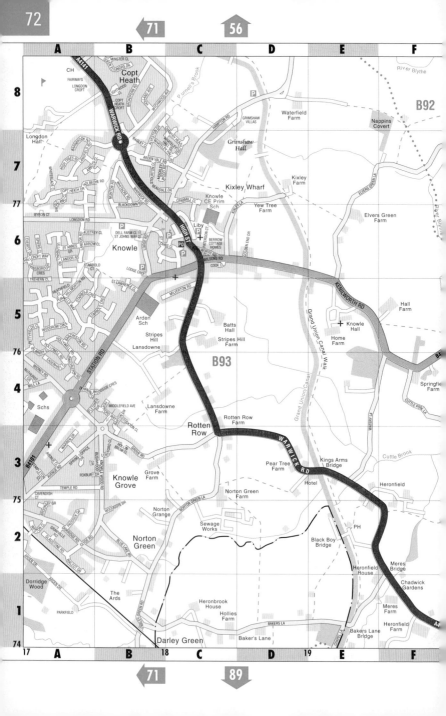

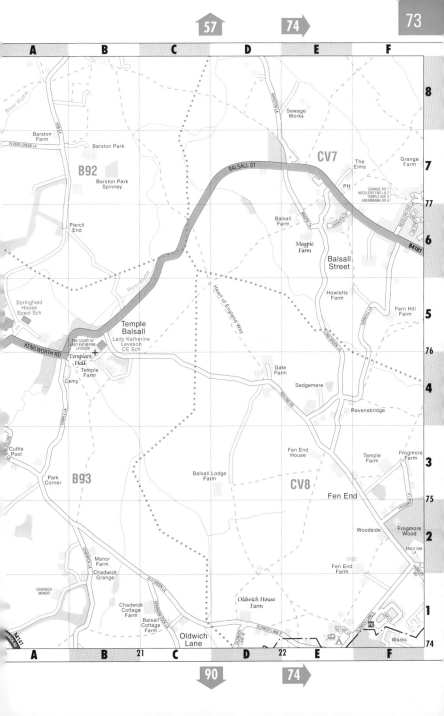

A B C D E F

8

River Blythe

Barston
Farm

Barston Park

ELVERS GREEN LA

VOG LA

B92

Barston Park
Spinney

Piercil
End

7

CV7

The
Elms

Grange
Farm

BALSALL ST

Balsall
Farm

Magpie
Farm

PH

GRANGE RD 1
NEEDLERS END LA 2
TEMPLE AVE 3
GREENBANK RD 4

Balsall
Street

77

6

B4101

Springfield
House
Specl Sch

River Blythe

Heart of England Way

Howletts
Farm

Fern Hill
Farm

5

KENILWORTH RD

Temple
Balsall

THE COURT OF
LADY KATHERINE
LEVESON

Lady Katherine
Leveson
CE Sch

LONG BROOK LA

FEN END LA

FERN HILL LA

76

Templars
Hall

Temple
Farm

Gate
Farm

Sedgemere

4

Cemy

Cuttle
Pool

TEMPLE LA

Park
Corner

B93

Balsall Lodge
Farm

Fen End
House

CV8

Ravensbridge

Temple
Farm

Frogmore
Farm

3

Fen End

75

Woodside

Frogmore
Wood

TABLE OAK
LA

2

CHADWICK LA

Manor
Farm

Chadwick
Grange

OLD GREEN LA

CHADWICK
MANOR

Chadwick
Cottage
Farm

Balsall
Cottage
Farm

BRADNOCKS DOCK LA

Oldwich House
Farm

Fen End
Farm

M101

Oldwich
Lane

OLDWICH LANE

OLDWICH LANE E

Works

74

1

21

C

22

E

F

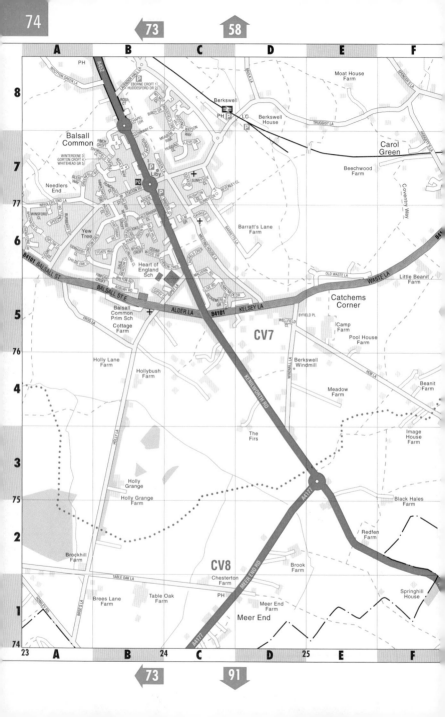

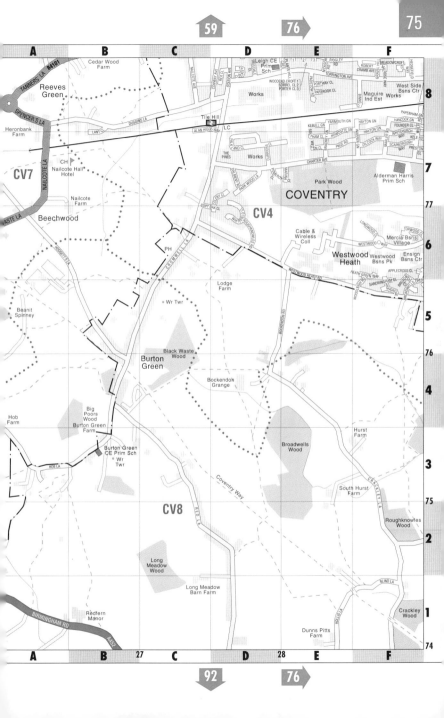

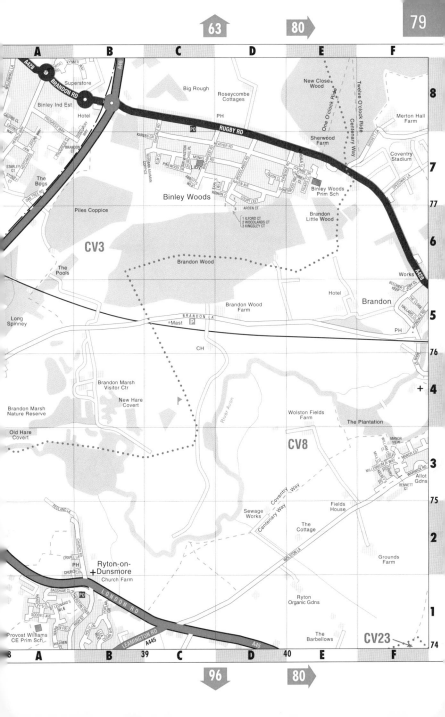

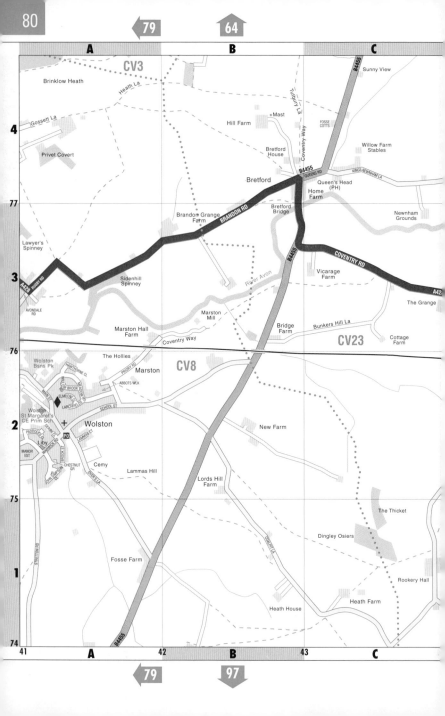

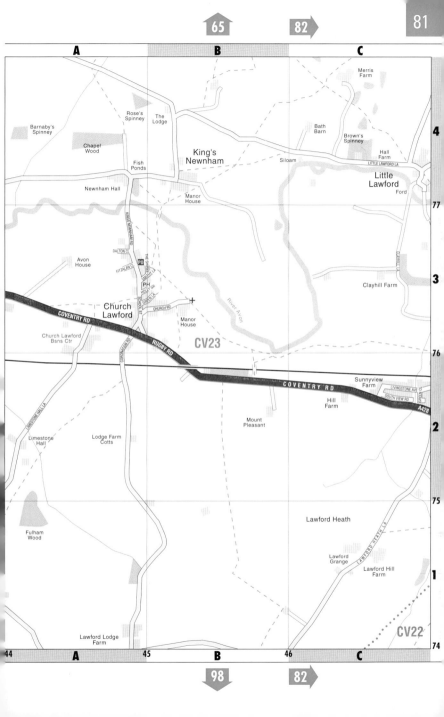

A
B
C

4

77

3

76

2

75

1

74

Merris
Farm

Barnaby's
Spinney

Rose's
Spinney

The
Lodge

Bath
Barn

Brown's
Spinney

Chapel
Wood

King's
Newnham

Siloam

Hall
Farm

LITTLE LAWFORD LA

Fish
Ponds

Little
Lawford

Newnham Hall

Ford

Manor
House

CLAYHILL LA

KING'S NEWNHAM RD

Avon
House

DALTON CL

FITZALAN CL

PO

Clayhill Farm

PH

THE SPINNEY

SMITH ST

HOLLY WK

Church
Lawford

SCHOOL ST

CHAPEL LA

CHURCH RD

Manor
House

COVENTRY RD

River Avon

CV23

Church Lawford
Bsns Ctr

CORONATION RD

RUGBY RD

Sunnyview
Farm

COVENTRY RD

Hill
Farm

LIVINGSTONE AVE

SOUTH VIEW RD

A428

Limestone
Hall

LIMESTONE HALL LA

Lodge Farm
Cotts

Mount
Pleasant

Lawford Heath

LAWFORD HEATH LA

Fulham
Wood

Lawford
Grange

Lawford Hill
Farm

Lawford Lodge
Farm

CV22

44
A
45
B
46
C

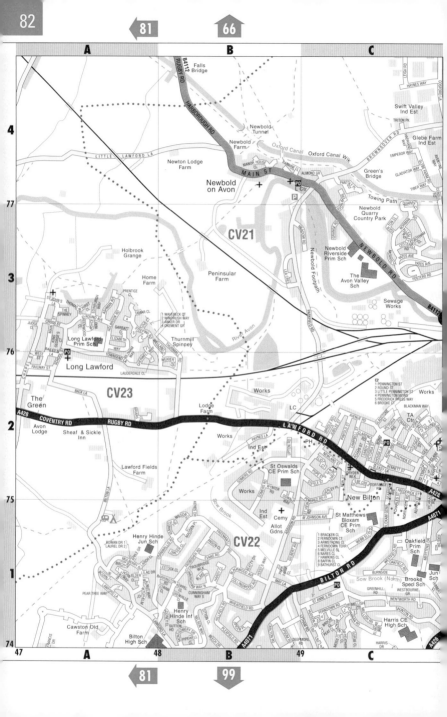

Newton House Farm

Brownsover

Brownsover Hall Hotel

Swift Valley Ind Est

Glebe Farm Ind Est

Swift Park

Swift Aqueduct

Midland Trad Est

Tribune Trad Est

Junction One Ret Pk

Hunters La Ind Est

CV21

CV23

Brownsover Com Sch

Newton Manor House

Boughton Leigh Inf & Jun Schs

Clifton Mill Farm

Sunnycroft Farm

Clifton-upon-Dunsmore CE Prim Sch

THE ELMS PADDOCK

THE BEECHES

Arches Bsns Ctr

Avon Ind Est

Sir Frank Whittle Bsns Ctr

Arches Ind Est

Butlers Leap Ind Est

Works

Woodside Bsns Pk

Webb Ellis Ind Pk

Rugby

St Andrew's Benn CE Prim Sch

Court TH

Court

Northlands Prim Sch

Whinfield Park

Cemy

Lawrence Sheriff Sch

Cambridge Ct

Cemy

Rugby Coll

Eastlands Prim Sch

Rugby Sch

1 MAFFEY CT
2 COLDWELLS CT
3 UNION CT
4 WARWICK ST

The Island

St Marie's RC Ind Sch

Bishop Wulstan RC Sch

St Cross

Ken Marriott L Ctr

Rec Gd

Abbots Farm Jun & Inf Schs

Rec Gd

4 KINGSWAY
5 CHARLESFIELD RD

RUGBY
CV22

HILLMORTON RD

Great Central Wlk

LEICESTER RD

NEWBOLD RD

DUNCHURCH RD

CHURCH ST

NORTH ST

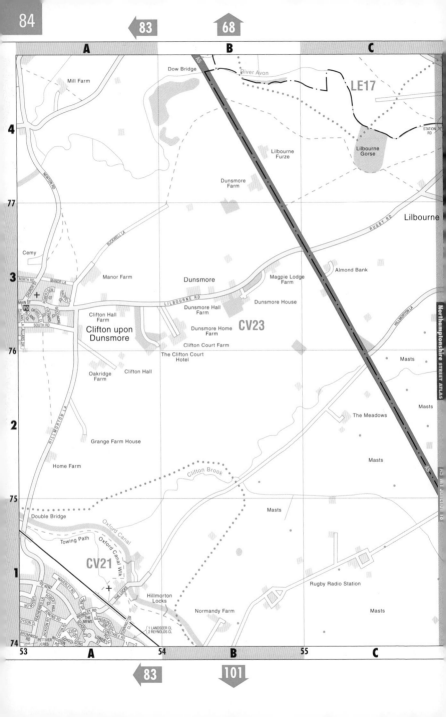

A   B   C

Dow Bridge

River Avon

LE17

Mill Farm

STATION RD

4

Lilbourne
Furze

Lilbourne
Gorse

Dunsmore
Farm

77

RUGBY RD

Lilbourne

BUCKWELL LA

Cemy

Dunsmore

Magpie Lodge
Farm

Almond Bank

NORTH RD

Manor Farm

3

MANOR LA

NORTH RD

LILBOURNE RD

HILLMORTON LA

MAIN ST

Clifton Hall
Farm

Dunsmore Hall
Farm

Dunsmore House

CV23

SOUTH RD

Clifton upon
Dunsmore

Dunsmore Home
Farm

Clifton Court Farm

76

Clifton Court
Hotel

The

Masts

Oakridge
Farm

Clifton Hall

HILLMORTON LA

Masts

2

The Meadows

Grange Farm House

Home Farm

Masts

Clifton Brook

75

Masts

Double Bridge

Oxford Canal

Towing Path

Oxford Canal Wlk

CV21

Rugby Radio Station

1

Hillmorton
Locks

Masts

1 LANDSEER CL
2 REYNOLDS CL

Normandy Farm

Masts

74

53   A   54   B   55   C

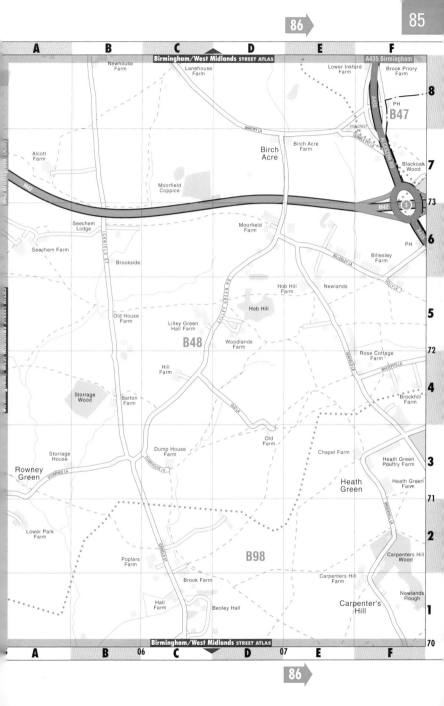

Birmingham/West Midlands STREET ATLAS

A435 Birmingham

8

Newhouse Farm

Lanehouse Farm

Lower Inkford Farm

Brook Priory Farm

PH

B47

Alcott Farm

BALE RY LA

Birch Acre

Birch Acre Farm

HILLCREST
PH
DIAMOND PIT LA

7

Blackoak Wood

Seechem Lodge

M42

Moorfield Coppice

Moorfield Farm

73

3

Seechem Farm

ICKNIELD ST

Brookside

Billesley Farm

PH

6

BILLESLEY LA

Moorfield Farm

Hob Hill Farm

Newlands

PITS LA

Old House Farm

LILLEY GREEN RD

Lilley Green Hall Farm

Hob Hill

5

B48

Woodlands Farm

Rose Cottage Farm

SEMINOLE

72

WHITEPITS LA

Storrage Wood

Hill Farm

Barton Farm

OLD LA

Brockhill Farm

4

Dump House Farm

FARMHOUSE LA

Old Farm

Chapel Farm

Heath Green Poultry Farm

3

Storrage House

STORRAGE LA

Rowney Green

Heath Green

Heath Green Farm

71

BROOKHILL LA

Lower Park Farm

B98

Carpenters Hill Wood

2

Poplars Farm

ROWNEY LA

Carpenters Hill Farm

Newlands Rough

Brook Farm

Hall Farm

Beoley Hall

Carpenter's Hill

1

70

Birmingham/West Midlands STREET ATLAS

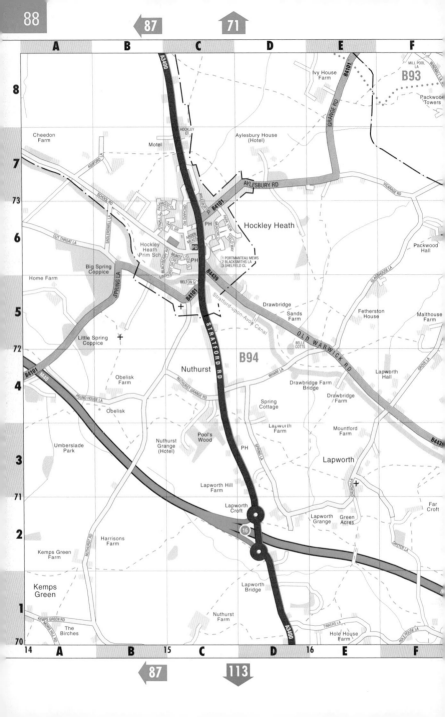

B93

MILL POOL LA

Packwood
Towers

Cheedon
Farm

Ivy House
Farm

Motel

HOCKLEY
CT

Aylesbury House
(Hotel)

AYLESBURY RD

GRANGE RD

B4101

VICARAGE RD

PH

B4101

Hockley Heath

Packwood
Hall

Hockley
Heath
Prim Sch

PH

PO

1 PORTMANTEAU MEWS
2 BLACKSMITHS LA
3 SHELFIELD CL

BELTON GR

B4101

Big Spring
Coppice

Home Farm

SPRING LA

BLANDHOUSE LA

Drawbridge

Stratford-upon-Avon Canal

Sands
Farm

Fetherston
House

Malthouse
Farm

Little Spring
Coppice

BELL'S
COTTS

OLD WARWICK RD

B94

B4101

A410

Nuthurst

Obelisk
Farm

NUTHURST GRANGE RD

WHARF LA

Drawbridge Farm
Bridge

SPRING LA

Lapworth
Hall

GROVE LA

STRATFORD RD

Drawbridge
Farm

Obelisk

ROUND HOUSE LA

Spring
Cottage

Mountford
Farm

B4439

Umberslade
Park

Pool's
Wood

Lapworth
Farm

Lapworth

Nuthurst
Grange
(Hotel)

PH

Lapworth Hill
Farm

Lapworth
Croft

Lapworth
Grange

Green
Acres

Far
Croft

NUTHURST RD

Harrisons
Farm

16

Kemps Green
Farm

OYSTER LA

Kemps
Green

KEMPS GREEN RD

The
Birches

Lapworth
Bridge

Nuthurst
Farm

TINKERS LA

Hole House
Farm

HOCKLEY HOUSE LA

A3400

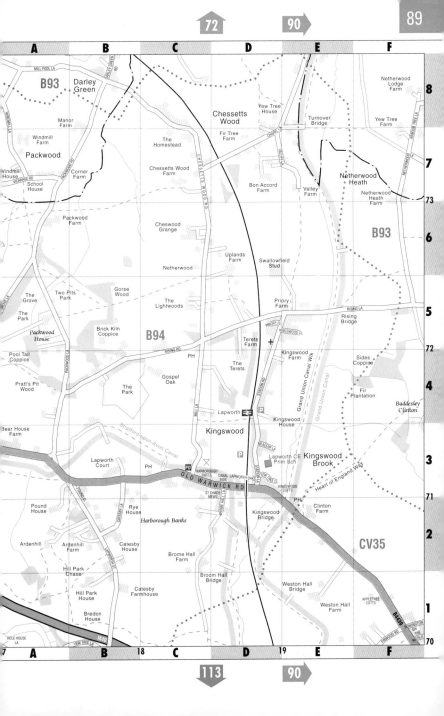

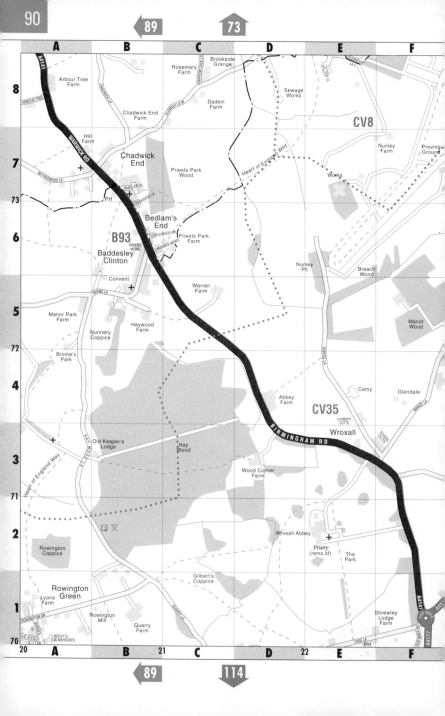

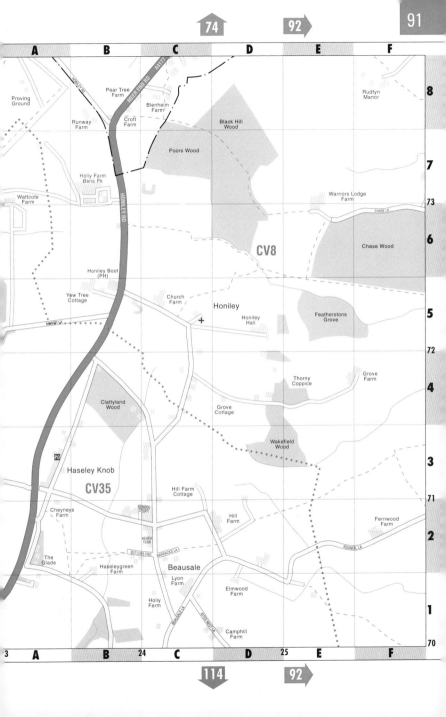

A **B** **C** **D** **E** **F**

8

Proving Ground

HONILEY RD

MEER END RD
A4177

Pear Tree Farm

Blenheim Farm

Croft Farm

Runway Farm

Rudfyn Manor

Black Hill Wood

Poors Wood

7

73

Holly Farm Bsns Pk

Wattcote Farm

HONILEY RD

Warriors Lodge Farm

CHASE LA

6

CV8

Chase Wood

Honiley Boot (PH)

Yew Tree Cottage

Church Farm

Honiley

Featherstons Grove

5

MARSH LA

+

Honiley Hall

72

Clattyland Wood

Grove Cottage

Thorny Coppice

Grove Farm

4

Wakefield Wood

3

PO

Haseley Knob

CV35

Hill Farm Cottage

71

Cheyneys Farm

SCHOOL CROFT

Hill Farm

Fernwood Farm

ROUNCIL LA

2

HEATH TERR

BUTLERS END

BARRACKS LA

The Glade

Haseleygreen Farm

Beausale

Lyon Farm

Elmwood Farm

1

Holly Farm

BEAUSALE LA

RISE BEAU LA

Camphill Farm

70

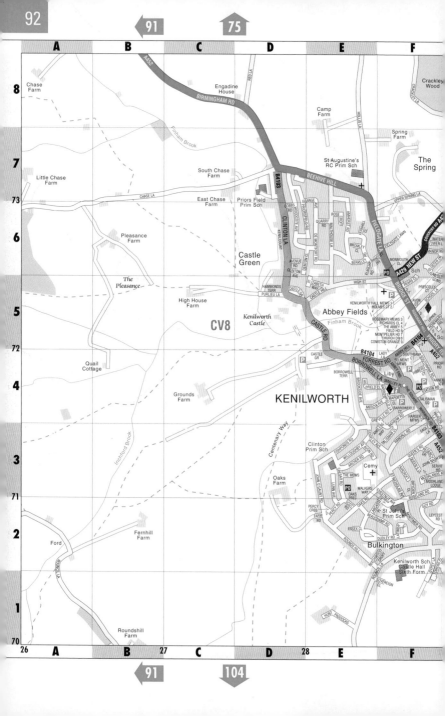

91
75

A **B** **C** **D** **E** **F**

8

Chase
Farm

Engadine
House

BIRMINGHAM RD

Camp
Farm

Crackley
Wood

7

Little Chase
Farm

South Chase
Farm

St Augustine's
RC Prim Sch

The
Spring

Spring
Farm

BEEHIVE HILL

73

CHASE LA

East Chase
Farm

Priors Field
Prim Sch

B4103

FIELDGATE LA

UPPER SPRING LA

COVENTRY RD

6

Pleasance
Farm

CLINTON LA

KENILCOURT

QUARRY
RD

ROSE
CROFT

A429 NEW ST

MANOR RD

Castle
Green

MONMOUTH

Sch

PO

5

The
Pleasance

High House
Farm

HAMMONDS
TERR
PURLIEU LA

AVENUE
RD
CLINTON
AVE

ELIZABETH WAY
CASTLE CT

CASTLE DR

HIGH ST

KENILWORTH HALL MEWS 2
HOLMES 2

Abbey Fields

CV8

Kenilworth
Castle

Finham Brook

ROSEMARY MEWS 3
RICHARDS CL 4
THE ABBEY 5
FIELD HO 6
MONTPELIER HO 7
CHURCH CL 8
CONISTON GRANGE 9

B4104

72

Quail
Cottage

CASTLE RD

CASTLE
GR

LADY
FORREST RD

Liby

P

BORROWELL LA

P

B4103

4

Grounds
Farm

BORROWELL
TERR

FIELD CL

BARROWFIELD

KENILWORTH

STATION RD

TALISMAN

P

A452

Inchford Brook

Centenary Way

Clinton
Prim Sch

HARGER
MEWS

3

Cemy

Oaks
Farm

The Mews

JOHN NASH SQ

SERVITE

MOORLANDS
LODGE

71

PERCY
CRES

WALKERS
WAY

OAKS
CRES

John O'Gaunt Rd

PO

ST JOHN'S
PRIM SCH

ROSELAND RD

LEYCEST
RD

2

Ford

Fernhill
Farm

COUNCIL LA

ESSEX CL

DUDLEY RD

ROUND HILL

Bulkington

Kenilworth Sch
Castle Hall
Sixth Form

SOVEREIGN

1

70

A 26 **B** 27 **C** **D** 28 **E** **F**

91
104

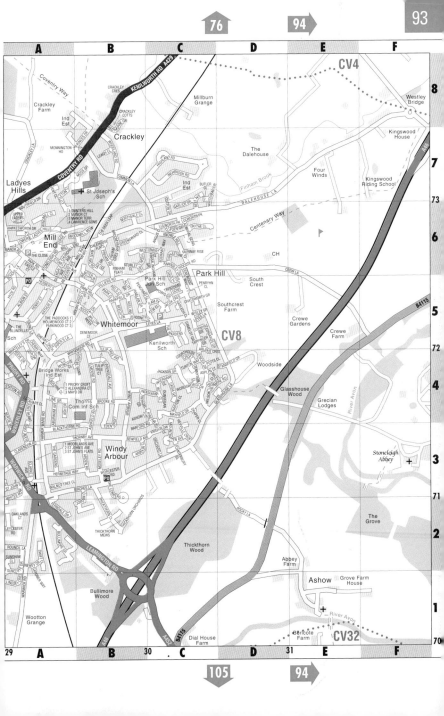

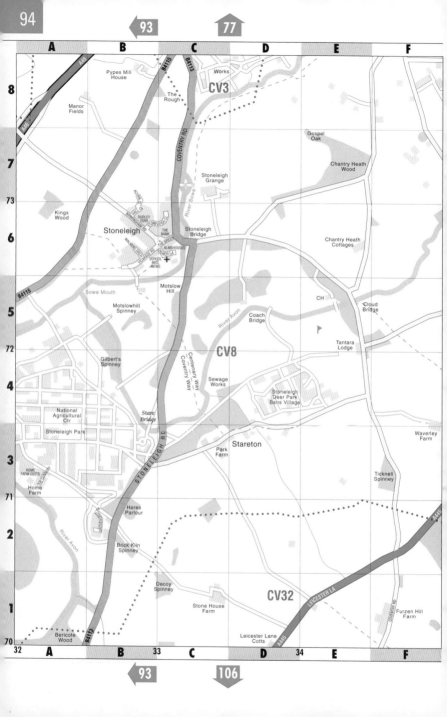

CV3

Ryton Lodge

A423

Rock Farm

Sewage Works

4

Rock Spinney

Centenary Way

Coventry Way

Sewage Works

River Avon

A445

Vehicle Test Track

73

Bubbenhall Bridge

The Bungalow

Ryton Pool

AVON TERR

P

P

Ryton Wood

3

Manor Farm

SPRING RD

PH

Visitor Ctr

P

Bubbenhall

Ryton Pools Country Park

Piece Barn

CV8

PAGET'S LA

Shrubs Wood

72

Old House Farm

Shrubs Lodge

Broomhill Farm

Glebe Farm

Burnt Hurst Wood

Bubbenhall Wood

Nunwood La

2

Bubbenhall House

Burnt Hurst Coppice

York Farm

CV23

Waverley Wood

71

Wappenbury Wood

Weston Fields Farm

CV33

1

CV32

Campbells Farm

B4453

Weston Wood

70

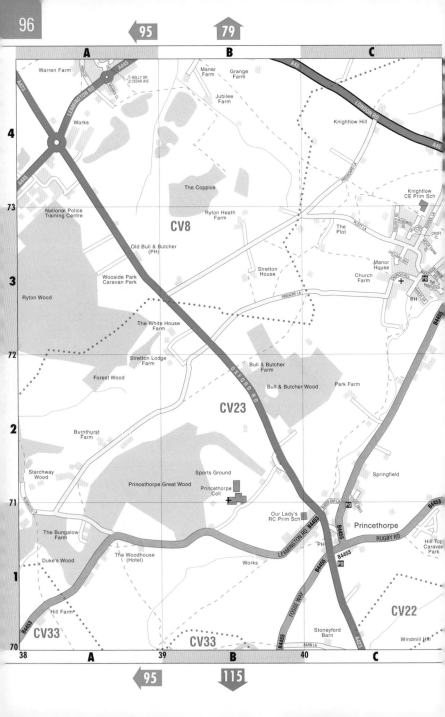

A **B** **C**

Warren Farm

A445

LEAMINGTON RD

HIGH ST

MAYPOLE CL

1 HOLLY DR
2 CEDAR AVE

A423

Manor
Farm

Grange
Farm

A45

LONDON RD

Works

Jubilee
Farm

Knightlow Hill

4

B445

Knightlow
CE Prim Sch

The Coppice

73

National Police
Training Centre

Ryton Heath
Farm

CV8

PRIORY RD

PLOTT LA

DR S BYFORD

GH S BYFORD

CROFT
CL

MOOR FARM

The
Plot

Old Bull & Butcher
(PH)

ORCHARD WAY

Manor
House

CHURCH HILL

Church
Farm

BIRCHWOOD DR

THE
PADDOCKS

MAPLE DRI

PO

3

Wooside Park
Caravan Park

PH

Ryton Wood

The White House
Farm

FINEACRE LA

72

Stretton Lodge
Farm

Stretton
House

Bull & Butcher
Farm

Forest Wood

OXFORD RD

Bull & Butcher Wood

Park Farm

CV23

2

Burnthurst
Farm

Starchway
Wood

Sports Ground

Springfield

Princethorpe Great Wood

Princethorpe
Coll

B4453

71

NEWBOLD LA

Our Lady's
RC Prim Sch

SHREE DIP LA

EDGES CRES

PO

B4453

Princethorpe

RUGBY RD

B4453

Hill Top
Caravan
Park

The Bungalow
Farm

LEAMINGTON RD

PH

B4453

PO

Duke's Wood

The Woodhouse
(Hotel)

Works

B4455

1

Hill Farm*

FOSSE WAY

CV22

CV33

B4453

Stoneyford
Barn

A423

Windmill Hill

70

CV33

BARN LA

38

A

39

B

40

C

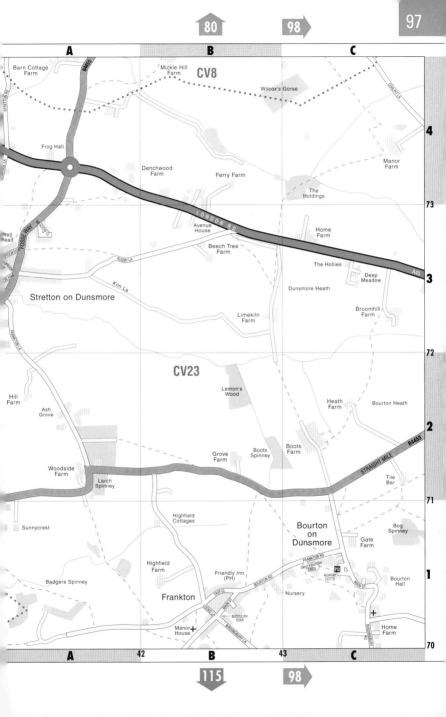

A   B   C

4

Lawford Heath

Lawford Heath Farm

Rose Grove Farm

North Lodge Farm

Lawford Heath Ind Est

Nursery

Works

Reservoir

CV22

73

Wolston Grange

Cawston Farm

Potford's Dam Farm

Cawston Spinney

A45

Park Farm

South Lodge Farm

Blue Boar Farm

3

Nursery

LONDON RD

A4071

Dunchurch Trad Est

Station Farm

72

Motel

B4453

A4071

STRAIGHT MILE

The Mill House

Northampton La

CV23

COVENTRY RD

Hotel

CH

B4453

A45

B44

2

Barnwells Barn Farm

Far Popehill Spinney

Thurlaston

Poultry Farm

71

Popehill Spinneys

BIGGIN HALL LA

Biggin Hall

CHURCH

Hill Farm

Thurlaston Grange

Grange Farm

Biggin House

Little Mead

1

Draycote Fields Farm

Water Wks

Draycote Water (Reservoir)

CV22

70

Chapel Farm

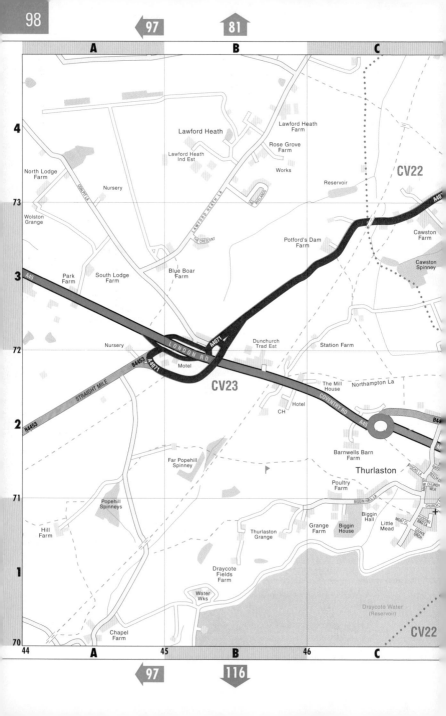

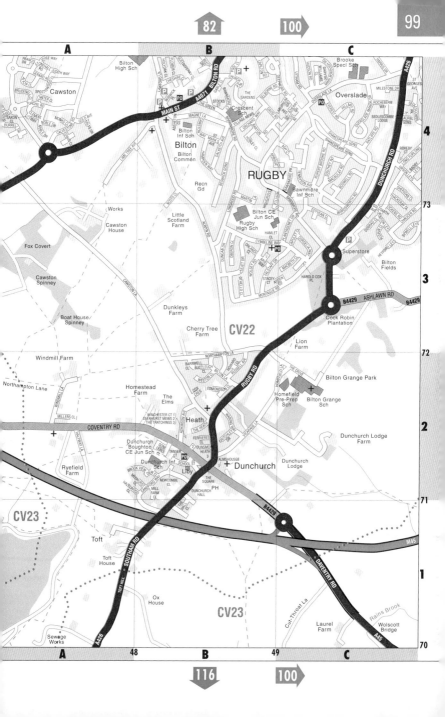

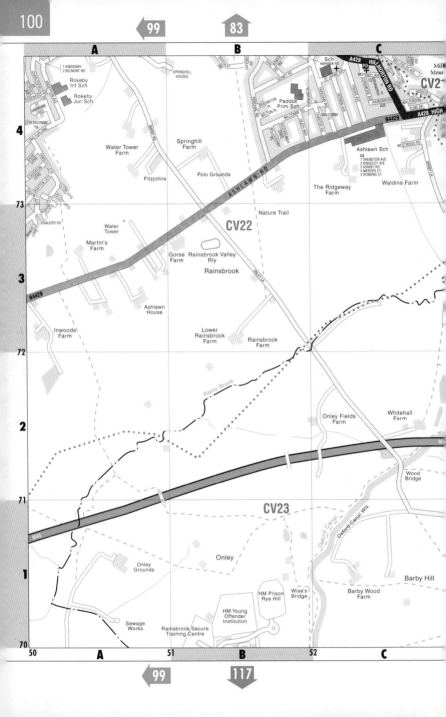

A   B   C

WILLOW TREE GDNS
DEANE PAR
LOWER ST
Sch
Cemy
HORNE CL
HIGH ST
Hillmorton

English Martyrs RC Prim Sch

Moat Farm

CRICK RD

Masts

Dollman Farm

Mast

A428 Northampton

4

Wharf Bridge

The Old Royal Oak (PH)

CV21

Marina

Eastfield Farm

73

Wharf Farm

Tarry's Bridge

Rains Brook

Croft Farm

Nortoft Farm

Barby Nortoft

Oxford Canal Wlk

Oxford Canal

Tower Farm

Nortoft Farm

3

Barby Lodge Farm

Norman's Bridge

RUGBY RD

Northamptonshire STREET ATLAS

72

Towing Path

BARBY LA

CV23

Danetre Farm

Rains Brook

2

B4038

Manor Works

Works

Kilsby

ESSEN LA

BARBY RD

Ash Tree Farm

71

M45

Home Farm

STEPHENSON CT

CASTLE MOUND

POSTLE CL 1
COWLEY WAY 2

M45 M1 Junction 17

The Arnold Arms

WARE RD

ALMOND CL

THE GREEN

RECTORY LA

Barby

1

ELKINGTON LA

CHURCH LA

HOLME WAY

Hopthorne Farm

THE REGIMENT

70

3   A   54   B   55   C

A448 Bromsgrove A441 Birmingham (A38) A4189 Warwi

A448

A4189 WARWICK HIGHWAY

BROMSGROVE HIGHWAY A448

Downsell Wood

CH

Morton Stanley Park

Callow Hill

Walkwood Coppice

Walkwood

Windmill La

PH

Oakenshaw Wood

Headless Cross

REDDITCH
Superstore

The Vaynor Fst Sch

Mid Sch

PO

Oakenshaw

B98

Harry Taylor Fst Sch

PO

Crabbs Cross

PH

ROUGH HILL DR

WINDMILL DR

B97

White House

Lanehouse Farm

Lovelyne Farm

Windrush

St Peter's Sch

CROFT RD

A4504

A448

THE SLOUGH

Slough Farm

The Moors

Hunt End

PH

St Augustine's RC Sch

Stonepits Copse

New Coppice

Thickwrney Brook

Chapel House Farm

Weavers Hill

Upper Huntend Farm

DAGTAIL LA

1 BROOKHAMPTON CL
2 ALDERMINSTER CL

Dagtail End

Monarch's Way

Eastern Hill

Foxpits

Wixon Brook

Astwood Hill Farm

The Wren's Nest Farm

Manor House La

Astwood Bank Fst Sch

EASTERN HILL

Eastern Hill Farm

EVESHAM RD

Yew Tree House

CROFTS LA

ASTWOOD LA

B96

Walnut Tree Farm

DARK LA

Ridgeway Trad Est

B4092

Sambour Lane Est

1 EASTWOOD CT
2 DEWBURY CL
3 POST OFFICE WLK
4 NEW RD

Astwood Court

Sewage Works

Doebank House

BADGER BROOK LA

AVENUE RD

PO

Astwood Bank

A441

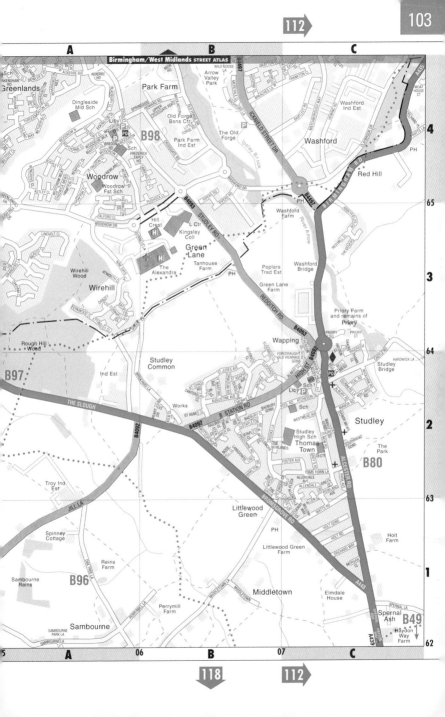

CV8

Chesford Bridge

Bericote Wood

Field Barn Farm

Hotel

Hotel

New Farm

Blackdown Manor

Tiger's Island

Cattle Brook

Wootton Spinnies

Works

B4113

69

Tower House

Hill Wootton

Meadow Cottage

Blackdown

HILL WOOTTON

Blackdown Hill Hotel

CV35

Sewage Works

Hill Wootton Farm

6

New House Farm

Woodland Grange

Cranford

5

All Saints CE Prim Sch

The Warwickshire Nuffield

H

Gaveston Lodge

River Avon

68

B4115

North Leamington Comm Sch & Art Coll

A429

Sandy Lane Farm

4

Church Farm

CV32

SANDY LA

Old Milverton

ROYAL LEAMINGTON SPA

3

Manor Farm

THE CLOISTERS 1
AMBASSADOR CT 2
BELL TOWER MEWS 3

Allot Gdns

67

Guy's Well

Guy's Cave

Guy's Cliffe

Patten's Grove

CV34

The Trinity RC Tech Coll

Milverton

2

Weir

Sch

Cemy

Sch

COVENTRY RD

1

Sch

PO

WARWICK

B4099

WARWICK ST

66

A1
1 LOWER VILLIERS ST
2 LANSDOWNE RD
3 KENNEDY SQ
4 ST PAUL'S SQ
5 MERCHANTS CT
6 LANSDOWNE CRES
7 WILLES RD
8 HANOVER GDNS
9 WHITTLE CT

A2
1 ACORN CT
2 STOCKTON GR
3 WHITACRE RD
4 SHUCKBURGH GR
5 HELLIDON CL
6 BROWNLOW ST

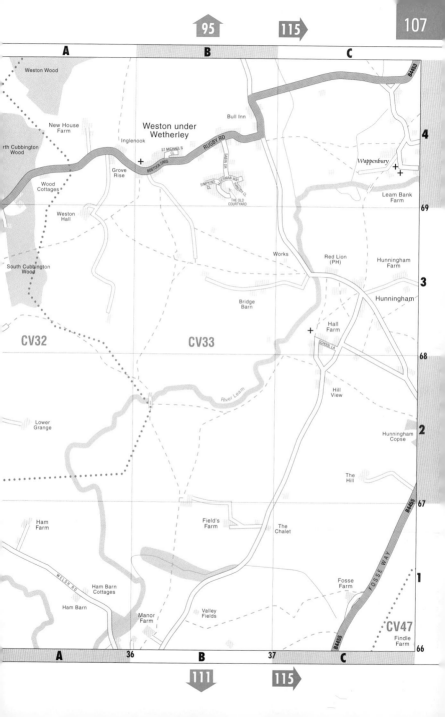

A
B
C

Weston Wood

New House Farm

rth Cubbington Wood

Inglenook

Weston under Wetherley

Bull Inn

4

Wappenbury

ST MICHAEL'S CL

RUGBY RD

JABIN DR

Grove Rise

BOSTOCK LANES

Leam Bank Farm

Wood Cottages

SIMPKINS CL

LEEMAN WAY

THEODORA CL

THE OLD COURTYARD

69

Weston Hall

South Cubbington Wood

Works

Red Lion (PH)

Hunningham Farm

3

Hunningham

Bridge Barn

Hall Farm

CV32

CV33

SCHOOL LA

68

River Leam

Hill View

Lower Grange

Hunningham Copse

2

The Hill

67

Ham Farm

Field's Farm

The Chalet

B4455

FOSSE WAY

1

WELSH RD

Ham Barn Cottages

Ham Barn

Manor Farm

Valley Fields

Fosse Farm

CV47

Findle Farm

A
36
B
37
C
66

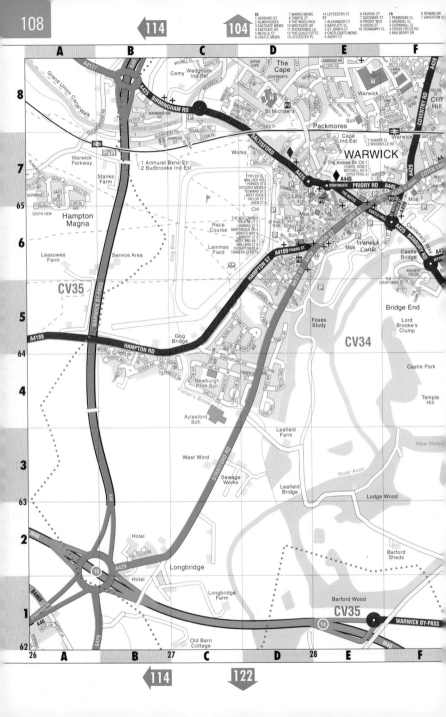

114
104
114
122

E6
1 GERRARD ST
2 ALMSHOUSES
3 EASTGATE MEWS
4 EASTGATE HO
5 NEVILLE CT
6 CASTLE MEWS

7 MARKS MEWS
8 TIBBITS CT
9 THE WOOLPACK
10 WESTGATE HO
11 PUCKERINGS LA
12 THE GUILD COTTS
13 LEYCESTER PL

14 LEYCESTER CT
F7
1 ALEXANDER CT
2 BARTLETT CL
3 ST JOHN'S CT
4 CASTLEGATE MEWS
5 AVERY CT

6 FAIRFAX CT
7 GOODWAY CT
8 PRIORY WLK
9 CROSS ST
10 YEOMANRY CL

F8
1 PEMBROKE CL
2 ARUNDEL CL
3 CORNWALL CL
4 CROSS FIELDS RD
5 MULBERRY DR

6 ROWAN DR
7 GAVESTON CL

WARWICK

CV35

CV34

CV35

105

110

122

110

B8
1 CHARLES CT
2 ST EDITH'S HO
3 ST EDITH'S GN
4 WHITTINGTON CL
5 PACKWOOD MEWS
6 HERALDS CT

D8
1 WESTGROVE TERR
2 CROSS RD
3 THE CEDARS MEWS
4 PENDINE CT
5 GOODWAY HO

E8
1 WOODBINE ST
2 WOODBINE COTTS
3 NEW BROOK ST
4 SOMERS PL
5 PORTLAND PLACE W
6 RIVERSDALE

F7
1 CHURCH WLK
2 SMITH ST
3 BATH PL
4 ABBOTTS ST

F8
1 EUSTON SQ
2 ROSEFIELD ST
3 ROSEFIELD WLK
4 ROSEFIELD PL
5 BEDFORD PL
6 REGENCY ARC

F8
7 ST PETER'S RD
8 CARLTON HO
9 PORTLAND CT
10 CHURCHILL HO
11 WINDSOR CT
12 ROYAL PRIORS

13 SATCHWELL CT
14 SATCHWELL WLK
15 DENBY BLDGS
16 KENILWORTH CT

F5
1 YEW TREE CT
2 GINGKO WLK
3 CONIFER GR
4 SPRUCE GR
5 SILVER BIRCH GR
6 WYCH ELM DR
7 BONNINGSEN CL
8 LOCKHEED CL

F6
1 PHILIP CT
2 FRANCES HAVERGAL CL
3 PRINCE REGENT CT
4 FETHERSTON CT
5 TATCHBROOK CT
6 CHARLES GARDNER CL
7 MARKET CNR

ROYAL
LEAMINGTON SPA

CV32

CV34

CV31

CV33

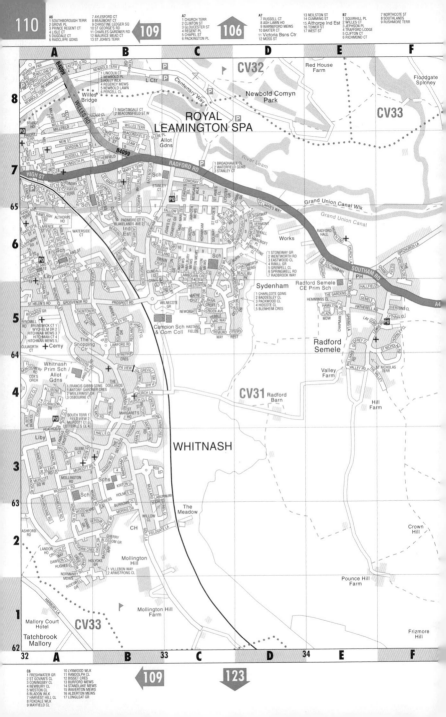

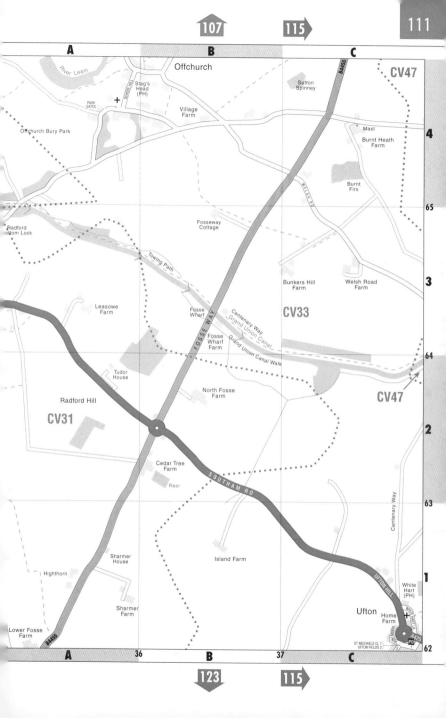

A
B
C

CV47

River Leam

Offchurch

Stag's Head (PH)

Sutton Spinney

PARK GATES

Village Farm

Mast

Burnt Heath Farm

4

Offchurch Bury Park

Burnt Firs

Radford Bottom Lock

65

WELSH RD

Fosseway Cottage

Towing Path

Bunkers Hill Farm

Welsh Road Farm

3

Leasowe Farm

FOSSE WAY

Fosse Wharf

Centenary Way
Grand Union Canal

CV33

Fosse Wharf Farm

Grand Union Canal Walk

64

Tudor House

North Fosse Farm

CV47

Radford Hill

CV31

2

Cedar Tree Farm

SOUTHAM RD

Resr

63

Centenary Way

Highthorn

Sharmer House

Island Farm

UFTON HILL

1

White Hart (PH)

Sharmer Farm

Ufton

Home Farm

Lower Fosse Farm

B4455

ST MICHAELS CL 1
UFTON FIELDS 2

PO

62

A
36
B
37
C

Scale: 1¼ inches to 1 mile

0   ¼   ½ mile

0 250m 500m 750m 1 km

A   B   C   D   E   F

Birmingham / West Midlands STREET ATLAS

DUDLEY LN
B4101

Pink Green

Green Hills Farm

B98

Mast
A4023
COVENTRY HIGHWAY

Gorcott Hall

PH

Gorcott Hill

Skilts Sch

1 KINGHAM CL
2 ILLSHAW CL
3 GATELY CL
4 FLAKEY CL
5 LONGHOPE CL
6 KINGAL CL
7 MEADFEN CL
8 PRESTBURY CL
9 LINDRIDGE CL
10 WEWENT CL
11 JAYS CL

Lower Skilts

Mappleborough Green

A4189

Mappleborough Green CE Prim Sch

PH

WARWICK HIGHWAY

HAYE LA

Cracknut Hill

Gattax Farm

Outhill

Trap's Green

Forde Hall

B94

Danzey Green

Danzey

Hilf Farm

River Alne

TANWORTH LA

Mockley Wood

Mockley Manor

Dean's Green

Botley Hi Farm

Blunt's Green

GENTLEMANS LA

Heath Farm

Oldberrow Hill Farm

Ullenhall

Halle

Cadborough Farm

Arden Way

Oldberrow

B95

Bishops Farm

Clarke's Green

Summerhouse Hill

Hardwick House

Field Farm

Castle Farm

Mars Hill

Morton Bagot Manor

MANOR DR

B80

Morton Bagot

Upper Wawensmoor

Lower Wavensmere

Arden Way
Heart of England Way

Morton Common Farm

Priory Earthworks

Netherstead

Greenhill Farm

Badbury Hill

B49

Cemy

St Giles Farm

Spernall Park

Round Hill

Shelfield

Elmhu

Works

River

SPERNALL LA

Spernall

BURFORD LA

08   A   09   B   10   C   11   D   12   E   13   F

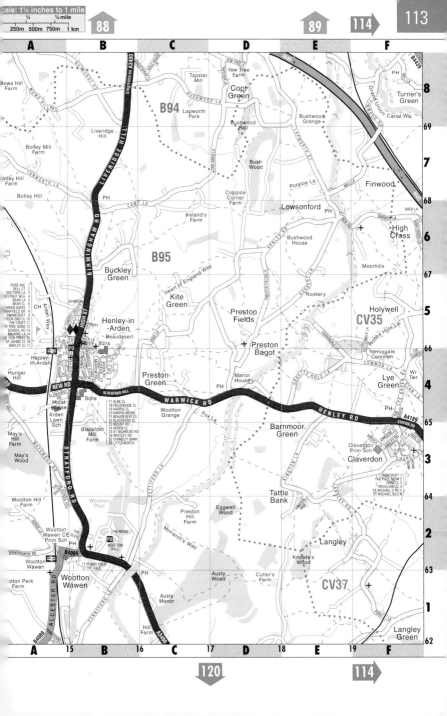

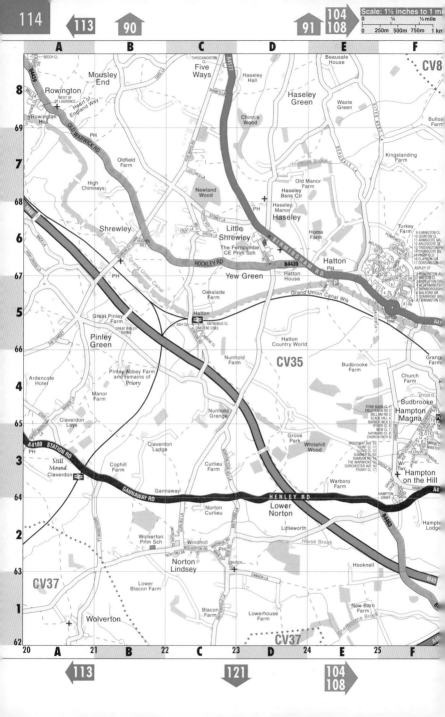

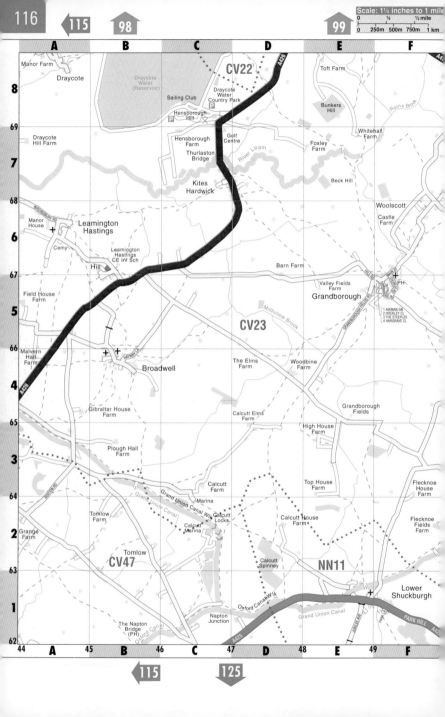

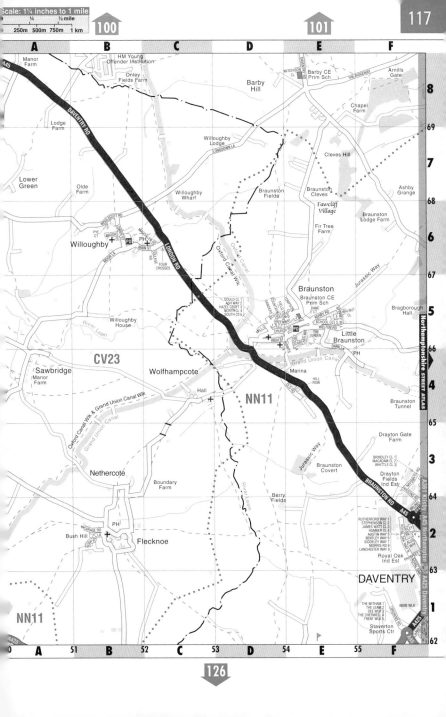

Scale: 1¼ inches to 1 mile

¼ ½ mile

250m 500m 750m 1 km

100

101

117

A **B** **C** **D** **E** **F**

Manor Farm

A45

DAVENTRY RD

HM Young Offender Institution

Onley Fields Farm

Barby CE Prim Sch

MITCHISON CL

Arnills Gate

Barby Hill

Chapel Farm

8

Lodge Farm

Willoughby Lodge

LONGDOWN LA

Cleves Hill

THE RIDGEWAY

69

7

Lower Green

Olde Farm

Willoughby Wharf

Braunston Fields

Braunston Cleves

Fawcliff Village

Ashby Grange

Braunston Lodge Farm

68

OXford Canal Wlk

Fir Tree Farm

MOOR LA

MOULSCOTT RD

PYE CT

BROOKS ST

MILL LA

PO

MAIN ST

COLLEGE RD

Willoughby

LONDON RD

FOUR CROSSES

Jurassic Way

6

67

Willoughby House

GOULD CL 1
ASH WAY 2
HAZEL CROFT 3
NORTH CL 4
SOUTH CL 5

Braunston

Braunston CE Prim Sch

DANE

WALNUT CL

Bragborough Hall

5

Northamptonshire STREET ATLAS

River Leam

Willoughby House

MILL CL

SANDERS RD

DRETTLE

GREENWAY

CHURCH RD

HIGH ST

LONGCROFT

WELTON RD

SCHOOL CL

PO

THE GREEN

Little Braunston

WALNUT CL

DARK LA

PH

66

CV23

Sawbridge

Wolfhampcote

Oxford Canal Wlk & Grand Union Canal Wlk

Grand Union Canal

Marina

HILL ROW

OLD RD

Grand Union Canal

NN11

Braunston Tunnel

4

65

Manor Farm

Hall

Nethercote

Boundary Farm

River Leam

Berry Fields

Jurassic Way

Braunston Covert

Drayton Gate Farm

BRINDLEY CL 1
MACADAM CL 2
WHITTLE CL 3

Drayton Fields Ind Est

BRAUNSTON RD

A45

A361 Kilsby A45 Northampton

3

64

PH

VICARAGE RD

Bush Hill

Flecknoe

RUTHERFORD WAY 1
STEPHENSON CL 2
JAMES WATT CL 3
HUMBER PL 4
AUSTIN WAY 5
BENTLEY WAY 6
SIDDELEY WAY 7
MORRIS RD 8
LANCHESTER WAY 9

Royal Oak Ind Est

A425 Daventry

2

63

DAVENTRY

NN11

A425

THE WITHAM 1
THE LEAM 2
DEE WLK 3
THE CHERWELL 4
TRENT WLK 5

NENE WLK

1

A425

Staverton Sports Ctr

62

A 51 **B** 52 **C** 53 **D** 54 **E** 55 **F**

Scale: 1¼ inches to 1 mile
0   ¼   ½ mile
0   250m 500m 750m 1 km

A   **B**   **C**   **D**   **E**   **F**

ASTWOOD LA
Mutton Hall
Astwood Farm
Monarch's Way
Tookeys Farm
NEW RD
ST. JOSEPH'S
Sambourne
PH
B80

Electricity Sub Sta
Ridgeway Mid Sch
Sambourne Warren Farm
1 WOOD TERR
2 TRUST COTTS
3 SAMBOURNE LA
4 MIDDLETOWN LA
Parkfield House Farm

Wheating Hill
Cemy
A441
Alcester Warren
WHITEMOOR HILL RD
Coughton

B4090
Brandon Brook
Shurnock Court
B96
EDGIOAKE LA
B4092
ORCHARD DR
PH
Coughton Park
SAMBOURNE LA
Coughton CE Prim Sch

Shurnock
SALT WAY
Edgiock
PH
New End
ALCESTER HEATH
COUGHTON LA

The Hill Farm
BRANDHEATH LA
Alcester Park Farm
Spittle Brook

Bouts Corner Farm
YES LA CLOSE
Hookey's Farm
BROOK LA
THE RIDGEWAY
Asplands Husk Coppice
Alcester Lodge

Bouts
GLADSWELL LA
Cladswell
ORANGE CLOSE
ELSHAM RD
Monarch's Way

B4092
Mearse Farm
LOWER CLADSWELL LA
CLADSWELL CLOSE
CHAMBERLAIN LA
Cookhill
Coldcomfort Wood

A422 Worcester
Little Bouts Farm
MEARSE LA
OAK TREE LA
Three Oak Hill Wood
Coldcomfort Farm

A422
Priory Piece Farm
Knowle Fields
The Old House
Old Park Wood
B49

APPLETREE LA
Little Nobury
Knighton
Priory Farm
A441
Thornhill Farm
PARK VIEW LA
Arrow

WR7
Great Nobury Farm
Piddle Brook
Little Knighton Farm
Cank
B4088
Thornhill Wood

Abbots Morton
Weethley Wood
Weethley Farm
Weethley
Pearson's Wood
Ragley Hall

Groom's Hill
Morton Spirt
Weethley Bank
Evesham Lodge

Weethley Gate
B4088

A 02   **B** 03   04   **C** 05   **D** 06   **E** 07   **F**

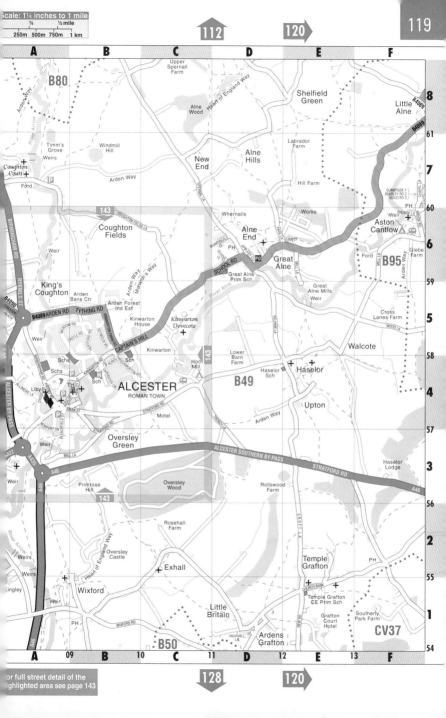

A   B   C   D   E   F

8

61

7

60

6

59

5

58

4

57

3

56

2

55

1

54

B80

Upper Spernall Farm

Alne Wood

Heart of England Way

Shelfield Green

Little Alne

B4089

B4089

Arden Way

Timm's Grove

Windmill Hill

Weirs

New End

Alne Hills

Labrador Farm

Coughton Court

P

Ford

Arden Way

VERNON LA

Hill Farm

143

Coughton Fields

COUGHTON FIELDS LA

Whernalls

Alne End

Works

Aston Cantlow

PH

SUNNYSIDE 1 BEARLEY RD 2 GUILD RD 3

Weir

B4090

BIRMINGHAM RD

Arden Way

Monarch's Way

School Rd

NIGHTINGALE LA

PH

APPLETREE RD

P Spd

Great Alne

PARK RD

GUNNER

MILL LA

Glebe Farm

B95

Ford

CHURCH LA

MILL LA

Arden Way

King's Coughton

Arden Bsns Ctr

Arden Forest Ind Est

Great Alne Prim Sch

River Alne

Great Alne Mills

Weir

RYKNILD ST

B4090

B4089 ARDEN RD   TYTHING RD

CAPTAIN'S HILL

Kinwarton House

Kinwarton Dovecote

Kinwarton

PELHAM LA

Cross Lanes Farm

WOOD LA

Weir

Schs

Schs

Sch

ALCESTER BY-PASS

Lib

H

TH

143

Hoo Mill

B49

Lower Barn Farm

Haselor Sch

Haselor

Walcote

ALCESTER

ROMAN TOWN

SWAN ST

Stratford Rd

Motel

TRENCH LA

Upton

Oversley Green

Arden Way

A435

A422

A46

Weir

MILL LA

ALCESTER SOUTHERN BY-PASS   STRATFORD RD

A46

Haselor Lodge

Weir

Primrose Hill

143

Oversley Wood

Rollswood Farm

CROFT LA

Haselor Hill

River Arrow

Weirs

Weirs

Oversley Castle

Heart of England Way

Rosehall Farm

Temple Grafton

PH

Singley

Weir

Exhall

Wixford

PH

WIXFORD RD

Little Britain

VAUXHALL LA

Ardens Grafton

CHURCH BANK

MILL RD

Temple Grafton CE Prim Sch

Grafton Court Hotel

Southerly Park Farm

CV37

B50

A   09   B   10   C   11   D   12   E   13   F

or full street detail of the highlighted area see page 143

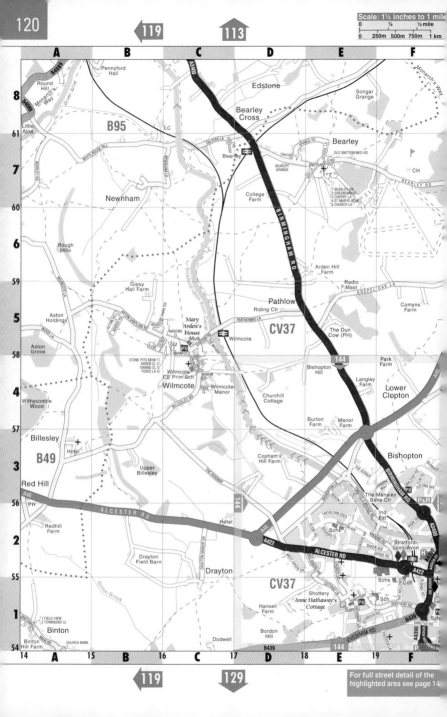

Scale: 1¼ inches to 1 mile

121
108
109

CV34

Brookside Farm

E8
1 RYE FIELDS
2 DUNSTALL CRES
3 ST CHADG RD
4 SEVEN ACRE CL
5 OVERBERRY ORCH
6 BRADFORD CL
7 COURT CL

Greys Mallory

Red House Farm

Hareway Farm

Debden Farm

Gooseberry Hall Farm

Bishop's Tachbrook

Tachbrook Hill Farm

CV33

F8
1 MILLWAY DR
2 FARM WLK
3 PENFOLD CL
4 ISLE GDNS
5 SANDYS WAY
6 CROFT CL
7 CHURCH LEES
8 VICARAGE RISE
9 RASSALL CL
10 BEALE CL
11 KINGSLEY RD
12 COMMANDER CL
13 PARSONAGE CL
14 WOODWARD CL
15 CHURCH HILL
16 BISHOPS CL
17 POWELL CL

Ryland Rd 1
Avon Cl 2
Verdon Pl 3

61

High St

Barford

1 Carter Dr
2 Keyes La
3 Fairfax Cl

Lower Watchbury Farm

Watchbury Hill

Plestowes House

Oakley Wood Farm

Middle Farm

Wilkins Cl 1
Mill La 2
Hemmings Mill 3
Elliotts Orch 4
Cedar Ho 5
Steeds Ct 6

Westham House

Dugard Pl

Sandy Way

Wasperton La

60

Wasperton Farm

Wasperton Hill

Oakley Wood

Wiggerland Wood Farm

Grovefields Farm

Holloway Farm

6

Crem

Tollgate Farm

59

Wasperton

Seven Elms

Thelsford Brook

Heathcote Farm

CV35

Ashorne House Farm

Ashorne Hall Nickelodeon

5

Thelsford Farm

Ashorne Hill Management Coll

Ashorne Hill

58

146

Coppington Farm

Middle Hill Farm

Woozeley Bridge

Ashorne

PH

4

Horticultural Research International

Newbold Pacey Hall

Newbold Pacey

Mill Farm

57

Little Hill Farm

Flint Hall

Little Morrell

Charlecote

Hotel

CV35

John Taylor Way 1
Chestnut Gr 2

Sewage Works

Moreton Morrell

3

Oaktree Cl
Oaktree Cl

Pillar Box La

Brook La

PH

The Terrace
Morton Morrell CE Prim Sch

Wilcox Leys

56

Kingsmead Farm

River Dene

Sewage Works

Sch

Wellesbourne

Wellesbourne CE Prim Sch

Moreton Morrell CE Prim Sch

2

Stratford Rd

Moreton Wood

Moreton Hill

55

Wellesbourne Airport

Wellesbourne CE Prim Sch

Staple Hill Farm

Staple Hill Ho

Warwickshire Coll
(Moreton Morrell Ctr)

Three Gates Stud

1

M40 Distribution Pk

Kineton Rd

Water Mill

Glebe House

Hill Farm

Hell Hole

Moreton Paddox

Lighthorne Rough

54

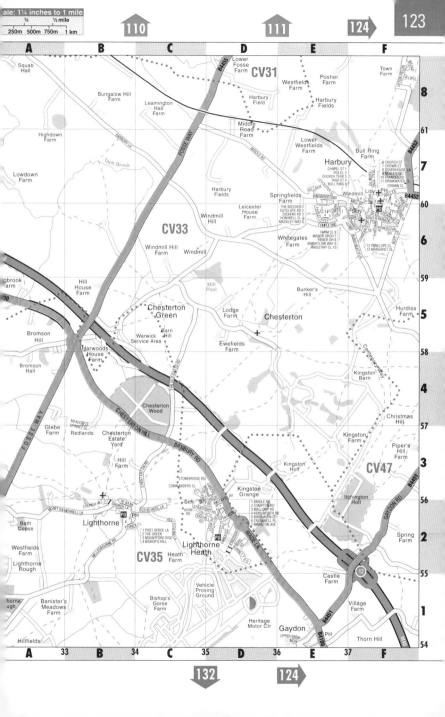

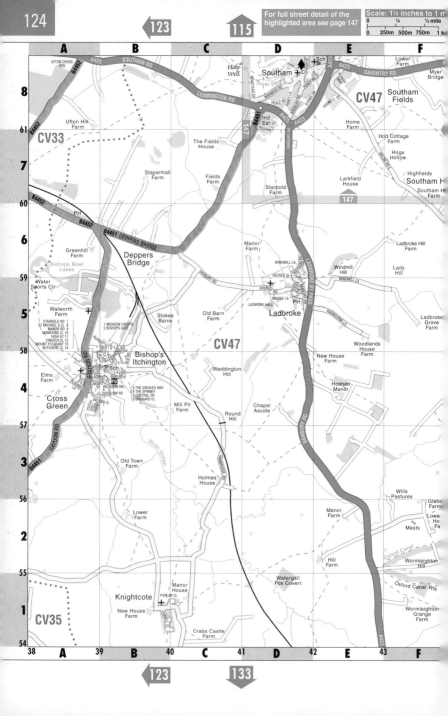

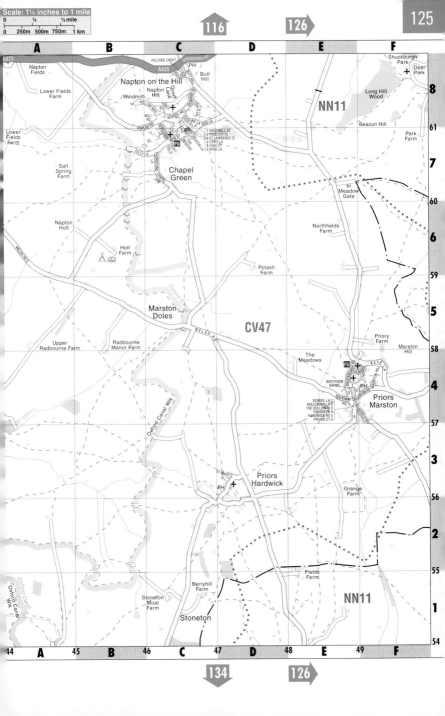

A   B   C   D   E   F

A425
Napton Fields
Lower Fields Farm

HILLSIDE CROFT
SHUCKBURGH RD
A425
PH
Butt Hill

8

Napton on the Hill
Windmill
Napton Hill
Grove Lane
THE BUTTS
MILL RD
SCHOOL
POPLAR RD

NN11
Long Hill Wood

Shuckburgh Park
Deer Park

Beacon Hill

Lower Fields Farm

1 HACKWELL ST
2 PADDOCK CL
3 ST LAWRENCE CL
4 COW'S LA
5 HIGH ST
6 ROSE LA

Park Farm

61

Salt Spring Farm

Chapel Green

7

In Meadow Gate

60

Napton Holt

Northfields Farm

6

Holt Farm

BRISE RD

Potash Farm

59

Oxford Canal

Marston Doles

CV47

5

Upper Radbourne Farm

Radbourne Manor Farm

WELSH RD

The Meadows

Priory Farm

Marston Hill

58

Oxford Canal Wlk

PO
VICARAGE
WESTFIELD BARNS
PH
KEYS LA
MARSTON HILL
SOUTHAM RD

Priors Marston

4

SCHOOL LA 1
HOLLYBUSH LA 2
THE HOLLOWAY 3
THE GREEN 4
HARDWICK RD 5
PRIORS CT 6

57

ST MARY'S
PH

Priors Hardwick

Grange Farm

3

56

Oxford Canal Wlk

Berryhill Farm

Fields Farm

55

NN11

Stoneton Moat Farm

Stoneton

2

1

Oxford Canal Wlk

54

44   A   45   B   46   C   47   D   48   E   49   F

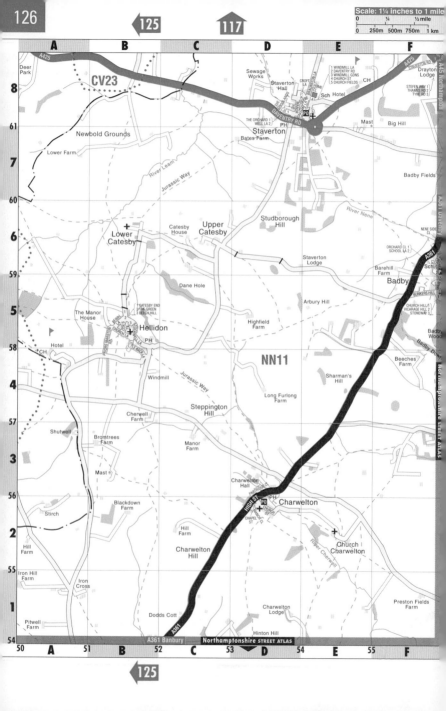

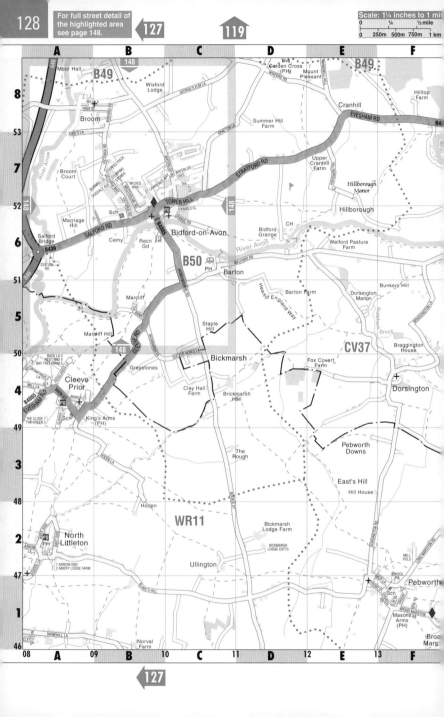

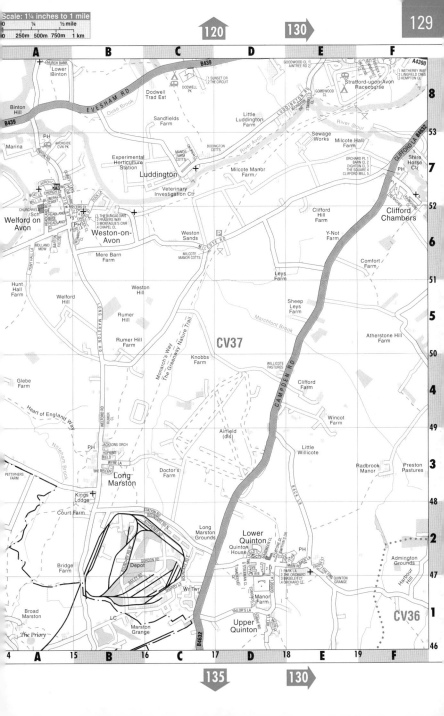

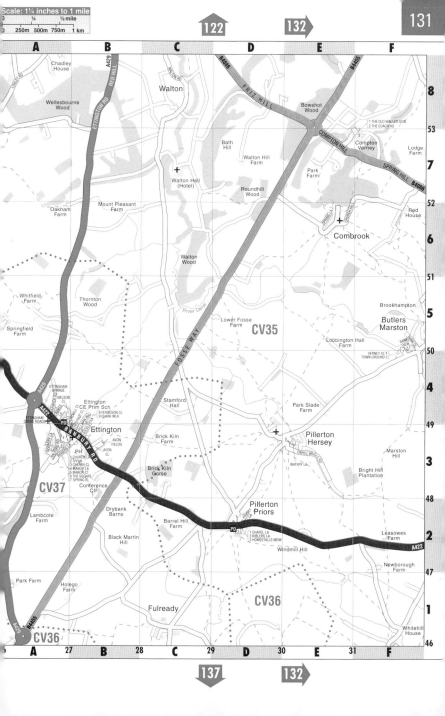

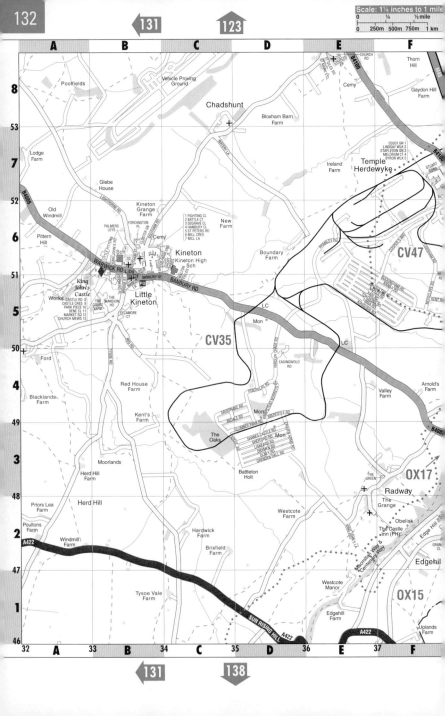

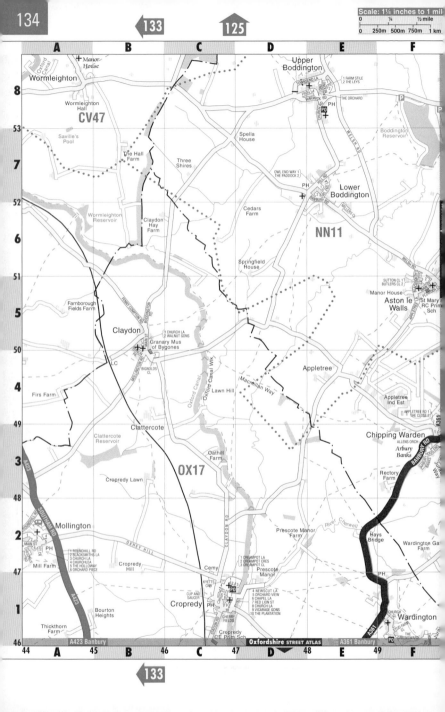

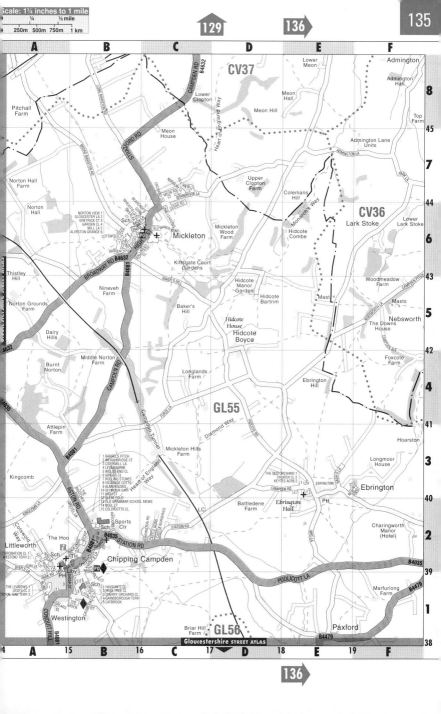

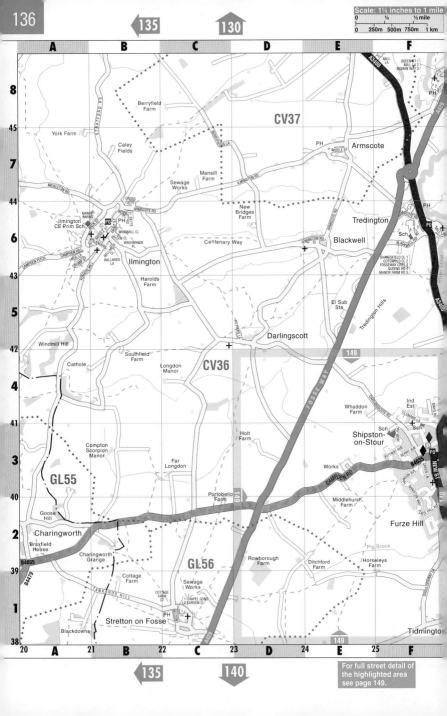

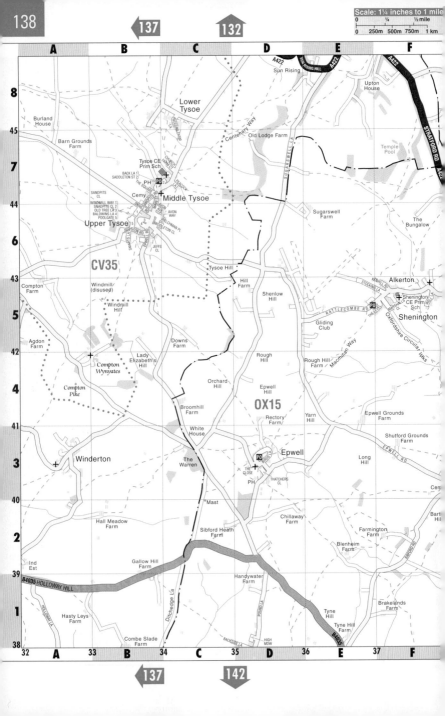

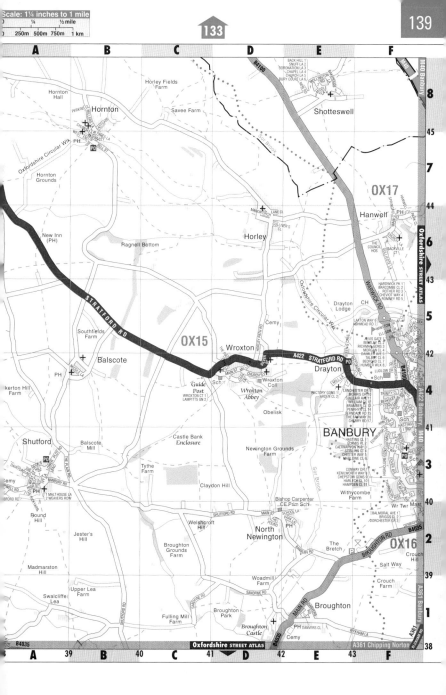

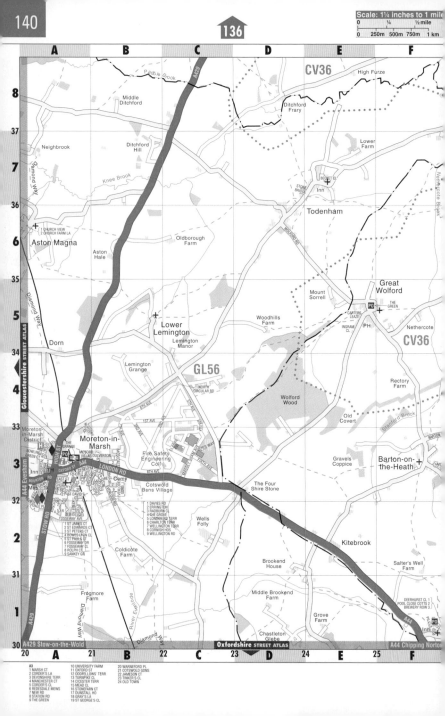

Scale: 1¼ inches to 1 mile

0   ¼   ½ mile
0 250m 500m 750m 1 km

A B C D E F

8
37
7
36
6
35
5
34
4
33
3
32
2
31
1
30

CV36
High Furze

Middle Ditchford
Ditchford Frary

Lower Farm

Neighbrook
Ditchford Hill

Knee Brook
Todenham

STONE BRIDGE
Inn

1 CHURCH VIEW
2 CHURCH FARM LA
Aston Magna
Oldborough Farm

Aston Hale

Great Wolford
THE GREEN

Mount Sorrell
Nethercote

Dorn
Lower Lemington
Woodhills Farm
CARTERS LEAZE
INGRAM CL
PH
CV36

Lemington Manor

Lemington Grange
GL56
Rectory Farm

NORTH CIRCULAR RD
Wolford Wood

1ST AVE
Old Covert

Moreton-in-Marsh District
Moreton-in-Marsh
Fire Safety Engineering Coll
Gravels Coppice
Barton-on-the-Heath

BOWLING GREEN CT
Inn
LONDON RD
The Four Shire Stone

Cemy
Cotswold Bsns Village

1 DAVIES RD
2 ERRINGTON
3 RADBURN CL
4 THE GROVE
5 LONDON RD TERR
6 CHARLTON TERR
7 WELLINGTON TERR
8 CORNISH HOS
9 WELLINGTON RD

Wells Folly

FOSSEWAY AVE
Coldicote Farm
Kitebrook

Salter's Well Farm

Brookend House

Frogmore Farm
Middle Brookend Farm

DEERHURST CL 1
POOL CLOSE COTTS 2
BREWERY ROW 3
Grove Farm

Chastleton Glebe
Inn

A429 Stow-on-the-Wold
A44 Chipping Norton

Oxfordshire STREET ATLAS

20 A 21 B 22 C 23 D 24 E 25 F

A3
1 MARSH CT
2 CORDER'S LA
3 DEVONSHIRE TERR
4 MANCHESTER CT
5 CORDER'S CL
6 RIDGSDALE MEWS
7 NEW RD
8 STATION RD
9 THE GREEN
10 UNIVERSITY FARM
11 OXFORD ST
12 ODDFELLOWS TERR
13 TURNPIKE CL
14 CICESTER TERR
15 MEAD CL
16 STONEFARM CT
17 DUNSTALL HO
18 GRAY'S LA
19 ST GEORGE'S CL
20 WARNEFORD PL
21 COTSWOLD GDNS
22 JAMESON CT
23 TINKER'S CL
24 OLD TOWN

Gloucestershire STREET ATLAS

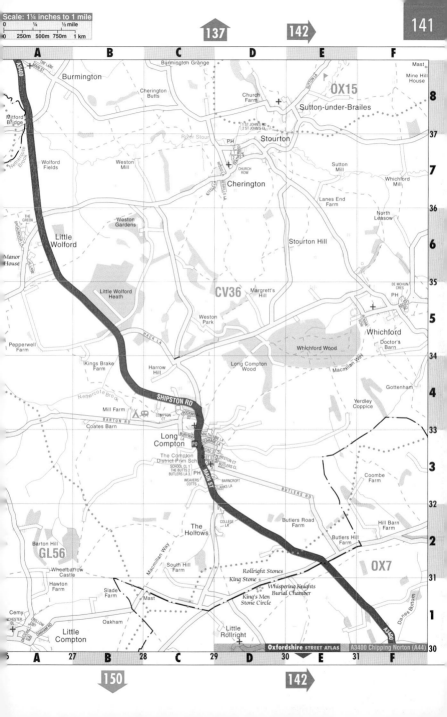

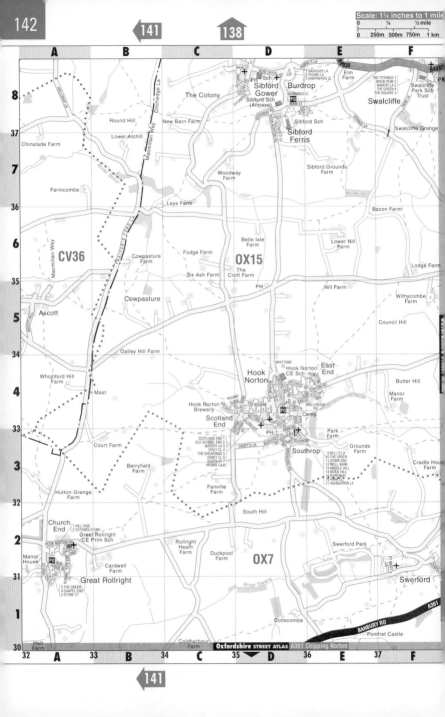

A   B   C   D   E   F

8
The Colony
Burdrop
Sibford
Gower
Sibford Sch
(Annexe)
Swalcliffe
Swalcliffe
Park Sch
Trust
Elm
Farm
THE TITHINGS 1
BRICK ROW 2
BAKERS LA 3
THE GREEN 4
THE SQUARE 5

37
Round Hill
Lower Atchill
New Barn Farm
Sibford
Ferris
Sibford Sch
Swalcliffe Grange
Chinslade Farm

7
Farnicombe
Woodway
Farm
Sibford Grounds
Farm

36
Leys Farm
Bacon Farm

6
Macmillan Way
CV36
Cowpasture
Farm
Fodge Farm
Belle Isle
Farm
OX15
The
Croft Farm
Lower Nill
Farm
Lodge Farm

35
Six Ash Farm
PH
Nill Farm
Withycombe
Farm

5
Ascott
Cowpasture
Council Hill

34
Oatley Hill Farm
Whichford Hill
Farm
Hook
Norton
East
End
Butter Hill

4
Mast
Hook Norton CE Sch
WHITTONS
Manor
Farm
Hook Norton
Brewery
Scotland
End
Cemy
Hollybush
Rd
Southrop
Park
Farm
Grounds
Farm
Cradle House
Farm

33
Court Farm
SCOTLAND END 1
OLD SCHOOL END 2
WATERY LA 3
DOILY CL 4
THE SHEARINGS 5
OSNEY CL 6
QUEEN ST 7
MOBBS LA 8
9 BELL'S LA
10 THE GREEN
11 DOWN END
12 WELL BANK
13 MIDDLE HILL
14 BRICK HILL
15 ROPEWAY
16 PAGE CL
17 ASHBURTON LA

3
Berryfield
Farm
Fanville
Farm

32
Hutton Grange
Farm
South Hill

2
Church
End
1 HILL RISE
2 COTSWOLD CNR
Great Rollright
CE Prim Sch
Rollright
Heath
Farm
Duckpool
Farm
OX7
Swerford Park

31
Manor
House
Cardwell
Farm
Great Rollright
3 THE GREEN
4 CHAPEL END
5 STONE CT
Swerford

1
Coltscombe
BANBURY RD
A361
Pomfret Castle

30
Hall
Farm
Coldharbour
Farm

32   A   33   B   34   C   35   D   36   E   37   F

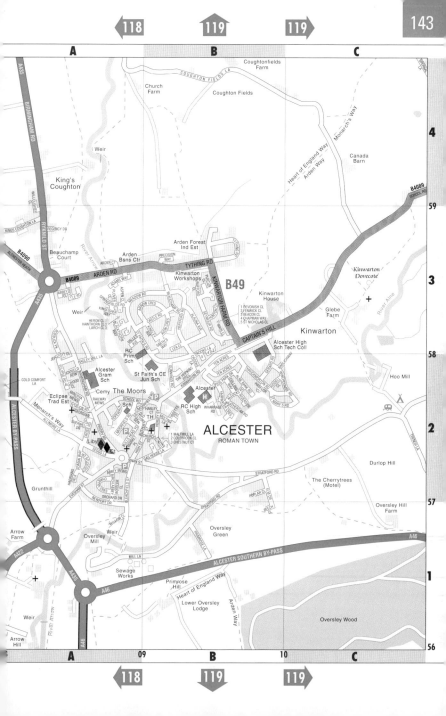

118 119 119

A B C

Coughtonfields Farm

COUGHTON FIELDS LA

Church Farm

Coughton Fields

Monarch's Way

4

Weir

King's Coughton

Canada Barn

Heart of England Way

Arden Way

B4089
BROSOL RD

59

B4089

BIRMINGHAM RD
A435

WALL COUGHTON LA

KINGS COUGHTON LA

RYKNILD ST

Regency Dr

B4090
ALCESTER HEATH

A435

Beauchamp Court

Arden Forest Ind Est

Kinwarton Dovecote

3

Arden Bsns Ctr

PRECISION WAY

TYTHING RD

B4089

ARDEN RD

Weir

River Arrow

Kinwarton Workshops

B49

Kinwarton House

Glebe Farm

River Alne

Kinwarton

HERON CL 1
HAWTHORN CL 2
LARCH CL 3

MEADOW RD

CASTLE RD

KINWARTON FARM RD

CAPTAIN'S HILL

1 BEVONISH CL
2 FENWICK CL
3 BEACON CL
4 CHAPMAN WAY
5 ST NICHOLAS CL

58

RC Prim Sch

Alcester Gram Sch

St Faith's CE Jun Sch

Alcester High Sch Tech Coll

Hoo Mill

Cemy

The Moors

RAGLEY MILL LA

TEN ACRES

Alcester

Hr

Alcester H
RC High Sch

Eclipse Trad Est

Monarch's Way

Railway Mews

SCHOOL RD

TH

WHARRAGE RD

ALCESTER BY-PASS

Lib

P

SWAN ST

GAS HOUSE LA

ST MARY'S RD

ALCESTER
ROMAN TOWN

2

Grunthill

ABBEY MEWS

STRATFORD RD

The Cherrytrees (Motel)

Durlop Hill

1 MALTMILL LA
2 COLEBROOK CL
3 CHESTNUT CT

A46

Arrow Farm

A422

Oversley Mill

ORCHARD DR

NEWPORT DR

Weir

Oversley Green

STRATFORD RD

POPLAR CL

Oversley Hill Farm

57

MILL LA

A453

Sewage Works

ALCESTER SOUTHERN BY-PASS

1

Primrose Hill

Heart of England Way

Arden Way

A46

Weir

A46

Lower Oversley Lodge

Oversley Wood

Arrow Hill

River Arrow

56

A 09 B 10 C

118 119 119

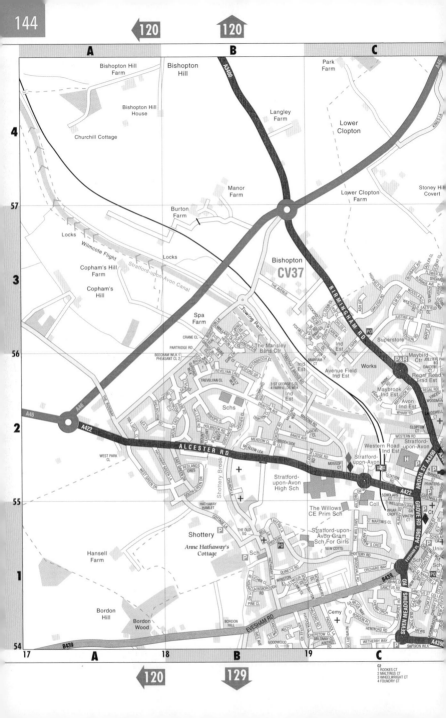

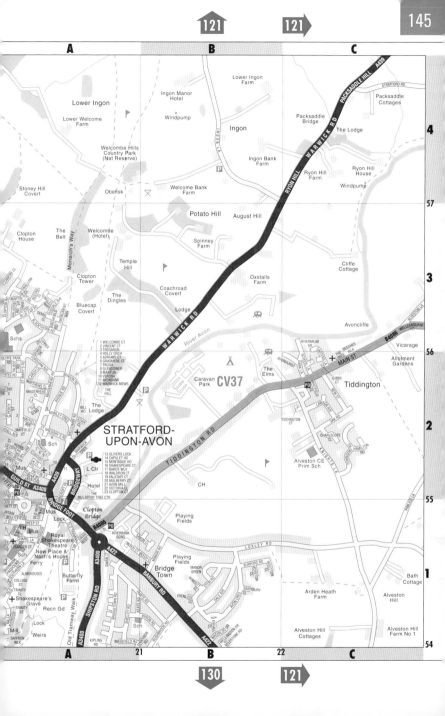

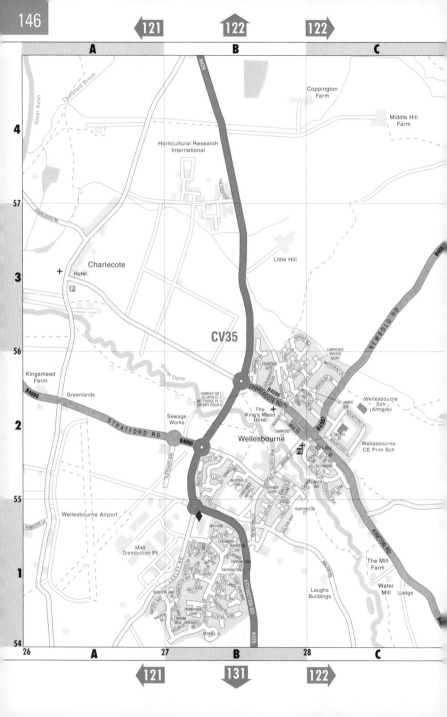

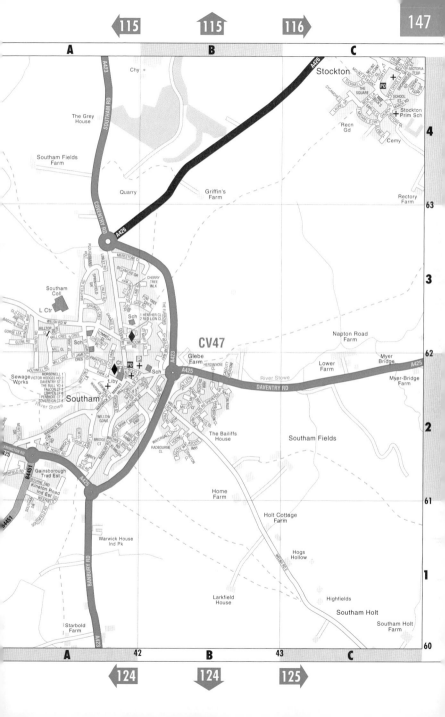

4

41

Shipston-on-Stour

3

CV36

40

2

GL56

39

1

Tidmington

38

Pleasure Farm

Wilhaven

Whaddon Farm

Waddon Hill

Shipston High Sch

Holt Farm

Mount Farm

Works

Mount Cottage

Mount Pleasant

THE TANNERY 1
THE CEDARS 2
COACH HOUSE CT 3
THE OLD BOWLING GN 4
GRANVILLE CT 5
BRINDLEY ALLEY 6
ELLIOT CT 7
ROTHERWICK CT 8
SPINNERS BRIDGE 9
RAINBOW FIELDS 10
WEAVERS CL 11
THE OLD SCHOOL 12
COMPTON CT 13

Portobello Farm

Middlehurst Farm

Hanson Hill

Furze Hill

Cemy

Rowborough Farm

Ditchford Farm

Pig Brook

Pig Brook Farm

Shoulderway House

Horseleys Farm

Ditchford Gorse

Ditchford Cottages

Tidmington Farm

Tidmington Lodge

Green Farm

GUNN END 1
HENWOODS CT 2
CRIPPLEGATE 3

Ind Est

Sch

PO

FOSSE WAY

CAMPDEN RD

DARLINGSCOTE RD

A429

B4035

LONDON RD A3400

CHURCH ST

NEW ST

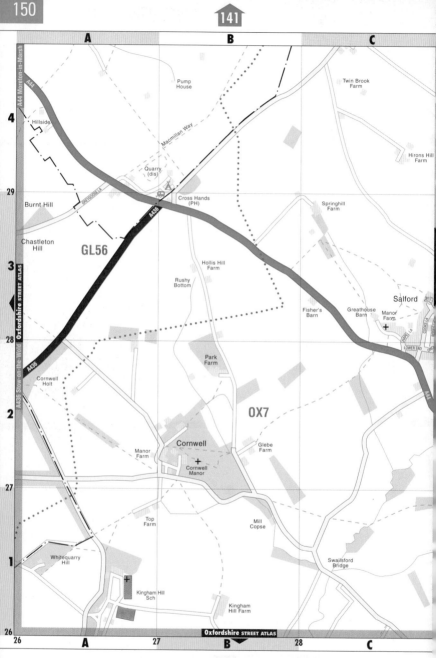

A   B   C

4

Pump
House

Twin Brook
Farm

A44 Moreton-in-Marsh

Hillside

Macmillan Way

Hirons Hill
Farm

29

Quarry
(dis)

GREYGOOSE LA

Cross Hands
(PH)

Springhill
Farm

Salford

Burnt Hill

A436

Chastleton
Hill

GL56

Hollis Hill
Farm

Rushy
Bottom

Fisher's
Barn

Greathouse
Barn

Manor
Farm

COOKS LA

GREEN LA

LEYS

LOWER END

3

28

A436 Stow-on-the-Wold

A436

Cornwell
Holt

Park
Farm

OX7

A44

2

Manor
Farm

Cornwell

Glebe
Farm

27

Cornwell
Manor

Top
Farm

Mill
Copse

Swailsford
Bridge

1

Whitequarry
Hill

Kingham Hill
Sch

Kingham
Hill Farm

26

26   A   27   B   28   C

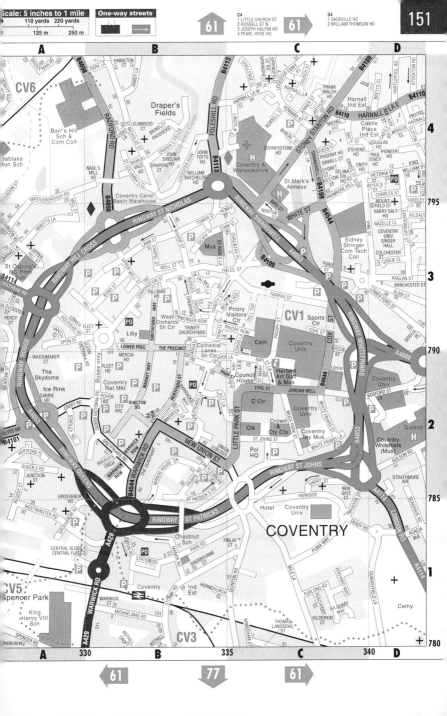

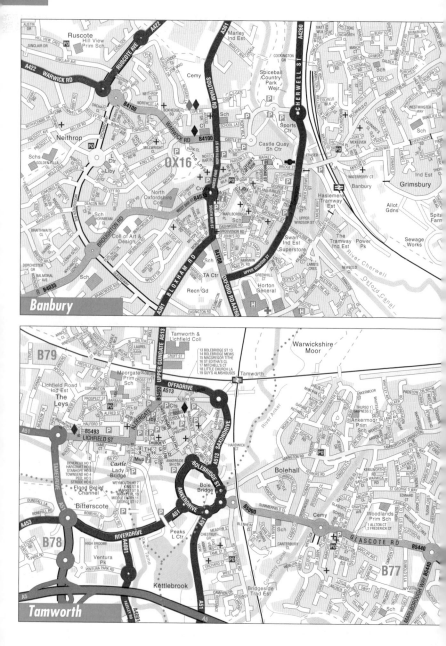

Banbury

Tamworth

Index

Church Rd 6 Beckenham BR2..........**53** C6

Place name	Location number	Locality, town or village	Postcode district	Page and grid square
May be abbreviated on the map	Present when a number indicates the place's position in a crowded area of mapping	Shown when more than one place has the same name	District for the indexed place	Page number and grid reference for the standard mapping

Public and commercial buildings are highlighted in magenta. Places of interest are highlighted in blue with a star★

Abbreviations used in the index

Acad	**Academy**	Comm	**Common**	Gd	**Ground**	L	**Leisure**	Prom	**Prom**
App	**Approach**	Cott	**Cottage**	Gdn	**Garden**	La	**Lane**	Rd	**Road**
Arc	**Arcade**	Cres	**Crescent**	Gn	**Green**	Liby	**Library**	Recn	**Recreation**
Ave	**Avenue**	Cswy	**Causeway**	Gr	**Grove**	Mdw	**Meadow**	Ret	**Retail**
Bglw	**Bungalow**	Ct	**Court**	H	**Hall**	Meml	**Memorial**	Sh	**Shopping**
Bldg	**Building**	Ctr	**Centre**	Ho	**House**	Mkt	**Market**	Sq	**Square**
Bsns, Bus	**Business**	Ctry	**Country**	Hospl	**Hospital**	Mus	**Museum**	St	**Street**
Bvd	**Boulevard**	Cty	**County**	HQ	**Headquarters**	Orch	**Orchard**	Sta	**Station**
Cath	**Cathedral**	Dr	**Drive**	Hts	**Heights**	Pal	**Palace**	Terr	**Terrace**
Cir	**Circus**	Dro	**Drove**	Ind	**Industrial**	Par	**Parade**	TH	**Town Hall**
Cl	**Close**	Ed	**Education**	Inst	**Institute**	Pas	**Passage**	Univ	**University**
Cnr	**Corner**	Emb	**Embankment**	Int	**International**	Pk	**Park**	Wk, Wlk	**Walk**
Coll	**College**	Est	**Estate**	Intc	**Interchange**	Pl	**Place**	Wr	**Water**
Com	**Community**	Ex	**Exhibition**	Junc	**Junction**	Prec	**Precinct**	Yd	**Yard**

Index of localities, towns and villages

Alcester 143 B2
Alderminster 130 D3
Allesley 60 B7
Alveston 121 D3
Ansley 27 A2
Ansty 51 D4
Appleby Magna 3 C4
Ash Green 49 C6
Astley 37 C4
Aston Cantlow 119 F6
Aston Flamville 32 E6
Aston le Walls 134 F5
Aston Magna 140 A6
Astwood Bank 102 C1
Atherstone 18 C4
Austrey 3 A1
Avon Dassett 133 C5
Badby 126 F5
Baddesley Ensor 11 B1
Baginton 77 F2
Balsall Common 74 A7
Banbury 139 E3
Barby 101 B1
Barford 122 B7
Barnacle 51 B6
Barston 57 B1
Barton-on-the-Heath .140 F3
Bascote 115 C2
Baxterley 17 B3
Bearley 120 E7
Beausale 91 C2
Bedworth 39 B1
Bentley Heath 71 E5
Berkswell 58 D3
Bickenhill 44 D1
Bidford-on-Avon 148 C2
Binley Woods 79 C7
Binton 120 A1
Birchley Heath 17 C1
Birdingbury 115 F7
Birmingham 33 D5
Bishops Itchington .124 B4
Bishops Tachbrook ..122 E7
Blackdown 105 F6
Bourton on Dunsmore .97 C1
Bradnock's Marsh 57 D3
Bramcote 40 E6
Brandon 79 F5
Braunston 117 E5
Bretford 80 B4
Brinklow 64 C2
Broadwell 116 B4
Broom 148 A4
Broughton 139 E1
Bubbenhall 95 B3
Bulkington 40 B1
Burmington 141 A8
Burton Green 75 C4
Burton Hastings 41 A4

Butlers Marston 131 F5
Catherine de Barnes .56 B6
Catthorpe 68 B1
Chadwick End 90 B7
Charwelton 126 D2
Cherington 141 D7
Cheswick Green 70 E4
Chipping Campden ..135 B2
Chipping Warden ...134 F3
Church Lawford 81 A3
Church Lench 127 A6
Churchover 67 B3
Claverdon 113 F3
Claybrooke Magna 43 B3
Claybrooke Parva 43 C2
Claydon 134 B5
Cleeve Prior 128 A4
Clifford Chambers ..129 F6
Clifton upon Dunsmore .84 A3
Coleshill 133 F6
Combrook 131 E6
Cookhill 118 D5
Corley 48 B7
Coughton 118 F7
Coventry 61 C4
Coventry 151 C1
Cropredy 134 C1
Cubbington 106 D6
Curdworth 23 B6
Darlingscott 136 D5
Daventry 117 F1
Dordon 10 C3
Dorridge 71 E3
Drayton 139 E4
Drayton Bassett 8 B3
Dunchurch 99 B2
Dunnington 127 E8
Earlswood 70 B1
Easenhall 65 C2
Ebrington 135 F3
Epwell 138 D3
Ettington 131 B3
Farnborough 133 F4
Fazeley 8 C3
Fenny Compton 133 D7
Fenny Drayton 19 D7
Fillongley 36 C2
Flecknoe 117 C2
Frankton 97 B1
Furnace End 25 C2
Gaydon 123 E1
Grandborough 116 B7
Great Alne 119 E6
Great Rollright 142 B1
Great Wolford 140 F5
Grendon 11 B2
Halford 137 A8
Hampton Lucy 121 F4
Hampton Magna 114 F4

Hampton-in-Arden 57 B8
Hanwell 139 F6
Harborough Magna 66 A2
Harbury 123 E7
Hartshill 19 A1
Harvington 127 C4
Hatton 114 E6
Hellidon 126 B5
Henley-in-Arden ...113 B5
Higham on the Hill ...21 A2
Hinckley 31 B8
Hockley Heath 88 D6
Hollywood 69 B8
Honiley 91 D3
Honington 137 A5
Hook Norton 142 D4
Horley 139 D6
Hornton 139 B8
Hurley 16 B2
Ilmington 94 B5
Kenilworth 92 D4
Keresley 48 F5
Kilsby 101 C2
Kineton 132 C6
Kingsbury 15 C3
Kinwarton 143 C3
Knightcote 124 B1
Knowle 72 B6
Ladbroke 124 D5
Lapworth 88 E3
Lawford Heath 98 B4
Lea Marston 24 A4
Leamington Hastings .116 B6
Leek Wootton 104 F7
Lighthorne 123 B2
Lighthorne Heath ..123 C2
Lilbourne 84 C3
Little Compton 141 A1
Little Packington ...45 C6
Long Compton 141 C3
Long Itchington ...115 D4
Long Lawford 82 A2
Long Marston 129 B3
Lower Boddington ..134 E7
Lower Brailes 137 F2
Lower Quinton 129 D2
Lower Shuckburgh ..116 F1
Lowsonford 113 E6
Loxley 130 F8
Luddington 129 C7
Lutterworth 55 C3
Mappleborough Green .112 B6
Marton 139 A3
Maxstoke 35 A1
Meer End 74 D1
Meriden 46 D1
Mickleton 135 C6
Middleton 8 A1
Minworth 22 C5

Mollington 134 A2
Monks Kirby 53 C1
Moreton Morrell ...122 F3
Moreton-in-Marsh ..140 B3
Napton on the Hill .125 C8
Nether Whitacre 25 A3
New Arley 37 A4
Newbold-on-Stour ..130 E1
Newton 68 A1
Newton Regis 2 B2
North Newington ..139 D2
Northend 133 B7
Norton 127 C2
Norton Lindsey 114 C2
Nuneaton 29 B6
Offchurch 111 B4
Offenham 127 D1
Old Arley 26 C1
Orton-on-the-Hill ...6 C2
Oxhill 137 F8
Pailton 66 A4
Pebworth 128 F1
Piccadilly 15 C4
Pillerton Hersey ...131 E3
Pillerton Priors ...131 D2
Polesworth 5 A1
Portway 86 A5
Preston Bagot 113 D5
Princethorpe 96 C1
Priors Hardwick ...125 D3
Priors Marston 125 F4
Radford Semele 110 E5
Ratley 133 A2
Redditch 102 C4
Rowington 114 A8
Rowington Green 90 A1
Rowney Green 85 A3
Royal Leamington Spa .109 C5
Rugby 83 A1
Ryton-on-Dunsmore ..79 B2
Salford 150 C3
Salford Priors 127 F6
Sambourne 118 D8
Seckington 2 A2
Shawell 68 B3
Shenington 139 F8
Sherbourne 121 F8
Shilton 51 F5
Shipston-on-Stour .149 C3
Shottteswell 139 E8
Shrewley 114 A6
Shustoke 24 C1
Shutford 139 A3
Shuttington 4 C4
Sibford Ferris 142 D7
Sibford Gower 142 D8
Snitterfield 121 B6
Solihull 71 B7
South Littleton ...127 F1

Southam 147 A2
Staverton 126 D7
Stockton 147 C4
Stoke Golding 21 B3
Stoneleigh 94 B6
Stratford-upon-Avon .145 A2
Stretton on Dunsmore .97 A3
Stretton on Fosse .136 B1
Stretton under Fosse .65 B4
Studley 112 C2
Sutton Coldfield 13 B3
Swalcliffe 142 F8
Swerford 142 F1
Tamworth 9 B3
Tanworth-In-Arden ..87 B2
Temple Grafton 119 E2
Temple Herdewyke ..132 E7
Thorpe Constantine ..1 C3
Thurlaston 98 C2
Tidbury Green 69 E4
Tiddington 145 C2
Todenham 140 E6
Tredington 136 F6
Twycross 23 C3
Tysoe 138 C7
Ufton 111 C1
Ullenhall 112 D6
Upper Boddington ..134 D8
Upper Brailes 137 E2
Upper Quinton 129 D1
Wardington 134 F1
Warmington 133 D2
Warton 5 C2
Warwick 108 F7
Water Orton 23 C3
Welford on Avon ...129 A6
Wellesbourne 146 B2
Weston under
  Wetherley 107 B4
Whatcote 137 D7
Whichford 141 F5
White Stitch 46 C3
Whitnash 110 C3
Wibtoft 43 A2
Wigston Parva 43 A2
Willey 54 C3
Willoughby 117 B6
Wilmcote 120 C4
Wishaw 14 B2
Witherley 20 F4
Withybrook 52 C3
Wolston 80 A2
Wolvey 41 B2
Wood End 10 B1
Wootton Wawen 113 B1
Wroxall 90 E3
Wroxton 139 D5
Wythall 69 B3

1

1st Ave GL56 .... 140 B4

2

2nd Ave GL56 .... 140 B4

3

3rd Ave GL56 .... 140 B3

5

5 Hos The CV23 .... 67 B3
5th Ave GL56 .... 140 C4

6

6th Ave GL56 .... 140 B4

7

7th Ave GL56 .... 140 B4

8

8th Ave GL56 .... 140 B3

A

Ab Lench Rd WR11 .... 127 A6
Abberley B77 .... 4 B1
Abberton Gr B90 .... 71 B7
Abberton Way CV4 .... 76 E3
Abbey CE Inf Sch CV11 .... 29 B5
Abbey Cl Alcester B49 .... 143 A3
 Southam CV47 .... 147 A2
Abbey Croft B78 .... 5 A1
Abbey Ct CV3 .... 78 B6
Abbey End CV8 .... 92 F4
Abbey Est CV2 .... 62 E5
Abbey Gate CV11 .... 29 C4
Abbey Gate Sh Ctr CV11 .... 29 C4
Abbey Gn CV11 .... 29 C4
Abbey Green Ct B78 .... 5 A1
Abbey Hill CV8 .... 92 E5
Abbey La CV47 .... 147 A2
Abbey Mews B49 .... 143 A2
Abbey Rd CV3 .... 78 A6
Abbey St Nuneaton CV11 .... 29 B5
 Rugby CV21 .... 83 B2
Abbey The CV8 .... 92 F5
Abbey View B78 .... 11 A4
Abbey Way CV3 .... 77 F6
Abbeydale Cl CV3 .... 62 F2
Abbofields Dr B80 .... 103 C3
Abbots Cl B93 .... 72 A7
Abbots Farm Jun & Inf Sch
 CV21 .... 83 C1
Abbots Way CV34 .... 108 D6
Abbots Wlk CV8 .... 80 A2
Abbots Wood Cl B98 .... 112 A6
Abbotsbury Cl CV2 .... 63 A4
Abbotsford Rd CV11 .... 29 F3
Abbotsford Sch CV8 .... 92 F6
Abbotts Gn LE10 .... 31 F5
Abbotts La CV1 .... 151 A3
Abbotts St 4 CV31 .... 109 F7
Abbotts Way CV21 .... 83 C1
Abbotts Wlk CV3 .... 79 C7
Abelia B77 .... 12 B1
Abercorn Rd CV5 .... 60 E2
Aberdeen Cl CV5 .... 60 A5
Aberdeen Rd CV11 .... 29 E1
Aberfoyle Rd CV5 .... 132 D4
Abergavenny Wlk CV3 .... 78 F6
Abingdon Way
 Birmingham B35 .... 22 A3
 Nuneaton CV11 .... 29 F7
Abu Sultan Rd CV47 .... 132 F5
Acacia Ave CV1 .... 61 E1
Acacia Gr CV21 .... 83 A2
Acacia Rd Nuneaton CV10 .... 28 C6
 Royal Leamington Spa
 CV32 .... 105 D1
Achal Cl CV6 .... 49 E2
Achilles Cl CV34 .... 109 F2
Achilles Rd CV6 .... 62 A7
Achray Cotts CV23 .... 97 C1
Acorn Cl Bedworth CV12 .... 49 C8
 Stoneleigh CV8 .... 94 B6
Acorn Ct 1 CV32 .... 106 A2
Acorn Dr CV22 .... 82 A1
Acorn St CV3 .... 78 B8
Acre Cl CV31 .... 110 A4
Acre Ditch OX15 .... 142 D8
Acton Ho CV4 .... 59 F3
Adam Rd 1 CV6 .... 61 F7
Adams St CV21 .... 82 C2
Adams Way B49 .... 143 A3
Adare Dr CV3 .... 77 C8
Adcock Dr CV8 .... 93 B5
Addenbrooke Rd CV7 .... 49 A6
Adderley St CV1 .... 61 E4

Addingham Cl 2 CV34 .... 104 E1
Addison Cl CV10 .... 28 A5
Addison Pl B46 .... 23 B3
Addison Rd Coventry CV6 .... 61 A8
 Rugby CV22 .... 82 B1
Adelaide Ct CV12 .... 39 A2
Adelaide Rd CV31,CV32 .... 109 E8
Adelaide St CV1 .... 151 D4
Adkins Croft CV7 .... 36 C2
Adkinson Ave CV22 .... 99 B2
Admington La CV36 .... 114 F5
Admington Rd CV36 .... 135 C8
Admiral Gdns CV8 .... 93 C6
Admirals Way CV11 .... 40 E6
Adrians Ct CV37 .... 145 A2
Agincourt Rd CV3 .... 77 E7
Aikman Gn CV23 .... 116 F5
Ainsbury Rd CV5 .... 76 E8
Ainsdale Cl CV6 .... 50 B4
Aintree Cl Bedworth CV12 .... 39 B4
 Coventry CV6 .... 61 E5
Aintree Dr CV32 .... 106 C3
Aintree Rd CV37 .... 144 B1
Airport Way B26 .... 44 C3
Ajax Cl CV21 .... 83 B3
Akon Ho CV6 .... 48 F2
Alan Bray Cl LE10 .... 30 D7
Alan Higgs Way CV4 .... 75 C8
Alandale Ave CV5 .... 59 E4
Alandale Ct CV12 .... 49 C8
Alauna Ave B49 .... 143 B3
Albany Ct CV1 .... 61 A2
Albany Rd Coventry CV5 .... 61 A1
 Stratford-u-A CV37 .... 144 C1
Albany Terr CV32 .... 105 E1
Albert Bean Cl CV31 .... 110 A4
Albert Cl B80 .... 103 C2
Albert Cres CV6 .... 49 B3
Albert Rd Allesley CV5 .... 59 A8
 Fazeley B78 .... 9 A4
Albert Sq CV21 .... 83 A2
Albert St Coventry CV1 .... 61 E4
 Nuneaton CV10 .... 28 E2
 Royal Leamington Spa
 CV32 .... 105 C1
 Rugby CV21 .... 83 A2
 Warwick CV34 .... 108 D7
Albion Cotts B46 .... 23 B3
Albion Ct CV11 .... 29 D3
Albion Ind Est CV6 .... 61 D7
Albion St CV8 .... 93 A5
Albion Terr Bedworth B50 .... 148 B4
 Water Orton B46 .... 23 B3
Albrighton Wlk CV11 .... 30 A2
Albury Rd B80 .... 103 C2
Alcester B-Pass B49 .... 143 A2
Alcester Gram Sch B49 .... 143 A2
Alcester Heath B49 .... 118 E6
Alcester High Sch B49 .... 143 B3
Alcester Highway B98 .... 102 C4
Alcester Hospl B49 .... 143 B2
Alcester Inf Sch B49 .... 143 A2
Alcester Rd
 Hollywood B47 .... 69 A8
 Portway B48 .... 85 F7
 Portway B48,B94,B98 .... 86 B4
 Stratford-u-A CV37 .... 144 B2
 Studley B80 .... 103 C2
 Wootton Wawen B95 .... 113 A1
Alcester Southern By-Pass
 B49 .... 143 B1
Alcocks Rd B49 .... 143 B2
Alcott Cl B93 .... 71 F2
Alcott Hall Jun & Inf Sch
 B37 .... 33 A2
Aldbourne Rd CV1 .... 61 C5
Aldbury Rise CV5 .... 60 C4
Alder Cl B47 .... 69 B6
Alder Cl CV7 .... 12 B1
Alder Dr B37 .... 33 B3
Alder La CV7 .... 74 C5
Alder Meadow Cl CV6 .... 49 D4
Alder Rd CV6 .... 50 A2
Alderbrooke Dr CV11 .... 40 A6
Alderhanger La B98 .... 112 B8
Alderman Callow Sch & Com
 Coll CV4 .... 76 A6
Alderman Gee Hall CV12 .... 39 A4
Alderman Harris Prim Sch
 CV4 .... 75 F7
Alderman Smith Sch
 CV10 .... 28 D2
Alderman Way CV33 .... 107 B4
Alderman's Green Com Prim
 Sch CV2 .... 50 C3
Alderman's Green Rd
 CV2 .... 50 D2
Alderminster Cl B97 .... 102 C2
Alderminster Rd
 Coventry CV5 .... 60 A4
 Solihull B91 .... 71 C8
Aldermoor Farm Prim Sch
 CV3 .... 78 B8
Aldermoor La CV3 .... 62 A1
Alderney Cl
 Bramcote CV11 .... 40 F6
 Coventry CV6 .... 49 B2
Alders Dr B98 .... 112 A2
Alders Gr CV34 .... 108 D4
Alders La CV10 .... 27 A4
Aldersgate Kingsbury B78 .... 15 B4
 Nuneaton CV11 .... 29 C4
Aldershaws B90 .... 70 A5
Alderton Mews 16 CV31 .... 110 C6

Aldrich Ave CV4 .... 59 E2
Aldridge Cl B78 .... 10 C4
Aldridge Rd LE10 .... 31 D6
Aldrin Way CV4 .... 76 D5
Aldwick Cl CV34 .... 106 A4
Alesworth Dr LE10 .... 31 F4
Alex Grierson Cl CV3 .... 78 E7
Alexander Ct 1 CV34 .... 108 F7
Alexander Rd CV12 .... 39 C3
Alexandra Ct
 Atherstone CV9 .... 18 C4
 Kenilworth CV8 .... 93 A4
 16 Rugby CV21 .... 83 A2
Alexandra Hospl The
 B98 .... 103 B3
Alexandra Rd
 Coventry CV1 .... 61 F4
 Royal Leamington Spa
 CV31 .... 110 B6
 Rugby CV21 .... 83 A2
Alexandra St CV11 .... 29 B4
Alexandra Terr CV6 .... 49 E2
Alfall Rd CV2 .... 62 B5
Alfred Green Cl CV22 .... 83 A1
Alfred Rd CV1 .... 61 F4
Alfreda Ave B47 .... 69 A8
Alfreton Cl LE10 .... 31 F5
Alfriston Rd CV3 .... 77 C4
Alice Arnold Ho 1 CV2 .... 50 B1
Alice Cl CV12 .... 38 F1
Alice Stevens Sch CV3 .... 78 A6
Alicia Cl CV22 .... 99 A4
Alison Sq CV6 .... 50 B4
All Saints CE Inf Sch
 CV12 .... 39 C2
All Saints CE Jun Sch
 CV34 .... 105 A1
All Saints CE Prim Sch
 Coventry CV1 .... 61 E1
 Leek Wootton CV35 .... 105 A5
 Nuneaton CV10 .... 29 C1
All Saints Cl CV7 .... 52 C3
All Saints La CV1 .... 61 F3
All Saints Rd
 Bedworth CV12 .... 38 F1
 Warwick CV34 .... 109 B8
All Souls RC Prim Sch
 CV5 .... 60 E2
Allan Rd CV6 .... 60 F4
Allans Cl CV23 .... 84 A3
Allans Dr CV23 .... 84 A3
Allans La CV23 .... 84 A3
Allard Ho CV3 .... 78 B6
Allard Way CV3 .... 78 C7
Allen Cl B80 .... 103 C2
Allendale Ave B80 .... 103 C2
Allendale Cres B80 .... 103 C2
Allendale Rd B80 .... 103 C2
Allens Cl CV9 .... 17 B4
Allens Orch OX17 .... 134 F3
Allerton Cl CV2 .... 62 E2
Allesley Croft CV5 .... 60 A6
Allesley Hall Dr CV5 .... 60 A5
Allesley Hall Prim Sch
 CV5 .... 60 B4
Allesley Old Rd CV5 .... 60 D3
Allesley Prim Sch CV5 .... 60 A7
Allesley Rd CV21 .... 82 C2
Alliance Cl CV11 .... 29 F3
Alliance Way CV2 .... 62 A5
Allibone Cl CV31 .... 110 A4
Allied Cl CV6 .... 49 D2
Allimore La B49 .... 143 A2
Allitt Gr CV8 .... 93 B5
Allwood Cl B49 .... 143 A2
Alma Cl CV11 .... 40 F6
Alma St CV1 .... 151 D3
Almond Ave
 Nuneaton CV10 .... 28 C6
 Royal Leamington Spa
 CV32 .... 105 F3
Almond Cl CV23 .... 101 B1
Almond Gr Rugby CV21 .... 82 C4
 Warwick CV34 .... 105 A1
Almond Tree Ave CV2 .... 50 C2
Almshouses
 Bedworth CV12 .... 39 B3
 Chipping Campden GL55 .... 135 B2
 Dunchurch CV22 .... 99 B2
 Rowington Green CV35 .... 90 A1
 Stoneleigh CV8 .... 94 C6
 Stratford-u-A CV37 .... 145 A1
 2 Warwick CV34 .... 108 E6
Alne Bank Rd B49 .... 143 A2
Alne Cl B95 .... 113 B4
Alpha Bsns Pk CV2 .... 50 D1
Alpha Ho CV2 .... 62 A4
Alpine Ct CV8 .... 93 A6
Alpine Rise CV3 .... 77 B4
Alspath La CV5 .... 59 F4
Alspath Rd CV7 .... 46 C1
Althorpe Dr B93 .... 71 E3
Althorpe Ho CV1 .... 110 A6
Althorpe Ind Est 15
 CV31 .... 110 A7
Alton Cl CV2 .... 50 D2
Alum Cl CV6 .... 61 D8
Alvecote Cotts B79 .... 4 B3
Alverley Rd CV6 .... 61 C6
Alverstone Rd CV2 .... 62 A4
Alverton Cl B77 .... 4 A2
Alveston CE Prim Sch
 CV37 .... 145 C2
Alveston Gr B93 .... 72 B7
Alveston Grange GL55 .... 135 B6

Alveston La CV37 .... 121 D3
Alveston Pl 7 CV32 .... 105 F1
Alveston Rd B47 .... 69 A7
Alvin Cl CV3 .... 62 F1
Alvis Gate OX16 .... 139 F4
Alvis Ret Pk CV5 .... 61 A3
Alvis Way NN11 .... 117 F2
Alvis Wlk B36 .... 22 E1
Alwyn B77 .... 9 C4
Alwyn Rd CV22 .... 99 C3
Alwynne Freeman Ct
 CV7 .... 49 A6
Ambassador Ct CV22 .... 105 F3
Ambassador Rd B26 .... 44 C4
Amber Bsns Village B77 .... 4 A2
Amber Cl B77 .... 4 A2
Amber Ct B77 .... 4 A2
Amberley Ave CV12 .... 40 C2
Ambien Rd CV9 .... 18 B4
Ambler Gr CV2 .... 62 C3
Ambleside Coventry CV2 .... 50 E2
 Rugby CV21 .... 83 B3
Ambleside Way CV11 .... 29 E6
Ambrose Cl CV21 .... 83 B3
Amelia Cl CV12 .... 40 C3
Amersham Cl CV5 .... 60 B4
Amery Lodge Farm
 WR11 .... 128 A2
Amherst Rd CV8 .... 92 E6
Amhurst Bsns Ctr CV34 .... 108 B7
Amicombe B77 .... 4 B1
Amington Heath Com Prim
 Sch B77 .... 4 A2
Amington Ind Est B77 .... 4 A2
Amington Rd B90 .... 70 A8
Amos Ave CV10 .... 29 B2
Amos Jacques Rd CV12 .... 39 A4
Amroth Mews CV31 .... 110 C6
Amy Cl CV6 .... 49 F4
Anchor La
 Harvington WR11 .... 127 D3
 Harvington WR11 .... 127 E3
Anchorway Rd CV3 .... 77 B4
Anderson Ave CV22 .... 100 A4
Anderson Dr CV31 .... 110 A2
Anderton Rd
 Bedworth CV12 .... 38 C1
 Coventry CV2,CV6 .... 50 B4
 Kenilworth CV8 .... 93 C6
Anker Dr CV23 .... 82 A3
Anker St CV11 .... 29 D3
Anker View B78 .... 11 A4
Ankerside B78 .... 5 A4
Ann Rd B47 .... 69 A3
Anne Cres CV3 .... 78 C5
Anne Hathaway's Cott*
 CV37 .... 144 B1
Annie Osborn Prim Sch
 CV2 .... 62 D7
Anns La CV23 .... 65 B4
Ansell Dr CV6 .... 50 A5
Ansell Rd CV34 .... 108 D7
Ansley Comm CV10 .... 26 C2
Ansley La CV7,CV10 .... 26 C2
Anson Cl Rugby CV22 .... 82 B1
 Wellesbourne CV35 .... 146 B1
Anson Ct B78 .... 9 A4
Anson Way CV2 .... 62 F8
Anstey Croft B37 .... 33 A4
Ansty Rd CV2 .... 62 E5
Antelope Gdns CV34 .... 108 C8
Anthony Way CV2 .... 62 F2
Anton Dr B76 .... 22 A6
Antony Gardner Cres
 CV31 .... 110 A4
Antrim Cl CV5 .... 60 B7
Antrobus Cl CV35 .... 114 F3
Apollo Way CV34 .... 109 D5
Appian Cl B77 .... 9 B4
Appian Way B90 .... 70 D4
Apple Gr CV22 .... 82 A1
Apple Pie La CV10 .... 19 A1
Applebee Rd LE10 .... 31 D6
Appleby Cl Banbury OX16 .... 139 F4
 Great Alne B49 .... 119 D6
Appleby Gr B90 .... 71 B6
Appleby Hill CV9 .... 23 A3
Applecross Cl CV4 .... 75 F6
Appledore Dr CV5 .... 59 F5
Appletree Cl B91 .... 56 B5
Appletree Cotts B79 .... 89 F1
Appletree Ind Est OX17 .... 134 F4
Appletree La
 Aston le W NN11 .... 134 F5
 Cookhill WR7 .... 118 A3
Appletree Rd OX17 .... 134 F3
Approach The CV31 .... 109 F6
Apsley Gr B93 .... 72 B5
Aqua Ho CV32 .... 106 A1
Aragon Dr CV34 .... 109 D6
Aragon Ho CV3 .... 77 C8
Arbor Way B37 .... 33 C1
Arboretum The CV4 .... 76 D5
Arbour Cl Kenilworth CV8 .... 93 B3
 Mickleton GL55 .... 135 B6
 Rugby CV22 .... 99 B4
Arbour Tree La B93 .... 89 F7
Arbury Ave
 Bedworth CV12 .... 39 A3

Arbury Ave continued
 Coventry CV6 .... 49 F2
Arbury Banks OX17 .... 134 F3
Arbury Cl CV32 .... 106 A4
Arbury Ct
 Henley-in-A B95 .... 113 B5
 Nuneaton CV10 .... 28 C3
Arbury Garth CV10 .... 28 C3
Arbury Hall Park & Gdns*
 CV10 .... 38 D7
Arbury Hall Rd B90 .... 70 D8
Arbury Rd CV10 .... 28 D2
Arbury Wlk B76 .... 22 D2
Arcade The CV3 .... 62 B2
Arch Rd CV2 .... 62 E5
Archer Ave NN11 .... 117 E5
Archer Cl B80 .... 103 B2
Archer Rd CV8 .... 92 E3
Archers Spinney CV21 .... 101 A4
Archery Fields CV34 .... 108 F6
Archery Rd Meriden CV7 .... 46 B1
 Royal Leamington Spa
 CV31 .... 109 C8
Arches Bsns Ctr CV21 .... 83 B3
Arches Ind Est CV21 .... 83 B3
Arches Ind Est The CV5 .... 61 A3
Arches La CV21 .... 83 B3
Arden Ave CV9 .... 18 C4
Arden Bldgs B93 .... 71 F3
Arden Bsns Ctr B49 .... 143 A3
Arden Cl
 Balsall Common CV7 .... 74 B7
 Drayton OX15 .... 139 E4
 Henley-in-A B95 .... 113 B4
 Meriden CV7 .... 46 C1
 Royal Leamington Spa
 CV31 .... 110 B5
 Rugby CV22 .... 99 B3
 Stratford-u-A CV37 .... 144 C2
 Warwick CV34 .... 105 A1
 Wilmcote CV37 .... 120 C5
Arden Croft B46 .... 23 F1
Arden Ct Alcester B49 .... 143 A3
 Binley Woods CV3 .... 79 D6
 Hampton-in-A B92 .... 57 A7
Arden Dr Dorridge B93 .... 72 A1
 Sutton Coldfield, Falcon Lodge
 B75 .... 13 A6
Arden Forest Est CV10 .... 18 A1
Arden Forest Ind Est
 B49 .... 143 B3
Arden Forest Inf Sch
 CV12 .... 40 B3
Arden Hill Inf Sch CV9 .... 18 C4
Arden Lawn Sch B95 .... 113 A4
Arden Leys B94 .... 86 D2
Arden Meads B94 .... 58 C6
Arden Rd Alcester B49 .... 143 A3
 Bulkington CV12 .... 40 C2
 Dorridge B93 .... 71 F2
 Henley-in-A B95 .... 113 B4
 Hollywood B47 .... 69 A4
 Kenilworth CV8 .... 93 B3
 Nuneaton CV11 .... 30 A1
 Tamworth B77 .... 9 C3
Arden Sch B93 .... 72 B5
Arden St Atherstone CV9 .... 18 C4
 Coventry CV5 .... 76 F8
Arden Vale Rd B93 .... 72 B7
Ardendale B90 .... 70 C8
Ardens Cl B98 .... 112 A5
Arderne Dr B37 .... 33 A1
Argyle St CV21 .... 83 B2
Argyle Way 5 CV33 .... 122 F8
Argyll St CV2 .... 62 A3
Ariel Way CV22 .... 99 B3
Arkle B77 .... 9 B2
Arkle Dr CV2 .... 62 F7
Arklet Cl CV10 .... 28 C5
Arlescote Cl CV35 .... 114 F6
Arleston Way B90 .... 70 D8
Arley La CV10 .... 27 B2
Arley Mews CV32 .... 105 E1
Arlidge Cres CV8 .... 93 C5
Arlington Ave CV32 .... 105 F2
Arlington Cl CV21 .... 105 F2
Arlington Mews 5
 CV32 .... 105 F2
Arlington Way CV11 .... 29 F2
Arlon Ave CV10 .... 28 D7
Armarna Dr CV5 .... 59 B8
Armfield St CV6 .... 62 A8
Armorial Rd CV3 .... 77 B7
Armour Cl LE10 .... 31 D5
Armscote Gr CV35 .... 114 E6
Armscote Rd
 Ilmington CV36 .... 136 B6
 Tredington CV36 .... 136 E6
Armscott Rd CV2 .... 62 C6
Armson Rd CV7 .... 39 A1
Armstrong Ave CV3 .... 62 B1
Armstrong Cl Rugby CV22 .... 82 C1
 Whitnash CV31 .... 110 A2
Armstrong Dr B36 .... 22 F1
Arna Ho CV3 .... 78 B6
Arncliffe Cl CV11 .... 30 A2
Arncliffe Way 4 CV34 .... 104 F1
Arne Rd CV2 .... 63 A6
Arnhem Cnr CV3 .... 78 D6
Arnold Ave CV3 .... 77 C5
Arnold Cl CV22 .... 83 A1
Arnold Lodge Sch CV32 .... 105 F2
Arnold Rd CV13 .... 21 A3
Arnold St CV21 .... 83 A2
Arnold Villas 17 CV21 .... 83 A2
Arnolds La B46 .... 34 C2
Arnside Cl CV1 .... 151 C4
Arran Cl CV10 .... 29 A3

Arran Dr B77 . . . . .9 C4
Arran Way B36 . . . . .33 B7
Arras Byd CV11 . . . . .108 A7
Arreton CI CV12 . . . . .72 A6
Arrow Cres B49 . . . . .143 B3
Arrow End WR11 . . . . .128 A2
Arrow La WR11 . . . . .127 F2
Arthingworth CI CV3 . . . . .62 E1
Arthur Alford Ho CV12 . . . . .38 D1
Arthur Rd CV37 . . . . .145 A2
Arthur St Coventry CV1 . . . . . . .151 C4
  Kenilworth CV8 . . . . .93 A5
Artillery Rd CV11 . . . . .40 F6
Artmess Dr CV34 . . . . .109 C5
Arun Way B76 . . . . .13 A1
Arundel B77 . . . . .9 B4
Arundel CI 2 CV34 . . . . .108 F8
Arundel PI OX16 . . . . .139 F3
Arundel Rd
  Bulkington CV12 . . . . .40 C3
  Coventry CV3 . . . . .77 D6
Asbury Rd CV7 . . . . .74 B5
Ascot CI Bedworth CV12 . . . . . . .39 B4
  Coventry CV3 . . . . .78 C6
  Stratford-u-A CV37 . . . . .144 B1
Ascot Dr B77 . . . . .9 B2
Ascot Rd CV35 . . . . .132 D3
Ascot Ride CV32 . . . . .106 C3
Ascote Way CV47 . . . . .147 B2
Ascott Hall CV36 . . . . .142 A5
Ascott Rd CV36 . . . . .141 F5
Asfare Bsns Pk LE10 . . . . .31 E1
Ash CI CV35 . . . . .114 C5
Ash Ct CV22 . . . . .99 C4
Ash Dr Kenilworth CV8 . . . . .93 A4
  Nuneaton CV10 . . . . .28 A8
Ash End House Farm*
  B78 .14 B8
Ash Gr Arley CV7 . . . . .26 C1
  Ash Green CV7 . . . . .49 C7
  Bagington B B 15 B4
  Southam CV47 . . . . .147 A3
  Stratford-u-A CV37 . . . . .144 C3
  Tamworth B77 . . . . .9 C3
Ash Green La CV7 . . . . .49 D6
Ash Green Sch CV7 . . . . .49 D6
Ash La Bearley CV37 . . . . .120 E7
  Newton Regis B79 . . . . .2 C3
Ash Lawn Ho 8 CV31 . . . . . . .110 A7
Ash Priors CI CV4 . . . . .60 A2
Ash Tree Ave CV4 . . . . .60 A2
Ash Tree CI CV35 . . . . .146 C2
Ash Tree Gr CV7 . . . . .51 E5
Ash Way NN11 . . . . .117 D5
Ashborough Dr B91 . . . . .71 C8
Ashbourne Way B90 . . . . .70 E8
Ashbridge Rd CV5 . . . . .60 C4
Ashbrook Cres B91 . . . . .71 C8
Ashbrook Rise CV10 . . . . .19 A1
Ashburton CI CV11 . . . . .32 A6
Ashburton La OX15 . . . . .142 D3
Ashburton Rd CV2 . . . . .62 E8
Ashby CI CV3 . . . . .78 F8
Ashby Ct CV11 . . . . .29 D3
Ashby Rd NN11 . . . . .117 E5
Ashcroft CI CV2 . . . . .59 F3
Ashcroft CI CV2 . . . . .63 A8
Ashcroft Way CV2 . . . . .63 B8
Ashdale CI CV3 . . . . .79 E7
Ashdene Gdns CV8 . . . . .93 B4
Ashdown CI CV3 . . . . .78 D8
Ashdown Dr CV10 . . . . .28 F2
Ashe Rd CV10 . . . . .28 B3
Ashfield Ave CV4 . . . . .59 D1
Ashfield Rd CV8 . . . . .93 B4
Ashford Dr CV12 . . . . .39 A3
Ashford Gdns CV31 . . . . .109 F3
Ashford La B94 . . . . .88 B7
Ashford Rd Hinckley LE10 . . . . . .31 B7
  Whitnash CV31 . . . . .109 F2
Ashfurlong CI CV7 . . . . .74 B6
Ashgrove CV36 . . . . .149 C2
Ashington Gr CV3 . . . . .78 A5
Ashington Rd CV12 . . . . .38 C1
Ashlawn Rd CV22 . . . . .100 B4
Ashlawn Sch CV22 . . . . .100 C4
Ashlea B78 . . . . .10 C3
Ashleigh CI CV23 . . . . .101 B1
Ashleigh Dr
  Nuneaton CV11 . . . . .29 F1
  Tamworth B77 . . . . .9 C4
Ashley Cres CV34 . . . . .109 B6
Ashley Way CV7 . . . . .74 A7
Ashman Ave CV23 . . . . .82 A3
Ashmead Rd OX17 . . . . .139 F5
Ashmore Rd CV6 . . . . .61 B4
Ashmores CI B97 . . . . .102 B3
Ashorne CI Coventry CV2 . . . . . . .50 C2
  Redditch B98 . . . . .103 B4
Ashorne Hall Nickelodeon*
  CV33 . . . . .123 B4
Ashorne Hill Management
  Coll CV33 . . . . .122 E5
Ashow CI CV8 . . . . .93 B4
Ashridge CI CV11 . . . . .39 F8
Ashstead CI B76 . . . . .22 B6
Ashurst CI CV6 . . . . .50 A4
Ashurst Way CV6 . . . . .60 F5
Ashwood Dr B37 . . . . .33 D3
Ashwood Rd CV10 . . . . .28 E5
Aspbury Croft B36 . . . . .22 C1
Aspen CI Alcester B49 . . . . .143 A3
  Coventry CV4 . . . . .59 D1
Aspen Dr Birmingham B37 . . . . . .44 C8
  Coventry CV6 . . . . .50 C6
Aspen Gr B47 . . . . .69 B5
Aspens The B78 . . . . .15 B4
Asplen CI CV8 . . . . .93 C4

Aspley Ct CV35 . . . . .114 F6
Aspley Heath B94 . . . . .86 D2
Aspley Heath La B94 . . . . .86 D2
Assheton CI CV22 . . . . .99 B4
Aster CI Hinckley LE10 . . . . .31 E6
  Nuneaton CV11 . . . . .30 A1
Aster Way LE10 . . . . .31 D6
Asthill Croft CV3 . . . . .77 C8
Asthill Gr CV3 . . . . .77 C8
Astley Ave CV6 . . . . .49 E2
Astley CI Redditch B98 . . . . . . .103 A4
  Royal Leamington Spa
  CV32 . . . . .105 D2
Astley La Bedworth CV12 . . . . . . .38 C4
  Fillongley CV7 . . . . .37 A2
  Nuneaton CV10 . . . . .28 B1
Astley Wlk CV47 . . . . .133 A7
Astley's PI CV21 . . . . .101 A4
Aston Cantlow Rd CV37,
  B95 . . . . .120 B5
Aston Flamville Rd LE10 . . . . . . .32 C7
Aston Hill CV37 . . . . .120 B5
Aston La LE10 . . . . .32 A6
Aston La Ind Est CV11 . . . . .29 B5
Aston Rd
  Chipping Campden GL55 . . . . .135 B3
  Coventry CV5 . . . . .60 F1
  Nuneaton CV11 . . . . .29 B5
Astwood Bank Fst Sch
  B96 . . . . .102 C1
Astwood La B96 . . . . .102 B1
Atch Lench Rd WR11 . . . . .127 A6
Atcheson CI B80 . . . . .103 C2
Athena Dr CV34 . . . . .109 E5
Athena Gdns CV6 . . . . .50 A1
Atherston PI CV4 . . . . .76 D6
Atherstone Ind Est
  CV37 . . . . .130 C6
Atherstone La CV9 . . . . .16 C3
Atherstone Rd
  Appleby Magna DE12 . . . . .3 C3
  Atherstone CV9 . . . . .12 B2
  Fenny Drayton CV13 . . . . .20 A3
  Furnace End B46 . . . . .25 C3
  Hartshill CV10 . . . . .19 A1
  Hurley CV9 . . . . .16 B2
Atherstone St B77,B78 . . . . .9 A4
Atherstone Sta CV9 . . . . .18 B4
Athol Rd CV2 . . . . .63 A6
Atholl Cres CV10 . . . . .28 E2
Atkins Way LE10 . . . . .31 E7
Atterton La CV9 . . . . .19 B4
Attleborough Fields Ind Est
  CV11 . . . . .29 F3
Attleborough La B46 . . . . .23 A1
Attleborough Rd CV11 . . . . .29 D3
Attoxhall Rd CV2 . . . . .62 E4
Attwood Cres CV2 . . . . .62 C7
Atworth CI B98 . . . . .103 A3
Auckland Dr B36 . . . . .33 B8
Auden CI CV10 . . . . .27 C2
Augusta PI CV32 . . . . .109 F8
Augustine Ave B80 . . . . .103 B2
Augustus CI B46 . . . . .23 F1
Augustus Dr B49 . . . . .143 A2
Augustus Rd CV1 . . . . .61 F4
Austcliff CI B97 . . . . .102 B3
Austcliff Dr B91 . . . . .71 C8
Austen CI CV10 . . . . .27 C3
Austen Ct CV32 . . . . .106 E5
Austin CI CV9 . . . . .18 B4
Austin Croft B36 . . . . .22 E1
Austin Dr Banbury OX16 . . . . . .139 F4
  Coventry CV6 . . . . .62 A7
Austin Edwards Dr
  CV34 . . . . .109 B8
Austin Way NN11 . . . . .117 F2
Austin's Way OX15 . . . . .142 E4
Austrey CE Prim Sch CV9 . . . . . . .3 A1
Austrey CI B93 . . . . .72 A6
Austrey La Austrey B79 . . . . .3 A3
  Newton Regis B79 . . . . .3 A2
Austrey Rd
  Appleby Magna CV9,DE12 . . . . . .3 B3
  Warton B79 . . . . .5 C3
Austwick CI CV34 . . . . .104 E1
Auxerre Ave B98 . . . . .103 A4
Auxerre Ho B98 . . . . .103 A4
Avebury CI CV11 . . . . .29 F2
Aventine Way CV21 . . . . .82 C4
Avenue CI B93 . . . . .72 A3
Avenue Farm CV37 . . . . .144 C3
Avenue Field Ind Est
  CV37 . . . . .144 C2
Avenue Rd
  Astwood Bank B96 . . . . .102 C1
  Dorridge B93 . . . . .72 A3
  Kenilworth CV8 . . . . .92 D6
  Nuneaton CV11 . . . . .29 C5
  Royal Leamington Spa
  CV31 . . . . .109 F7
  Rugby CV21 . . . . .82 C2
  Stratford-u-A CV37 . . . . .145 A2
Avenue The Coventry CV3 . . . . .78 F8
  Rowington Green CV35 . . . . . . .90 A1
  Stratford-u-A CV37 . . . . .144 B3
Avery CI 6 CV34 . . . . .108 F7
Avernake CI CV10 . . . . .29 A3
Avill B77 . . . . .10 A3
Avocet CI CV2 . . . . .50 B3
Avon B77 . . . . .10 A4
Avon Aquatics* CV37 . . . . .130 A3
Avon Carrow CV47 . . . . .133 D4
Avon CI Barford CV35 . . . . .122 B8
  Bulkington CV12 . . . . .40 B6
  Ettington CV37 . . . . .131 B3
Avon Cres Alcester B49 . . . . . . .143 B3

Avon Cres continued
  Stratford-u-A CV37 . . . . .145 B1
Avon Ct Kenilworth CV8 . . . . .92 F5
  Offenham WR11 . . . . .127 D1
  Rugby CV21 . . . . .83 A3
Avon Dassett Rd CV47 . . . . . . .133 D6
Avon Fields CV37 . . . . .131 B3
Avon Ho CV4 . . . . .76 C6
Avon Ind Est Rugby CV21 . . . . . .83 B3
  Stratford-u-A CV37 . . . . .144 C2
Avon Mill CV37 . . . . .145 A2
Avon Rd Coventry CV4 . . . . .76 B6
  Kenilworth CV8 . . . . .93 B5
  Lighthorne Heath CV33 . . . . . .123 D2
  Whitnash CV31 . . . . .110 A3
Avon St Clifton u D CV23 . . . . . .83 C2
  Coventry CV2 . . . . .62 B5
  Rugby CV21 . . . . .83 A2
Avon Terr CV8 . . . . .95 B3
Avon Valley Sch The
  CV21 . . . . .82 C3
Avon Way CV35 . . . . .138 C6
Avonbank CV37 . . . . .145 A2
Avonbank CI B97 . . . . .102 B3
Avonbank Dr CV37 . . . . .129 E8
Avonbank Paddocks
  CV37 . . . . .145 A1
Avonbrook CI CV37 . . . . .144 B2
Avoncroft WR11 . . . . .127 D1
Avoncroft Ho B37 . . . . .33 A2
Avondale Rd Brandon CV8 . . . . . .79 F5
  Coventry CV5 . . . . .77 A8
Avonfields CI CV37 . . . . .121 D3
Avonhurst CV37 . . . . .145 C2
Avonlea Rise CV32 . . . . .105 D2
Avonmeadow CI CV37 . . . . .144 C1
Avonmere CV21 . . . . .82 C4
Avonside CV37 . . . . .145 A1
Avonside Cvn Pk CV37 . . . . .129 A7
Awson St CV6 . . . . .61 F6
Axholme Rd CV2 . . . . .62 E4
Axminster CI CV11 . . . . .29 F5
Aylesbury CI B94 . . . . .88 C6
Aylesbury Rd B94 . . . . .88 D7
Aylesdene Ct CV5 . . . . .76 F8
Aylesford CI 7 Redditch B98 . . .110 A6
Aylesford Dr B37 . . . . .44 A7
Aylesford Sch CV34 . . . . .108 C4
Aylesford St Coventry CV1 . . . . . .61 F4
  Royal Leamington Spa
  CV31 . . . . .110 A6
Aylstone CI CV37 . . . . .129 D2
Aynho CI CV5 . . . . .60 A3
Aysgarth CI CV11 . . . . .30 A2
Azalea CI LE10 . . . . .31 E6
Azalea Dr LE10 . . . . .31 E6
Azalea Wlk LE10 . . . . .31 E5

B

Babbacombe Rd CV3 . . . . .77 D5
Bablake CI CV6 . . . . .60 F8
Bablake Jun Sch CV1 . . . . .151 A4
Bablake Sch CV1 . . . . .61 B4
Bachelors Bench CV9 . . . . .18 B4
Back Ends GL55 . . . . .135 B2
Back Hill OX17 . . . . .139 E8
Back La Birdingbury CV23 . . . . .115 F7
  Claverdon CV35 . . . . .114 A6
  Claybrooke Magna LE17 . . . . . . .43 C3
  Cleeve Prior WR11 . . . . .128 A4
  Harborough Magna CV23 . . . . . .66 A2
  Henley-in-A B95 . . . . .113 B5
  Long Compton CV36 . . . . .141 D3
  Long Lawford CV23 . . . . .82 A2
  Lower Quinton CV37 . . . . .129 E2
  Meriden CV7 . . . . .58 E1
  Mickleton GL55 . . . . .135 B6
  Pebworth CV37 . . . . .128 E1
  Shustoke B46 . . . . .24 C1
  Sibford Ferris OX15 . . . . .142 D8
  Solihull B90 . . . . .70 C6
  Tysoe CV35 . . . . .138 B7
  Warwick CV34 . . . . .108 E6
Back St Ilmington CV36 . . . . . .136 B6
  Nuneaton CV11 . . . . .29 C5
Backside La OX15 . . . . .142 D8
Badbury CI B80 . . . . .103 B2
Badbury Gdns B80 . . . . .103 B2
Badby Leys CV22 . . . . .100 A4
Badby Sch NN11 . . . . .126 F6
Baddesley CI CV31 . . . . .110 B5
Baddesley Clinton* B93 . . . . . .89 F4
Badger Brook La B96 . . . . .102 C1
Badger CI B90 . . . . .70 D4
Badger Rd CV3 . . . . .78 D8
Badgers Cres CV36 . . . . .149 C4
Badgers Farm La CV35 . . . . . . .138 C6
Badgers Field OX15 . . . . .135 B2
Baffin CI CV22 . . . . .99 C3
Baginton Fields Sch CV3 . . . . . . .78 B4
Baginton Rd
  Birmingham B35 . . . . .22 B4
  Coventry CV3 . . . . .77 C5
Bagot Way CV34 . . . . .109 E3
Bagshaw CI CV8 . . . . .79 A1
Bailey Ave B77 . . . . .9 C2
Bailey Rd CV37 . . . . .129 B1
Bailey's La CV23 . . . . .82 A2
Bakehouse La
  Chadwick End B93 . . . . .90 B6
  Nether Whitacre B46 . . . . .24 C1
  Rugby CV21 . . . . .83 A2
  Shottesfield OX17 . . . . .139 E8

Baker Ave
  Royal Leamington Spa
  CV31 . . . . .109 F6
  Stratford-u-A CV37 . . . . .144 B2
Baker Dr CV35 . . . . .146 B2
Baker St CV6 . . . . .50 B6
Baker's Hill GL55 . . . . .135 C5
Bakers Croft CV9 . . . . .11 B1
Bakers Ct CV9 . . . . .18 B4
Bakers La Coventry CV5 . . . . .60 E2
  Knowle B93 . . . . .72 D1
  Swalcliffe OX15 . . . . .142 F8
  Bakers Mews B95 . . . . .90 B6
Bakers Wlk B77 . . . . .9 C3
Bakewell CI CV3 . . . . .78 F8
Balcombe Ct CV22 . . . . .100 C4
Balcombe Rd CV22 . . . . .100 B4
Balding CI CV23 . . . . .53 C2
Baldwin Croft CV6 . . . . .50 B1
Baldwins La CV35 . . . . .138 B6
Balfour CI LE10 . . . . .31 E7
Ballantine Rd CV6 . . . . .61 B6
Ballard Wlk B37 . . . . .33 A6
Ballards CI GL55 . . . . .135 B6
Ballards Ct CV36 . . . . .149 C3
Ballards La CV36 . . . . .136 B6
Ballingham CI CV4 . . . . .60 A2
Balliol Rd Coventry CV2 . . . . .62 C4
  Hinckley LE10 . . . . .31 F6
Balmoral Ave
  Banbury OX16 . . . . .139 F3
  Banbury, Crouch Hill OX16 . . . .139 F2
Balmoral CI CV2 . . . . .62 E6
Balmoral Ct CV10 . . . . .28 E6
Balmoral Rd B36 . . . . .33 A7
Balmoral Way CV32 . . . . .106 C6
Balsall Common Prim Sch
  CV7 .74 B5
Balsall St B93,CV7 . . . . .73 D7
Balsall St E CV7 . . . . .74 B5
Balthazar CI CV34 . . . . .109 E4
Bamburgh B77 . . . . .9 B4
Bamburgh Gr CV32 . . . . .105 E2
Ban Brook Copse WR11 . . . . . .127 F6
Ban Brook Rd WR11 . . . . .127 F6
Banbury Rd
  Chipping Warden OX17 . . . . . .134 F3
  Ettington CV37 . . . . .131 B3
  Kineton CV35 . . . . .132 C5
  Ladbroke CV47 . . . . .124 C4
  Lighthorne Heath CV35 . . . . . .123 C3
  Lower Boddington NN11 . . . . . .134 E7
  North Newington OX15 . . . . . .139 E2
  Shutford OX15 . . . . .139 A3
  Southam CV47 . . . . .147 A3
  Southam CV47 . . . . .147 A2
  Stratford-u-A CV37 . . . . .130 D7
  Swerford OX7 . . . . .142 E1
  Warmington OX17 . . . . .133 D1
  Warwick CV34 . . . . .109 A3
Banbury St CV35 . . . . .132 B5
Bancroft PI CV37 . . . . .145 A2
Bangley La
  Drayton Bassett B78 . . . . .7 C3
  Fazeley B78 . . . . .8 A4
Bangor Ho B37 . . . . .33 A4
Banister Way CV34 . . . . .149 C3
Bank CI CV35 . . . . .131 F5
Bank Croft CV31 . . . . .110 C5
Bank Rd CV9 . . . . .18 C4
Bank St CV21 . . . . .83 A2
Bank The
  Bidford-on-A B50 . . . . .148 B2
  Bidford-on-A, Marlcliff B50 . . . .148 B1
  Lighthorne CV35 . . . . .123 B2
  Stoneleigh CV8 . . . . .94 C3
Bank View CV35 . . . . .131 F5
Bankfield Dr CV12 . . . . .105 C1
Banks Rd CV6 . . . . .61 A5
Bankside CI CV3 . . . . .78 A6
Bankside Cl CV4 . . . . .59 E1
Banks La CV8 . . . . .59 D2
Banners La B97 . . . . .102 C3
Banquo App
  Royal Leamington Spa
  CV34 . . . . .109 F2
Bantam Gr CV6 . . . . .49 A3
Bantock Rd CV4 . . . . .59 E2
Bar Rd CV3 . . . . .77 E8
Barber Wlk CV35 . . . . .114 F4
Barbers La B91 . . . . .56 C6
Barbican Rise CV2 . . . . .62 E4
Barbourne CI B91 . . . . .71 B7
Barbridge CI CV12 . . . . .40 C2
Barbridge Rd CV12 . . . . .40 C2
Barby CE Prim Sch
  CV23 . . . . .117 E8
Barby La CV22 . . . . .101 A2
Barby Rd Kilsby CV23 . . . . .101 C2
  Rugby CV22 . . . . .100 A4
Barchestion Dr CV35 . . . . .114 E6
Barcheston Rd B93 . . . . .71 F4
Barcombe CI OX16 . . . . .139 F5
Bardley Dr CV6 . . . . .61 C6
Bardon View Rd B78 . . . . .11 A4
Bards Wlk CV37 . . . . .145 A2
Bardswell Ct CV37 . . . . .145 A2
Barford App CV31 . . . . .110 B2
Barford CI CV3 . . . . .78 D8
Barford Rd CV8 . . . . .93 A3
**Barford St Peter's CE Prim
  Sch** CV35 . . . . .122 B7
Barham CI B90 . . . . .71 A5
Bari Rd CV35 . . . . .132 E5
Barker's Butts La CV6 . . . . .61 A4
Barkers La B47 . . . . .69 A1
Barkers' Butts La CV6 . . . . .61 A5

Barkus CI CV47 . . . . .147 B2
Barle Gr B36 . . . . .33 A7
Barley CI Henley-in-A B95 . . . . . .113 B4
Barley Croft CV22 . . . . .101 A4
Barley Ct CV32 . . . . .105 F2
Barley Lea Ho CV3 . . . . .78 B8
Barley Lea The CV3 . . . . .78 C8
Barlichway B49 . . . . .143 B2
Barling Ct B78 . . . . .15 B3
Barlow Rd CV2 . . . . .50 D2
Barn CI
  Clifford Chambers CV37 . . . . . .129 F7
  Coventry CV5 . . . . .60 C5
  Dordon B78 . . . . .10 C3
  Whitnash CV31 . . . . .110 B3
Barn End Rd B79 . . . . .5 C2
Barn La CV23 . . . . .96 C1
Barnack Ave CV3 . . . . .77 B5
Barnack Dr CV34 . . . . .104 E1
Barnacle La CV12 . . . . .40 C1
Barnard CI
  Birmingham B37 . . . . .33 D1
  Royal Leamington Spa
  CV32 . . . . .106 C3
Barnbrook Rd B93 . . . . .72 A7
Barncroft CV36 . . . . .141 C3
Barne CI CV11 . . . . .40 B7
Barnfield Ave CV5 . . . . .60 B6
Barnsley CI CV9 . . . . .3 A1
Barnstaple CI CV5 . . . . .59 F5
Barnwell CI CV22 . . . . .99 B2
Baron's Croft CV3 . . . . .77 E7
Baron's Field Rd CV3 . . . . .77 E8
Barons Croft CV10 . . . . .28 C4
Barpool Rd CV10 . . . . .28 D4
Barr La Brinklow CV23 . . . . .64 C2
  Higham on t H CV13 . . . . .21 A2
Barr's Hill Sch & Com Coll
  CV1 . . . . .151 A4
Barra Croft B35 . . . . .22 B4
Barrack Ct B75 . . . . .13 A6
Barrack St CV34 . . . . .108 E7
Barracks Gn CV35 . . . . .130 F7
Barracks La CV35 . . . . .91 C2
Barracks Way CV1 . . . . .151 B2
Barras Gn CV2 . . . . .62 A4
Barras Gn CV2 . . . . .62 A4
Barras La CV1 . . . . .61 B3
Barrels Pitch GL55 . . . . .135 B2
Barretts La CV7 . . . . .74 B6
Barrington Rd CV22 . . . . .82 B1
Barrow CI CV2 . . . . .63 B6
Barrow Rd CV8 . . . . .92 F4
Barrowfield Ct CV8 . . . . .92 F4
Barrowfield La CV8 . . . . .92 F4
Barry Ho CV2 . . . . .50 D1
Barsby CI CV9 . . . . .18 B4
Barston CI CV6 . . . . .50 A2
Barston La
  Balsall Common CV7 . . . . .73 D8
  Barston B92 . . . . .57 C1
  Catherine de B B91 . . . . .56 B2
  Hampton-in-A B92 . . . . .56 D3
Bartholomew Ct CV3 . . . . .78 A6
Bartleet Rd B98 . . . . .103 C4
Bartlett CI Coventry CV6 . . . . . . .49 C2
  2 Warwick CV34 . . . . .108 F7
Barton Cres CV31 . . . . .110 C6
Barton Dr B93 . . . . .72 B4
Barton Fields CV37 . . . . .129 A6
Barton Rd Bedworth CV12 . . . . . .39 A4
  Coventry CV6 . . . . .49 F2
  Long Compton CV36,GL56 . . . .141 B4
  Nuneaton CV10 . . . . .29 C1
  Rugby CV22 . . . . .99 B4
Barton's Mdw CV2 . . . . .62 B6
Barwell CI Dorridge B93 . . . . .71 F4
  Royal Leamington Spa
  CV32 . . . . .105 F3
Basant CI CV34 . . . . .109 A7
Bascote Rd CV47 . . . . .115 C3
Bascote Rise CV47 . . . . .147 A3
Baseley Way CV6 . . . . .49 F4
Basford Brook Dr CV6 . . . . .49 F4
Basildon Wlk 3 CV2 . . . . .63 A8
Basin Bridge La CV13 . . . . .21 B2
Bassett Rd CV6 . . . . .61 A5
Bastyan Ave CV37 . . . . .129 D2
Bateman Rd B46 . . . . .23 F1
Bateman's Acre S 1 CV6 . . . . . .61 A4
Bates CI B76 . . . . .22 B8
Bates La B94 . . . . .86 E7
Bates Rd CV5 . . . . .76 E8
Bath PI 3 CV31 . . . . .109 F7
Bath Rd Atherstone CV9 . . . . .18 C4
  Nuneaton CV11 . . . . .29 C5
  Royal Leamington Spa
  CV31 . . . . .109 F7
Bathurst CI CV6 . . . . .61 A6
Bathway Rd CV3 . . . . .77 A5
Batsford CI B98 . . . . .103 A4
Batsford Rd CV6 . . . . .60 F4
Battalion Ct CV4 . . . . .49 A1
Battle Ct CV35 . . . . .132 B6
Baulk La CV7 . . . . .58 D1
Bawnmore Ct CV22 . . . . .99 B4
Bawnmore Inf Sch CV22 . . . . . . .99 B4
Bawnmore Pk CV22 . . . . .99 C4
Bawnmore Rd CV22 . . . . .99 B4
Baxter CI CV4 . . . . .59 D2
Baxter Ct B CV31 . . . . .110 A7
Baxters Gn B90 . . . . .70 B8

Baxters Rd B90 ....70 B8
Bay Tree Cl CV2 ....50 D1
Bay Tree Farm WR11 ....128 A4
Bayley La CV1 ....151 C2
Bayliss Ave CV6 ....50 A4
Bayton Rd CV7 ....50 B7
Bayton Road Ind Est CV7 50 B8
Bayton Way CV7 ....50 D2
Baywell Cl B90 ....71 A7
Bazzard Rd CV11 ....41 A3
Beacon Cl B49 ....143 B3
Beacon Rd CV6 ....49 D3
Beaconsfield Ave CV22 ..83 A1
Beaconsfield Ct CV11 ...29 D5
Beaconsfield Rd CV2 ....62 B2
Beaconsfield St CV31 ...110 B7
Beaconsfield St W CV31 .110 B8
Beake Ave CV6 ....61 B7
Beale Cl Birmingham B35 .22 A2
16 Bishops Tachbrook
CV33 ....122 F8
Beamish Cl CV2 ....63 A6
Beanacre Rd OX15 ......142 D3
Beanfield Ave CV3 ....76 F4
Bear Cl B95 ....113 B5
Bear La B95 ....113 A5
Bear La Cl B78 ....5 A1
Bearcroft Gdns GL55 ...135 C6
Bearley Croft B90 ......70 C8
Bearley Gn CV37 ....120 E7
Bearley Grange CV37 ...120 D7
Bearley Halt B95 ....120 D7
Bearley Rd
Aston Cantlow B95 .....120 A7
Snitterfield CV37 ....121 A7
Beatty Dr CV22 ....82 B1
Beauchamp Ave CV32 ...105 F1
Beauchamp Cl
11 Birmingham B37 ......33 B2
Sutton Coldfield B76 .....22 B7
Beauchamp Ct **11** CV8 .105 F1
Beauchamp Gdns CV34 .109 B6
Beauchamp Hill CV32 ...105 E1
Beauchamp Ind Pk B77 ..9 B4
Beauchamp Rd
Alcester B49 ....143 B3
Kenilworth CV8 ....92 F2
Royal Leamington Spa
CV32 ....105 F1
Tamworth B77 ....9 C4
Warwick CV34 ....109 B8
Beaudesert Cl
Henley-in-A B95 ....113 B4
Hollywood B47 ....69 A7
Beaudesert La B95 .....113 B5
Beaudesert Rd
Coventry CV5 ....61 A1
Hollywood B47 ....69 A6
Beaufell Cl CV4 ....60 A2
Beaufort Ave CV32 .....106 C5
Beaufort Cl Hinckley LE10 .31 E4
Wellesbourne CV35 .....146 B1
Beaufort Dr CV3 ....78 F7
Beaulieu Pk CV31 ......110 D6
Beaumaris Cl
Banbury OX16 ....139 F4
Coventry CV5 ....59 F5
Beaumont Ave LE10 ....31 A7
Beaumont Cl CV47 .....133 A7
Beaumont Cres CV6 ....61 A4
Beaumont Ct
10 Coventry CV6 ....61 A4
B Royal Leamington Spa
CV31 ....110 A6
Beaumont Pl CV11 ......29 A4
Beaumont Rd
Keresley CV7 ....49 A6
Nuneaton CV11 ....29 A4
Beausale Croft CV5 ....60 A3
Beausale Dr B93 ....72 C7
Beausale La CV35 ......114 E2
Beck's Cl CV47 ....147 C4
Beck's La CV47 ....147 C4
Beckbury Rd CV2 ....62 F6
Becket Cl GL56 ....140 E7
Beckfoot Cl CV21 ......83 B4
Beckfoot Dr CV2 ....50 F1
Beckford Croft B93 ....71 F3
Becks La CV7 ....47 A5
Beconsfield Cl B93 .....71 F2
Bedale Rd CV35 ....132 D4
Bede Arc CV12 ....39 B3
Bede Rd Bedworth CV12 .39 A4
Coventry CV6 ....61 B6
Nuneaton CV10 ....28 D3
Bedford Cl CV16 ....139 F4
Bedford Ho B36 ....33 B6
Bedford Pl **15** CV32 ..109 F8
Bedford St Coventry CV1 .61 A2
Royal Leamington Spa
CV32 ....109 F8
Bedlam La CV6 ....49 E2
Bedworth Cl CV12 .....40 B2
Bedworth La CV12 .....38 D4
Bedworth Rd
Bedworth CV12 ....39 F2
Bulkington CV12 ....40 A2
Coventry CV6,CV7 .....50 A5
Bedworth Sta CV12 ....39 C2
Beech Ave B37 ....33 A3
Beech Cl Alcester B49 ..143 B1
Hurley CV9 ....16 B3
Kingsbury B78 ....15 B4
Nuneaton CV10 ....28 A8
Rowington CV35 ....114 A8

Beech Cl continued
Southam CV47 ....147 A2
Stratford-u-A CV37 ....145 B1
Beech Cliffe CV34 .....108 F8
Beech Ct
Royal Leamington Spa
CV34 ....109 E2
Rugby CV22 ....100 C4
Stratford-u-A CV37 ....145 A1
Beech Dr Kenilworth CV8 .93 B5
Rugby CV22 ....99 B4
Thurlaston CV23 ....98 C2
Beech Gr Arley CV7 ....26 C1
Warwick CV34 ....108 B4
Beech Hill NN11 ....126 B5
Beech Rd Coventry CV6 .61 B5
Hollywood B47 ....69 B6
Oxhill CV35 ....137 F8
Beech Tree Ave CV4 ...60 B2
Beecham Ind Est CV37 .130 C5
Beecham Wlk CV37 ....144 B2
Beechcroft Bedworth CV12 .38 F1
Long Itchington CV47 ...115 D4
Beechcroft Rd B36 ....22 C1
Beecher's Keep CV8 ...79 F5
Beeches The
Bedworth CV12 ....38 E2
Clifton u D CV23 ....83 C3
Harbury CV33 ....123 E7
Nuneaton CV10 ....19 A1
Polesworth B78 ....11 A4
Beeches Wlk CV37 ....145 C2
Beechnut Cl CV4 ....59 D2
Beechtree Pk B50 .....148 C3
Beechwood Ave
Coventry CV5 ....76 F8
Hinckley LE10 ....31 E6
Beechwood Cl B90 ....70 D4
Beechwood Croft CV8 ..92 F2
Beechwood Ct CV5 ....76 F8
Beechwood Rd
Bedworth CV12 ....39 C3
Nuneaton CV10 ....28 D6
Beehive Hill CV8 ....92 E7
Beehive La B76 ....23 C6
Beeston Cl CV3 ....78 F8
Begonia Cl LE10 ....31 E5
Begonia Dr IF10 ......31 E5
Belcony GL56 ....136 C1
Belfry Cl LE10 ....31 D4
Belgrave Dr CV21 .....83 B3
Belgrave Rd Coventry CV2 .62 E4
Tamworth B77 ....9 C4
Belgrave Sq CV2 ......62 E4
Belgravia Ct B37 ......33 A5
Bell Brook CV37 ....121 B6
Bell Cl B36 ....33 B6
Bell Ct
Royal Leamington Spa
CV32 ....105 F2
Stratford-u-A CV37 ....145 A1
Bell Dr CV7 ....49 E7
Bell Green Rd CV6 .....62 A8
Bell Hill OX15 ....142 D4
Bell La Monks Kirby CV23 .53 C1
Snitterfield CV37 ......121 B6
Stratford-u-A CV37 ....144 B1
Studley B80 ....103 C2
Bell Mead B80 ....103 C2
Bell St
Claybrooke Magna LE17 .43 C3
Hornton OX15 ....139 B7
Bell Tower Mews CV32 .105 F1
Bell Wlk CV21 ....101 A4
Bell's La OX15 ....142 D4
Bellairs Ave CV12 .....38 E1
Bellam Rd CV35 ....114 F4
Bellbrooke Cl CV6 ....50 B1
Belle Cotts B94 ....88 C3
Belle Vue CV10 ....28 E3
Belle Vue Terr B92 ....57 A6
Bellemere Rd B92 .....57 B6
Bellfield B94 ....87 A2
Bellingham B77 ....4 B1
Bellington Croft **5** B90 .71 A6
Bells La OX15 ....137 E3
Bellview Way CV6 .....50 B1
Belmont Ct CV32 ......106 A4
Belmont Dr CV32 ......106 A4
Belmont Mews CV8 ....92 F4
Belmont Rd Coventry CV6 .62 A7
Rugby CV22 ....83 A1
Belmont Row CV37 ....136 B6
Belvedere Rd CV5 .....77 A8
Belvoir B77 ....9 B4
Benedict Sq CV2 ......62 C8
Benedictine Rd CV3 ...77 C8
Bengrove Cl H98 ......103 A4
Benn Rd CV12 ....40 B2
Bennet St CV13 ....21 F4
Bennett Cl CV8 ....79 F3
Bennett Dr CV34 ......109 C7
Bennett Pl CV36 ......136 B6
Bennett's Rd CV7 .....82 C2
Bennett's Rd N CV7 ...48 F7
Bennett's Rd S CV6 ...48 F2
Bennfield Rd CV21 ....83 A2
Benson Rd Coventry CV6 .49 A1
Stratford-u-A CV37 ....145 A2
Benthall Rd CV6 ....49 F3
Bentley Cl Banbury OX16 .139 F4
Royal Leamington Spa
CV32 ....106 B3
Bentley Ct Coventry CV6 .61 B5
Nuneaton CV11 ....29 A4

Bentley Farm Cl B93 ..71 E4
Bentley Heath CE Prim Sch
B93 ....71 F5
Bentley Heath Cotts B93 .71 F5
Bentley La B46 ....35 B2
Bentley Rd Bedworth CV7 .39 A1
Nuneaton CV11 ....29 A4
Benton Green La CV7 ..58 F2
Bentree The CV3 ......78 B8
Beoley La B98 ....86 B1
Berenska Dr CV32 ....106 A2
Beresford Ave CV6 ....49 E1
Bericote Rd CV32 .....105 E8
Berkeley Cl
Banbury OX16 ....139 F4
Nuneaton CV11 ....29 B3
Redditch B98 ....112 A6
Berkeley Rd CV8 ....92 E6
Berkeley Rd N CV5 ....61 A1
Berkeley Rd S CV5 ....77 A8
Berkett Rd CV6 ....49 B2
Berkshire Cl CV10 .....28 E3
Berkswell CE Prim Sch
CV7 ....58 C3
Berkswell Hall CV7 ....58 B2
Berkswell Rd
Coventry CV6 ....50 B2
Meriden CV7 ....58 E7
Berkswell Sta CV7 ....74 C8
Berkswell Windmill*
CV7 ....74 D8
Bermuda Bsns Pk CV10 .39 A7
Bermuda Ind Est CV10 .39 B8
Bermuda Rd CV10 .....29 A1
Berners Cl CV4 ....59 E2
Berrills La CV36 ......141 D7
Berrington Rd
Chipping Campden GL55 .135 C2
Nuneaton CV10 ....28 D7
Royal Leamington Spa
CV31 ....110 B6
Berrow Cottage Homes
B93 ....72 C6
Berry Ave CV36 ....149 C3
Berry Cl CV36 ....149 C3
Berry Hall La B91,B92 .56 B4
Berry La NN11 ....126 B5
Berry Mdw CV47 ......133 E7
Berry St CV1 ....61 E4
Berryfields Cl CV7 .....36 C3
Berryfields La CV36,
CV37 ....136 C7
Berrymound View B47 ..69 C7
Bertie Rd CV8 ....93 A4
Bertie Terr CV22 ......105 E1
Berwick Cl Coventry CV6 .60 E4
Warwick CV34 ....104 E2
Berwicks La B37 ......33 B1
Berwood Pk B35 ......22 A2
Berwyn Ave CV6 ......49 A1
Berwyn Way CV10 ....28 C4
Besbury Cl B93 ....71 E2
Besford Gr B90 ....71 B6
Best Ave CV8 ....93 C7
Beswick Gdns CV22 ...99 B4
Bettina Cl CV10 ....28 B3
Bettman Cl CV3 ....77 E6
Bettridge Pl CV35 .....146 B2
Beverley Ave CV10 ....28 B2
Beverley Cl
Astwood Bank B96 ....102 C1
Balsall Common CV7 ...74 C7
Beverley Rd CV32 .....105 D1
Beverly Dr CV4 ....76 D2
Bevington Cres CV6 ..60 E5
Bewdley Ho B36 ......33 B6
Bexfield Cl CV6 ....60 A6
Beyer Cl B77 ....4 A1
Biart Pl CV21 ....83 B2
Bicester Sq B35 ......22 B4
Bickenhill Green Ct B92 .44 D1
Bickenhill La
Birmingham B26,B37,B40 .44 D4
Birmingham B37 ......44 C2
Catherine de B B92 ....56 C6
Bickenhill Parkway B37 .44 C6
Bickenhill Rd B37 ....44 B7
Bickmarsh La B50 ....148 B1
Bickmarsh Lodge Cotts
WR11 ....128 D2
Bidavon Ind Est B50 ..148 C3
Biddles Hill B94 ....86 C6
Bidduiph Terr CV23 ...97 B1
Bideford Rd CV2 ......62 C7
Bidford on Avon CE Prim Sch
B50 ....148 B2
Bidford Rd B50 ....148 A4
Biggin Cl B35 ....22 A3
Biggin Cl B35 ....22 A3
Biggin Hall Cres CV3 ..62 B2
Biggin Hall La CV23 ...98 F1
Bignolds Cl OX17 .....134 B4
Bigwood Dr B75 ......13 A5
Bilberry Rd CV2 ....50 D2
Bilbury Cl B97 ....102 B3
Billesden Cl CV3 ......78 E8
Billesley La B48 ....85 E6
Billing Rd CV5 ....60 C3
Billingham Cl B91 .....71 B8
Billinton Cl CV2 ......62 E2
Bills La B90 ....69 F7
Bilton CE Jun Sch CV22 .99 B3
Bilton Grange Sch CV22 .99 C2
Bilton High Sch CV22 ..82 A1
Bilton Inf Sch CV22 ...99 B3
Bilton Inf Sch CV22 ...99 B3
Bilton La Dunchurch CV22 .99 B3

Bilton La continued
Long Lawford CV22,CV23 ..82 A2
Bilton Rd CV22 ....82 C1
Binley Ave CV3 ....78 F7
Binley Bsns Pk CV3 ...63 A1
Binley Gr CV3 ....70 A8
Binley Gr CV3 ....78 F7
Binley Ind Est CV3 ....79 A8
Binley Rd CV2,CV3 ....62 D1
Binley Woods Prim Sch
CV3 ....79 E7
Binns Cl CV4 ....75 F8
Binswood Ave CV32 ...105 F2
Binswood Cl CV2 .....50 D2
Binswood End CV33 ...123 E7
Binswood Mans **16**
CV32 ....105 F2
Binswood St CV32 ....105 E1
Binton Rd Coventry CV2 .50 D2
Welford on A CV37 ....129 A7
Bintonhill CV37 ....120 A1
Birbeck Ho B36 ....33 B6
Birch Abbey B49 ......143 A2
Birch Cl Bedworth CV12 .39 D4
Coventry CV5 ....59 F6
Kingsbury B78 ....15 B4
Birch Coppice Distribution
Pk B78 ....10 C2
Birch Croft B37 ....33 C1
Birch Ct CV34 ....109 C7
Birch Dr CV22 ....82 A1
Birch End CV34 ....109 B8
Birch Gr
Balsall Common CV7 ...74 B8
Polesworth B78 ....10 B4
Wellesbourne CV35 ...146 C2
Birches La CV8 ....93 B3
Birches The CV12 .....40 B4
Birchfield Cl CV9 .....10 B1
Birchfield Rd
Coventry CV6 ....60 F8
Stratford-u-A CV37 ...145 A3
Birchgrave Cl CV6 ....62 A7
Birchley Heath Rd CV10 .17 C1
Birchmoor Rd B78 ....10 C4
Birchtree Rd CV10 ....28 C6
Birchwood Cl CV22 ...105 C1
Birchwood Ave CV8 ...10 C4
Birchwood Prim Sch B78 .10 C4
Birchwood Rd CV3 ....79 C7
Birchy Cl B90 ....69 E6
Birchy Leasowes La B90 .69 E5
Bird Grove Ct CV1 ....61 D5
Bird Rd
Lighthorne Heath CV33 .123 D2
Royal Leamington Spa
CV34 ....105 E1
Bird St CV1 ....151 C3
Birdhaven Cl CV33 ...123 D2
Birdhope B77 ....4 B1
Birdingbury La CV23 ..115 E8
Birdingbury Rd
Birdingbury CV23 .....115 F8
Marton CV23 ....115 B7
Birds Bush Prim Sch B77 .9 C4
Birds Bush Rd B77 ....9 C4
Birds La OX15 ....133 C6
Birkdale Cl Coventry CV6 .49 B4
Nuneaton CV11 ....30 A1
Birmingham Bsns Pk
B40 ....44 B4
Birmingham Int Airport
B40 ....44 B4
Birmingham Int Sta B40 .44 D4
Birmingham Rd
Alcester B49 ....143 A2
Allesley CV5 ....59 E7
Ansley CV10 ....27 A2
Burton Green CV8 .....75 A1
Coleshill B46 ....33 E5
Henley-in-A B95 ......113 B6
Kenilworth CV8 ....75 B8
Little Packington CV7 ..45 E3
Nether Whitacre B46,B76 .24 B4
Shrewley CV35 ....114 D6
Stoneleigh CV8 ....94 B6
Stratford-u-A CV37 ...144 C3
Studley B80 ....103 C4
Warwick CV34 ....108 B8
Water Orton B46 ......23 A3
Wilmcote CV37,B95 ...120 D6
Wroxall B93,CV35 .....90 D3
Birstall Dr CV21 ......83 B4
Birvell Ct CV12 ....39 C2
Bishop Carpenter CE Prim
Sch Ox15 ....139 D2
Bishop St CV1 ....151 B3
Bishop Ullathorne RC Sch
CV3 ....76 F4
Bishop Wilson CE Prim Sch
B37 ....33 A5
Bishop Wulstan RC Sch
CV22 ....83 A1
Bishop's Cl B37 ....44 E8
Bishop's Hill CV35 ...123 B2
Bishop's Itchington Prim Sch
CV47 ....124 B4
Bishop's Tachbrook CE Prim
Sch CV33 ....122 F8
Bishopgate Bsns Pk CV1 .61 D5
Bishopgate Ind Est CV1 .61 D5
Bishops Bowl Lakes Water
Sports Ctr CV47 ......124 A5
Bishops Cl
16 Bishops Tachbrook
CV33 ....122 F8
Stratford-u-A CV37 ...144 B2
Bishops Cleeve CV9 ...3 A1

Bishops Gate CV47 ...124 B5
Bishops Wlk CV5 .....77 B8
Bishopton Cl CV5 ....60 B3
Bishopton La CV37 ...144 B3
Bishopton Prim Sch
CV37 ....144 B2
Bisset Cres **11** CV31 ...110 C6
Bitham Rd CV33 ......123 D3
Bixhill La B46 ....25 A2
Black Bank CV7 ....39 B1
Black Hall La CV7 ....36 B2
Black Horse Hill DE12 ..3 C4
Black Horse Rd CV6 ..50 B6
Black La CV32 ....106 C2
Black Prince Ave CV3 ..77 E6
Black-a-Tree Ct CV10 ..28 F5
Black-A-Tree Rd CV10 ..28 E4
Blackberry Ave B94 ...88 C6
Blackberry Cl CV23 ...83 B4
Blackberry La
Ash Green CV7 ....49 C5
Coventry CV2 ....62 D6
Blackbird Croft B36 ..33 A7
Blackburn Rd CV6 ....49 F3
Blackcat Cl B37 ....33 A3
Blackdown B77 ....4 B1
Blackdown Rd B93 ...72 B6
Blackfirs La B37,B46 ..44 D7
Blackford Cl B95 .....113 B4
Blackford Hill B95 ...113 B4
Blackford Rd B90 .....70 C8
Blackford Way CV35 ..137 F8
Blackgreaves La B76 ..14 F1
Blacklow Rd CV34 ...105 A1
Blackman Way CV21 ..82 C2
Blackshaw Dr CV2 ....62 F6
Blacksmith's La NN11 .134 F5
Blacksmiths Cl WR11 ..127 F1
Blacksmiths La
Hockley Heath B94 ....88 C6
Mollington OX17 ......134 A2
Northend CV47 ....133 B7
South Littleton WR11 ..127 F1
Blacksmiths Yd CV13 ..21 B4
Blackthorn Cl CV4 ....76 D5
Blackthorn Gr CV11 ...29 F2
Blackthorn Rd CV37 ..145 A3
Blackthorn Way B49 ..143 A3
Blackthorne Rd CV8 ..93 A3
Blackwatch Rd CV6 ...61 C8
Blackwell Rd
Coventry CV6 ....61 E8
Tredington CV36 ......136 F6
Blackwood Ave CV22 ..82 B1
Blackwood Rd B77 ....4 A3
Blacon Way CV37 .....144 B2
Bladon Cl CV11 ....30 A5
Bladon Wlk **13** CV31 ...110 C6
Blaenavon Pl LE10 ...31 E4
Blake Cl Nuneaton CV10 .28 A5
Rugby CV22 ....82 B1
Blake's Hill WR11 ....128 B1
Blakelands Ave CV31 ..110 B6
Blakenhurst WR11 ...127 C4
Blandford Ave B36 ....22 E1
Blandford Dr CV2 ....62 F5
Blandford Rd CV32 ...105 C1
Blandford Way CV35 ..108 A7
Blanning Ct B93 ......71 E3
Blaze La B96,B97 ....102 A2
Bleaberry CV21 ....83 B4
Bleachfield St B49 ....143 A2
Blenheim Ave CV6 ....49 C2
Blenheim Cl
Bidford-on-A B50 .....148 B3
Nuneaton CV11 ....29 F2
Blenheim Cres CV31 ..110 C5
Blenheim Ways B35 ..22 B2
Blenheim Wlk
Coventry CV6 ....49 B4
Wellesbourne CV35 ...146 B1
Bletchley Dr Coventry CV5 .60 B4
Tamworth B77 ....9 B4
Blew Gates OX15 .....137 F2
Blewitt Cl B36 ....22 D2
Blick Rd CV34 ....109 C4
Blind La Berkswell CV7 ..58 D4
Chipping Campden GL55 .135 A1
Kenilworth CV8 ....75 F1
Tanworth-In-A B94 ...86 D1
Blindpit La B76 ....23 B8
Bliss Cl CV4 ....59 E3
Blockley Rd CV12 .....39 C4
Blockley's Yd **4** LE10 ..31 D8
Blondvil St CV3 ....77 D7
Bloxam Gdns CV22 ...82 C1
Bloxam Pl **12** CV21 ...83 A2
Bloxham Rd OX16 ....139 F1
Blue Cap Rd CV37 ....145 A3
Blue Coat CE Sch CV1 .61 F3
Blue La CV35 ....130 E6
Blue Lake Rd B93 ....72 B2
Blue Lias Ind Est CV47 .115 B4
Bluebell Cl CV23 ......83 B4
Bluebell Dr
Bedworth CV12 ....38 E2
Birmingham B37 ......33 D1
Bluebell Wlk CV4 .....59 F1
Bluebellwood Cl B76 ..13 A3
Blundells Croft CV37 ..129 A7
Blundells The CV8 ....93 A5
Blyth Ave CV7 ....74 C5
Blyth Cl CV12 ....38 C1
Blyth Ct CV11 ....29 C3
Blythe Cl B97 ....102 B4
Blythe Gate B90 ....70 F3
Blythe Rd Coleshill B46 ..34 A4

Blythe Rd continued
Coventry CV1 ....61 E4
Blythe Special Sch B46 ...34 A2
Blythe Valley Pk B90 ......70 F2
Boar Croft CV4 ....59 F2
Boat La CV37 ....129 A7
Bockenden Rd CV4 ....75 E5
Boddington Cl CV32 ....106 E5
Boddington Rd OX17 ......134 B5
Bodington Cotts CV37 ....129 D7
Bodmin Rd CV2 ....62 F5
Bodnant Way CV8 ....93 B6
Bodymoor Heath La B76 ..15 A2
Bohun St CV4 ....59 F1
Boleyn Cl CV9 ....109 E3
Bolingbroke Dr CV34 ....109 E3
Bolingbroke Rd CV3 ......62 A1
Bolton Cl CV3 ....77 E5
Bolyfant Cl CV11 ....110 A2
Bond B35 ....22 A3
Bond End CV23 ....53 C2
Bond Gate CV11 ....29 C4
Bond St Coventry CV1 ...151 B3
Nuneaton CV11 ....29 C5
Rugby CV21 ....82 C2
Boningale Way B93 ....71 E3
Bonington Dr CV12 ....39 A4
Bonneville Cl CV5 ....59 B8
Bonniksen Cl [7] CV31 ..109 F5
Bonnington Cl CV21 ....84 A1
Boot Hill CV9 ....11 B1
Booths Fields CV6 ....49 E2
Bordesley Ct CV32 ....106 A3
Bordon Hill CV37 ....144 B1
Bordon Pl CV37 ....144 C1
Borough The LE10 ....31 D8
Borrowdale CV21 ....83 B4
Borrowdale Cl CV6 ....61 A8
Borrowdale Dr CV32 .....105 D2
Borrowell La CV8 ....92 E4
Borrowell Terr CV8 ....92 E4
Boscobel Rd B90 ....70 D5
Bosley Cl CV36 ....149 C2
Bostock Cres CV33 ......107 B4
Boston Pl CV6 ....61 D8
Boswell Dr CV2 ....63 A7
Boswell Gr CV34 ....104 D1
Boswell Rd CV22 ....99 C4
Bosworth Dr B37 ....33 A2
Bosworth Wood Prim Sch
B36 ....22 F1
Boteler Cl B49 ....143 A2
Botoner Rd CV1 ....61 F2
Bott Rd CV5 ....76 D8
Bott's La DE12 ....3 C4
Bottom St CV47 ....133 B7
Bottrill St CV11 ....29 B5
Botts Green La B46 ....25 B3
Boucher Cl CV37 ....144 B1
Boughton Leigh Inf Sch
CV21 ....83 B4
Boughton Leigh Jun Sch
CV21 ....83 B4
Boughton Rd CV21 ....83 B3
Boulters La CV9 ....10 B1
Boultons La B97 ....102 B3
Boundary Rd CV21,CV22 ..83 B1
Boundary Rd E CV37 ....129 C2
Boundary Rd N CV37 ....129 B2
Boundary Rd W CV37 ....129 B2
Bourne Brook Cl CV7 .....36 C2
Bourne Cl CV9 ....12 C1
Bourne End CV47 ....147 A2
Bourne La OX15 ....142 D4
Bourne Rd CV3 ....62 C1
Bourne The OX15 ....142 D4
Bournebrook CE Prim Sch
CV7 ....36 C2
Bournebrook View CV7 ...36 C1
Bourton Dr CV31 ....110 B5
Bourton La CV23 ....115 F8
Bourton Rd Frankton CV23 .97 B1
Moreton-in-M GL56 .....140 A3
Bouts La B97 PH96 ......118 B5
Bovey Croft B76 ....22 A7
Bovingdon Rd B35 ....22 A3
Bow Ct CV5 ....76 D8
Bow Fell CV21 ....83 B4
Bow La CV7,CV23 ....53 A2
Bowbrook Av B90 ....71 A5
Bowden Way CV3 ....62 F1
Bowen Rd CV22 ....83 B1
Bowers Croft CV32 ......106 A5
Bowes Lyon Cl GL56 ....140 A2
Bowfell Cl CV5 ....60 B4
Bowley's La DE12 ....3 C4
Bowling Green Ave B77 ...9 C4
Bowling Green Ct CV34 ..148 A4
Bowling Green La CV7,
CV12 ....49 E8
Bowling Green St CV34 ..108 D5
Bowls Ct CV5 ....60 F3
Bowman Gn LE10 ....31 F6
Bowness Cl CV6 ....61 A8
Bowshot Cl B36 ....22 D1
Box Cl CV31 ....110 B3
Box Rd B37 ....44 C8
Box Trees Rd B93 ....71 C1
Boxhill The CV3 ....62 B1
Boyce Way B93 ....82 A3
Boyd Cl CV2 ....63 A8
Boyslade Rd LE10 ....31 F6
Boyslade Rd E LE10 ......31 F5
Bracadale Cl CV3 ....63 A2
Bracebridge Cl CV7 ......74 B6
Bracebridge Rd
Atherstone CV9 ....18 B4
Kingsbury B78 ....15 B3

Bracebridge St CV11 .....29 B3
Bracken Cl CV22 ....82 C1
Bracken Croft [3] B37 ...33 C3
Bracken Dr Rugby CV22 ..82 C1
Sutton Coldfield B75 .....13 A5
Wolvey LE10 ....41 B2
Brackendale Dr
Barby CV23 ....101 B1
Nuneaton CV10 ....28 F3
Brackenhurst Rd CV6 .....61 A7
Bracklesham Way B77 ....4 A3
Brackley Cl CV6 ....60 F7
Bracknell Wlk [1] CV2 ...63 A7
Braddock Cl CV3 ....63 A1
Braden Cl CV8 ....93 B7
Bradestone Rd CV11 .....29 D1
Bradewell Rd B36 ....22 D1
Bradfield Cl CV5 ....60 C5
Bradford Cl CV33 ....122 E8
Brading Rd CV10 ....29 D6
Bradley Croft CV7 ....74 B6
Bradmore Cl B91 ....71 A8
Bradney Gn CV4 ....75 E7
Bradnick Pl CV4 ....59 F1
Bradnock's Marsh La
B92 ....57 E2
Braemar Cl CV2 ....62 E6
Braemar Rd CV32 ....106 B4
Braemar Way CV10 ....29 A2
Braeside Croft B37 ......33 D2
Brafield Leys CV22 ......100 A3
Braggington La CV37 ...128 F5
Braggs Farm La B90 .....70 A4
Braids Cl CV21 ....83 B2
Brailes CE Prim Sch
OX15 ....137 E2
Brain St B77 ....4 A1
Brakesmead CV31 ....109 F5
Bramber Cl OX16 ....139 F4
Bramble Cl
[3] Coleshill B46 ....33 F7
Nuneaton CV11 ....29 F2
Bramble St CV1 ....61 E2
Brambles The B76 ....22 A8
Brambling B77 ....10 A4
Brambling Cl CV23 ....83 B4
Bramcote Cl CV12 ....40 D2
Bramcote Hospl CV11 ....40 E7
Bramdene Ave CV10 ......29 D8
Bramley Dr B47 ....69 B6
Bramley Rd CV35 ....132 E6
Bramley Way B50 ....148 B3
Brampton Way CV12 .....40 B3
Bramshall Dr B93 ....71 E3
Bramston Cres CV4 ......59 F1
Bramwell Gdns CV6 ......49 F5
Brancaster Cl A17 ....4 A3
Brandfield Rd CV6 ....60 F8
Brandon Cl CV3 ....79 A7
Brandon La CV3,CV8 .....79 C5
Brandon Marsh Nature
Reserve* CV3 ....79 B4
Brandon Marsh Visitor Ctr*
CV3 ....79 B4
Brandon Par CV32 ......110 A8
Brandon Rd
Bretford CV8,CV23 ....80 B3
Coventry CV3 ....79 A8
Hinckley LE10 ....31 B7
Branksome Rd CV6 ....60 E6
Bransdale Ave CV6 ....49 D3
Bransford Ave CV4 ....76 D5
Bransford Rise B91 ......56 B5
Brascote Rd LE10 ....30 F8
Bratches The GL55 .....135 B3
Brathay Cl CV3 ....77 D6
Braunston CE Prim Sch
NN11 ....117 E5
Braunston Cl B76 ....13 A2
Braunston La NN11 .....126 E8
Braunston Pl CV22 .....100 B4
Braunston Rd NN11 ....117 F2
Bray Bank B46 ....25 B2
Bray's La CV2 ....62 A3
Brayford Ave CV3 ....77 C6
Brays Cl CV23 ....64 C2
Braytoft Cl CV6 ....49 C2
Brazil St CV4 ....59 E2
Breach La CV35 ....113 A7
Breach Oak La CV7 ....37 B2
Breaches La B98 ....103 B4
Bream B77 ....9 B4
Bream Cl B37 ....33 C2
Brechin Cl LE10 ....31 A8
Bredon Ave CV3 ....78 F8
Bredon Ho B98 ....103 A4
Bredon View CV37 ....102 B4
Bree Cl CV5 ....60 A7
Bree's La CV8 ....64 A1
Brendan Cl B46 ....23 B6
Brendan Cl B46 ....34 A3
Brendon B77 ....4 A1
Brendon Way CV10 ....28 A3
Brenfield Dr LE10 ....31 A8
Brent B77 ....9 C4
Brentwood Ave CV3 ......77 C3
Brentwood Gdns CV3 ....77 C3
Brese Ave CV34 ....104 F1
Bretch Hill OX16 ....139 F3
Bretford Rd CV2 ....50 C1
Bretshall Cl B90 ....70 F5
Bretts Cl CV1 ....151 D4
Bretts Hall Est CV10 ....28 A7
Brewer Rd CV12 ....40 D2
Brewers Cl CV3 ....63 A1

Brewery La OX15 ....142 C4
Brewery Row GL56 ......140 F1
Brewery St CV37 ....144 C2
Brewster Cl CV2 ....62 E2
Briansway CV6 ....49 E3
Briar B77 ....4 A2
Briar Cl Hinckley LE10 ...31 F6
Royal Leamington Spa
CV32 ....106 B2
Briar Coppice B90 ....70 D4
Briar Croft CV37 ....144 C1
Briar Hill Inf Sch CV31 ..110 B3
Briardene Ave CV12 ......39 B2
Briarmead LE10 ....31 E4
Briars Cl Coventry CV2 ...62 C2
Long Lawford CV21 ....82 A2
Nuneaton CV11 ....29 E5
Briarwood Cl B90 ....70 D4
Brick Hill OX15 ....142 D3
Brick Hill La CV11 ....59 E8
Brick Kiln La
Middleton B78 ....14 D6
Solihull B90,B91 ....70 F8
Brick Kiln St LE10 ....31 C8
Brick Row OX15 ....142 F8
Brickall The CV37 ....129 B3
Brickhill Cl CV36 ....149 C3
Brickhill Dr B37 ....33 A2
Brickkiln La CV9 ....16 A2
Brickyard La B80 ....103 B2
Bridal Path The CV5 .....60 B6
Bridge Cl CV47 ....147 A2
Bridge End
Southam CV47 ....147 A2
Warwick CV34 ....108 F5
Bridge Foot CV37 ......145 A1
Bridge Ho CV31 ....110 A8
Bridge La Ladbroke CV47 .124 D5
Witherley CV9 ....19 A4
Bridge Meadow Dr B93 ..71 F6
Bridge Rd LE10 ....31 D7
Bridge St Barford CV35 .122 A7
Coventry CV6 ....62 A7
Fenny Compton CV47 ...133 D7
Hampton Lucy CV35 ....121 F4
Hurley CV9 ....16 B2
Kenilworth CV8 ....92 F5
Kineton CV35 ....132 B5
Nuneaton CV11 ....29 C2
CV11 ....29 C2
Polesworth B78 ....5 A1
Rugby CV21 ....83 B2
Stratford-u-A CV37 .....145 A1
Warwick CV34 ....109 C8
Wellesbourne CV35 ......146 B2
Bridge Town Prim Sch
CV37 ....145 A1
Bridge View Baginton CV8 .77 D3
[3] Coleshill B46 ....33 F7
Bridgecote CV3 ....63 F2
Bridgecote Gdns CV3 ....63 F2
Bridgecote CV3 ....78 E6
Bridgeman Rd CV6 ....61 B4
Bridget St CV22 ....82 C2
Bridgetown Rd CV37 ...145 A1
Bridgeway CV37 ....145 A2
Bridle Brook La CV5,CV7 .48 A3
Bridle Rd
Lighthorne Heath CV33 .123 D2
Rugby CV21 ....82 C2
Bridport Cl CV2 ....62 A5
Brierley Rd CV2 ....62 C8
Briggs Cl OX16 ....139 F2
Bright St CV6 ....61 E6
Brightmere Rd CV6 ......61 B4
Brighton St CV2 ....61 F4
Brighton Rd CV3 ....77 D7
Brightwell Cres B93 .....71 E3
Brill Cl CV4 ....76 C5
Brindle Ave CV3 ....62 C2
Brindley Allee CV6 ......149 C3
Brinley Cl
Atherstone CV9 ....12 B1
Daventry NN11 ....117 F3
Brindley Paddocks CV1 .151 B4
Brindley Rd Bedworth CV7 .50 B8
Hinckley LE10 ....30 E8
Rugby CV21 ....84 A1
Brinklow Rd B98 ....103 B4
Brinklow Rd Coventry CV3 .63 A2
Easenhall CV23 ....65 C2
Brisbane Ct CV3 ....39 A2
Brisbane Ct CV12 ....39 A2
Briscoe Rd CV6 ....49 D4
Bristol Rd CV5 ....60 F2
Bristol Way CV35 ....146 B1
Britannia Rd LE10 ....32 A5
Britannia St CV2 ....62 A3
Briton Rd CV2 ....62 A4
Brittania Sh Ctr [3] LE10 .31 D8
Britten Cl CV11 ....40 A7
Brixfield Way B90 ....70 D3
Brixham Cl CV11 ....29 F5
Brixham Dr CV2 ....62 E7
Brixworth Cl CV3 ....78 B8
Broad Cl CV33 ....123 F8
Broad Heath Com Prim Sch
CV6 ....61 E6
Broad La Coventry CV5 ..59 D4
Fillongley CV7 ....36 A2
Tanworth-In-A B98 ....86 E3
Broad Marston Rd
Mickleton GL55,GL55 ...135 B7
Pebworth CV37 ....128 F1
Broad Oaks B76 ....13 A1
Broad Park Rd CV2 ......62 D8
Broad St Brinklow CV23 ..64 C2

Broad St continued
Coventry CV6 ....61 E7
Long Compton CV36 ....141 C3
Stratford-u-A CV37 ....144 C1
Warwick CV34 ....108 F7
Broad Street Jetty CV6 ..61 E7
Broad Wlk CV37 ....144 C1
Broadfern Rd B93 ....72 B8
Broadgate CV1 ....151 B3
Broadhaven Cl CV31 ....110 C7
Broadlands Cl CV5 ....60 C2
Broadlee B77 ....4 B1
Broadmead Ct CV5 ......60 C2
Broadmeadow La CV37 .144 C2
Broadmere Rise CV5 ....60 A2
Broadmoor La CV36 ....141 A6
Broadsword Way LE10 ...31 D4
Broadwater CV5 ....77 A8
Broadway Cubbington CV32 .106 E5
Cubbington CV32 ....106 E5
Broadway Mans CV5 .....61 A1
Broadway Rd GL55 .....135 B6
Broadwell Ct CV4 ....75 F6
Broadwells Cres CV4 ....76 A5
Brockenhurst Way CV6 ..50 B6
Brockhill La B98 ....85 F2
Brockhurst Ave LE10 ....31 D4
Brockhurst Dr CV4 ......59 D2
Brockhurst La
Monks Kirby CV23 ......53 C2
Solihull B90 ....70 B5
Sutton Coldfield B75 .....7 A4
Brodick Cl LE10 ....31 A8
Brodick Rd LE10 ....30 F8
Brodick Way CV10 ....28 F3
Bromage Ave B78 ....15 B3
Brome Hall La B94 ....89 D2
Bromford Way CV37 ....144 B2
Bromleigh Dr CV2 ....62 C2
Bromleigh Villas CV8 ....77 F2
Bromley Cl CV6 ....92 E6
Bromsgrove Highway
B98 ....102 C4
Bromsgrove Rd B80 ....103 B1
Bromwich Cl CV3 ....78 C8
Bromwich Rd CV21 ......83 C1
Bromyard Ave B76 ....22 A8
Bronte Cl Nuneaton CV10 .27 C3
Rugby CV21 ....83 B2
Bronze Cl CV11 ....39 E8
Brook Ave B77 ....10 A4
Brook Cl Coventry CV1 ...61 E4
Kingsbury B78 ....15 B3
Shipston-on-S CV36 ....149 C3
Brook Cottage Cl B46 ...25 B2
Brook Cotts CV36 ....147 B2
Brook Croft B37 ....44 B7
Brook End B78 ....9 A4
Brook End Cl B95 ....113 A4
Brook End Dr CV5 ....60 B3
Brook Farm Ind Est B94 .70 B2
Brook Farm Wlk B37 .....33 D2
Brook Green La B92 .....57 A1
Brook La
Moreton Morrell CV35 ...122 F3
Newbold-on-S CV37 ....130 E1
Nuneaton CV10 ....29 C6
Brook Piece Wlk B35 ....22 B3
Brook Rd CV10 ....27 C2
Brook St Bedworth CV12 .39 B5
Fenny Compton CV47 ..133 D7
Warwick CV34 ....108 E6
Wolston CV8 ....80 A2
Brook View CV22 ....99 B2
Brook Wlk CV37 ....18 C4
Brookdale
Harvington WR11 ....127 C4
Hinckley LE10 ....31 B7
Brookdale Rd CV10 ......29 E7
Brooke Cl CV34 ....108 F5
Brooke Ct [3] CV21 .....82 C2
Brooke Rd CV8 ....93 B4
Brooke Specl Sch
Rugby CV22 ....82 C1
Rugby CV22 ....99 C4
Brookfield Cl B97 ......102 B2
Brookfield Dr LE10 ......41 B2
Brookfield Rd
Cubbington CV32 ....106 E5
Hinckley LE10 ....31 C6
Brookford Ave CV6 ......49 A3
Brookhampton St B97 ..102 C2
Brookhurst Ct CV32 ....105 C1
Brookhurst Prim Sch
CV32 ....105 C1
Brookhus Farm Rd B76 ..22 A8
Brooklands Way B37 .....44 A8
Brooklea CV12 ....38 F2
Brooklime Dr CV23 ......83 C4
Brooklyn Rd CV1 ....61 D6
Brooks Cl CV23 ....117 B6
Brooks Croft B35 ....22 A2
Brooksby Gr B93 ....72 A2
Brookshaw Way CV2 ....62 F8
Brookside
Cheswick Green B90 ....70 D3
Hinckley LE10 ....31 E7
Hook Norton OX15 .....142 D8
Snitterfield CV37 ....121 B7
Stretton on D CV23 ......96 C3
Brookside Ave
Coventry CV5 ....60 C4
Kenilworth CV8 ....92 E4
Wellesbourne CV35 ....146 C2
Brookside Cl Rugby CV22 .83 C1
Stratford-u-A CV37 ....144 B2
Brookside Rd CV37 ....144 B2

Brookside Way B77 ......10 A3
Brookstray Flats CV5 ....60 B3
Brookvale Ave CV3 ......62 E1
Brookvale Rd CV37 ....144 C1
Brookweed B77 ....4 A2
Broom Cl CV22 ....82 C1
Broom La B90 ....70 A6
Broome Croft CV6 ....49 B3
Broomey Croft Childrens
Farm* B76 ....15 A4
Broomfield Ave B78 ......9 A3
Broomfield Pl CV5 ....61 A2
Broomfield Rd CV5 ......61 A1
Broomfield Rise CV10 ...28 F2
Broomybank CV8 ....93 B6
Broughton Rd OX15,
OX16 ....139 F2
Browett Rd CV6 ....61 A5
Brown Ave B77 ....9 B4
Brown's Bridge Rd
CV47 ....147 A3
Brown's La Allesley CV5 ..48 C1
Dordon B78 ....11 A3
Browning Ave CV34 ....108 C5
Browning Cl CV10 ....28 A5
Browning Rd
Coventry CV2 ....62 C3
Rugby CV21 ....101 A4
Brownley Rd B90 ....70 E7
Brownlow St [6] CV32 ..106 A2
Browns La B93 ....71 E6
Browns Rd NN11 ....117 F1
Brownshill Ct CV6 ....60 F8
Brownshill Green Rd
CV6 ....48 E1
Brownsover Cl B36 ......22 B1
Brownsover Com Sch
CV23 ....83 B4
Brownsover La CV21 ....83 A4
Brownsover Rd
Rugby CV21 ....82 C4
Rugby CV21 ....83 A4
Broxell Cl CV34 ....104 C1
Bruce Rd Bedworth CV7 ..49 F7
Coventry CV6 ....61 B8
Bruce Williams Way
CV22 ....83 A1
Brudenell Cl CV22 ....99 A4
Brunel Cl Coventry CV2 ..61 F3
Daventry NN11 ....117 F2
Whitnash CV31 ....110 B2
Brunel Rd LE10 ....31 C8
Brunel Wlk B78 ....5 A2
Brunes Ct CV21 ....83 B4
Brunswick Cl CV21 ......83 B3
Brunswick Rd CV1 ......110 A5
Brunswick St CV31 ....110 A5
Bruntingthorpe Way B78 .78 E8
Brunton Cl CV3 ....63 B1
Brutus Dr B46 ....23 E1
Bryan Mews B50 ....148 C2
Bryanston Cl CV2 ....63 A4
Bryant Rd CV7 ....50 A7
Brympton Rd CV3 ....62 C2
Bryn Jones Cl CV3 ....78 F7
Bryn Rd CV6 ....61 F7
Bryony Cl CV12 ....38 C1
Buccleuch Cl CV22 ......99 B2
Buchan Cl CV10 ....27 C2
Buchanan Rd CV22 ......82 C1
Buckbury Croft B90 ......71 B6
Buckden B77 ....4 B1
Buckden Cl [3] CV34 ...104 F1
Buckfast Cl CV3 ....77 E5
Buckingham Cl CV10 ....29 B1
Buckingham Rd CV47 ..132 F5
Buckingham Rise CV5 ...60 B4
Buckland Rd CV6 ....49 B2
Buckle St WR11,B50 ...128 C3
Buckler's Yd CV12 ....39 A2
Buckley Ho CV5 ....60 B1
Buckley Rd CV32 ....106 C2
Buckminster Dr B93 .....71 E4
Bucknill Cres CV21 .....101 A4
Buckridge La B90 ....70 A5
Bucks Hill CV10 ....28 C6
Buckwell La CV23 ......84 A3
Budbrooke Cl CV2 ....50 D2
Budbrooke Ind Est
CV34 ....108 B7
Budbrooke Prim Sch
CV35 ....114 F4
Budbrooke Rd CV34 ....108 B7
Bufferys Cl B91 ....71 B8
Bulkington La CV11 ......40 A7
Bulkington Rd
Bedworth CV12 ....39 D2
Shilton CV7 ....51 E6
Wolvey LE10 ....41 B2
Bull Ring Harbury CV33 .123 F6
Nuneaton CV10 ....29 B2
Bull Ring Farm Rd CV33 .123 F7
Bull St Nuneaton CV11 ..29 C4
Southam CV47 ....147 A2
Stratford-u-A CV37 ....144 C1
Bull Yd CV1 ....151 B2
Bull Yd The CV47 ....147 A2
Bull's Head La CV3 ......62 B2
Bull's La B76 ....13 E1
Bullaces La LE17 ....68 B2
Bullfield Ave CV4 ....59 E1
Bullfurlong La LE10 .....31 F4
Bullimore Gr CV8 ....93 A2

Bullivents Cl B93 71 F5
Bulls Head Yd B49 143 A2
Bulwer Rd CV6 61 A6
Bulwick Cl CV3 63 B1
Bungalows The CV37 129 B7
Bunkers Hill NN11 126 F5
Burbage Ave CV37 144 C3
Burbage CE Inf Sch LE10 32 A5
Burbage CE Jun Sch
LE10 31 F6
Burbage Rd LE10 32 A7
Burbages La CV6 49 D4
Burberry Gr CV7 74 A6
Burbury Cl Bedworth CV12 39 C4
Royal Leamington Spa
CV32 106 C2
Burbury Ct CV34 109 B8
Burford La B49,B80 112 C1
Burford Mews 13 CV31 110 C6
Burford Rd Hollywood B47 69 A6
Stratford-u-A CV37 145 B1
Burgage Pl CV11 29 C4
Burgage Wlk CV11 29 B5
Burges CV1 151 B3
Burges Gr CV34 104 F1
Burghley Cl CV11 29 F2
Burhill Way B37 33 B5
Burleigh Cl CV7 74 B7
Burlington Ct B78 9 A4
Burlington Rd
Coventry CV2 61 F4
Nuneaton CV10 39 B7
Burman Dr B46 34 A3
Burnaby Cl CV10 28 B5
Burnaby Rd CV6 49 B1
Burnaston Cres B90 71 C6
Burnell Cl B50 148 B3
Burnett Rd CV33 123 D2
Burnham Rd CV3 78 A6
Burnham Rise CV11 30 A6
Burns Ave CV34 108 C5
Burns Cl B97 102 B4
Burns Rd Coventry CV2 62 B3
Royal Leamington Spa
CV32 106 B4
Burns Wlk CV12 39 C1
Burnsall Gr CV5 76 D8
Burnsall Rd CV5 76 D8
Burnside Coventry CV3 63 A2
Rugby CV22 82 C1
Burnthurst Cres B90 71 A7
Burrow Hill La CV7 48 D7
Burrows Cl CV31 110 B3
Burrows The CV37 130 E1
Burton Cl CV5 48 C2
Burton Dassett Hills Ctry
Pk* CV47 133 B7
Burton Green CE Prim Sch
CV8 75 B3
Burton La CV11 40 F7
Burton Rd CV9 3 C1
Bury Court La OX17 139 E8
Bury Ho CV4 59 F3
Bury Rd CV31 109 F7
Burycroft Rd OX15 142 D3
Buryway La CV36 141 C3
Busby Cl CV3 78 F7
Busbys Piece CV23 53 C2
Bush Cl CV4 59 F3
Bush Ct CV2 62 B6
Bush Heath La CV33 123 F6
Bush Hill La CV23 117 B2
Bushbery Ave CV4 59 F2
Bushbury Croft B37 33 C3
Bushley Cl B98 103 A4
Bushley Croft B91 71 B8
Bushwood Dr B93 72 B3
Bushwood La B94,B95 113 C8
Bushy End CV34 109 E4
Butcher's La CV5 60 C6
Butchers Cl
Bishops Itchington CV47 124 A4
Brinklow CV23 64 C2
Butchers La OX15 137 F2
Butchers Rd B92 57 A6
Butler Cl CV8 93 C7
Butler St B96 102 C1
Butlers Cl
Aston le W NN11 134 F5
Long Compton CV36 141 D3
Butlers Cres CV7 39 A1
Butlers End CV35 91 C2
Butlers La Grendon CV9 11 B1
Long Compton CV36 141 C3
Butlers Leap CV21 83 B3
Butlers Leap Ind Est
CV21 83 B2
Butlers Rd CV36,OX7 141 E3
Butlin Rd Coventry CV6 49 C4
Rugby CV21 83 B2
Butt Hill CV47 125 C8
Butt La Allesley CV5 60 B7
Harbury CV33 123 F6
Butter St B49 143 B2
Buttermere Rugby CV21 83 B4
Tamworth B77 10 A4
Buttermere Ave CV11 30 A6
Buttermere Cl CV3 78 F7
Buttermilk La CV35 113 F5
Butterworth Dr CV4 76 A6
Butts CV1 61 A2
Butts Cl CV9 3 A1
Butts La B94 87 B2
Butts Rd CV1 61 B2
Butts The
Long Compton CV36 141 C3
Napton on t H CV47 125 C8
Warwick CV34 108 E7
Buxton Ave B78 9 A4
By Pass Rd B77 4 A3
Byfield Pl CV7 74 D5
Byfield Rd
Chipping Warden OX17 134 F4
Coventry CV6 60 E5
Priors Marston CV47 125 F4
Byford Ct CV10 28 F4
Byford St CV10 28 F4
Byford Way B37 44 B8
Byron Ave Bedworth CV12 39 D2
Warwick CV34 108 C4
Byron Ct B93 72 A6
Byron Rd Redditch B97 102 B4
Stratford-u-A CV37 145 B1
Byron St CV1 151 C4
Byron Wlk CV47 132 F7
Bywater Cl CV3 77 B5

C

Cable & Wireless Coll
CV4 75 E6
Cadbury Dr B35 22 A2
Cadden Dr CV4 60 B2
Cadman Cl CV12 39 C3
Cadogan Rd B77 9 B3
Caen Cl CV35 108 A7
Caernarfon Dr CV11 29 D3
Caernarvon Way OX16 139 F3
Caesar Rd CV8 92 E3
Caesar Way B46 23 E1
Caister B77 4 A3
Caistor Cl B78 8 A4
Caithness Cl CV5 60 A4
Calcott Ho CV3 78 B5
Calcutt Mdw CV47 147 B2
Calcutt Way B90 70 A6
Caldecote Cl CV10 29 C8
Caldecote Hall Dr CV10 19 C2
Caldecote Rd CV6 61 C5
Caldecott Pl CV21 83 B1
Caldecott St CV21,CV22 83 B1
Caldeford Ave B90 71 A7
Calder B77 4 A1
Calder Cl Bulkington CV12 40 B2
Coventry CV3 77 E7
Calder Dr B76 22 A7
Calder Wlk CV31 110 C6
Caldon Cl LE10 31 B8
Caldwell Ct CV11 29 D1
Caldwell Rd CV11 29 D1
Calf's La GL55 135 B2
Caliban Mews CV34 109 E3
Callaways Rd CV36 149 C2
Callendar Cl CV11 30 A7
Callis Wlk B77 9 C3
Callow Hill La B97 102 A3
Calmere Cl CV2 62 F8
Calpurnia Ave CV34 109 E2
Caludon Castle Sch CV2 62 E4
Caludon Lodge CV2 62 E5
Caludon Park Ave CV2 62 E5
Caludon Rd CV2 62 A4
Calvert Cl Coventry CV3 77 D6
Rugby CV21 83 C4
Calvestone Rd CV22 99 A4
Camberwell Terr CV31 110 A7
Camborne Dr CV11 29 F5
Cambourne Rd LE10 32 A6
Cambria Cl B90 69 E7
Cambrian B77 4 A1
Cambridge Ct CV21 83 B2
Cambridge Dr
Birmingham B37 33 A1
Nuneaton CV10 28 E3
Cambridge Gdns CV32 106 A1
Cambridge St
Coventry CV1 61 E5
Rugby CV21 83 B2
Camden Cl GL56 140 F3
Camden St CV2 62 A4
Camellia Rd 1 CV2 50 B2
Camelot Gr CV8 93 C5
Cameron Cl Allesley CV5 60 A7
Royal Leamington Spa
CV32 106 A4
Camhouses B77 4 A1
Camp Hill Dr CV10 28 D7
Camp Hill Prim Sch CV10 28 E6
Camp Hill Rd CV10 28 C7
Camp La Henley-in-A B95 113 B6
Warmington OX17 133 B2
Campbell Cl CV10 28 A4
Campbell St CV21 82 C2
Campden Ave CV36 135 F5
Campden Cl B97 102 B3
Campden Gr CV35 114 F6
Campden Lawns CV37 130 D3
Campden Pitch CV36 136 A6
Campden Rd
Ebrington GL55 135 D3
Lower Quinton CV37 129 D4
Mickleton GL55 135 B4
Shipston-on-S CV36 149 B3
Campden St CV36 136 A6
Campion Cl CV3 77 D6
Campion Gn CV32 106 A2
Campion Rd CV32 106 A2
Campion Sch & Com Coll
CV31 110 C5
Campion Terr CV32 106 A1
Campion Way Rugby CV23 83 B4
Campion Way *continued*
Solihull B90 70 A5
Camplea Croft B37 33 A2
Campling Cl CV12 40 B2
Campriano Dr CV34 109 A8
Campton Cl LE10 31 E7
Camville CV3 63 A2
Canada La CV35 114 D1
Canal Rd Coventry CV6 61 F8
Hatton CV35 114 E5
Canal Way LE10 30 F7
Canalside B94 89 D3
Canberra Cl CV35 146 B1
Canberra Ct 2 CV12 38 F2
Canberra Rd CV2 50 C4
Canberra Way LE10 31 E4
Canford Cl CV3 77 C3
Canley Ford CV4,CV5 76 E7
Canley Rd CV5 76 D8
Canley Sta CV5 60 D1
Cannes Ct CV4 76 D6
Cannocks La CV4 76 D6
Cannon Cl CV4 76 F6
Cannon Hill Rd CV4 76 D5
Cannon Park District Ctr
CV4 76 C6
Cannon Park Prim Sch
CV4 76 D5
Cannon Park Rd CV4 76 E5
Canon Dr CV7 49 D6
Canon Evans CE Inf Sch
CV12 39 A2
Canon Hudson Cl CV3 78 C6
Canon Maggs CE Jun Sch
CV12 39 B2
Canon Young Rd CV31 110 B3
Canterbury Cl
Kenilworth CV8 93 C3
Studley B80 103 B2
Canterbury Dr B37 44 A7
Canterbury St CV1 151 D3
Canterbury Way CV11 30 A8
Cantlow Cl CV5 60 A3
Canton La B46 24 A3
Canwell Dr B75 7 A3
Cape Ind Est CV34 108 E7
Cape Rd CV34 108 D8
Capmartin Rd CV6 61 C7
Captain's Hill B49 143 B3
Capulet Cl Coventry CV3 78 C6
Rugby CV22 99 C3
Capulet Dr CV34 109 E3
Capulet Ho CV37 145 A2
Caradoc B77 4 A1
Caradoc Cl CV2 62 D7
Caradoc Hall CV2 62 D7
Cardale Croft 1 CV3 78 F8
Cardiff Cl CV3 78 D5
Cardigan Rd CV12 38 C1
Cardinal Newman RC Sch &
Com Coll CV6 48 F2
Cardinal Wiseman RC Sch
CV2 50 E1
Carding Cl CV5 59 F4
Carew Cl CV37 144 C3
Carey B77 10 A3
Carey St CV6 62 B8
Cargill Cl CV6 49 F5
Carhampton Rd B75 13 A5
Carisbrook Rd CV10 29 D6
Carisbrooke B77 4 A1
Carisbrooke Ave B37 33 C2
Carlcroft B77 4 A1
Carlton Cl CV12 40 B3
Carlton Ct CV5 60 F2
Carlton Gdns CV5 77 A8
Carlton Ho 8 CV32 109 F8
Carlton Rd Coventry CV6 49 F1
Rugby CV22 82 B1
Carlyle Cl CV10 27 C3
Carlyon Rd CV9 18 C4
Carlyon Rd Ind Est CV9 18 C4
Carlyon Road Ind Est
CV9 12 C1
Carmelite Rd CV1 61 E2
Carnbroe Ave CV3 78 F7
Carnegie Cl CV3 78 B5
Carnoustie B77 4 B3
Carnoustie Cl CV11 40 C8
Caroline Cl CV11 39 F7
Carpenters Cl LE10 31 F5
Carrie Ho CV1 151 A2
Carroway Head Hill B78 7 B3
Carsal Cl CV7 49 D5
Carson Cl GL56 136 C1
Cart's La CV9 11 B1
Carter Dr CV35 122 A7
Carter Rd CV3 78 A8
Carters La CV37 145 C2
Carters Leaze CV36 140 E5
Carthusian Rd CV3 77 C7
Cartmel Cl CV5 60 A4
Carvell Cl CV5 48 B1
Carver Cl CV2 62 E2
Cascade Cl CV3 77 E6
Case La CV35 114 B8
Casern View B75 13 A6
Cash's Bsns Ctr CV1 61 D5
Cash's La CV1 61 D6
Cashmore Ave CV31 109 F5
Cashmore Rd
Bedworth CV12 38 E1
Kenilworth CV8 93 C4
Casia Gr CV8 93 C4
Caspian Way CV2 63 A8
Cassandra Cl CV4 76 D3
Cassandra Gr CV34 109 D4
Castello Dr B36 22 D1
Castle Bromwich Bsns Pk
B35 22 A1
Castle Cl Coventry CV3 77 D6
Fillongley CV7 36 C1
Henley-in-A B95 113 B4
Warwick CV34 108 E6
Castle Cres CV35 132 B5
Castle Ct Hinckley LE10 31 D6
Kenilworth CV8 93 A6
Castle Dr Astley CV10 37 C4
Coleshill B46 33 F5
Castle Gdns GL55 135 C2
Castle Gn CV8 92 D5
Castle Gr CV8 92 E4
Castle Hill Kenilworth CV8 92 E5
Upper Brailes OX15 137 E3
Warwick CV34 108 E6
Castle Hill La OX15 137 E2
Castle La Maxstoke B46 34 C4
Warwick CV34 108 E6
Castle Mews 6 CV34 108 E6
Castle Mound CV23 101 B1
Castle Mound Way CV23 67 B1
Castle Nurseries GL55 135 C2
Castle Place Ind Est
CV1 151 D4
Castle Rd Alcester B49 143 B3
Henley-in-A B95 113 B4
Kenilworth CV8 92 E5
Kineton CV35 132 B6
Nuneaton CV10 29 C7
Studley B80 103 C2
Tamworth B77 9 C3
Castle St
Astwood Bank B96 102 C1
Coventry CV1 151 D4
Hinckley LE10 31 D8
Rugby CV21 83 A2
Warwick CV34 108 E6
Castle Vale Ind Est B76 22 A5
Castle Vale Sec Sch B35 22 B3
Castle Vale Sports Ctr
B35 22 B2
Castle View CV10 19 A1
Castleditch La B98 102 C4
Castlegate Mews 4
CV34 108 F7
Castlehall B77 4 A1
Caswell Rd CV31 110 B6
Catbrook GL55 135 A1
Catbrook Cl GL55 135 B1
Catesby End NN11 126 B5
Catesby La B94 89 B2
Catesby Rd Coventry CV6 61 B8
Rugby CV22 83 B1
Cathedral Lanes Sh Ctr
CV1 151 B3
Catherine de Barnes La
Bickenhill B92 44 D1
Catherine de B B92 56 C7
Catherine St CV2 61 F3
Catherine Ward Hall
CV12 39 B5
Catherines Cl B91 56 B4
Cathiron La CV23 65 B1
Cattell Dr B75 13 B5
Cattell Rd CV34 108 E7
Catthorpe Manor LE17 68 C1
Catthorpe Rd LE17 68 B2
Cavalier Cl CV11 29 E2
Cavans Cl CV3 79 A8
Cavans Way CV3 79 A8
Cave Cl CV22 99 A4
Cavendish Ct B93 72 A3
Cavendish Rd CV4 59 E2
Caversham Cl CV11 30 A7
Cawdon Gr B93 71 F3
Cawnpore Rd CV6 49 B2
Cawston La CV22 99 A3
Cawston Way CV22 99 B4
Cawthorne Cl 1 CV1 61 E4
Cecil Ct CV31 110 A8
Cecil Leonard Knox Cres
CV11 40 F6
Cecily Rd CV3 77 E7
Cedar Ave CV8 79 B1
Cedar Cl Kingsbury B78 15 B3
Royal Leamington Spa
CV32 106 A4
Stratford-u-A CV37 145 A2
Cedar Ct Allesley CV5 60 A6
Hinckley LE10 32 A6
Cedar Dr CV37 121 B7
Cedar Gr CV34 105 A1
Cedar Ho CV35 122 A7
Cedar Rd Mickleton GL55 135 C6
Nuneaton CV10 28 D6
Cedar Wlk 6 B37 33 B2
Cedar Wood Dr CV7 74 B6
Cedars Ave CV6 60 F5
Cedars Mews The 3
CV32 109 D8
Cedars Rd CV7 39 B1
Cedars The CV36 149 C3
Cedric Cl CV3 78 C5
Celandine CV23 83 B4
Celandine Rd CV2 50 D2
Celandine Way CV12 38 E2
Cemetery La CV10 19 A1
Centaur Rd CV5 60 F2
Centenary Bsns Ctr CV11 29 E3
Centenary Rd CV4 76 D7
Central Ave Coventry CV2 62 A2
Nuneaton CV11 29 B5
Royal Leamington Spa
CV31 109 F6
Central Bldgs
Coventry CV3 151 B1
Central Bldgs *continued*
16 Rugby CV21 83 A2
Central Bvd
Coventry CV6,CV7 49 A5
Keresley CV7 48 F6
Central City Ind Est CV6 61 F5
Central Dr CV47 124 B4
Central Flats CV3 151 B1
Central Park Dr CV23 67 B1
Centrovell Ind Est CV11 29 C2
Centurion Cl B46 23 F1
Centurion Pk B77 10 A3
Centurion Way B77 10 A3
Century Pk B26 44 C6
Ceolmund Cres B37 33 B2
Chace Ave CV3 78 C6
Chace Prim Sch CV3 78 C6
Chaceley Cl CV2 63 A8
Chadbury Croft 1 B91 71 B8
Chadbury Rd WR11 127 A1
Chadshunt Cl B36 22 D2
Chadstone Cl B90 71 B6
Chadwick Cl CV5 60 B3
Chadwick La
Chadwick End B93 90 B8
Knowle B93 73 B2
Chadwick Manor B93 73 A1
Chadwick Mews
Chadwick End B93 90 B6
Redditch B98 103 A4
Chadworth Ave B93 71 E3
Chaffinch Dr B36 33 B7
Chalfont Cl
Bedworth CV12 39 A4
Coventry CV5 60 B4
Chalford Way B90 70 C8
Challenge Bsns Pk CV1 61 D5
Challenge Cl CV1 151 C4
Chamberlain Cl CV32 106 E5
Chamberlain La B49 118 D5
Chamberlain Rd CV21 101 A4
Chamberlain Wlk 10 B46 33 F7
Chamberlaine St CV12 39 B3
Chance Fields CV31 110 F6
Chancellors Cl CV4 76 D4
Chancery Ct CV10 28 A7
Chancery La CV10 28 B7
Chanders Rd CV34 104 D1
Chandlers CV31 109 D7
Chandlers Cl B97 102 B4
Chandlers Dr B77 4 A3
Chandlers Rd CV31 110 A2
Chandos Ct 13 CV32 105 F1
Chandos St Coventry CV2 62 A3
Nuneaton CV11 29 A4
Royal Leamington Spa
CV32 105 F1
Change Brook Cl CV11 29 F8
Chantries The CV1 61 E5
Chantry Cl B47 69 A7
Chantry Cres B49 143 A2
Chantry Heath Cres B93 72 C7
Chantry The CV34 105 A1
Chapel Cl
Bidford-on-A B50 148 B2
Welford on A CV37 129 B6
Chapel Ct B96 102 C1
Chapel Dr
Balsall Common CV7 74 B8
Wythall B47 69 A3
Chapel End OX7 142 A2
Chapel Farm Cl CV3 78 C6
Chapel Gdns GL56 136 C1
Chapel Gn CV47 125 C7
Chapel Hill OX7 142 F2
Chapel La
Aston Cantlow B95 119 F7
Barnacle CV7 51 B6
Bidford-on-A B50 148 B2
Cropredy OX17 134 C1
Lapworth B94 89 D7
Mickleton GL55 135 B6
Newbold-on-S CV37 130 E1
Pillerton Priors CV35 131 D2
Ratley OX15 133 A2
Ryton-on-D CV8 79 B2
Salford OX7 150 C3
Shotteswell OX17 139 E8
Stratford-u-A CV37 145 A1
Ullenhall B95 112 E6
Witherley CV9 19 B4
Chapel Rd B96 102 C1
Chapel Row CV34 108 E7
Chapel St
Astwood Bank B96 102 C1
Bedworth CV12 39 C3
Bishops Itchington CV47 124 A4
Charwelton NN11 126 D2
Coventry CV1 151 B3
Harbury CV33 123 F6
Hook Norton OX15 142 D4
Long Lawford CV23 82 A2
Nuneaton CV11 29 C4
5 Royal Leamington Spa
CV31 110 A7
Rugby CV21 83 A2
Stratford-u-A CV37 145 A1
Warmington OX17 133 D2
Warwick CV34 108 E7
Welford on A CV37 129 B6
Wellesbourne CV35 146 B2
Chapel Wlk B50 148 B2
Chapelhouse Rd B37 33 A1
Chapelon B77 4 A1
Chapman Cl CV31 110 E5
Chapman Ct CV34 109 C8
Chapman Way B49 143 B3
Chard Rd CV3 78 D8

Charingworth Dr CV35 ....114 F5
Chariot Way CV21 ....83 A4
Charity Hos The CV23 ......67 B3
Charity Rd CV7 ....49 A7
Charlbury Mews CV31 ......110 C6
Charlecote Cl CV37 ....145 C2
Charlecote Croft B90 .....70 C8
Charlecote Fields CV35 ...146 B2
Charlecote Gdns CV31 .....110 D5
Charlecote Pk* CV35 ......121 F3
Charlecote Rd
  Coventry CV6 ....49 A2
  Wellesbourne CV35 ......146 B2
Wellesbourne, Charlecote
  CV35 ....146 A3
Charlecote Wlk CV11 ......39 F8
Charles Cl
  Warwick, Budbrooke Ind Est
  CV34 ....108 C7
  ■ Warwick, Emscote
  CV34 ....109 B8
Charles Eaton Rd CV12 ...38 F3
Charles Gardner Rd ■
  CV31 ....109 F6
Charles Lakin Cl CV7 .....51 C5
Charles Rd CV9 ....18 C4
Charles St Arley CV7 ......37 A4
  Coventry CV1 ....151 D4
  Hurley CV9 ....16 B3
  Nuneaton CV11 ....29 A5
  Rugby CV21 ....82 C2
  Warwick CV34 ....109 A8
Charles Warren Cl CV21 ..83 A2
Charlesfield Rd CV22 ....100 A4
Charlesworth Ave B90 ....71 B6
Charlewood Rd CV6 ....49 B2
Charlotte St
  Royal Leamington Spa
  CV31 ....109 F6
  Rugby CV21 ....83 A2
Charlton Terr GL56 ......140 B3
Charminster Dr CV3 ......77 D4
Charnwood Ave CV10 .....28 E2
Charnwood Dr CV10 ......19 A1
Charnwood Way CV32 ....106 C3
Charter App CV34 ....108 D5
Charter Ave CV4 ....76 B7
Charter Ho CV4 ....76 A7
Charter Rd CV22 ....100 C4
Charterhouse Rd CV1 ....61 E2
Chartley Cl B93 ....71 E3
Chartwell Cl CV11 ....29 F1
Chartwell Dr B90 ....70 D5
Charwelton Dr CV21 ......83 C3
Chase Cl CV11 ....29 E6
Chase La CV8 ....92 B7
Chater Dr B76 ....13 A1
Chaters Orch CV47 ......115 D4
Chatham Cl CV3 ....78 C8
Chatillon Cl CV34 ....109 E3
Chatsworth Cl
  Cheswick Green B90 .....70 E5
  Hinckley LE10 ....31 F6
Chatsworth Cres CV11 ....29 F2
Chatsworth Gdns CV31 ..110 D6
Chatsworth Gr CV8 ....93 C5
Chatsworth Rise CV3 .....77 E6
Chattaway Dr CV7 ....74 B6
Chattle Hill B46 ....23 E2
Chaucer Dr CV10 ....28 A4
Chaucer Rd CV22 ....99 C3
Chauntry Pl CV1 ....151 C3
Chauson Gr B91 ....71 A8
Chaytor Rd B78 ....11 A4
Cheadle Cl CV2 ....50 A4
Cheam Cl CV6 ....50 A1
Cheatle St B77 ....9 B3
Cheedon Cl B93 ....71 E2
Chelmarsh CV6 ....61 C6
Chelmsley Ave B46 ....33 F6
Chelmsley Circ B37 ......33 B3
Chelmsley La B37 ....44 A8
Chelmsley Rd B37 ....33 C2
Chelmsley Wood Ind Est

Cherry Rd QX16 ....139 F4
Cherry St
  Stratford-u-A CV37 .....144 C1
  Warwick CV34 ....108 F7
Cherry Tree Ave CV10 .....28 E6
Cherry Tree Cres WR11 ..127 F6
Cherry Tree Wlk CV47 ...147 A3
Cherry Way CV8 ....93 A5
Cherry Wlk B47 ....69 B5
Cherrybrook Way CV2 .....50 C1
Cherryfield Cl CV10 ......19 A1
Cherrywood Cres ■ B91 ..71 C8
Cherrywood Gr CV5 ....59 F5
Cherwell Cl LE10 ....31 A8
Cherwell The NN11 ....117 F1
Cherwell Way CV23 ....82 A2
Chesford Cres
  Coventry CV6 ....50 B2
  Warwick CV34 ....105 B1
Chesford Gr CV37 ....144 B2
Chesham St CV31 ....110 B7
Cheshire Cl CV22 ....99 B4
Chesholme Rd CV6 ....49 B2
Cheshunt Ho ■ B37 ......33 B2
Chesils The CV3 ....77 B6
Chessetts Wood Rd B94 ..89 C7
Chester Cl ■ B37 ....33 A2
Chester Ct ■ B37 ....33 D2
Chester Rd
  Birmingham, Chelmsley Wood
  B37 ....44 F8
  Hampton-in-A B46,B92,CV7 ..45 B5
Chester St Coventry CV1 ..61 B3
  Rugby CV21 ....83 B2
Chester Way CV16 ....139 F3
Chesterton Cl B97 ......102 B2
Chesterton Dr
  Nuneaton CV10 ....28 A5
  Royal Leamington Spa
  CV31 ....110 C5
Chesterton Hill CV35 ...123 B4
Chesterton Rd
  Coventry CV6 ....61 A7
  Lighthorne CV35 ....123 C3
Chesterwood Rd CV44 ....69 A6
Chestnut Ave CV8 ....92 F3
Chestnut Cl
  Ettington CV37 ....131 B3
  Kingsbury B78 ....15 B3
Chestnut Cres CV10 ......28 E5
Chestnut Ct Alcester B49 .143 B2
  Coventry CV3 ....78 B8
  Royal Leamington Spa
  CV34 ....109 E2
Chestnut Dr CV11 ....29 E3
Chestnut Field CV21 ......83 A2
Chestnut Gr Coleshill B46 ..34 A4
  Coventry CV4 ....60 A2
  Moreton Morrell CV35 ..122 E3
  Wolston CV8 ....80 A2
Chestnut Pl CV47 ....147 A3
Chestnut Rd
  Astwood Bank B96 .....102 C1
  Bedworth CV12 ....39 D4
  Mollington OX17 ....134 A2
Chestnut Sch CV1 ....151 B1
Chestnut Sq
  Royal Leamington Spa
  CV32 ....106 B2
  Wellesbourne CV35 ....146 B2
Chestnut Tree Ave 60 A2
Chestnut Wlk
  ■ Birmingham B37 ......33 B2
  Henley-in-A B95 ....113 A5
  Stratford-u-A CV37 ....144 C1
Chestnuts The CV12 ......38 E2
Cheswick Cl Coventry CV6 ..62 A7
  Redditch B98 ....112 A6
Cheswick Green Prim Sch
  B90 ....70 C4
Cheswick Way B90 ....70 D4
Cheswood Dr B76 ....22 B6
Chetton Ave CV6 ....61 C6
Chetwode Cl CV5 ....60 B4
Chetwynd Ave B78 ....11 A4
Chetwynd Dr CV11 ....40 B7
Chetwynd Jun Sch CV11 ..40 A7
Cheveral Ave CV6 ....61 B6
Cheveral Rd CV12 ....39 A3
Cheverel Pl CV11 ....29 B2
Cheverel St CV11 ....29 B3
Cheviot B77 ....4 B1
Cheviot Cl CV10 ....28 B3
Cheviot Rise CV32 ....106 C3
Cheviot The CV4 ....76 D6
Cheviot Way QX16 ....139 F5
Chewton Ho CV3 ....78 C8
Cheylesmore CV1 ....151 B2
Chichester Cl CV11 ......30 A7
Chichester Gr B37 ....33 B1
Chichester La CV35 .....114 F3
Chicory Dr CV23 ....83 B4
Chidock Hill CV3 ....77 B6
Chiel Cl CV5 ....59 F4
Chigwell Cl B35 ....22 A3
Childs Cl CV37 ....144 C3
Childs Oak Cl CV7 ....74 A6
Chilham Dr B37 ....33 C2
Chillaton Rd CV6 ....49 B2
Chillingham B77 ....4 C1
Chiltern Ct ■ CV6 ....61 A5
Chiltern Ho CV5 ....60 B4
Chiltern Leys ■ CV6 ....61 A4
Chiltern Rd B77 ....4 B1
Chilterns The CV5 ....60 B4
Chilvers Coton Com Inf Sch
  CV11 ....29 B3
Chilvers Coton Craft Ctr
  CV11 ....29 C2

Chilvers Ct CV11 ....29 C4
Chilworth Cl CV11 ....39 E8
Chines The CV10 ....29 D7
Chingford Rd CV6 ....50 A4
Chingley Bank B95 ......113 B4
Chipping Campden Sch
  GL55 ....135 B2
Chipping Norton Rd
  OX15 ....142 D4
Chipstone Cl ■ B93 .....71 C8
Chiswick Wlk B37 ....33 E2
Chivenor Ho ■ B35 ......22 A2
Chivenor Jun & Inf Sch
  B35 ....22 A2
Chivington Cl B90 ....71 B6
Chorley Way CV6 ....61 C6
Choyce Cl CV9 ....12 B1
Christ the King RC Inf Sch
  CV6 ....60 F6
Christ the King RC Jun Sch
  CV6 ....60 F7
Christchurch Cl CV31 ...110 B4
Christchurch Rd CV6 ....61 A5
Christine Ledger Sq ■
  CV31 ....110 A6
Christopher Hooke Ho
  CV6 ....61 E8
Chub B77 ....9 B4
Chudleigh Rd CV2 ....62 E7
Church Ave B46 ....23 B3
Church Bank
  Binton CV37 ....129 A8
  Temple Grafton B49 ...119 E1
Church Cl Arley CV7 .....26 C1
  Birmingham B37 ....33 A6
Bishops Itchington CV47 ..124 A4
  Drayton Bassett B78 ....8 C3
  Ebrington GL55 ....135 E3
  Harborough Magna CV23 ..66 A2
  Hinckley LE10 ....32 A5
  Luddington CV37 ......129 C7
  Nuneaton CV10 ....28 B8
  Ryton-on-D CV8 ....79 B2
  Stoke Golding CV13 ....21 B4
  Wardington OX17 ....134 F1
  Whitnash CV31 ....110 B4
  Wolvey LE10 ....41 C2
  Wood End CV9 ....10 B1
Church Cotts B46 ....25 B2
Church Ct CV6 ....48 F1
Church Down Cl B97 ....102 B3
Church Dr Cookhill B49 ..118 D5
  Kenilworth CV8 ....92 F5
Church End
  Great Rollright OX7 ...142 A2
  Radford Semele CV31 ..110 E6
  Charwelton NN11 ......126 D2
  Chipping Campden GL55 .135 B2
  Churchover CV23 ....67 B3
  Clifton u D CV23 ....84 A3
  Coventry CV4 ....151 C4
  Fenny Compton CV47 ..133 D7
  Hampton Lucy CV35 ....121 F4
  Harbury CV33 ....123 F6
  Harvington WR11 ......127 D3
  Hinckley LE10 ....32 A5
  Marton CV23 ....115 C7
  Moreton-in-M GL56 ....140 A3
  Nuneaton CV11 ....29 D4
  Offenham WR11 ....127 D1
  Royal Leamington Spa
  CV31 ....110 A7
  Rugby CV21 ....83 A2
  Shipston-on-S CV36 ...149 C3
  Staverton NN11 ....126 D8
  Stockton CV47 ....147 C4
  Stratford-u-A CV37 ...144 C1
  Studley B80 ....103 C2
  Warwick CV34 ....108 E6
  Welford on A CV37 ....129 A7
  Wellesbourne CV35 ....146 B2
  Wroxton OX15 ....139 D4
Church Terr
  Cubbington CV32 ......106 E5
  Harbury CV33 ....123 F7
  ■ Royal Leamington Spa
  CV31 ....110 A7
Church View
  Aston Magna GL56 ....140 A6
  Tamworth B77 ....9 C4
  Warton B79 ....5 C2
Church Way CV12 ....39 B2
Church Wlk Allesley CV5 .60 C6
  Atherstone CV9 ....18 C4
  Barby CV23 ....101 B1
  Hinckley LE10 ....31 D8
  Norton WR11 ....127 C2
  ■ Royal Leamington Spa
  CV31 ....109 F7
  Rugby CV21,CV22 ....83 A1
  Rugby, Bilton CV22 .....99 B4
  Thurlaston CV23 ....98 C2
  Wellesbourne CV35 ....146 B2
Church Wks CV13 ....21 B4
Churchdale Cl CV10 ......28 C4
Churchfield CV37 ....129 A7
Churchill Ave
  Coventry CV6 ....61 E8
  Kenilworth CV8 ....93 A6
Churchill Cl CV34 ....131 A4
Churchill Ho ■ CV32 ...109 F8
Churchill Par B76 ....13 A1
Churchill Rd Rugby CV22 ..83 A1
  Sutton Coldfield B75 ....13 A5
Churchlea OX17 ....134 A2
Chylds Ct CV5 ....60 A5
Cicero App CV34 ....109 F3
Cicester Terr ■ GL56 ...140 A3
Cicey La CV11 ....41 A4
Cidermill La GL55 ......135 B2

Cinder La CV9 ....6 A4
Circle The CV10 ....28 E4
Circuit The CV37 ....129 C8
Circus Ave B37 ....33 C2
City Arc CV1 ....151 B2
City Coll Coventry CV1 ...61 A2
City Coll Coventry (Butts Ctr)
  CV1 ....61 B1
City College Coventry (Tile
  Hill Ctr) CV4 ....59 F1
City Tech Coll The B37 ...33 A4
Cladswell Cl B49 ....118 D5
Cladswell La B49,B96 ...118 C6
Clapham Sq CV31 ....110 B7
Clapham St CV31 ....110 B6
Clapham Terr CV31 ......110 B7
Clapham Terrace Com Prim
  Sch CV31 ....110 B7
Clara St CV2 ....62 A2
Clare Cl CV22 ....106 C2
Clare Ct CV21 ....82 C2
Claremont Cl CV12 ......40 B4
Claremont Rd
  Royal Leamington Spa
  CV31 ....109 F6
  Rugby CV21 ....83 B2
Claremont Wlk CV5 ......60 C6
Clarence St ■ LE10 ......31 E8
Clarence Rd Hinckley LE10 ..31 E8
  Rugby CV21 ....82 C2
  Stratford-u-A CV37 ...144 B2
Clarence St
  ■ Coventry CV1 ....61 E4
  Nuneaton CV11 ....29 A4
  Royal Leamington Spa
  CV31 ....110 A6
Clarence Terr ■ CV32 ...105 F1
Clarendon Ave CV32 ....105 F1
Clarendon Cres CV32 ...105 E1
Clarendon Ct ■ CV21 ....83 A2
Clarendon Ho LE10 ....31 B7
Clarendon Pl CV32 .....105 E1
Clarendon Rd
  Hinckley LE10 ....31 C7
  Kenilworth CV8 ....93 A3
Clarendon Sq CV32 .....105 F1
Clarendon St
  Coventry CV5 ....60 F1
  Royal Leamington Spa
  CV32 ....106 A1
Clarewell Ave B91 ....71 B8
Clark Cl CV36 ....149 C3
Clark St CV6 ....50 A1
Clark Wlk CV37 ....131 B4
Clarke Ave GL56 ....140 C3
Clarke's Ave CV8 ....93 A3
Clarks La CV36 ....141 D3
Clarkson Dr CV31 ....110 A4
Claverdon Cl B97 ....102 B2
Claverdon Prim Sch
  CV35 ....113 F3
Claverdon Rd CV5 ....60 B3
Claverdon Sta CV35 ....114 A3
Clay Ave CV11 ....29 F7
Clay Bank OX15 ....142 D4
Clay La Allesley CV5 .....47 E3
  Coventry CV2 ....62 A4
Clay Pit La B90 ....70 A5
Claybrook Dr B98 ....103 C4
Claybrooke Prim Sch
  LE17 ....43 C2
Claydon Gr CV35 ....114 F6
Claydon Rd OX17 ....134 C2
Claymore B77 ....9 C4
Clayton Rd CV6 ....60 E5
Clayton Wlk B35 ....22 A2
Cleasby B77 ....4 B1
Cleaver Gdns CV10 ......29 C6
Cleeve Ct B50 ....148 B1
Cleeve Prior CE Fst Sch
  WR11 ....128 A4
Cleeve Rd
  Bidford-on-A B50 ......148 B1
  South Littleton WR11 ..127 F2
Cleeves Ave CV34 ....109 D6
Clematis B77 ....4 A2
Clements St CV11 ....110 A7
Clement St CV11 ....29 B3
Clement Way CV21 ....99 A4
Clements St CV2 ....62 A3
Clennon Rise CV2 ....62 D8
Clent Ave B97 ....102 B4
Clent Dr CV10 ....28 B3
Cleobury La B94,B90 .....70 A3
Cleopatra Gr CV34 .....109 E4
Clevedon Gn WR11 ......128 A1
Cleveland Ct ■ CV32 ...105 F2
Cleveland Rd
  Bulkington CV12 ....40 B3
  Coventry CV2 ....62 A4
  Hinckley LE10 ....31 C8
Cleveley Dr CV11 ....28 B8
Clews Rd B98 ....102 C4
Clifden Gr CV8 ....93 C6
Cliff Hall La B78 ....9 A1
Cliffe Cl CV32 ....105 D1
Cliffe Rd CV32 ....105 D1
Cliffe Way CV34 ....109 A8
Clifford Bridge Prim Sch
  CV3 ....63 A3
Clifford Bridge Rd CV3 ..62 F4
Clifford La CV37 ....130 A8
Clifford Mill CV37 ......129 F7
Clifford Rd B93 ....71 F4
Clifford Way 1 B3

Draycote Water Ctry Pk*
CV23 ....116 C8
Draycott Rd CV2 ....62 C7
Drayton Ave CV37 ....144 B2
Drayton Cl
  Bidford-on-A B50 .....148 B3
  Fenny Drayton CV13 ....19 C3
  Nuneaton CV10 ....28 A8
  Redditch B98 ....103 B4
  Stratford-u-A CV37 ...144 B2
Drayton Cres CV5 ....59 D5
Drayton Ct Hartshill CV10 ..19 A1
  Warwick CV34 ....104 C2
Drayton Fields Ind Est
  NN11 ....117 F2
Drayton La
  Drayton Bassett B78 .....8 B3
  Fenny Drayton CV13 ....19 C3
Drayton Leys CV22 ....100 A4
Drayton Manor Dr
  Drayton Bassett B78 .....8 C4
  Fazeley B78 ....8 C4
  Stratford-u-A CV37 ...120 C2
Drayton Manor Pk* B78 ..8 C4
Drayton Rd
  Bedworth CV12 ....39 D2
  Solihull B90 ....70 E8
Drayton Sch OX16 ....139 F4
Drayton Way
  Daventry NN11 ....117 F2
  Nuneaton CV10 ....28 C7
Drem Croft B35 ....22 A2
Drew Cres CV8 ....93 A4
Dreyer Cl CV22 ....82 B1
Driftway The CV36 ...149 C3
Drinkwater Cl CV33 ..123 F6
Drinkwater Ho 7 CV1 ..61 B2
Drive The Coleshill B46 ..34 A3
  Coventry CV2 ....62 E3
  Dunchurch CV22 ....99 C2
Drivers La GL56 ......141 A1
Dronfield Rd CV2 ....62 E6
Drovers Way CV47 ....147 B2
Droylsdon Park Rd CV3 ..77 B3
Druid Rd CV2 ....62 B3
Drummond Cl CV6 ......60 F7
Drummond Way B37 ....33 C2
Drury La CV21 ....83 A2
Drybrooks Cl CV7 ......74 B6
Dryden Cl Kenilworth CV8 ..92 F3
  Nuneaton CV10 ....27 C3
Dryden Pl CV22 ....82 C2
Dryden Wlk CV22 ....82 C2
Drymen Rd CV35 ......132 D3
Duck La CV37 ....129 B7
Duck Lake DE12 ....3 C4
Dudley Gn CV32 ....106 B2
Dudley Rd CV8 ....92 F2
Dudley Rise LE10 ....31 D6
Dudley St Atherstone CV9 ..18 B4
  Coventry CV6 ....50 A1
Dudley Terr CV8 ....94 B6
Duffy Pl CV21 ....101 A4
Dugard Pl CV35 ....122 B7
Dugdale Ave
  Bidford-on-A B50 .....148 B3
  Stratford-u-A CV37 ...145 A3
Dugdale Ct 5 CV31 ...110 A6
Dugdale Ho CV11 ....29 C3
Dugdale Rd CV6 ....61 B6
Dugdale St CV11 ....29 C4
Duggins La CV4,CV7 ....75 B8
Duke Barn Field CV2 ...62 A5
Duke St Coventry CV5 ...60 F2
  Nuneaton CV11 ....29 B4
  Royal Leamington Spa
  CV32 ....106 A1
  2 Rugby CV21 ....83 A2
Dukes Jetty 8 CV21 ....83 A2
Dukes Rd B78 ....11 A3
Dulverton Ave CV5 .....60 D4
Dulverton Ct CV5 ......60 D4
Dulverton Pl GL56 ....140 B3
Dumble Pit La B98 ......85 F7
Dumphouse La B48 ......85 C3
Dunblane Dr CV32 ....106 C5
Duncan Dr CV22 ....99 B2
Dunchurch Boughton CE Jun
  Sch CV22 ....99 B2
Dunchurch Cl CV7 ......74 B7
Dunchurch Hall CV22 ...99 B2
Dunchurch Highway CV5 ..60 A4
Dunchurch Inf Sch CV22 ..99 B2
Dunchurch Rd CV22 ....99 C4
Dunchurch Trad Est
  CV23 ....98 B2
Duncombe Gn 13 B46 ...33 F7
Duncroft Ave CV6 ......60 F7
Duncumb Rd B75 ....13 A5
Dunedin B77 ....4 A1
Dunham Croft B93 .....71 D3
Dunhill Ave CV4 ....59 E3
Dunkirk Pl CV3 ....78 F7
Dunley Croft B90 ......70 F6
Dunlop Rd B97 ....102 B3
Dunn's La B78 ....11 A3
Dunnerdale CV21 ....83 B4
Dunnington CE Prim Sch
  B49 ....127 E8
Dunnose Cl CV6 ....61 E8
Dunottar Cl CV22 ......62 E2
Dunsmore Ave
  Coventry CV3 ....78 C6
  Rugby CV22 ....100 C4
Dunsmore Heath CV22 ..99 B2

Dunstall Cres 2 CV33 .122 E8
Dunstall Ho 17 GL56 ..140 A3
Dunstan Croft B90 .....70 C8
Dunster B77 ....9 B4
Dunster Pl CV6 ....49 D3
Dunster Rd B37 ....33 D2
Dunsville Dr CV2 ....62 F8
Dunton Hall Rd B90 ....70 A8
Dunton La B76 ....14 C1
Dunvegan Cl Coventry CV3 ..63 A2
  Kenilworth CV8 ....93 C4
Duport Rd LE10 ....31 F7
Durbar Ave CV6 ....61 D8
Durham Cl CV7 ....48 F4
Durham Cres CV5 ......60 B7
Durham Croft B37 .....33 B2
Durlston Cl B77 ....4 A3
Durrell Dr CV22 ....99 A4
Dursley La B98 ....112 A6
Dutton Rd CV2 ....50 D3
Duttons Cl CV37 ......121 B7
Duxford Cl Redditch B97 ..102 A4
  Wellesbourne CV35 ...146 B1
Dwarris Wlk CV34 ....104 E2
Dyas Rd B47 ....69 A7
Dyce Cl B35 ....22 A4
Dyer's La
  Chipping Campden GL55 ..135 A2
  Wolston CV8 ....80 A2
Dyers La B94 ....87 D8
Dyers Rd CV11 ....40 F6
Dymond Rd CV6 ....49 D3
Dysart Cl CV1 ....83 C1
Dyson Cl CV21 ....83 C1
Dyson St CV4 ....59 E3

E

Eacott Cl CV6 ....49 A3
Eadie St CV10 ....28 D4
Eagle Cl CV11 ....40 B8
Eagle Dr B77 ....4 B2
Eagle Gr B36 ....33 A8
Eagle Ho CV1 ....61 D5
Eagle La CV8 ....92 F3
Eagle St Coventry CV1 ....61 D5
  Royal Leamington Spa
  CV31 ....110 A6
Eagle St E CV1 ....61 D5
Ealingham B77 ....4 A1
Earl Place Bsns Pk CV4 ..60 E1
Earl St Bedworth CV12 ....39 C2
  Coventry CV1 ....151 C2
  Royal Leamington Spa
  CV32 ....106 A1
  Rugby CV21 ....83 A2
Earl's Croft The CV3 ...77 D7
Earl's Wlk CV3 ....79 D7
Earles Cl CV47 ....147 C4
Earls Rd CV11 ....29 A5
Earls Rivers Ave CV34 ..109 D3
Earlsdon Ave N CV5 ...77 A8
Earlsdon Ave S CV5 ...77 A8
Earlsdon Bsns Ctr CV5 ..76 F8
Earlsdon Prim Sch CV5 ..61 A1
Earlsdon St CV5 ....76 F8
Earlsmere B94 ....70 A1
Earlswood Comm B94 ..87 A6
Earlswood Rd B93 .....71 D2
Earlswood Sta B94 ....69 D1
Earlswood Trad Est B94 ..86 C6
Easedale Cl Coventry CV3 ..77 B6
  Nuneaton CV11 ....30 A6
Easenhall Cl B93 ......72 A4
Easenhall Rd CV23 ....66 A1
Easingwold Rd CV35 ..132 D4
East Ave Bedworth CV12 ..39 C2
  Coventry CV2 ....62 A2
East Car Park Rd B40 ..44 F4
East Cl LE10 ....31 D7
East Dene CV32 ....106 B2
East End OX15 ....142 D4
East Gr CV31 ....110 A6
East Green Dr CV37 ..144 B2
East House Dr CV9 ....16 B2
East Side CV11 ....29 D6
East St Coventry CV1 ....61 E3
  Long Compton CV36 ...140 A1
  Moreton-in-M GL56 ...140 A3
  Rugby CV21 ....83 B2
  Tamworth B77 ....9 B3
East Union St CV22 ...83 A1
East Way B32 ....45 B3
Eastboro Ct CV11 .....29 E2
Eastboro Fields CV11 ..30 A4
Eastboro Way CV11 ....29 F2
Eastbourne Cl CV6 ....60 E6
Eastcote La B92 ......56 F4
Eastcotes CV4 ....60 B1
Eastern Green Jun Sch
  CV5 ....59 D5
Eastern Green Rd CV5 ..59 D4
Eastern Hill B96 .....102 C1
Eastfield Cl CV37 ....144 C3
Eastfield Pl 6 CV21 ..83 A2
Eastfield Rd
  Nuneaton CV10 ....29 D6
  Royal Leamington Spa
  CV32 ....110 A8
Eastgate CV35 ....139 B8
Eastgate Ho 6 CV34 ..108 E6
Eastgate Mews 3 CV34 .108 E6
Eastlands Gr CV5 .....60 B4
Eastlands Rd CV21 ....83 B2
Eastlands Prim Sch CV21 ..83 B1
Eastlands Rd CV21 ....83 B2
Eastling Gr CV7 ....36 C2

Eastleigh Ave CV5 .....76 F7
Eastleigh Croft B76 ...22 A7
Eastley Cres CV34 ....108 B8
Eastnor Gr CV31 ....110 B7
Easton Gr B47 ....69 B7
Eastway B40 ....44 E3
Eastwood Cl CV31 ....110 D6
Eastwood Ct B96 ......102 C1
Eastwood Gr CV21 ...101 B4
Easy La CV21 ....82 C2
Eathorpe Cl Coventry CV2 ..50 C1
  Redditch B98 ....103 C4
Eaton Cl CV32 ....105 D2
Eaton Ct CV32 ....105 D1
Eaton Rd CV1 ....151 B1
Eaves Green La CV7 ...46 E1
Ebbw Vale Terr CV3 ...77 D7
Eborall Cl CV34 ......104 E2
Eborne Croft CV7 ......74 C8
Ebourne Cl CV8 ....93 A4
Ebrington Gl55 ......135 E3
Ebrington Dr CV35 ...114 F5
Ebro Cres CV3 ....62 F1
Ebsdorf Cl B50 ....148 C3
Eburne Prim Sch CV2 ..50 C2
Eburne Rd CV2 ....50 C3
Eccles Cl CV2 ....62 C8
Eckington Cl B98 ....103 A4
Eclipse Rd B49 ......143 A2
Eclipse Trad Est B49 ..143 A2
Ecton Leys CV22 .....100 A4
Edale B77 ....4 A1
Edale Gn LE10 ....31 F6
Edale Way CV6 ....62 A7
Eddens Wood Cl B78 ...8 C3
Eddie Miller Ct CV12 ..39 A2
Eden Cl B80 ....103 B2
Eden Croft CV8 ....93 B3
Eden Ct CV32 ....106 D3
Eden Gr B37 ....33 D1
Eden Rd Coventry CV2 ..63 A8
  Rugby CV21 ....83 C1
Eden St CV6 ....61 F7
Edge Hill CV9 ....10 A1
Edge La B95 ....113 C5
Edgecote Cl CV21 .....83 C1
Edgefield Rd CV2 .....63 A8
Edgehill Ctry Pk* OX17 ..133 B3
Edgehill Pl CV4 ....59 C1
Edgehill Rd CV35 ....137 A3
Edgewick Com Prim Sch
  CV6 ....61 E8
Edgioake La B96 ......118 C7
Edgwick Park Ind Est
  CV6 ....61 F8
Edgwick Rd CV6 ....61 F7
Edinburgh Cl OX16 ...139 F4
Edinburgh Cres CV31 ..109 F6
Edinburgh Rd Hurley CV9 ..16 B3
  Nuneaton CV10 ....28 D6
Edinburgh Way
  Banbury OX16 ....139 F3
  Long Lawford CV23 ....82 A3
Eringale Rd CV2 ....62 F8
Edison Rd Coleshill B76 ..23 F4
  Lea Marston B46 ....24 A2
Edmondes Cl CV34 ....104 F1
Edmonds Cl CV37 ....129 D1
Edmondscote Rd CV32 ..109 D8
Edmondson Cl CV22 ....99 B2
Edmund Rd CV1 ....61 D5
Edmunds Rd OX16 ....139 F3
Edstone Cl B93 ....71 F4
Edward Bailey Cl CV3 ..78 E7
Edward St 11 CV21 ....83 A2
Edward Rd Bedworth CV12 ..39 C3
  Coventry CV6 ....49 B3
  Nuneaton CV11 ....29 C3
Edward St Coventry CV1 ..151 A4
  Nuneaton CV11 ....29 D3
  Royal Leamington Spa
  CV32 ....105 C1
  Rugby CV21 ....83 B2
  Warwick CV34 ....108 D7
Edward Tyler Rd CV7 ...39 A1
Edwards Ctr 7 LE10 ...31 D8
Edwards Gr CV8 ....93 C5
Edwards Rd B24 ....22 A6
Edyth Rd CV2 ....62 E4
Edyvean Cl CV22 ....99 C3
Edyvean Walker Ct CV11 ..29 B5
Egerton Cl CV21 ....82 C3
Egginton Way CV34 ..109 F3
Egret Wlk CV2 ....50 B3
Eileen Gdns B37 ....33 A4
Elan Cl CV32 ....106 C3
Elborow St 5 CV21 ....83 A2
Elbury Croft B93 ......71 F6
Eld Rd CV6 ....61 E7
Elder Cl Kingsbury B78 ..15 B4
  Rugby CV22 ....82 A1
Elderberry Way CV2 ...62 B6
Elderfield Gr B91 .....71 B7
Eldorado Cl B80 .....103 B2
Elford Gr B37 ....33 B1
Elgar Cl CV11 ....40 A7
Elgar Rd CV6 ....62 B6
Eliot Cl CV34 ....104 E2
Eliot Ct CV22 ....82 C2
Elizabeth Ave B78 ......5 A1
Elizabeth Ct
  5 Coventry CV5 ....61 A4
  Warwick CV34 ....108 F6
Elizabeth Rd CV31 ...109 F6
Elizabeth Way
  Kenilworth CV8 ....92 E5
  Long Lawford CV23 ...82 A3

Elkington Croft B90 ....71 A5
Elkington La CV23 ....101 A1
Elkington St CV6 ......61 F8
Ell La CV23 ....64 C2
Ellacombe Rd CV2 ....62 C6
Ellen Badger Com Hospl
  CV36 ....137 A4
Ellerbeck B77 ....4 A1
Ellerdene Cl B98 .....102 B4
Ellerman Gdns CV6 ....49 F3
Ellesmere Rd CV12 ....39 A2
Ellice Dr B36 ....33 B7
Elliot Cl B50 ....148 B3
Elliot Ct CV36 ....149 C3
Elliot Dr CV35 ....146 B4
Elliott's Field Ret Pk
  CV21 ....83 A3
Elliotts Orch CV35 ...122 A7
Ellis Park Dr CV3 .....63 B1
Ellison Dr OX17 ......139 F5
Elliston Gr CV31 .....110 C6
Ellys Rd CV1 ....61 C5
Elm Bank Cl CV32 ....106 A4
Elm Cl Binley Woods CV3 ..79 C7
  Ilmington CV36 ....136 B6
  Pebworth CV37 ....128 F1
  Southam CV47 ....147 A2
Elm Ct CV5 ....59 B8
Elm Dr B49 ....143 B2
Elm Gr Arley CV7 ......26 C1
  Balsall Common CV7 ...74 C6
  Brinklow CV23 ....35 F3
  Bromsgrove B61 ......135 F3
Elm La LE17 ....68 C1
Elm Lodge B92 ....57 A7
Elm Rd
  Royal Leamington Spa
  CV32 ....106 B3
  Shipston-on-S CV36 ..149 C2
  Stratford-u-A CV37 ..144 C3
Elm Row CV47 ....115 F3
Elm Tree Ave CV4 ......60 B2
Elm Tree Cl B78 ....15 B3
Elm Tree Dr LE10 ......31 F8
Elm Tree Rd Bulkington CV12 ..40 D2
Elm Tree Rise B92 ....57 B8
Elm Way CV10 ....28 A8
Elmbank Rd CV8 ....92 E6
Elmbridge Dr B90 .....70 F6
Elmdene Cl Hatton CV35 ..114 C5
  Wolston CV8 ....80 A2
Elmdene Rd CV8 ....93 B4
Elmdon Cl B37 ....44 A7
Elmdon La
  Birmingham B37 ....44 A6
  Birmingham B26 ....44 A4
Elmdon Rd CV3 ....78 A8
Elmdon Trad Est B37 ..44 A5
Elmfield Rd CV10 ......29 C7
Elmhurst Cl B97 ......102 B2
Elmhurst Rd CV6 ......49 A4
Elms Ct CV9 ....3 A1
Elms Dr Austrey CV9 ....3 A1
Elms Paddock The CV23 ..83 C3
Elms The Bedworth CV12 ..38 D2
  Leek Wootton CV35 ...104 F6
  Stratford-u-A CV37 ..145 A2
Elmsdale Ave CV6 .....49 F2
Elmstone Cl CV37 ....102 B3
Elmwood Ave CV6 .....60 F5
Elmwood Cl CV7 ......151 B4
Elmwood Dr B47 ....69 A6
Elphin Cl CV6 ....49 A4
Elsee Rd CV21 ....83 A2
Elter Cl CV21 ....83 B4
Eltham Rd CV3 ....77 E7
Elton Cl CV32 ....106 C6
Elton Croft B93 ....71 F4
Elva Croft B36 ....22 F1
Elvers Green La B93,B93 ..72 E7
Elwy Circ CV7 ....49 C6
Ely Cl Birmingham B37 ..33 B2
  Coventry CV2 ....63 A6
Ely Gdns CV37 ....144 C1
Ely St CV37 ....145 A1
Embassy Wlk CV2 ......62 D8
Emerald Way CV31 ...109 F5
Emerson Rd CV2 ....62 C6
Emery Cl CV2 ....62 E7
Emily Smith Ho 2 CV2 ..50 B1
Emmott Dr CV31 ......110 B5
Emperor Way CV21 ....82 C4
Emscote Inf Sch CV34 ..109 B8
Emscote Lawn Prep Sch
  CV34 ....109 A8
Emscote Rd Coventry CV3 ..62 F1
  Warwick CV34 ....109 B7
Ena Rd CV1 ....61 D5
Endemere Rd CV6 .....61 D7
Enderby Cl B93 ....71 F4
Endsleigh Gdns CV31 ..110 B6
Enfield Rd Coventry CV2 ..62 B3
  Redditch B98 ....103 B3
Engine La B77 ....4 A1
England Cres CV31 ...109 E7
England Ho 9 CV32 ....105 F2
Engleton Rd CV6 ......60 F5
English Martyrs RC Prim Sch
  CV21 ....101 A4
Ennerdale B77 ....83 B4
Ennerdale Cl CV32 ...105 D2

Ennerdale Cres CV11 ...29 F6
Ennerdale La CV2 ......62 F4
Ennersdale Bglws B46 ..23 F1
Ennersdale Cl B46 ....23 F1
Ennersdale Rd B46 ...23 F1
Enright Cl CV32 .....105 E2
Ensign Bsns Ctr CV4 ..75 F6
Ensign Cl CV4 ....59 D1
Ensor Cl CV11 ....30 A6
Ensor Dr B78 ....4 A1
Enterprise Ho B92 .....57 A6
Enville Cl B37 ....33 B1
Epperston Ct CV31 ...109 F7
Epping Way CV32 ....106 C4
Epsom Cl Bedworth CV12 ..39 B4
  Redditch B97 ....102 B4
Tamworth B77 ....9 B2
Epsom Dr CV3 ....78 C6
Epsom Rd
  Royal Leamington Spa
  CV32 ....106 C4
  Rugby CV22 ....82 B1
Erdington Rd CV9 ......18 B4
Eric Grey Cl CV2 ......62 A5
Erica Ave CV12 ....38 F2
Erica Dr CV31 ....110 B2
Eringden B77 ....4 A1
Erithway Rd CV3 ....77 B4
Ernesford Grange Prim Sch
  CV3 ....62 E1
Ernesford Grange Sch & Com
  Coll CV3 ....78 D8
Ernest Richards Rd CV12 ..39 B4
Ernsford Ave CV3 ......62 B1
Ernsford Cl B93 ....71 F2
Errington GL56 ......140 B3
Esher Dr CV3 ....77 E7
Eskdale CV21 ....83 B4
Eskdale Rd LE10 ....31 A7
Eskdale Wlk CV3 ......78 D7
Essen La CV23 ....101 C2
Essex Cl Coventry CV5 ..59 B8
  Kenilworth CV8 ....92 E2
Essex Ct CV34 ....108 E8
Essex Gn CV47 ....132 F7
Essex St CV21 ....83 A2
Esterton Cl CV6 ....49 C2
Ethelfield Rd CV2 .....62 B3
Ethelfleda Rd B77 ......9 C3
Ethelfleda Terr B77 ..145 B1
Etone Com Sch CV11 ...29 C5
Etone Ct CV11 ....29 B5
Ettingham Cross Roads
  CV37 ....131 A4
Ettingham Grange CV37 ..131 A4
Ettingley Cl B98 .....103 A3
Ettington CE Prim Sch
  CV37 ....131 A4
Ettington Cl Dorridge B93 ..71 D2
  Wellesbourne CV35 ...146 B1
Ettington Rd Coventry CV5 ..60 A3
  Wellesbourne CV35 ...146 B1
Eunal Ct B97 ....102 C3
Europa Way CV34 ....109 D5
Eustace Rd CV12 ......40 D1
Euston Cres CV3 ......78 C6
Euston Pl CV32 ......109 F8
Euston Sq 11 CV32 ...109 F8
Evans Cl Bedworth CV12 ..39 C3
  Stratford-u-A CV37 ..144 B1
Evans Gr CV31 ....110 A2
Evans Rd CV22 ....82 B1
Evelyn Ave CV6 ....49 F2
Evenlode Cl CV37 ....145 B1
Evenlode Cres CV6 ....60 E5
Evenlode Gdns GL56 ..140 B3
Evenlode Rd GL56 ....140 A3
Everard Cl CV23 ....84 A3
Everard Ct CV11 ....29 E2
Everdon Cl CV22 .....100 C4
Everdon Rd CV6 ....49 B2
Everest Rd CV22 ....99 C4
Everglade Rd CV9 ......12 B1
Everitt Dr B93 ....72 A6
Eversleigh Rd CV6 ....60 F5
Eversley Rd CV47 ....144 C1
Evesham Rd
  Bidford-on-A B50,CV37 ..128 C8
  Church Lench WR11 ...127 A6
  Cookhill B49 ....118 D5
  Harvington WR11 .....127 D4
  Redditch, DaggVal End B98,
  B97 ....102 C2
  Redditch, Headless Cross
  B97 ....102 B3
  Salford Priors WR11 ..127 F5
  South Littleton WR11 ..127 F3
  Stratford-u-A CV37 ...144 C1
Evesham St B49 ......143 A2
Evesham Wlk CV4 .....76 B4
Evreux Way CV21 ......83 A2
Exbury Way CV11 ......39 E8
Exeter Cl CV3 ....78 D8
Exeter Dr B37 ....44 A8
Exhall Cedars Inf Sch
  CV7 ....49 D2
Exhall Cl CV37 ....145 B1
Exhall Gn CV7 ....49 C3
Exhall Grange Sch CV7 ..49 C5
Exhall Rd CV7 ....48 D4
Exham Cl CV34 ....104 E1
Exhibition Way B40 ...44 D4
Exis Ct CV11 ....29 E2
Exmiinster Rd CV3 ....77 D4
Exmoor Dr CV32 .....106 C4
Exmouth Cl CV2 ....50 C2

Exton Cl CV7 . . . . 49 C6
Eydon Cl CV21 . . . . 83 C3
Eyffler Cl CV34 . . . . 108 D7

F

Fabian Cl CV21 . . . . 78 D7
Fabius Cl LE10 . . . . 31 C7
Fair Cl CV23 . . . . 97 B1
Fair Isle Dr CV10 . . . . 28 F2
Fairbanks Cl CV2 . . . . 63 A7
Fairbourne Gdns B97 . . . . 102 B4
Fairbourne Way CV6 . . . . 60 E8
Faircroft CV8 . . . . 92 F3
Faircroft Rd B36 . . . . 22 D1
Fairfax Cl CV35 . . . . 122 A7
Fairfax St **6** CV1 . . . . 108 F7
Fairfax St CV1 . . . . 151 C3
Fairfield Cl CV3 . . . . 78 A7
Fairfield Rise CV7 . . . . 46 C1
Fairfields Hill B78 . . . . 10 C4
Fairfields Wlk CV37 . . . . 144 B2
Fairhurst Dr CV32 . . . . 105 E3
Fairlands Pk CV4 . . . . 76 F6
Fairlawn Cl CV32 . . . . 105 D1
Fairlawns B76 . . . . 22 A8
Fairmile Cl CV3 . . . . 78 C8
Fairview Mews **9** B46 . . . . 33 F7
Fairview Wlk CV6 . . . . 49 E2
Fairwater Cres B49 . . . . 143 B2
Fairway Nuneaton CV11 . . . . . . 40 B8
Tamworth B77 . . . . 9 C3
Fairway Ct Rugby CV21 . . . . . . 83 B2
Tamworth B77 . . . . 4 A2
Fairway Rise CV8 . . . . 93 C6
Fairway The
Banbury OX16 . . . . 139 F4
Hinckley LE10 . . . . 31 F7
Fairways B93 . . . . 72 A8
Fairways Cl CV5 . . . . 60 A6
Fairways The CV32 . . . . 105 D2
Faicon B77 . . . . 10 A3
Falcon Ave CV3 . . . . 78 F8
Falcon Cl CV11 . . . . 40 B8
Falcon Cres B50 . . . . 148 C3
Falcon Ct CV47 . . . . 147 A2
Falcon Lodge Cres B75 . . . . . . 13 A6
Falconers Gn LE10 . . . . 31 F6
Falcons The B75 . . . . 13 B5
Falkener Ho CV6 . . . . 61 E7
Falkland Cl CV4 . . . . 75 D7
Falkland Pl CV47 . . . . 133 A7
Falkland Way B36 . . . . 33 B5
Falkwood Gr B93 . . . . 71 F6
Fallow Hill CV31 . . . . 110 C6
Fallowfields CV6 . . . . 49 C4
Falmouth Cl CV11 . . . . 30 A5
Falstaff Ave B47 . . . . 69 A6
Falstaff Cl Nuneaton CV11 . . . . 30 A1
Sutton Coldfield B76 . . . . 22 B7
Falstaff Ct
Stratford-u-A CV37 . . . . 145 A2
Sutton Coldfield B75 . . . . 13 C5
Falstaff Dr CV22 . . . . 99 B3
Falstaff Gr CV34 . . . . 109 E3
Fancott Rd CV8 . . . . 59 E1
Fancott Dr CV8 . . . . 29 F6
Fant Hill OX15 . . . . 137 E3
Far Gosford St CV1 . . . . 61 E2
Far Lash LE10 . . . . 31 F7
Far Moor La B98 . . . . 112 A6
Far Pool Mdw CV35 . . . . 113 F3
Faraday Ave Coleshill B76 . . . . 23 E5
Lea Marston B46 . . . . 24 A2
Faraday Rd Hinckley LE10 . . . . . 30 E7
Rugby CV22 . . . . 83 B1
Farber Rd CV2 . . . . 63 A6
Farcroft Ave CV5 . . . . 59 D4
Fareham Ave CV22 . . . . 100 C4
Faringdon B77 . . . . 4 A1
Farley Ave CV33 . . . . 123 E6
Farley St CV31 . . . . 110 B7
Farlow Cl CV6 . . . . 62 A6
Farm Cl Coventry CV6 . . . . 49 B3
Harbury CV33 . . . . 123 C6
Shipston-on-S CV36 . . . . 149 C3
Farm Gr CV22 . . . . 83 B1
Farm La Easenhall CV23 . . . . . . 65 C2
Grendon CV9 . . . . 11 C3
South Littleton WR11 . . . . 127 F1
Farm Rd Hinckley LE10 . . . . 31 C6
Kenilworth CV8 . . . . 92 E2
Royal Leamington Spa
CV32 . . . . 106 B3
Farm St CV33 . . . . 123 E6
Farm Stile NN11 . . . . 134 E8
Farm Wlk **2** CV33 . . . . 122 F8
Farman Rd CV5 . . . . 61 A2
Farmcote Cl B97 . . . . 102 B2
Farmcote Lodge CV2 . . . . 50 B4
Farmcote Rd CV2 . . . . 50 B4
Farmer Ward Rd CV8 . . . . 93 A3
Farmhouse Way B90 . . . . 71 B7
Farmside CV3 . . . . 78 D5
Farmstead The CV3 . . . . 78 B8
Farnborough Dr B90 . . . . 70 F6
Farnborough Hall*
OX17 . . . . 133 F4
Farnborough Rd B35 . . . . 22 B3
Farndale Ave CV6 . . . . 49 D3
Farndon Ave B37 . . . . 44 B7
Farndon Cl CV12 . . . . 40 B3
Farnworth Gr B36 . . . . 22 E1
Farr Dr CV4 . . . . 60 B2
Farren Rd CV2 . . . . 62 E5
Farriers Ct CV23 . . . . 65 B4

Farriers Way
Hinckley LE10 . . . . 31 F6
Nuneaton CV11 . . . . 29 F2
Farrington Cl CV35 . . . . 146 B1
Farrington Ct CV35 . . . . 146 B1
Farther Sand Cl CV35 . . . . . . 121 F4
Farthing La B76 . . . . 23 C6
Farvale Rd B76 . . . . 22 C6
Faseman Ave CV4 . . . . 59 F3
Fasson Cl B77 . . . . 9 B4
Faulconbridge Ave CV5 . . . . . . 59 E4
Faulconbridge Way
CV34 . . . . 109 E3
Faultlands Cl CV11 . . . . 39 F8
Fawley Cl CV3 . . . . 78 C6
Fawsley Leys CV22 . . . . 100 A4
Faygate Cl CV3 . . . . 62 F3
Fearnings Cotts B97 . . . . 102 B3
Featherbed La
Bascote CV47 . . . . 115 B1
Cherington CV36 . . . . 141 D7
Coventry CV4 . . . . 76 A5
Redditch B97 . . . . 102 B3
Rugby CV21 . . . . 84 A1
Wilmcote CV37 . . . . 120 D5
Withybrook CV7 . . . . 52 C3
Featherston Dr LE10 . . . . 31 E6
Featherstone Cl CV10 . . . . 29 C2
Feckenham Rd
Astwood Bank B96 . . . . 102 C1
Redditch, Headless Cross
B97 . . . . 102 B4
Redditch, Hunt End B97 . . . . . 102 B2
Feilding Cl CV2 . . . . 63 A6
Feilding Way CV10 . . . . 28 A5
Felgate Cl B90 . . . . 71 A6
Fell Gr CV32 . . . . 106 C3
Fell Mill La CV36 . . . . 137 A3
Fell's La CV47 . . . . 125 C8
Fellmore Gr CV31 . . . . 110 D7
Fellows Way CV21 . . . . 100 C4
Felspar Rd B77 . . . . 4 A2
Felstead Cl B77 . . . . 9 B2
Felton Cl CV2 . . . . 50 E1
Fen End Rd CV8 . . . . 73 E4
Fencote Ave B37 . . . . 33 A4
Fenn Lanes CV13 . . . . 20 B4
Fennell Ho **10** CV1 . . . . 61 B2
Fennis Cl B93 . . . . 72 A5
Fenny Compton Rd
OX17 . . . . 134 B5
Fentham Cl B92 . . . . 57 A6
Fentham Ct B92 . . . . 57 A6
Fentham Gr B92 . . . . 57 A7
Fentham Rd B92 . . . . 57 A6
Fenton Rd B47 . . . . 69 A7
Fenwick Cl B49 . . . . 143 B3
Fenwick Dr CV21 . . . . 101 A4
Ferguson Cl CV37 . . . . 131 B3
Fern Cl Coventry CV2 . . . . 50 C2
Rugby CV23 . . . . 83 B4
Salford Priors WR11 . . . . 127 D6
Fern Dale Rd CV7 . . . . 73 F6
Fern Gr CV12 . . . . 38 E2
Fern Hill Way LE10 . . . . 41 B2
Ferncumbe CE Prim Sch The
CV35 . . . . 114 D6
Ferndale Cl CV11 . . . . 29 E5
Ferndale Cl B46 . . . . 34 A3
Ferndale Dr CV8 . . . . 93 A2
Ferndale Mews B46 . . . . 34 A3
Ferndale Rd
Banbury OX16 . . . . 139 F4
Binley Woods CV3 . . . . 79 D7
Coleshill B46 . . . . 34 A3
Ferndown Cl CV4 . . . . 60 A3
Ferndown Ct CV22 . . . . 82 C1
Ferndown Rd CV22 . . . . 82 C1
Ferndown Terr CV22 . . . . 82 C1
Fernhill Cl CV8 . . . . 92 E6
Fernhill Dr CV32 . . . . 106 B1
Fernhill La CV7,CV8 . . . . 75 B8
Fernwood Cl B98 . . . . 103 A3
Ferrers Cl CV4 . . . . 59 F2
Ferreres Cl CV22 . . . . 99 B2
Ferry La CV37 . . . . 121 D3
Fetherston Cres CV8 . . . . 79 B1
Fetherston Ct **4** CV31 . . . . . 109 F6
Fiddlers Gn B92 . . . . 57 A7
Field Barn Rd CV35 . . . . 108 A7
Field Cl Harbury CV33 . . . . . . 123 F8
Kenilworth CV8 . . . . 93 B5
Warwick CV34 . . . . 109 B7
Field Ct CV2 . . . . 62 B8
Field Gate La CV47 . . . . 133 E7
Field Head La CV34 . . . . 109 B6
Field Ho CV8 . . . . 92 F5
Field La B91 . . . . 56 A5
Field View CV22 . . . . 100 B4
Field View Binton CV37 . . . . . . 120 A1
Braunston NN11 . . . . 117 C5
Whitnash CV31 . . . . 110 B3
Field View Cl CV7 . . . . 50 A8
Field Way B94 . . . . 88 C6
Fieldfare Cl CV2,CV23 . . . . 83 B4
Fieldfare Croft B36 . . . . 33 A8
Fieldgate La
Kenilworth CV8 . . . . 92 F6
Whitnash CV31 . . . . 110 B3
Fieldgate Lawn CV8 . . . . 92 F6
Fieldhouse Cl B95 . . . . 113 B4
Fielding Cl CV9 . . . . 12 B1
Fields Ct CV34 . . . . 108 F8
Fields Park Dr B49 . . . . 143 B2
Fieldside La CV3 . . . . 62 F2
Fieldways Cl B47 . . . . 69 A7
Fife Rd CV5 . . . . 60 F2
Fife St CV11 . . . . 29 A4

Fifield Cl CV11 . . . . 29 D2
Fighting Cl CV35 . . . . 132 B6
Fillingham Cl B37 . . . . 33 D1
Fillongley Rd
Maxstoke B46,CV7 . . . . 35 B2
Meriden CV7 . . . . 46 E3
Filton Croft B35 . . . . 22 A4
Finch Cl CV6 . . . . 49 C2
Finch Croft CV7 . . . . 74 B7
Finch La WR11 . . . . 127 D3
Findley Cl CV9 . . . . 19 C3
Findon Cl CV12 . . . . 40 C3
Fineacre La CV8,CV23 . . . . 96 B3
Finford Croft CV7 . . . . 74 B6
Fingal Cl CV3 . . . . 78 C6
Fingest Cl CV5 . . . . 60 B4
Finham Cres CV8 . . . . 93 B6
Finham Flats CV8 . . . . 93 B6
Finham Gr CV3 . . . . 77 C3
Finham Green Rd CV3 . . . . 77 B3
Finham Park Sch CV3 . . . . 77 A4
Finham Prim Sch CV3 . . . . 77 B3
Finham Rd CV8 . . . . 93 B6
Finings Ct **7** CV32 . . . . 105 F2
Finlay Ct CV1 . . . . 151 C1
Finmere CV21 . . . . 83 B3
Finnemore Cl CV3 . . . . 77 B5
Finwood Rd CV35 . . . . 113 F8
Fir Gr CV4 . . . . 60 A2
Fir Tree Ave CV4 . . . . 60 B2
Fir Tree Gr CV11 . . . . 39 D8
Fircroft B78 . . . . 15 B4
Fircroft Ho B37 . . . . 33 A2
Fire Safety Engineering Coll
GL56 . . . . 140 C3
Fire Station Rd B26 . . . . 44 C5
Firethorn Cres CV31 . . . . 110 A2
Firleigh Dr CV12 . . . . 40 D2
Firs Dr CV22 . . . . 82 C1
Firs The Bedworth CV12 . . . . . . 38 E2
Coventry CV5 . . . . 77 B8
Kingsbury B78 . . . . 15 B4
Lower Quinton CV37 . . . . 129 E2
Meriden CV7 . . . . 46 B1
Wroxton OX15 . . . . 139 D4
First Ave
Birmingham, Tyburn B76 . . . . . 22 A5
Coventry CV3 . . . . 62 A3
First Exhibition Ave B40 . . . . . . 44 D4
Firth Ave GL56 . . . . 140 C3
Firtree Cl OX16 . . . . 139 F5
Firtree La CV7 . . . . 37 A4
Fisher Ave CV22 . . . . 100 C4
Fisher Rd
Bishops Itchington CV47 . . . . . 124 A4
Coventry CV6 . . . . 61 E8
Fisher's Ct CV34 . . . . 108 D4
Fishers Cl CV23 . . . . 101 A1
Fishers Dr B90 . . . . 69 F5
Fishponds Rd CV8 . . . . 92 E3
Fishpool La CV7 . . . . 44 B5
Fitton St CV11 . . . . 29 B3
Fitzalan Cl CV23 . . . . 84 A3
Fitzroy Cl CV2 . . . . 63 B6
Five Lane Ends LE10 . . . . 41 C3
Five Ways CV7 . . . . 90 F1
Five Ways Rd CV35 . . . . 114 C7
Fivefield Rd CV7 . . . . 48 E5
Fladbury Cl B98 . . . . 103 A4
Flamboro' Cl CV3 . . . . 78 F8
Flamville Rd LE10 . . . . 32 B5
Flats La CV9 . . . . 3 A1
Flaunden Cl CV5 . . . . 60 A4
Flavel Cres CV31 . . . . 109 F7
Flavel Ct CV9 . . . . 3 A1
Flaxley Cl B98 . . . . 112 A6
Flecknoe Cl B36 . . . . 22 C1
Flecknose St CV3 . . . . 78 E8
Fleet Cres CV21 . . . . 83 C1
Fleet Ho CV1 . . . . 151 B2
Fleet St CV1 . . . . 151 B3
Fleming Rd LE10 . . . . 30 F7
Fletchamstead Highway
CV5 . . . . 76 D7
Fletcher Gr B93 . . . . 72 B4
Fletcher Rd LE10 . . . . 31 E7
Fletchers Way CV35 . . . . 146 B2
Fletchworth Gate CV5 . . . . 76 D8
Fleur-de-lys CV37 . . . . 130 B8
Flint Cl CV9 . . . . 12 C1
Florence Cl
Atherstone CV9 . . . . 12 B1
Bedworth CV12 . . . . 49 B8
Florian Way LE10 . . . . 21 C1
Flower Rd CV37 . . . . 144 C3
Flowerdale Dr CV2 . . . . 62 B6
Floyd Gr CV7 . . . . 74 C7
Flude Rd CV7 . . . . 49 A6
Flying Fields Rd CV47 . . . . 147 B2
Flynt Ave CV5 . . . . 60 B6
Foldyard Cl B76 . . . . 22 A6
Foleshill CE Prim Sch
CV6 . . . . 50 A2
Foleshill Rd CV1,CV6 . . . . 61 D6
Folkland Gn CV6 . . . . 61 A7
Folkes Rd CV37 . . . . 145 A2
Folly La
Baddesley Ensor CV9 . . . . 17 B4
Napton on t H CV47 . . . . 125 B7
Folly The B97 . . . . 102 B4
Fontmell Cl CV2 . . . . 63 A4
Ford Cotts CV33 . . . . 106 F2
Ford La CV37 . . . . 113 F1
Ford St Coventry CV1 . . . . 151 C4
Nuneaton CV10 . . . . 28 E4
Fordbridge Inf Sch B37 . . . . . . 33 A5
Fordbridge Rd B37 . . . . 33 A5

Forde Hall La B94,B95 . . . . . . 112 D7
Fordham Ave CV37 . . . . 145 A2
Fordington Pl CV35 . . . . 132 B6
Fordrift The B37 . . . . 44 A6
Fordrough The B90 . . . . 69 C7
Fordwell Cl CV5 . . . . 60 F3
Foredraught B80 . . . . 103 C2
Foregate St B96 . . . . 102 C1
Foreland Way CV6 . . . . 49 A3
Forest Ct Coventry CV5 . . . . . . 60 A4
Dorridge B93 . . . . 71 F3
Forest Oak Specl Sch
B36 . . . . 22 E1
Forest Rd Dorridge B93 . . . . . . 71 F3
Hinckley LE10 . . . . 31 F6
Forest Way B90 . . . . 70 C2
Forest Way Hollywood B47 . . . 69 B6
Nuneaton CV10 . . . . 28 E2
Forester's Rd CV3 . . . . 77 E6
Foresters Pl CV21 . . . . 101 A4
Forfield Pl CV31 . . . . 110 A7
Forfield Rd CV6 . . . . 60 E5
Forge Croft B76 . . . . 22 B6
Forge La B76 . . . . 22 B5
Forge Rd Kenilworth CV8 . . . . . 93 A6
Shustoke B46 . . . . 25 A2
Forge Way CV6 . . . . 49 C3
Forknell Ave CV2 . . . . 62 C5
Fornside Cl CV21 . . . . 83 B4
Forrest Rd CV8 . . . . 92 E4
Forresters Cl LE10 . . . . 31 F6
Forresters Rd LE10 . . . . 31 F6
Forryan Rd LE10 . . . . 31 F7
Forshaw Heath La B94 . . . . 86 A7
Forshaw Heath Rd B94 . . . . . . 69 C1
Forth Dr B37 . . . . 33 B4
Forties B77 . . . . 9 C4
Forum Dr CV21 . . . . 83 A3
Forum Rd B40 . . . . 44 E3
Forward Rd B26 . . . . 44 A3
Fosberry Cl CV34 . . . . 108 F8
Fossdale Rd B77 . . . . 10 A4
Fosse Cotts CV23 . . . . 80 C4
Fosse Cres CV23 . . . . 96 C2
Fosse Way
Ettington CV35,CV37 . . . . 131 C5
Harbury CV33 . . . . 123 C7
Moreton Morrell CV35 . . . . . . 123 A3
Shipston-on-S CV36,GL56 . . . 149 A3
Stretton u F CV23 . . . . 65 A4
Tredington CV36,GL56 . . . . . . 136 E4
Ufton CV33,CV31 . . . . 111 A3
Wolvey CV23 . . . . 42 C1
Fosseway Ave CV6 . . . . 140 A2
Fosseway Cl GL56 . . . . 140 A2
Fosseway Cres CV36 . . . . 136 F6
Fosseway Dr CV6 . . . . 50 A4
Fosseway Gdns LE17 . . . . 43 C3
Fosseway Rd CV3 . . . . 77 B4
Foster Ave B80 . . . . 103 C2
Foster Rd CV6 . . . . 61 B7
Fosterd Rd CV21 . . . . 82 C3
Founder Cl CV4 . . . . 76 A8
Foundry La **4** CV37 . . . . 144 C2
Fountain Gdns CV35 . . . . 146 B2
Fountain Way CV37 . . . . 145 A1
Four Ashes Rd B93 . . . . 71 E4
Four Crosses CV23 . . . . 117 C6
Four Oaks B93 . . . . 89 C8
Four Pounds Ave CV5 . . . . 60 F3
Fourfields Way CV7 . . . . 37 A4
Fourways CV9 . . . . 18 C4
Fow Oak CV4 . . . . 59 C2
Fowey Cl B76 . . . . 22 A7
Fowler Rd Coventry CV6 . . . . . 61 B4
Sutton Coldfield B75 . . . . 13 B5
Fox Ave CV10 . . . . 29 D7
Fox Cl CV21 Harbury CV33 . . . 123 F6
Rugby CV21 . . . . 84 A1
Fox Hill Rd B75 . . . . 7 A1
Fox Hollies Rd B76 . . . . 13 B2
Fox's Covert CV13 . . . . 19 C3
Foxbury Dr B93 . . . . 72 B3
Foxcote Cl B90 . . . . 70 D8
Foxcote Dr B90 . . . . 70 D8
Foxcote Hill CV36 . . . . 136 B6
Foxcovert La CV13 . . . . 21 A4
Foxdale Wlk **8** CV31 . . . . . . 110 C6
Foxes La CV37 . . . . 120 C5
Foxes Mdw B76 . . . . 22 A8
Foxes Way
Balsall Common CV7 . . . . 74 B6
Warwick CV34 . . . . 108 D4
Foxfield CV23 . . . . 66 A4
Foxford Cl B36 . . . . 22 D1
Foxford Cres CV2 . . . . 50 E4
Foxglove B77 . . . . 4 A2
Foxglove Cl
Bedworth CV12 . . . . 38 E1
Coventry CV6 . . . . 49 C2
Rugby CV23 . . . . 83 C4
Foxglove Croft CV12 . . . . 38 C1
Foxholes La B97 . . . . 102 A3
Foxland Cl
Birmingham B37 . . . . 33 D2
Cheswick Green B90 . . . . 70 D4
Foxley Dr B91 . . . . 56 A5
Foxon's Barn Rd CV21 . . . . 83 B3
Foxtail Cl CV37 . . . . 144 B3
Foxton Rd CV3 . . . . 62 E1
Foxwood Rd B78 . . . . 10 C4
Framlingham Gr CV8 . . . . 93 C6
Frampton Cl B37 . . . . 33 D3
Frampton Wlk CV2 . . . . 62 F4
Frances Ave CV34 . . . . 109 A7

Frances Cres CV12 . . . . 39 A3
Frances Havergal Cl **2**
CV31 . . . . 109 F6
Frances Rd Baginton CV8 . . . . . 77 F3
Harbury CV33 . . . . 123 F6
Francis Cl B78 . . . . 5 A1
Francis Dr CV22 . . . . 99 A4
Francis Gibbs Gdns
CV31 . . . . 110 A4
Francis St CV6 . . . . 61 E7
Franciscan Rd CV3 . . . . 77 D8
Frank St CV11 . . . . 29 B3
Frank Walsh Ho CV1 . . . . 151 C4
Frankholmes Dr B90 . . . . 71 A6
Frankland Rd CV6 . . . . 50 A1
Franklin Ct CV11 . . . . 29 D1
Franklin Gr CV4 . . . . 59 E1
Franklin Rd
Nuneaton CV11 . . . . 29 D1
Whitnash CV31 . . . . 110 A3
Frankpledge Rd CV3 . . . . 77 E7
Frankton Ave CV3 . . . . 77 C5
Frankton Cl B98 . . . . 103 C4
Frankton La CV23 . . . . 82 A3
Frankton Rd CV23 . . . . 97 C1
Frankwell Dr CV2 . . . . 50 E1
Fraser Cl CV10 . . . . 28 B6
Fraser Rd CV6 . . . . 49 A1
Frasers Way CV37 . . . . 129 B6
Fred Lee Gr CV3 . . . . 77 D4
Frederick Bird Prim Sch
CV2 . . . . 61 F5
Frederick Early Ho B98 . . . . . 103 A4
Frederick Neal Ave CV5 . . . . . . 59 C4
Frederick Press Way **5**
CV21 . . . . 82 C2
Frederick Rd CV7 . . . . 37 A4
Frederick St CV21 . . . . 82 C2
Freeboard La CV8,CV23 . . . . . 96 C4
Freeburn Cswy CV4 . . . . 76 C7
Freehold St CV1 . . . . 61 F4
Freeman Cl CV10 . . . . 28 D4
Freeman St CV6 . . . . 61 F6
Freeman's La LE10 . . . . 32 A5
Freemans Cl CV32 . . . . 105 E2
Freemantle Rd CV22 . . . . 82 B1
Freer St CV11 . . . . 29 E2
Freesland Rise CV10 . . . . 28 B6
Frensham Cl B37 . . . . 33 C2
Frensham Dr CV10 . . . . 28 B5
Freshfield Cl CV5 . . . . 48 C1
Freshwater Gr **1** CV31 . . . . . 110 C6
Freswick Cl LE10 . . . . 21 C1
Fretton Cl CV6 . . . . 61 F7
Frevill Rd CV6 . . . . 62 A8
Friar's Gate CV9 . . . . 18 B4
Friars Cl CV3 . . . . 79 E7
Friars La OX15 . . . . 137 F2
Friars St CV34 . . . . 108 D6
Friars Wlk B37 . . . . 33 D2
Friary Ave CV5 . . . . 59 C2
Friary Cl CV5 . . . . 151 A4
Friary Rd CV9 . . . . 71 A6
Friary Rd CV5 . . . . 114 F3
Friary Rd CV9 . . . . 12 B1
Friary St CV11 . . . . 29 B5
Friday Cl B50 . . . . 148 B3
Friday Furlong B50 . . . . 148 B3
Friday La B92 . . . . 56 D4
Friday St
Lower Quinton CV37 . . . . 129 E2
Pebworth CV37 . . . . 128 F1
Frilsham Way CV5 . . . . 60 B4
Frisby Ct CV11 . . . . 29 E2
Frisby Rd CV4 . . . . 59 E2
Friswell Dr CV6 . . . . 61 F8
Friswell Ho **3** CV2 . . . . 62 D8
Friz Hill CV35 . . . . 131 D8
Frobisher Rd
Coventry CV3 . . . . 77 C5
Rugby CV22 . . . . 82 B1
Frog La
Balsall Common CV7 . . . . 74 A5
Ilmington CV36 . . . . 136 A6
Upper Boddington NN11 . . . . . 134 E8
Welford on A CV37 . . . . 129 B6
Froglands La WR11 . . . . 128 A4
Frogmore Ct CV5 . . . . 60 C6
Frogmore La CV8 . . . . 73 F2
Frogmore Rd CV37 . . . . 121 B6
Frolesworth La LE17 . . . . 43 C4
Front St Ilmington CV36 . . . . . 136 B6
Pebworth CV37 . . . . 128 E1
Frost St CV5 . . . . 146 B2
Frost Rd CV35 . . . . 146 B2
Fryer Ave CV32 . . . . 105 E3
Frythe Cl CV8 . . . . 93 C6
Fuchsia Cl **1** CV2 . . . . 50 B4
Fulbrook La CV35 . . . . 121 F8
Fulbrook Rd CV2 . . . . 50 C2
Fulford Dr B76 . . . . 22 B5
Fulford Hall Rd B90,B94 . . . . . 69 D3
Fulford Wlk B90 . . . . 71 A5
Fuller Pl CV35 . . . . 122 F3
Fullers Cl CV6 . . . . 60 F7
Fullwood Cl CV2 . . . . 50 E2
Fulwell Mews B37 . . . . 44 B8
Furlong Mdw CV36 . . . . 149 C2
Furlong Rd CV1 . . . . 151 C1
Furnace Cl CV12 . . . . 39 D3
Furnace Rd CV12 . . . . 39 D4
Furness Cl CV21 . . . . 83 B4
Furrow Cl CV21 . . . . 83 B2
Furrows The CV47 . . . . 147 B3
Furze Hill Rd CV36 . . . . 149 C2

Furze La
Chipping Campden GL55 . . . . . .**135** C4
Redditch B98 . . . .**112** A6
Fylde Ho CV2 . . . .**62** D4
Fynford Rd CV6 . . . .**61** B5

G

Gables Cl CV22 . . . .**99** B4
Gables The B78 . . . .**5** A1
Gabor Cl CV21 . . . .**83** B3
Gadsby Ct CV11 . . . .**29** E3
Gadsby St CV11 . . . .**29** E3
Gadshill CV34 . . . .**109** E4
Gainford Rise CV3 . . . .**63** A3
Gainsborough Cres
Knowle B93 . . . .**72** A6
Rugby CV21 . . . .**84** A1
Gainsborough Dr
Bedworth CV12 . . . .**39** A4
Fazeley B78 . . . .**8** A4
Royal Leamington Spa
CV31 . . . .**110** D6
Gainsborough Rd CV37 . . . . .**144** B1
Gainsborough Terr
GL55 . . . .**135** C1
Gainsborough Trad Est
CV47 . . . .**147** A2
Galena Cl B77 . . . .**4** A1
Galey's Rd CV3 . . . .**77** D8
Gallagher Bsns Pk CV6 . . . .**49** E5
Gallagher Rd CV12 . . . .**39** A2
Gallagher Ret Pk CV6 . . . .**61** F8
Galley Common Inf Sch
CV10 . . . .**27** C2
Galliards The CV4 . . . .**76** D4
Galliers Cl B77 . . . .**9** C3
Gallows Hill CV34 . . . .**109** B4
Galmington Dr CV3 . . . .**77** B6
Gannaway Rd CV35 . . . .**114** B3
Garden Cl Hinckley LE10 . . . . . .**31** D6
Knowle B93 . . . .**71** F6
Mickleton GL55 . . . .**135** B6
Garden Ct
Warwick, Emscote CV34 . . . . . .**109** C8
Warwick, Packmores CV34 .**108** F7
Garden Flats CV5 . . . .**59** D5
Garden Cl CV12 . . . .**49** F8
Garden Terr CV35 . . . .**146** B2
Gardenia Dr CV5 . . . .**60** B6
Gardens The
Kenilworth CV8 . . . .**93** A3
Radford Semele CV31 . . . .**118** E5
Rugby CV22 . . . .**99** B4
Thurlaston CV23 . . . .**98** C2
Gardner Ho CV11 . . . .**61** B2
Gardner Way CV8 . . . .**93** A2
Garlands Croft CV7 . . . .**49** A6
Garlick Dr CV8 . . . .**93** C6
Garnette Ct CV10 . . . .**28** B5
Garrard Cl WR11 . . . .**127** F6
Garratt Cl CV23 . . . .**82** A3
Garrett St CV11 . . . .**29** E2
Garrick Cl CV5 . . . .**59** C4
Garrick Way CV37 . . . .**144** C1
Garrigill B77 . . . .**4** A1
Garth Cres CV3 . . . .**78** D8
Garth Ho CV3 . . . .**78** D8
Garton Cl DE12 . . . .**3** C4
Garway Cl CV32 . . . .**105** F4
Garyth Williams Cl CV22 . . . .**99** C4
Gas House La B49 . . . .**143** B2
Gas St
Royal Leamington Spa
CV31 . . . .**109** F7
Rugby CV21 . . . .**83** A2
Gate Farm Dr CV23 . . . .**53** C2
Gate La Dorridge B93 . . . .**71** C3
Nether Whitacre B46 . . . .**24** C3
Gatehouse CV31 . . . .**109** D7
Gatehouse Cl CV21 . . . .**101** A4
Gatehouse La CV12 . . . .**39** A1
Gateley Cl B98 . . . .**112** A6
Gateside Rd CV6 . . . .**49** F2
Gatwick Rd B35 . . . .**22** B4
Gaulby Wlk CV3 . . . .**63** A1
Gaveston Cl CV34 . . . .**108** F8
Gaveston Rd Coventry CV6 .**60** F6
Royal Leamington Spa
CV32 . . . .**105** C1
Gaydon Cl CV6 . . . .**62** A8
Gaydon Rd CV47 . . . .**124** A3
Gayer St CV6 . . . .**50** A1
Gayhurst Cl CV3 . . . .**78** F8
Gayle B77 . . . .**4** A1
Gaza Cl CV4 . . . .**60** A1
Gazelle Cl CV1 . . . .**151** D3
Geeson Cl B35 . . . .**22** B4
Gentian Way CV23 . . . .**83** C4
Gentlemans La B94 . . . .**112** C7
Geoffery Cl CV2 . . . .**62** B5
Geoffrey Cl B76 . . . .**22** B7
George Birch Cl CV23 . . . .**64** C2
George Eliot Ave CV12 . . . . . .**39** D2
George Eliot Com Sch
CV11 . . . .**29** D1
George Eliot Hospl CV10 . . .**29** B2
George Eliot Rd CV1 . . . .**61** D5
George Eliot Sch CV11 . . . . . .**39** D8
George Eliot St CV11 . . . .**29** C2
George Fentham Prim Sch
B92 . . . .**57** B6
George Fox La CV13 . . . .**20** A3

George Hodgkinson Cl
CV4 . . . .**59** F3
George La GL55 . . . .**135** B1
George Marston Rd CV3 . . . .**62** E1
George Park Cl Ansty CV7 .**51** D3
Coventry CV2 . . . .**50** C1
George Poole Ho CV11 . . . . . .**61** B2
George Rd
Warwick CV34 . . . .**109** A8
Water Orton B46 . . . .**23** C3
George Robertson Cl
CV3 . . . .**78** E7
George St Arley CV7 . . . .**37** A4
Coventry CV1 . . . .**61** E5
Hinckley LE10 . . . .**31** D8
Nuneaton CV11 . . . .**29** E2
Royal Leamington Spa
CV31 . . . .**110** A7
Rugby CV21 . . . .**82** C2
Stockton CV47 . . . .**115** F3
George Street Ringway
CV12 . . . .**39** B3
George's Elm La B50 . . . . .**148** C4
Georgian Cl B49 . . . .**143** A2
Gerandria Ct CV22 . . . .**100** C4
Gerard Ave CV4 . . . .**76** B8
Gerard Rd Alcester B49 . . . . .**143** B2
Rugby CV22 . . . .**99** A4
Gerrard St CV34 . . . .**108** E6
Gerrards Rd CV36 . . . .**149** C3
Gibbet Hill Rd CV4 . . . .**76** B3
Gibbet La LE17 . . . .**68** A3
Gibbons Cl CV4 . . . .**59** F2
Gibbs Cl CV2 . . . .**63** B6
Gibbs Ct CV37 . . . .**145** C2
Gibbs La WR11 . . . .**127** D1
Gibson Cres CV12 . . . .**39** A1
Gibson Dr CV21 . . . .**84** A1
Gielgud Way CV2 . . . .**63** B8
Giffard Way CV34 . . . .**104** E1
Gifford Rd CV33 . . . .**123** D3
Gifford Wlk CV37 . . . .**144** B2
Gigg La B76 . . . .**14** B3
Gilberry Cl B93 . . . .**72** A4
Gilbert Ave CV22 . . . .**82** B1
Gilbert Cl Coventry CV1 . . . . .**61** E3
9 Royal Leamington Spa
CV32 . . . .**144** C3
Gilberts Rugby Football
Mus* CV21 . . . .**82** C3
Giles Cl CV6 . . . .**49** C2
Gilfil Rd CV10 . . . .**29** B1
Gilkes La CV35 . . . .**137** F8
Gillet Cl CV11 . . . .**29** B3
Gillett's La OX15 . . . .**137** E2
Gillians Wlk CV2 . . . .**63** A8
Gillows Croft B90 . . . .**71** A7
Gilquart Way CV1 . . . .**151** C1
Gilson Dr B46 . . . .**33** D8
Gilson Rd B46 . . . .**33** E8
Gingko Wlk 2 CV31 . . . .**109** F5
Gipsy Cl CV7 . . . .**74** B5
Gipsy La
Balsall Common CV7 . . . .**74** C5
Nuneaton CV10,CV11 . . . .**39** D7
Wolvey LE10 . . . .**41** C4
Girdlers Cl CV3 . . . .**77** B5
Girtin Cl CV12 . . . .**39** A4
Girvan Gr CV32 . . . .**106** C5
Gisburn Cl CV34 . . . .**104** F1
Givens Ho 9 CV1 . . . .**61** B2
Glade The CV5 . . . .**59** F3
Gladiator Way CV21 . . . .**82** C4
Gladstone Rd B93 . . . .**72** A2
Gladstone St CV21 . . . .**82** C2
Gladstone Terr LE10 . . . .**31** E8
Glaisdale Ave CV6 . . . .**49** E3
Glamis Pl OX16 . . . .**139** F3
Glamorgan Cl CV3 . . . .**78** D5
Glaramara Cl CV21 . . . .**83** B4
Glascote Heath Prim Sch
B77 . . . .**4** A1
Glascote La B77 . . . .**9** C4
Glasshouse La
Kenilworth CV8 . . . .**93** D4
Tamworth-in-A B94 . . . .**88** F6
Glaston Dr B91 . . . .**71** A8
Gleave Rd CV31 . . . .**110** A3
Glebe Ave CV12 . . . .**38** E1
Glebe Cl Bidford-on-A B50 .**148** B2
Coventry CV4 . . . .**76** A7
Stockton CV47 . . . .**147** C4
Glebe Cotts WR11 . . . .**127** D3
Glebe Cres Kenilworth CV8 .**93** A3
Rugby CV21 . . . .**82** C2
Glebe Est CV37 . . . .**131** A3
Glebe Farm (Mus)*
CV37 . . . .**120** C5
Glebe Farm Ind Est CV21 .**82** C4
Glebe Farm Rd CV21 . . . .**82** C4
Glebe Fields B76 . . . .**23** B6
Glebe Fold GL55 . . . .**135** B2
Glebe La Nuneaton CV11 . . . . .**29** F6
Staverton NN11 . . . .**126** E8
Glebe Pl CV31 . . . .**110** A6
Glebe Rd Claverdon CV35 . . .**113** F3
Hinckley LE10 . . . .**31** F8
Nuneaton CV11 . . . .**29** C4
Southam CV47 . . . .**147** A3
Stratford-u-A CV37 . . . .**144** B2
Glebe Rise CV9 . . . .**3** A1
Glebe The Corley CV7 . . . .**48** C7
Hook Norton OX15 . . . .**142** D4
Wootton Wawen B95 . . . .**113** B2
Glebe Way CV7 . . . .**74** A7
Glebefarm Gr CV3 . . . .**62** F3
Gleeson Dr CV34 . . . .**104** E1

Glen Cl CV36 . . . .**149** C3
Glenbarr Cl LE10 . . . .**31** A8
Glenbarr Dr LE10 . . . .**31** A8
Glencoe Rd CV3 . . . .**62** B1
Glendale Ave CV8 . . . .**93** A6
Glendale Ct B77 . . . .**10** A3
Glendale Inf Sch CV10 . . . .**28** F2
Glendale Way CV4 . . . .**59** C2
Glendon Gdns CV12 . . . .**40** A1
Glendon Way
Dorridge B93 . . . .**71** D3
Dorridge B93 . . . .**71** E3
Glendower App CV34 . . . .**109** E3
Glendower Ave CV5 . . . .**60** D3
Gleneagles B77 . . . .**4** A3
Gleneagles Cl
Hinckley LE10 . . . .**31** D4
Nuneaton CV11 . . . .**30** C1
Gleneagles Rd CV2 . . . .**62** E6
Glenfern Gdns CV8 . . . .**78** A2
Glenfield Ave CV10 . . . .**29** D7
Glenfield Cl
Redditch B97 . . . .**102** B3
2 Solihull B91 . . . .**71** C8
Glenhurst Rd B95 . . . .**113** A4
Glenmore Dr CV6 . . . .**49** F5
Glenmount Ave CV6 . . . .**49** F5
Glenn St CV6 . . . .**49** D3
Glenridding Cl CV6 . . . .**49** F5
Glenrosa Wlk CV4 . . . .**76** A7
Glenroy Cl CV2 . . . .**62** E6
Glentworth Ave CV6 . . . .**49** A2
Glentworth Dr B76 . . . .**13** A2
Glenville Ave CV9 . . . .**10** B1
Glenwood Dr B90 . . . .**70** D4
Glenwood Gdns CV12 . . . .**39** A5
Gloster Dr CV8 . . . .**92** F6
Gloster Gdns CV35 . . . .**146** A4
Gloucester Cl CV11 . . . .**30** A7
Gloucester La GL55 . . . .**135** B6
Gloucester St
Coventry CV1 . . . .**61** B3
1 Royal Leamington Spa
CV31 . . . .**110** A7
Gloucester Way B37 . . . .**33** A1
Glover Cl CV34 . . . .**108** B4
Glover Rd B75 . . . .**13** A5
Glover St CV3 . . . .**77** D8
Glover's Cl CV9 . . . .**12** C1
Glovers Cl CV7 . . . .**46** C1
Godfrey Cl CV31 . . . .**110** E5
Godiva Pl CV1 . . . .**151** D3
Godiva Trad Est CV6 . . . .**61** F8
Godsons La CV47 . . . .**125** C8
Gofton B77 . . . .**10** A4
Gigaurt Way CV1 . . . .**99** A4
Gold Ave CV22 . . . .**99** A4
Gold Cl CV11 . . . .**39** E8
Goldacre Cl CV31 . . . .**109** F4
Goldcrest B77 . . . .**10** A3
Goldcrest Croft B36 . . . .**33** A8
Golden Acres La CV3 . . . .**78** F7
Golden End Dr B93 . . . .**72** D6
Goldicote Bsns Pk CV37 .**130** E5
Goldicote Mews CV37 . . . . .**130** E6
Goldicote Rd CV35 . . . .**130** F7
Goldsborough B77 . . . .**4** A1
Goldsmith Ave
Rugby CV22 . . . .**99** C3
Warwick CV34 . . . .**108** B4
Goldthorn Cl CV5 . . . .**59** D4
Golf Dr CV11 . . . .**30** B1
Golf La CV31 . . . .**110** B2
Good Shepherd RC Sch
CV6 . . . .**49** F1
Goodacre Cl CV23 . . . .**84** A3
Goode Cl CV34 . . . .**108** C7
Goode Croft CV4 . . . .**59** F2
Goodere Ave B78 . . . .**11** A4
Goodere Dr B78 . . . .**5** A1
Goodeve Wlk B75 . . . .**13** B5
Goodfellow St CV32 . . . .**105** C1
Goodman Way CV4 . . . .**59** C1
Goodway Ct 7 CV34 . . . .**108** F7
Goodway Ho 8 CV32 . . . . . .**109** D8
Goodwood Cl
Coventry CV3 . . . .**78** C6
Stratford-u-A CV37 . . . .**129** E8
Goodyers End La CV12 . . . . .**38** E1
Goodyers End Prim Sch
CV12 . . . .**49** E8
Goose La CV37 . . . .**129** D1
Goosehills Rd LE10 . . . .**31** E5
Gorcott Hill B98 . . . .**112** B7
Gorcott La B90 . . . .**70** A5
Gordon Cl CV12 . . . .**39** C4
Gordon Rd CV37 . . . .**129** C2
Gordon St Coventry CV1 . . . . .**61** B2
7 Royal Leamington Spa
CV31 . . . .**110** A7
Goring Rd CV2 . . . .**62** A4
Gorse Cl CV22 . . . .**82** C1
Gorse Farm Rd CV11 . . . .**40** B8
Gorse La B95 . . . .**113** A4
Gorse Lea CV47 . . . .**147** A3
Gorseway CV5 . . . .**60** C3
Gorsey Cl B96 . . . .**118** C8
Gorsey La Coleshill B46 . . . . .**23** F2
Wythall B47 . . . .**69** A6
Gorsey Way B46 . . . .**23** E2
Gorsy Bank Rd B77 . . . .**9** C3
Gorsy Way CV10 . . . .**28** D5
Gorton Croft CV7 . . . .**74** B7
Gosford Ind Est CV1 . . . .**61** F2
Gosford Park Prim Sch
CV1 . . . .**61** F2
Gosford St CV1 . . . .**151** D2
Gospel Oak La CV37 . . . .**120** F5

Gospel Oak Rd CV6 . . . .**49** B4
Gosport Rd CV6 . . . .**61** E8
Gossett La CV8 . . . .**79** F7
Gould Cl NN11 . . . .**117** D5
Gould Rd CV35 . . . .**108** A7
Governor's Ct CV34 . . . .**108** D8
Grace Rd CV5 . . . .**59** A8
Grafton Cl B98 . . . .**103** A4
Grafton Ct CV4 . . . .**76** B7
Grafton La B50 . . . .**148** C3
Grafton St CV1 . . . .**61** F2
Graham Ho CV1 . . . .**50** B1
Graham Rd CV21 . . . .**83** B3
Graham St CV11 . . . .**29** C5
Granary Mus of Bygones
OX17 . . . .**134** B4
Granborough Cl CV3 . . . .**78** F8
Granborough Ct CV32 . . . . .**106** A2
Granbrook La GL55 . . . .**135** C7
Granby Cl LE10 . . . .**31** C7
Granby Rd Hinckley LE10 . . . . .**31** C7
Honington CV36 . . . .**137** A5
Nuneaton CV10 . . . .**28** C7
Grand Depot Rd CV11 . . . .**40** F6
Grandborough Fields Rd
CV23 . . . .**116** C5
Grange Ave
Coventry, Binley CV3 . . . .**78** F7
Coventry, Finham CV3 . . . .**77** B5
Kenilworth CV8 . . . .**92** E7
Grange Ct Nuneaton CV10 .**28** C7
Ratley OX15 . . . .**132** B7
Southam CV47 . . . .**147** A3
Tamworth B77 . . . .**9** B4
Warwick CV34 . . . .**109** C8
Grange Dr LE10 . . . .**31** E5
Grange Farm Dr CV47 . . . . . .**147** C4
Grange Farm Prim Sch
CV3 . . . .**78** F8
Grange Gdns CV35 . . . .**146** B3
Grange La
Harvington WR11 . . . .**127** D3
Sibford Ferris OX15 . . . .**142** E8
Grange Mews The 1
CV32 . . . .**105** D1
Grange Pk CV37 . . . .**145** A2
Grange PRU The CV6 . . . .**48** E1
Grange Rd
Balsall Common CV7 . . . .**73** F7
Bearley CV37 . . . .**120** E7
Bidford-on-A B50 . . . .**148** C2
Coventry CV6 . . . .**50** B5
Dorridge B93 . . . .**71** E2
Hartshill CV10 . . . .**19** A1
Royal Leamington Spa
CV32 . . . .**106** B3
Rugby CV21 . . . .**99** B4
Seckington B79 . . . .**2** A2
Shawell LE17 . . . .**68** B3
Shrewley CV35 . . . .**114** D6
Shustoke B46 . . . .**24** C1
Snitterfield CV37 . . . .**121** B6
Stoke Golding CV13 . . . .**21** C4
Stoneleigh CV8 . . . .**94** C6
Swalcliffe OX15 . . . .**142** F8
Tamworth B77 . . . .**4** A3
Tanworth-In-A B94 . . . .**87** A2
Grange St CV21 . . . .**67** B3
Greenace's Cl B77 . . . .**4** B3
Greenacres B76 . . . .**22** A8
Greenacres Prim Sch B77 .**4** A3
Greenbank Rd CV7 . . . .**73** F6
Greendale Cl CV9 . . . .**18** C4
Greendale Rd
Atherstone CV9 . . . .**18** C4
Coventry CV5 . . . .**60** D3
Greenfield Ave CV7 . . . .**74** A7
Greenfields Cl CV36 . . . .**149** C3
Greenfinch Cl B36 . . . .**33** A7
Greenfinch Rd B36 . . . .**33** A7
Greenheart B77 . . . .**4** A2
Greenhill Cl B77 . . . .**9** C3
Greenhill Rd Rugby CV22 .**82** C1
Stoke Golding CV13 . . . .**21** B4
Warwick CV34 . . . .**110** B4
Greenhill St CV37 . . . .**144** C2
Greenland Ave CV5 . . . .**59** F5
Greenland Ct CV5 . . . .**59** F5
Greenlands Ave B98 . . . .**103** A4
Greenlands Dr B98 . . . .**102** C4
Greenlands Rd B37 . . . .**33** C1
Greenlea B77 . . . .**10** A4
Greenmoor Rd
Hinckley LE10 . . . .**31** D5
Nuneaton CV10 . . . .**29** A3
Greenodd Dr CV6 . . . .**49** F4
Greenore Bank CV6 . . . .**49** A1
Greens Yd CV12 . . . .**39** C3
Greenside B90 . . . .**70** C4
Greenside Cl CV11 . . . .**30** C1
Greensleeves Cl CV6 . . . .**49** B2
Greenspire Ct CV6 . . . .**93** B6
Greensward The
Coventry CV3 . . . .**63** A2
Wolvington OX17 . . . .**134** F1
Greenswood CV37 . . . .**120** E7
Greenway
Braunston NN11 . . . .**117** D5
Nuneaton CV11 . . . .**40** B8
Tamworth B77 . . . .**5** A2
Warwick CV34 . . . .**104** C1
Greenway Cl CV36 . . . .**149** C3
Greenway Nature Trail The*
CV37 . . . .**129** C5
Greenway Rd CV36 . . . .**149** C3
Greenway The B37 . . . .**44** A6
Greenways Ct CV36 . . . .**149** C3
Greenways The CV32 . . . .**106** B1

Greaves The B76 . . . .**22** F6
Greaves Way The CV47 . . . .**124** B4
Green Cl
Long Lawford CV23 . . . .**81** C2
Studley B80 . . . .**103** C2
Whitnash CV31 . . . .**110** B4
Wythall B47 . . . .**69** A3
Green Ct CV21 . . . .**83** B2
Green End CV47 . . . .**115** C4
Green Farm End CV35 . . . . .**132** B6
Green Field The CV3 . . . .**78** B8
Green Gables B47 . . . .**69** A7
Green Gates B95 . . . .**113** B5
Green La Arley CV10 . . . .**26** C4
Balsall Common CV7 . . . .**74** B7
Brinklow CV23 . . . .**64** B2
Church Lawford CV23 . . . .**81** B3
Coleshill B46 . . . .**33** F5
Corley CV7 . . . .**47** D6
Coventry CV3 . . . .**77** B4
Grendon B78 . . . .**14** B6
Middleton B78 . . . .**14** A4
Nuneaton CV10 . . . .**28** C7
Oxhill CV35 . . . .**137** F8
Polesworth B77,B78 . . . .**10** B4
Redditch B97 . . . .**102** A4
Shipston-on-S CV36 . . . .**149** C3
Shrewley CV35 . . . .**114** C6
Studley B80 . . . .**103** A3
Swalcliffe OX15 . . . .**139** A1
Warwick CV34 . . . .**108** F8
Wibtoft LE17 . . . .**43** A2
Wolvey LE10 . . . .**41** C3
Green Lane Cl CV36 . . . .**149** C3
Green The Austrey CV9 . . . .**3** A1
Barby CV23 . . . .**101** B1
Braunston NN11 . . . .**117** C5
Chipping Campden GL55 . . .**135** B1
Claverdon CV35 . . . .**113** F4
Cleeve Prior WR11 . . . .**128** A4
Dordon B78 . . . .**10** B2
Great Rollright OX7 . . . .**142** A2
Great Wolford CV36 . . . .**140** E5
Hellidon NN11 . . . .**126** B5
Hook Norton OX15 . . . .**142** D4
Hornton OX15 . . . .**139** B7
Kingsbury B78 . . . .**15** B3
Lighthorne CV35 . . . .**123** B2
Little Compton CV36 . . . .**141** A6
Long Itchington CV47 . . . .**115** D6
9 Moreton-in-M GL56 . . . .**140** A3
Nuneaton CV11 . . . .**29** E2
Orton-on-t-H CV9 . . . .**6** B2
Priors Marston CV47 . . . .**125** E4
Ratley CV35 . . . .**132** F3
Rugby CV22 . . . .**99** B4
Seckington B79 . . . .**2** A2
Shawell LE17 . . . .**68** B3
Shrewley CV35 . . . .**114** D6
Shustoke B46 . . . .**24** C1
Snitterfield CV37 . . . .**121** B6
Stoke Golding CV13 . . . .**21** C4
Stoneleigh CV8 . . . .**94** C6
Swalcliffe OX15 . . . .**142** F8
Tamworth B77 . . . .**4** A3
Tanworth-In-A B94 . . . .**87** A2

Greenwood Cl CV23 82 A3
Greenwood Ct
Nuneaton CV11 29 E3
Royal Leamington Spa
CV32 106 B1
Greenwood Rd CV13 21 C4
Greenwood Sq 5 B37 33 B2
Greenwood Way B37 33 B2
Gregory Ave CV3 77 A6
Gregory Hood Rd CV3 77 E4
Grenden Hall Rd CV35 132 D3
Grendon Cl CV4 59 C1
Grendon Dr CV21 83 C4
Grendon Rd B78 11 A4
Grenfell Cl CV31 110 D6
Grenville Ave CV2 62 B3
Grenville Cl CV22 82 B1
Gresham Ave CV32 106 B2
Gresham Pl CV32 106 B2
Gresham Rd CV10 39 B8
Gresham St CV2 62 A2
Gresley Rd CV2 62 D7
Greswold Cl CV4 59 F1
Greswoldes The CV31 110 F6
Gretna Rd CV3 76 F4
Grevel La GL55 135 B2
Greville Rd Alcester B49 143 A3
Kenilworth CV8 92 F4
Warwick CV34 105 B1
Greville Smith Ave
CV31 110 B4
Grewcock Cl LE17 43 C3
Grey Mill Cl B90 70 F6
Grey Tree Cres B93 71 E3
Grey's Rd B80 103 C2
Greycoat Rd CV6 49 A2
Greyfriars Ct CV6 61 A7
Greyfriars La CV1 151 B2
Greyfriars Rd CV1 151 B2
Greygoose La GL56 150 A3
Greyhurst Croft 5 B91 71 B8
Greyrick Ct GL55 135 B6
Greys Cl OX16 139 F3
Griff La Nuneaton CV10 39 A6
Nuneaton CV10 39 B6
Griff Specl Sch The CV10 39 B8
Griffin Rd CV34 109 C7
Griffiths Ho CV21 83 B4
Griggs Cl GL55 135 B2
Grimshaw Villas B93 72 D8
Grimston Cl CV3 63 A2
Grindle Rd CV6 49 F4
Grindley Ho 5 CV1 61 B2
Grindsbrook B77 10 A4
Grizebeck Dr CV5 60 A5
Grizedale CV21 83 B4
Grosvenor Cres LE10 32 A6
Grosvenor Ct 2 CV32 105 F1
Grosvenor Ho CV1 151 A2
Grosvenor Rd
Coventry CV1 151 A1
Royal Leamington Spa
CV31 110 A5
Rugby CV21 83 B2
Grouse Cl CV37 144 B3
Grove Croft CV35 114 F3
Grove Ct CV5 77 B8
Grove Fields CV10 29 D8
Grove La Keresley CV7 48 F7
Lapworth B94 88 F4
Wishaw B76 13 F2
Grove Pk
Hampton Magna CV35 114 F3
Hinckley LE10 32 A6
Grove Pl Nuneaton CV10 28 D3
2 Royal Leamington Spa
CV31 110 A6
Grove Rd Ansty CV7 51 D3
Atherstone CV9 18 B4
Dorridge B93 72 B3
Hinckley LE10 32 A6
Nuneaton CV10 28 D3
Stratford-u-A CV37 144 C1
Grove St Coventry CV1 151 C3
Royal Leamington Spa
CV32 109 E8
Grove The Bedworth CV12 39 C3
Coleshill B46 33 F4
Hampton-in-A B92 45 A1
Hinckley LE10 31 C8
Moreton-in-M GL56 140 B3
Studley B80 103 B2
Grovefield Cres CV7 74 C8
Grovehurst Pk CV8 94 B2
Grovelands Ind Est CV7 50 A6
Grump St CV36 136 B6
Guardhouse Rd CV6 61 B8
Guernsey Dr B36 33 B6
Guild Cotts The 12 CV34 108 E6
Guild Rd
Aston Cantlow B95 119 F6
Coventry CV6 61 D7
Guild St CV37 145 A2
Guildford Ct CV6 61 D7
Guillemard Ct B37 33 B1
Guilsborough Rd CV3 78 E8
Guinness Cl B98 102 B4
Gulistan Ct 6 CV32 105 E1
Gulistan Rd CV32 105 E1
Gullet The B78 4 C1
Gullicote La OX17 139 F6
Gulliman's Way CV31 110 D7
Gulliver's Cl OX15 139 D6
Gulson Hospl CV1 151 D2
Gulson Rd CV1 61 E2
Gun Hill CV7 37 A4
Gun Hill Inf Sch CV7 37 A4
Gun La CV2 62 A5
Gundry Cl CV31 110 A7
Gunn Ct B49 119 E6
Gunn End CV36 149 C4
Gunner Gr B75 13 A6
Gunners La B80 103 C2
Gunnery Terr 3 CV32 105 D1
Gunnings Rd B49 143 B2
Gunton Ave CV3 78 C6
Guphill Ave CV5 60 D2
Guphill La CV5 60 D3
Gurnard B77 9 B3
Gurney Cl CV4 59 E3
Gutteridge Ave CV6 49 A2
Guy Pl E 11 CV32 105 F1
Guy Pl W 10 CV32 105 F1
Guy Rd CV8 92 F2
Guy St
Royal Leamington Spa
CV32 105 F1
Warwick CV34 108 F7
Guy's Cl CV34 109 A8
Guy's Cliffe Ave CV32 105 D2
Guy's Cliffe Rd CV32 109 E8
Guy's Cliffe Terr CV34 108 F7
Guy's Cross Park Rd
CV34 108 F8
Gypsy La Atherstone CV9 12 B1
Dordon B78 11 A2
Kenilworth CV8 92 F2
Water Orton B46 23 D2

H

Hack La CV36 141 C5
Hackwell St CV47 125 C8
Haddon End CV3 77 E6
Haddon Rd CV32 106 B2
Haddon St CV6 62 A8
Hadfield Cl CV23 84 A3
Hadfield Way B37 33 A4
Hadleigh Croft B76 22 A6
Hadleigh Rd CV3 77 C4
Hadley Cl B47 69 A5
Hadleys Croft B78 15 B3
Hadrian Cl CV32 106 B4
Hadrian Dr B46 23 F1
Hadrians Cl B77 9 B4
Hadrians Way CV21 82 C4
Hadrians Wlk B49 143 A2
Halberd Cl LE10 31 D5
Haldale B77 4 B1
Hales Cl CV37 121 B7
Hales Park Ind Est CV6 49 E4
Hales St CV1 151 C3
Halford Gr CV35 114 F5
Halford La CV6 49 A2
Halford Lodge CV6 49 A2
Halford Rd
Ettington CV37 131 A3
Stratford-u-A CV37 144 C1
Whatcote CV36 137 C7
Halfpenny Field Wlk B35 22 A3
Halfway La CV22 99 A2
Halifax Cl Allesley CV5 60 A7
Wellesbourne CV35 146 A1
Hall Brook Rd CV6 49 A4
Hall Cl CV8 94 B6
Hall Cl The CV22 99 B1
Hall Dr Baginton CV8 77 E3
Birmingham B37 44 A7
Stoke Golding CV13 21 C4
Hall End CV11 29 D2
Hall End Pl CV11 29 D2
Hall Gr CV23 64 C2
Hall Green Rd CV2,CV6 50 B2
Hall La Coventry CV2 62 F6
Harbury CV33 123 F7
Witherley CV9 19 A4
Wolvey LE10 41 B2
Hall Rd Hinckley LE10 31 D5
Royal Leamington Spa
CV32 105 F1
Wolvey LE10 41 B2
Hall Wlk B46 33 F4
Hall's Cl CV31 110 B3
Hallam Rd CV6 49 B2
Hallams Cl CV8 79 F5
Hallcroft Way B93 72 A6
Hallfields CV31 110 E5
Hallway Dr CV7 51 E6
Halstead Gr B91 71 A8
Haltonlea B77 10 A4
Hamar Way B37 33 B1
Hambridge Rd CV47 124 C3
Hames La B79 2 B2
Hamilton Cl CV12 38 C1
Hamilton Ct
Coventry CV1 151 B4
Nuneaton CV10 28 D4
Hamilton Dr B80 103 B2
Hamilton Rd Coventry CV2 62 A3
Radford Semele CV31 110 E5
Redditch B97 102 B4
Tiddington CV37 145 C2
Hamilton Terr CV32 109 F8
Hamlet Cl Nuneaton CV11 30 B1
Rugby CV22 99 B3
Hamlet The
Bidford-on-A B50 148 B1
Leek Wootton CV35 105 A7
Hammersley St CV12 38 E1
Hammerton Way CV35 146 B1
Hammond Bsns Ctr CV11 29 E3
Hammond Cl CV11 29 E3
Hammond Gn CV35 146 B2
Hammond Rd CV2 61 F4
Hammonds Terr CV8 92 D5
Hampden Cl OX16 139 F3
Hampden Ct CV47 133 A7
Hampden Way CV22 99 B4
Hampdon Way CV35 146 B1
Hampshire Cl CV3 78 F8
Hampstead Norreys Rd
CV35 132 D4
Hampton Ave CV10 28 B4
Hampton Cl Coventry CV6 61 F6
Redditch B98 103 A4
Hampton Croft CV35 114 F2
Hampton Ct B92 57 B6
Hampton Gr CV32 106 B1
Hampton Grange CV7 46 B1
Hampton La Meriden CV7 57 E8
Solihull B91 56 B5
Hampton Lucy CE Prim Sch
CV35 121 F4
Hampton Rd Coventry CV6 61 F6
Knowle B93 72 C8
Warwick CV34 108 B5
Hampton St CV34 108 D6
Hampton-in-Arden Sta
B92 57 B7
Hams La B76 23 F6
Hanbury Cl CV35 132 B6
Hanbury Rd
Bedworth CV12 39 C4
Dorridge B93 71 F4
Hancock Gn CV4 75 F8
Hancox Cl CV33 107 B4
Handcross Gr CV3 77 A5
Handley Gr CV34 104 D1
Handley's Cl CV8 79 A1
Hands Paddock CV37 130 E1
Handsworth Cres CV5 59 E4
Hanford Cl CV6 61 E6
Hanger Rd B26 44 A3
Hangmans La B79 2 A1
Hanley Ct B49 143 B2
Hanlith B77 10 A4
Hanover Ct Hinckley LE10 31 E6
Redditch B98 102 B4
Hanover Gdns
8 Royal Leamington Spa
CV32 106 A1
Rugby CV21 83 A2
Hanover Glebe CV11 29 C2
Hans Cl CV2 61 F4
Hansell Dr B93 71 E2
Hanson Ave CV36 149 C3
Hanson Ct 2 LE10 31 D8
Hanson Way CV6 50 A4
Hanson's Bridge Rd B24 22 A4
Hanwell Cl B76 22 B7
Hanwell Ct OX17 139 F6
Hanwood Cl CV5 59 D4
Hanworth Cl CV32 106 C2
Hanworth Rd CV34 108 D8
Harbet Dr B40 44 E4
Harborough Cotts B94 89 D3
Harborough Dr B36 22 D1
Harborough Rd
Coventry CV6 49 B2
Rugby CV21,CV23 82 B4
Harbour Cl B50 148 B2
Harbury CE Prim Sch
CV33 123 F6
Harbury Cl B76 22 B6
Harbury La Harbury CV33 123 B7
Royal Leamington Spa
CV33,CV34 109 E2
Harbury Rd CV47 124 C6
Harby Cl B37 44 B8
Harcourt CV3 78 E5
Harcourt Gdns CV11 29 C3
Hardingwood La CV7 35 C2
Hardwick Cl CV5 60 A4
Hardwick La B80 112 B3
Hardwick Pk OX16 139 F5
Hardwick Rd CV47 125 E4
Hardwyn Cl CV3 63 A1
Hardy Cl Nuneaton CV10 28 A4
Rugby CV22 82 B1
Hardy Rd CV6 61 A8
Hare & Hounds La CV10 29 A2
Harebell B77 4 A2
Harebell Way CV23 83 B4
Harebell Wlk 1 B37 33 D2
Harefield Ho CV2 62 B3
Harefield La CV12 38 F8
Harefield Rd Coventry CV2 62 B3
Nuneaton CV11 29 C4
Haresfield B90 70 A5
Hareway La CV35 122 C7
Harewood Rd CV5 60 C2
Harger Ct CV8 92 F4
Harger Mews CV8 92 F4
Hargrave Cl Coventry CV3 63 A1
Grandborough CV23 116 F5
Water Orton B46 23 B3
Harington Rd CV6 61 A5
Harlech Cl Banbury OX16 139 F3
Kenilworth CV8 93 C5
Harley St CV2 62 A3
Harlow Wlk 8 CV2 63 A7
Harmar Cl CV34 104 D1
Harmer Cl CV2 63 A7
Harmony Ct CV10 29 B2
Harnall Cl B90 70 E7
Harnall Ind Est CV1 151 C4
Harnall La CV1 151 C4
Harnall La E CV1 61 E4
Harnall La W CV1 151 C4
Harnall Row Coventry CV1 61 E2
Coventry CV1 61 E3
Harold Cox Pl CV22 99 C3
Harold Rd CV2 62 D2
Harold St CV11 29 C3
Harpenden Dr CV5 60 A5
Harper Rd CV1 61 E2
Harpers La CV9 19 A4
Harrier Parkway LE17 55 B4
Harrington Ct CV3 62 F2
Harrington Way CV10 39 A7
Harriott Dr CV34 109 D4
Harris CE High Sch CV22 82 C1
Harris Cl B95 113 B4
Harris Dr CV22 99 C4
Harris Mews B95 113 B4
Harris Rd Coventry CV3 62 B2
Warwick CV34 108 C8
Harrison Cl CV21 101 A4
Harrison Cres CV12 39 A2
Harrison Rd B97 102 B4
Harrison Way CV31 109 F5
Harrow Cl CV6 50 A4
Harrow Rd CV31 110 B3
Harrowbrook Ind Est
LE10 30 E7
Harrowbrook Rd LE10 30 E7
Harry Caplan Ho CV5 60 B6
Harry Edwards Ho 2
CV2 62 D8
Harry Rose Rd CV2 62 E3
Harry Salt Ho CV1 151 D3
Harry Stanley Ho CV6 62 A8
Harry Taylor Fst Sch
B97 102 C3
Harry Truslove Cl CV6 61 A7
Harry Weston Rd CV3 63 A1
Hart Cl CV21 83 B1
Hartington Cl B93 71 E3
Hartington Cres CV5 60 F1
Hartington Gn LE10 31 E6
Hartland Ave CV2 62 B5
Hartlebury Cl B93 71 F3
Hartlepool Rd CV1 151 D4
Hartley Gdns CV47 147 A2
Hartleyburn B77 10 A4
Hartridge Wlk CV5 60 B4
Hartshill Hayes Ctry Pk*
CV10 18 C1
Hartshill Hayes Ctry Pk
Woodland* CV10 19 A1
Hartshill Hayes Visitors Ctr*
CV10 18 C1
Hartshill Sch CV10 28 B8
Harvard Cl CV35 146 B1
Harvest Hill Cl 7 CV31 110 C6
Harvest Hill La CV5,CV7 47 C4
Harvesters Cl CV3 63 A2
Harvey Cl CV5 60 A7
Harvington CE Fst Sch
WR11 127 D4
Harvington Dr B90 71 B6
Harvington Way B76 22 A8
Harwood Dr B77 9 B2
Harwood Gr 1 B90 70 C8
Haselbech Rd CV3 62 F1
Haselbury Cnr CV10 28 F1
Haseley Bsns Ctr CV35 114 D7
Haseley Cl CV31 110 B5
Haseley Rd CV2 50 C1
Haselor Cl B49 143 B2
Haselor Sch B49 119 D4
Hasilwood Sq CV3 62 B2
Haslucks Green Rd B90 69 E7
Hassall Cl 9 CV33 122 F8
Hastang Fields CV31 110 C5
Hastings Cl
Banbury OX16 139 F3
Tamworth B77 9 C3
Hastings High Sch LE10 31 F7
Hastings Rd
Banbury OX16 139 F4
Coventry CV2 62 A4
Wellesbourne CV35 146 B2
Haswell Cl CV22 83 B1
Hatchford Wlk B37 33 B1
Hathaway Cl
Balsall Common CV7 74 B7
South Littleton WR11 127 F1
Hathaway Dr
Nuneaton CV11 30 A1
Warwick CV34 104 E2
Hathaway Green La
CV37 144 C3
Hathaway Hamlet CV37 144 B1
Hathaway La CV37 144 B1
Hathaway Rd CV4 59 D1
Hatherden Dr B76 13 A2
Hatherell Rd CV31 110 E5
Hatters Dr CV9 12 B1
Hatton Bank La CV37 121 D5
Hatton Cl CV35 114 E5
Hatton Ctry World*
CV35 114 D5
Hatton Sta CV35 114 C5
Hatton Terr CV35 114 F5
Haunch La B76 24 A4
Haunchwood Park Dr
CV10 27 C2
Haunchwood Park Ind Est
CV10 27 C2
Haunchwood Rd CV10 28 D4
Havendale Cl CV6 61 B5
Hawbridge Cl B90 71 B6
Hawfinch B77 10 A3
Hawk Cl CV11 40 B8
Hawke Way LE17 55 B4
Hawke's La OX15 142 E8
Hawkes Dr CV34 109 D4
Hawkes Mill La CV5 48 B2
Hawkesbury Fields Sch
CV2 50 C3
Hawkesbury La CV2 50 D5
Hawkeshead CV21 83 B4
Hawkeswell La B46 34 A2
Hawkesworth Dr CV8 93 A6
Hawkinge Dr B35 22 A4
Hawkins Cl CV22 82 C1
Hawkins Rd CV5 61 A2
Hawkshead Dr B93 71 F6
Hawkside B77 10 A4
Hawkswood Dr CV7 74 B7
Hawksworth Dr 1 CV1 61 B3
Hawlands CV21 83 B3
Hawley Rd LE10 31 D7
Hawnby Gr B76 13 A2
Hawthorn Ave CV9 16 B3
Hawthorn Cl B49 143 A3
Hawthorn Cres LE10 31 E4
Hawthorn Ct CV4 59 E1
Hawthorn La CV4 59 E1
Hawthorn Rd CV31 109 F6
Hawthorn Terr CV23 66 A2
Hawthorn Way
Nuneaton CV10 28 A8
Rugby CV22 82 A1
Shipston-on-S CV36 149 C2
Hawthorne Ave CV7 37 A4
Hawthorne Cl CV8 80 A2
Hawthorne Dr B47 69 B6
Hawthorne Terr CV10 28 F5
Hawthorns The B78 15 B4
Hay La Coventry CV1 151 C2
Solihull B90 71 A6
Hay Mdw CV36 149 C3
Hay Pool OX17 133 F5
Hay Wood La B93,CV35 90 A3
Haybarn The B76 22 A8
Haydock Cl Coventry CV6 50 B4
Stratford-u-A CV37 144 C1
Tamworth B77 9 B2
Haydon Cl Dorridge B93 71 F2
Studley B80 103 C3
Haydon Way B49 118 F8
Haydons Cl GL55 135 B2
Haye La B80 112 A5
Hayes Cl CV21 83 B4
Hayes Green Rd CV12 49 F8
Hayes La CV7 50 A8
Hayes Rd CV10 28 A8
Hayle Ave CV34 104 F1
Hayle Cl CV11 30 A5
Haynes Way CV21 82 C4
Haynestone Rd CV6 60 E6
Hays La LE10 31 B7
Haysum's Cl GL55 135 B1
Hayton Gn CV4 75 F8
Haytor Rise CV2 62 C7
Hayward Cl CV35 114 F3
Hayward's Gn CV6 61 A7
Hayway La CV23 116 B4
Hazel Cl Nuneaton CV10 28 A8
Royal Leamington Spa
CV32 106 A2
Hazel Croft
Birmingham, Chelmsley Wood
B37 33 B1
Braunston NN11 117 E5
Hazel Dr B47 69 B5
Hazel Gr Bedworth CV12 39 D3
Hockley Heath B94 88 C6
Hazel Rd Coventry CV6 50 B1
Nuneaton CV10 28 D5
Hazelcroft B78 15 B4
Hazelgarth B77 10 A4
Hazelhead St Georges (Ind
Est) CV1 61 F2
Hazell Way CV10 29 A1
Hazeltree Gr B93 71 E3
Hazelwood Cl CV22 99 A2
Hazlemere Cl CV5 60 B4
Headborough Rd CV2 62 A5
Headington Ave CV6 49 A2
Headland Cl CV37 129 A6
Headland Rd CV37 129 A6
Headland Rise CV37 129 A6
Headlands The CV5 60 D4
Headley Ct B97 102 B4
Healey Cl CV21 83 B4
Healey Ct CV34 108 F7
Health Centre Rd CV4 76 C4
Heanley La CV9 16 B3
Hearsall Com Prim Sch
CV5 60 F2
Hearsall Comm CV5 60 F2
Hearsall Ct CV4 60 D2
Hearsall Golf Course
CV5 76 E7
Hearsall La CV5 60 F2
Heart of England Sch
CV7 74 C6
Heart of England Way
CV11 29 F3
Heath Ave CV12 38 E1
Heath Cres CV2 62 A6
Heath End La CV37 121 D7
Heath End Rd CV10 28 F2
Heath Farm La CV35 123 C2
Heath Green Way CV4 75 F6
Heath La CV23 64 C1
Heath Rd Bedworth CV12 38 F1
Coventry CV2 62 A4
Hollywood B47 69 A7
Heath Terr Beausale CV35 91 C2
Royal Leamington Spa
CV32 105 E1
Heath The CV22 99 B2

Heath Way CV22 ....100 B4
Heathcote Cl B77 ....10 A4
Heathcote Ct CV6 ....61 A7
Heathcote Ind Est CV34 .109 D4
Heathcote La
  Royal Leamington Spa
    CV34 ....109 D4
  Warwick CV34 ....109 A5
Heathcote Rd CV31 ....110 A4
Heathcote St CV6 ....61 A7
Heathcote Way CV34 ....109 D4
Heather Cl
  Birmingham B36 ....33 A8
  Nuneaton CV10 ....28 F3
  Rugby CV22 ....42 A1
  Southam CV47 ....147 A3
  Stratford-u-A CV37 ......144 B2
Heather Ct CV9 ....12 B1
Heather Dr CV12 ....38 C2
Heather Rd
  Binley Woods CV3 ....79 D7
  Coventry CV2 ....50 C2
Heathfield Cl B93 ....72 A5
Heathfield Rd
  Coventry CV5 ....60 C2
  Norton WR11 ....127 B2
Heathfields Inf Sch B77 ...9 C3
Heathgreen Cl B37 ....33 D3
Heathley La B78 ....8 C3
Hebden B77 ....10 A4
Hebden Ave CV34 ....104 F1
Hebden Way CV11 ....30 A2
Heber Dr CV33 ....123 E6
Heckley Rd CV7 ....50 A7
Heddle Gr CV6 ....62 B8
Hedgefield Way CV4 ....75 F8
Hedgerow Wlk CV6 ....49 B4
Hedgerows The
  Nuneaton CV10 ....28 F6
  Tamworth B77 ....9 C4
Hedges Cl CV47 ....124 D6
Hedgetree Croft B37 ....33 C2
Hedging La B77 ....9 C3
Hedging Lane Ind Est B77 ..9 C3
Hedingham Gr B37 ....33 D2
Heelley Croft B35 ....22 B4
Heemstede La CV32 ....106 A2
Heera Cl CV6 ....61 A8
Hele Rd CV3 ....77 D6
Helen St CV6 ....61 F6
Helena Cl CV10 ....28 F3
Hellidon Cl **5** CV32 ......106 A2
Hellidon Rd CV47 ....125 F4
Hellidon Rd CV23 ....83 A3
Helmsdale Rd CV32 ....106 B5
Helmswood Dr B37 ....44 C8
Helston Cl CV11 ....30 A5
Helvellyn Way CV21 ....83 B4
Hemdale CV11 ....30 A4
Heming Rd B98 ....103 C4
Hemingford Rd CV2 ....63 A8
Hemlingford Croft B37 .....44 A7
Hemlingford Rd
  Kingsbury B78 ....15 B2
  Sutton Coldfield B76 ......22 A6
Hemmings Cl CV31 ....110 E5
Hemmings Mill CV35 ....122 A7
Hemsby Cl CV4 ....76 A7
Hemsworth Dr CV12 ....46 B2
Hen La CV6 ....49 D3
Henbrook La OX15 ....137 E2
Hendre Cl CV5 ....60 D2
Henley Cl CV11 ....29 F8
Henley Coll CV2 ....62 C8
Henley Cl CV2 ....62 D7
Henley Mill La CV2 ....62 C7
Henley Park Ind Est CV2 ..62 E7
Henley Rd
  Claverdon CV35 ....113 E4
  Coventry CV2 ....62 D7
  Lowsonford B95 ....113 D6
  Norton Lindsey CV35 .....114 D3
  Royal Leamington Spa
    CV31 ....110 B5
Henley St Alcester B49 ....143 B2
  Stratford-u-A CV37 ....145 A2
Henley Wlk CV2 ....62 D8
Henley-in-Arden High Sch
  B95 ....113 B4
Henley-in-Arden Prim Sch
  B95 ....113 B4
Henley-in-Arden Sta
  B95 ....113 A4
Henleydale **4** B90 ....70 C8
Henrietta St CV6 ....61 E5
Henry Boteler Rd CV4 ......76 B7
Henry Hinde Inf Sch
  CV22 ....82 B1
Henry Hinde Jun Sch
  CV22 ....82 A1
Henry St Coventry CV1 ....151 B3
  Kenilworth CV8 ....93 A5
  Nuneaton CV11 ....29 C2
  Rugby CV21 ....83 A2
Henry Tandey Ct **4**
  CV32 ....105 E1
Hensborough B90 ....70 A5
Henson Rd CV12 ....38 E1
Henwood La B91 ....56 B4
Henwoods CV36 ....149 C4
Hepworth Rd CV3 ....83 A5
Herald Ave CV5 ....60 D1
Herald Bsns Pk CV3 ......78 F7
Herald Rd B26 ....44 C4
Herald Way Coventry CV3 ..79 A7

Herald Way continued
  Hinckley LE10 ....31 D4
Heralds Ct **5** CV34 ....109 B8
Herbert Art Gall & Mus*
  CV1 ....151 C2
Herbert Fowler Jun Sch
  CV7 ....26 C1
Herbert St CV10 ....28 E3
Herbert's La CV8 ....93 A5
Hercules Rd B35 ....22 B2
Herdwycke Cl CV47 ....147 B2
Hereford Cl CV10 ....28 E4
Hereford Rd CV11 ....40 F6
Hereward Coll CV4 ....59 F1
Hereward Way CV10 ....31 F6
Heritage Ct CV4 ....76 D3
Heritage Dr CV6 ....50 C6
Heritage Motor Ctr*
  CV35 ....123 D1
Hermes Cl CV34 ....109 E5
Hermes Cres CV2 ....62 E6
Hermes Rd B26 ....44 C4
Hermit's Croft CV3 ....77 D8
Hermitage Cl LE17 ....68 C1
Hermitage Dr B76 ....13 A4
Hermitage Rd CV2 ....62 D4
Hermitage Way CV8 ....93 A3
Heron Cl Alcester B49 .....143 A3
  Cheswick Green B90 ......70 D4
Heron Ho CV3 ....62 B2
Heron La CV37 ....144 B3
Heron Way CV37 ....130 E1
Heronbank CV4 ....59 C2
Herrick Rd CV2 ....62 D3
Herring Rd CV9 ....18 C4
Hertford Pl CV1 ....151 A2
Hertford Rd Alcester B49 ..143 B3
  Stratford-u-A CV37 ......144 C1
Hertford St CV1 ....151 B2
Hertford Way B93 ....72 B4
Hesleden B77 ....10 A4
Heslop Cl CV3 ....78 F8
Hetton Cl **1** CV34 ....104 F1
Hewitt Ave CV6 ....61 B4
Hexby Cl CV2 ....63 A6
Hexworthy Ave CV3 ....77 B5
Heybrook Cl CV2 ....62 E6
Heycroft CV4 ....76 D4
Heydons Terr OX17 ....133 F4
Heyford Cl CV2 ....50 D3
Heyford Gr B91 ....71 C8
Heyford Leys CV22 ....99 C3
Heyford Way B35 ....22 B5
Heyville Croft CV8 ....93 C3
Heywood Cl CV6 ....62 A7
Hibberd Ct CV8 ....92 F4
Hibbert Cl CV22 ....83 A1
Hickman Rd CV10 ....27 C3
Hicks Cl CV34 ....104 E2
Hidcote Ave B76 ....22 A8
Hidcote Cl Nuneaton CV11 .39 F8
  Royal Leamington Spa
    CV31 ....110 C5
Hidcote Gr B37 ....44 A7
Hidcote Manor Gdn*
  GL55 ....135 D5
Hidcote Rd
  Ebrington GL55 ....135 D3
  Kenilworth CV8 ....93 C6
High Ash Cl CV7 ....49 F7
High Beech CV5 ....60 A6
High Brink Rd B46 ....33 F7
High Cross La CV35 ....113 F6
High Cross Rd LE17 ....43 B3
High La OX15 ....137 E1
High Mdw OX15 ....138 D1
High Meadow Inf Sch
  B46 ....33 F8
High Park Cl CV5 ....59 F3
High St Alcester B49 ......143 A2
  Astwood Bank B96 ......102 C1
  Barford CV35 ....122 B8
  Bedworth CV12 ....39 B2
  Bidford-on-A B50 ....148 C2
  Bidford-on-A, Broom B50 .148 A4
  Bishops Itchington CV47 ..124 A4
  Braunston NN11 ....117 D5
  Charwelton NN11 ....126 C8
  Chipping Campden GL55 ..135 B2
  Coleshill B46 ....33 F7
  Coventry CV1 ....151 C2
  Coventry, Keresley CV6 ...48 F1
  Cropredy OX17 ....143 D4
  Cubbington CV32 ....106 E5
  Fenny Compton CV47 ....133 D7
  Great Rollright OX7 ......142 A2
  Hampton-in-A B92 ....57 A7
  Harbury CV33 ....123 F6
  Henley-in-A B95 ....113 B5
  Hook Norton OX15 ......142 D4
  Hurley CV9 ....16 B3
  Kenilworth CV8 ....92 E5
  Knowle B93 ....72 C6
  Lower Brailes OX15 .....137 F2
  Marton CV23 ....115 C7
  Mickleton GL55 ....135 C6
  Moreton-in-M GL56 ......140 A3
  Napton on t H CV47 .....125 C7
  Nuneaton CV11 ....29 A4
  Polesworth B78 ....5 A1
  Ratley OX15 ....133 A2
  Royal Leamington Spa
    CV31 ....110 A7
  Rugby CV21 ....83 A2
  Rugby, Hillmorton CV21 ..101 A4
  Ryton-on-D CV8 ....79 B1
  Shipston-on-S CV36 .....149 C3
  Shutford OX15 ....139 A3

High St continued
  Southam CV47 ....147 A2
  Stockton CV47 ....147 C4
  Stoke Golding CV13 ....21 B4
  Stratford-u-A CV37 ......145 A1
  Studley B80 ....103 C2
  Tamworth B77 ....9 B3
  Warwick CV34 ....108 E6
  Welford on A CV37 ......129 A7
High Trees Cl B98 ....102 C4
High Trees Rd B93 ....72 A7
High View Dr CV7 ....49 C7
High View Rd CV32 ....106 C5
Higham La Nuneaton CV11 .29 E7
  Stoke Golding, Wykin LE10 .21 C2
Higham Lane Sch CV10 ...29 D6
**Higham on the Hill CE Prim
  Sch** CV13 ....21 A2
Higham Way LE10 ....31 A7
Higham Way Ho LE10 ......31 E7
Highbury Gn CV10 ....28 C7
Highclere Gdns OX16 .....139 F3
Highcliffe Rd B77 ....9 B4
Highcroft CV35 ....113 F3
Highcroft Cres CV32 ......105 C1
Highdown Cres **3** B90 ..71 A6
Highdown Rd CV31 ....110 B6
Highfield Hatton CV35 ....114 F6
  Meriden CV7 ....46 C1
Highfield Ave
  Redditch B97 ....102 B4
  Tamworth B77 ....4 A3
Highfield Cl
  Kenilworth CV8 ....92 E4
  Sutherland CV37 ....121 B7
Highfield La CV7 ....37 B1
Highfield Rd Coventry CV2 .61 F4
  Nuneaton CV10 ....29 E2
  Redditch B97 ....102 B4
  Stratford-u-A CV37 ......144 C3
  Studley B80 ....103 B2
Highfield Terr CV32 ....105 D1
Highgrove Coventry CV4 ...75 F5
  Rugby CV22 ....99 B4
Highland Rd Coventry CV5 .60 F1
  Kenilworth CV8 ....93 C7
  Royal Leamington Spa
    CV32 ....106 B4
Highland Way B98 ....103 A4
Highlands OX16 ....139 F5
Highlands Cl CV34 ....109 A8
Highlands Ct B90 ....70 E8
Highlands Rd B90 ....70 E8
Highview B80 ....103 A8
Highwaymans Croft CV4 ..76 D5
Higol Coll CV11 ....30 A1
Hijker Gr **3** B37 ....33 D2
Hilary Bevins Cl CV13 .....20 C2
Hilary Dr B76 ....13 A3
Hilary Rd Coventry CV4 ....76 E6
  Nuneaton CV10 ....29 D2
Hill Cl Northend CV47 ....133 B7
  Royal Leamington Spa
    CV32 ....106 A3
Hill Cres CV23 ....96 C3
Hill Crest CV32 ....106 D4
Hill Crest Farm Cl B79 ......5 C2
Hill Crest Hospl B98 .....103 B3
Hill Farm Ave CV11 ....30 B1
Hill Farm Prim Sch CV6 ...61 B7
Hill Fray Dr CV3 ....78 A5
Hill Ho CV37 ....145 A2
Hill La Sutton Coldfield B75 ..7 A1
  Upper Brailes OX15 ......137 E3
  Upper Quinton CV37 ....129 D1
Hill Rd
  Grandborough CV23 .....116 E6
  Keresley CV7 ....48 F6
  Lower Boddington NN11 .134 E7
Hill Rise OX7 ....142 A2
Hill Row NN11 ....117 E4
Hill Side Coventry CV2 ....62 A6
  Kingsbury B78 ....15 B2
Hill St Bedworth CV12 ......39 B5
  Coventry CV1 ....151 A3
  Hinckley LE10 ....31 E8
  Nuneaton CV10 ....28 D4
  Royal Leamington Spa
    CV32 ....106 A1
  Rugby CV21 ....83 A2
  Warwick CV34 ....109 B8
Hill The CV37 ....145 A2
Hill Top
  Baddesley Ensor CV9 .....11 A1
  Coventry CV1 ....151 C3
Hill View CV47 ....124 A4
Hill View Cl GL55 ....135 C7
Hill View Rd B50 ....148 C3
Hill Wootton Rd CV32,
  CV35 ....105 C6
Hillary Rd CV22 ....99 C4
Hillborough La B50 ....128 E7
Hillcrest Pk B47 ....85 F8
Hillcrest Rd
  Nuneaton CV10 ....28 E5
  Polesworth B78 ....11 A4
Hillfield Mews **3** B91 ...71 B8
Hillfield Rd Rugby CV22 ...82 B1
  Solihull B91 ....71 B8
Hillfields Ho **1** CV1 .....61 E3
Hillhurst Gr B36 ....22 D1
Hilliard Cl CV12 ....39 B4
Hillman Dr B36 ....22 F1
Hillman Ho CV1 ....151 B3
Hillman Way CV37 ....131 B3
Hillmorton La
  Clifton u CV23 ....84 A2

Hillmorton La continued
  Lilbourne CV23 ....84 C3
Hillmorton Prim Sch
  CV21 ....101 A4
Hillmorton Rd
  Coventry CV2 ....50 C1
  Knowle B93 ....83 B1
  Rugby CV22 ....83 B1
Hillrise LE10 ....31 F8
Hillside Appleby Magna DE12 .3 C4
  Harbury CV33 ....123 E7
  Napton on t H CV47 .....125 C8
  Nuneaton CV10 ....28 A8
Hillside Croft CV47 ....125 C8
Hillside Ct CV9 ....12 B1
Hillside N CV2 ....62 A6
Hillside Rd Hinckley LE10 ..31 C6
  Stratford-u-A CV37 ......144 B2
Hilltop Cl Honiley CV8 .....90 E8
  Southam CV47 ....147 B3
Hillwood Ave B90 ....71 A6
Hillyard Rd CV47 ....147 A3
Hilmore Way B77 ....9 C4
Hilton Ave CV10 ....28 B6
Hilton Ct CV5 ....60 F2
Himbleton Croft **1** B90 ..71 A6
Himley Rd CV12 ....38 D2
Hinchwick Cl B98 ....70 E4
Hinckley & District Hospl
  LE10 ....31 D8
Hinckley Bsns Pk LE10 ...30 F8
Hinckley La CV13 ....21 B2
Hinckley Rd
  Ansty CV2,CV7 ....51 C2
  Aston Flamville LE10 .....32 D7
  Aston Flamville LE9 ......32 D8
  Burton Hastings CV11 ....31 A1
  Coventry CV2 ....63 A8
  Hinckley LE10 ....32 A6
  Nuneaton CV11 ....29 E5
  Stoke Golding CV13 ....21 A8
  Wolvey LE10 ....41 C4
Hinckley Sta LE10 ....31 D7
Hind Cl CV34 ....104 F2
Hinde Cl CV21 ....83 B4
Hindlip Cl B98 ....112 A6
Hintons Coppice B93 ....71 E6
Hipsley Cl B36 ....22 C1
Hipsley La CV9 ....16 C3
Hipswell Highway CV2 ...62 D3
Hipton Hill WR11 ....127 B3
Hirdemonsway B90 ....70 A5
Hiron Croft CV3 ....77 C8
Hiron The CV3 ....77 C8
Hiron Way CV34 ....108 B7
Hirst Cl CV23 ....82 A3
Hitchman Cl CV47 ....147 B3
Hitchman Mews CV31 ....110 A5
Hitchman Rd CV31 ....110 A5
Hithersand Cl CV35 ....121 F4
Hitherside B90 ....70 B5
HM Prison Rye Hill
  CV23 ....100 B1
**HM Young Offender
  Institution** CV23 ....100 B1
Hoarestone Ave CV11 .....40 A7
Hob La
  Balsall Common CV7 ......74 E4
  Burton Green CV8 ....75 A3
  Knowle B92 ....73 A8
Hobbins The CV36 ....149 C3
Hobley Cl CV22 ....99 B4
Hockett St CV3 ....77 D8
Hocking Rd CV2 ....62 E4
Hockley Cl CV23 ....116 F5
Hockley Ct B94 ....88 C7
Hockley Heath Prim Sch
  B94 ....88 C6
Hockley La Coventry CV5 ..59 C5
  Ettington CV37 ....131 B3
Hockley Rd
  Shrewley CV35 ....114 C6
  Wolvey LE10 ....41 C2
Hoden La WR11 ....128 A3
Hodge La B77 ....4 A3
Hodgett's La
  Berkswell CV7 ....74 F7
  Coventry CV7,CV8 ....75 B6
Hodgson Rd CV37 ....144 C3
Hodnell Cl B36 ....22 C1
Hodnell Dr CV47 ....147 B2
Hodnet Cl CV8 ....93 B5
Hogarth Cl CV12 ....39 A4
Hogarth Rd CV37 ....144 B1
Hogg End CV47 ....134 F3
Hoggrills End La B46 ....25 A2
Holbeche Cres CV7 ....36 C2
Holbeche Rd Knowle B93 ..72 A7
  Sutton Coldfield B75 ......13 A5
Holbein Cl CV12 ....39 A4
Holborn Ave CV6 ....49 C2
Holbrook Ave CV21 ....83 A2
Holbrook Gr B37 ....33 B1
Holbrook La CV6 ....49 D2
Holbrook Park Est CV6 ....61 D8
Holbrook Prim Sch CV6 ...49 E1
Holbrook Rd
  Long Lawford CV23 ....82 A3
  Stratford-u-A CV37 ......144 B2
Holbrook Way CV7 ....49 D1
Holcot Leys CV22 ....100 A4
Holder Cl B50 ....148 B3
Hole House La B94 ....88 F1
Holioak Dr CV34 ....109 B6
Holland Ave B93 ....72 B8
Holland Cl B50 ....148 B2
Holland Croft B76 ....15 A1
Holland Rd CV6 ....61 A6

Holland Rd CV6 ....61 A6
Hollberry Cl B98 ....112 A6
Hollick Cres CV7 ....37 A4
Hollicombe Terr CV2 ......62 D8
Hollin Rd B78 ....11 A4
Hollies The CV23 ....67 C3
Hollin Brow Cl B93 ....72 B3
Hollings Gr B91 ....71 C8
Hollington Way B90 ....71 A7
Hollinwell Cl CV11 ....40 C8
Hollis La CV8 ....92 C8
Hollis Rd CV3 ....62 A2
Hollow Cres CV6 ....61 B5
Hollow Way CV47 ....125 C8
Holloway Field CV6 ....61 A6
Holloway Hill OX15 ....138 A1
Holloway La CV15 ....138 A1
Holloway The
  Mollington OX17 ....134 A2
  Priors Marston CV47 ....125 E4
  Warwick CV34 ....108 D6
Hollowell Way CV21 ....83 B4
Hollows The CV11 ....29 F1
Holly Bank CV5 ....77 A8
Holly Bank Est CV9 ....3 A1
Holly Cl LE10 ....33 A5
Holly Dr Hollywood B47 ...69 B7
  Hurley CV9 ....16 B2
  Ryton-on-D CV8 ....79 B1
Holly Farm Bsns Pk CV8 ..91 B7
Holly Gr
  Church Lawford CV23 .....81 A3
  Coventry CV4 ....60 B2
Holly La Atherstone CV9 ...12 B1
  Balsall Common CV7 ......74 B3
  Portway B48 ....85 F6
  Wishaw B76 ....13 D4
Holly Lane Ind Est CV9 ..12 B1
Holly Lodge CV35 ....146 B2
Holly Lodge Wlk B37 ......33 A2
Holly Orch CV37 ....145 A2
Holly Rd CV36 ....149 C2
Holly St CV32 ....106 B1
Holly Stitches Rd CV10 ...28 E6
Holly Tree Wlk LE17 ....43 C3
Holly Wlk Baginton CV8 ...77 E2
  Nuneaton CV11 ....29 F2
  Royal Leamington Spa
    CV32 ....106 A1
  Stratford-u-A CV37 ......144 B2
Hollyberry Ave B91 ....71 A8
Hollybush La
  Coventry CV6 ....50 A4
  Priors Marston CV47 ....125 E4
Hollyfast La CV7 ....48 B7
Hollyfast Prim Sch CV6 ..60 E7
Hollyfast Rd CV6 ....60 E6
Hollyhurst Bedworth CV12 .38 F1
  Water Orton B46 ....23 C2
Hollyhurst Gr B90 ....70 E8
Hollyland B46 ....24 C1
Hollywell Rd B93 ....72 A5
Holman Way CV11 ....29 D3
Holmcroft CV2 ....62 F8
Holme Cl CV21 ....83 B3
Holme Way CV23 ....101 B1
Holmes Ct CV8 ....92 F5
Holmes Dr CV5 ....59 D5
Holmes Rd CV31 ....110 B8
Homewood Cl CV8 ....93 B5
Holmewood Ct CV8 ....93 B5
Holmfield Rd CV2 ....62 B3
Holmsdale Rd CV6 ....61 E7
Holroyd Ho CV4 ....59 F2
Holsworthy Cl CV11 ....40 C8
Holt Ave CV33 ....122 E8
Holt Gdns B80 ....103 C1
Holt Leys CV47 ....147 B2
Holt Rd Hinckley LE10 .....31 E6
  Studley B80 ....103 C1
Holt The Mollington OX17 .133 F7
  Royal Leamington Spa
    CV32 ....106 A3
Holte Rd CV9 ....18 B4
Holtom St CV37 ....144 C1
Holwick B77 ....4 A4
Holy Cross Ct CV2 ....62 E4
Holy Cross Prim Sch B76 .13 A3
Holy Family RC Prim Sch
  CV6 ....49 B3
Holyhead Rd CV5 ....60 E5
Holyoak Cl Bedworth CV12 .38 F1
  Rugby CV22 ....99 B4
Holyoke Gr CV31 ....110 B2
Holyrood Ct CV10 ....28 B6
Home Cl Bubbenhall CV8 ..95 B3
  Staverton NN11 ....126 D8
Home Farm CV35 ....104 F6
Home Farm *
  Pailton CV23 ....66 A4
  Witherley CV9 ....19 A4
Home Farm Cotts CV6 .....49 A3
Home Furlong CV35 ....146 B1
Home Mdw CV35 ....113 F3
Home Park Rd CV11 ....29 C3
Homefield La CV22 ....99 B4
Homefield Pre-Prep Sch
  CV22 ....99 B4
Homer Cl CV34 ....109 E5
Homestalls Mdw CV35 ...131 D2
Homeward Way CV3 ....63 A1
Honeybourne CV5 ....59 B4

Honeybourne Rd B50 . . . .148 C2
Honeyfield Rd CV1 . . . . . . .61 D5
Honeysuckle Cl CV23 . . . . .83 B4
Honeysuckle Dr CV2 . . . . . .50 B2
Honeywick Cir CV2 . . . . . . .50 D1
Honiley Rd Honiley CV8 . . .91 B6
    Meer End CV8 . . . . .74 A1
Honiley Way CV2 . . . . .50 D1
Honington Hall* CV36 . . . .137 A5
Honiton Rd CV2 . . . . .62 C5
Honiwell Cl CV23 . . . . . . .123 E6
Hoo La GL55 . . . . .135 A2
Hood St CV1 . . . . .61 E3
Hood's Way CV22 . . . . .82 B1
Hook Norton Brewery*
    OX15 . . . . .142 C4
Hook Norton CE Sch
    OX15 . . . . .142 D4
Hook Norton Rd
    Great Rollright OX7 . . . . .142 A2
    Sibford Ferris OX15 . . . . .142 D8
Hoopers La B96 . . . . .102 C1
Hope Aldridge Bsns Cctr
    CV10 . . . . .29 C6
Hope St CV1 . . . . .61 B2
Hopedale Cl CV2 . . . . .62 E3
Hopkins Field CV37 . . . . .129 B3
Hopkins Prec The B49 . . . .143 B2
Hopkins Rd CV6 . . . . .61 A6
Hopper's La CV35 . . . . . . .146 B2
Hopton Cl CV5 . . . . .60 A4
Hopton Crofts CV12 . . . . .105 C2
Horley Path Rd OX15 . . . . .139 D5
Hornbeam B77 . . . . .4 A2
Hornbeam Dr CV4 . . . . . . .59 D1
Hornbeam Gr CV31 . . . . . .110 C6
Hornchurch Cl CV1 . . . . . .151 B1
Horndean Cl CV6 . . . . .61 E8
Horne Cl CV21 . . . . .101 A4
Horninghold Cl CV3 . . . . . .78 E8
Hornsey Cl CV2 . . . . .62 E7
Hornton Prim Sch OX15 . .139 B7
Horse Shoe Rd CV6 . . . . . . .50 A4
Horsefair CV36 . . . . .149 C3
Horsefair The 8 LE10 . . . .31 D8
Horsepool LE10 . . . . .32 A5
Horsewell CV47 . . . . .147 A2
Horsfall Rd B75 . . . . .13 A5
Horsford Rd CV3 . . . . .77 E6
Horsham Cl OX16 . . . . . . .139 F5
Horton Cl B49 . . . . .143 B3
Horton Cres CV22 . . . . . . .83 A1
Horton Gr B90 . . . . .71 A5
Hosiery St CV12 . . . . .39 C2
Hoskyn Cl CV21 . . . . .100 C4
Hospital La CV12 . . . . .38 B1
Hospital of St Cross
    CV22 . . . . .83 A1
Hospital Rd GL56 . . . . . . .140 A3
Hotchkiss Cl CV35 . . . . . .146 B1
Hotchkiss Way CV37 . . . . .79 A7
Hothorpe Cl CV3 . . . . .62 F1
Houldsworth Cres CV6 . . . .49 C4
Houndsfield Cl B47 . . . . . .69 B6
Houndsfield Farm B47 . . . .69 B5
Houndsfield Gr B47 . . . . . .69 A5
Houndsfield La B47 . . . . . .69 C6
Houston Rd CV21 . . . . .83 B3
Houting B77 . . . . .9 B3
Hove Ave CV5 . . . . .59 E4
Hovelands Cl CV12 . . . . . . .62 C8
Howard Cl
    Bidford-on-A B50 . . . . . .148 B2
    Coventry CV5 . . . . .59 E4
    Dunchurch CV22 . . . . .99 B2
Howard Rd
    Nuneaton CV10 . . . . .29 A3
    Redditch B98 . . . . .103 B4
Howard St CV1 . . . . .151 C4
Howard Wlk CV31 . . . . . .109 D6
Howat Rd CV7 . . . . .48 F7
Howcombe La CV47 . . . . .125 C7
Howcotte Gn CV4 . . . . .75 E8
Howe Green La CV7,CV10 .37 B2
Howells Cl CV12 . . . . .38 D1
Howes Com Prim Sch
    CV3 . . . . .77 E5
Howes Croft B35 . . . . .22 A2
Howes La CV3 . . . . .77 D3
Howkins Rd CV21 . . . . .83 B3
Howlette Rd CV4 . . . . .59 E2
Hoylake B77 . . . . .4 A2
Hoylake Cl CV11 . . . . .30 B1
Huckson Rd CV47 . . . . . . .124 B4
Huddesford Dr CV7 . . . . . .74 C8
Huddisdon Cl 4 CV34 . . . .104 F1
Hudson Ave B46 . . . . .33 F6
Hudson Rd CV22 . . . . .82 C1
Huggins Cl CV7 . . . . .74 C7
Hugh Rd CV3 . . . . .62 A2
Hughes Cl
    Harvington WR11 . . . . . . .127 D4
    Warwick CV34 . . . . .104 D2
    Whitnash CV31 . . . . .110 A2
Hughes Hill CV35 . . . . . . .114 B6
Hughes La WR11 . . . . .127 D4
Hughes The CV34 . . . . . . .108 E6
Hulme Cl CV3 . . . . .63 B1
Humber Ave Coventry CV1 .61 F1
    Coventry CV3 . . . . .61 F2
    Sutton Coldfield B76 . . . . . .22 A2
Humber Cl NN11 . . . . .117 F2
Humber Gr B36 . . . . .22 F1
Humber Rd CV3 . . . . .78 A8
Humber Wlk OX16 . . . . . .139 F4
Humberstone Rd 4 CV6 . .61 A5

Humphrey Burton's Rd
    CV3 . . . . .77 C8
Humphrey-Davy Rd
    CV12 . . . . .49 D8
Humphris St CV34 . . . . . .109 B8
Hungerfield Rd B36 . . . . . .22 C1
Hunningham Gr 6 B91 . . .71 B8
Hunscote La CV35 . . . . . . .121 F1
Hunt Cl CV35 . . . . .114 F3
Hunt End La B97 . . . . .102 B3
Hunt Hall La CV37 . . . . . .129 A6
Hunt La CV9 . . . . .19 A4
Hunt Paddocks CV8 . . . . . .92 E1
Hunt Terr CV4 . . . . .76 B7
Hunter Blvd LE17 . . . . .55 A3
Hunter St CV21 . . . . .83 B2
Hunter Terr CV3 . . . . .76 D8
Hunters Cl CV3 . . . . .63 A2
Hunters La
    Fenny Drayton CV13 . . . . . .20 A3
    Rugby CV21 . . . . .83 A3
Hunters Lane Ind Est
    CV21 . . . . .83 A3
Hunters Pk CV9 . . . . .11 B1
Hunters Wlk CV9 . . . . .3 A4
Huntingdon Rd CV5 . . . . . .77 A8
Huntingdon Way CV10 . . . .28 E3
Huntington Ct CV35 . . . . .146 C2
Hunts Rd CV37 . . . . .145 B1
Hurdlers La CV37 . . . . . . .121 B6
Hurlbutt Rd CV34 . . . . . . .109 C4
Hurley Cl CV32 . . . . .106 A2
Hurley Comm CV9 . . . . . . .16 B3
Hurley La B46 . . . . .25 B3
Hurley Prim Sch CV9 . . . . .16 B2
Hurn Way CV6 . . . . .50 B4
Hurricane Way 3 B35 . . . .22 A2
Hurst Green Rd
    Bentley Heath B93 . . . . . . .71 F4
    Minworth B76 . . . . .22 D6
Hurst Rd Bedworth CV12 . .39 B3
    Coventry CV6 . . . . .50 A4
    Hinckley LE10 . . . . .31 D8
    Southam CV47 . . . . .147 A2
Hurst The B47 . . . . .69 A6
Hurst Wlk CV6 . . . . .50 B4
Husbandmans Cl CV34 . . .109 C3
Hyacinth Way LE10 . . . . . .31 D5
Hyde Pl CV32 . . . . .109 E8
Hyde Rd Coventry CV2 . . . .62 E4
    Kenilworth CV8 . . . . .93 A5
Hydes La LE10 . . . . .30 E4
Hypericum Gdns CV2 . . . . .62 C4

Ibex Cl CV3 . . . . .62 F1
Ibstock Rd CV6 . . . . .50 A5
Icknield Cl B50 . . . . .148 C2
Icknield Ct B50 . . . . .148 C2
Icknield Row B49 . . . . . . .143 A2
Icknield St
    Bidford-on-A B50 . . . . . . .148 C2
    Rowney Green B48 . . . . . . .85 B6
Icknield Street Dr B98 . . . .103 B4
Iden Rd CV1 . . . . .61 E4
Idlicote Rd CV36 . . . . .137 B8
Ilam Pk CV8 . . . . .93 C5
Ilex Cl CV34 . . . . .109 A7
Ilford Cl CV12 . . . . .39 A3
Ilford Ct CV3 . . . . .79 D7
Ilford Dr CV3 . . . . .77 B5
Ilfracombe Gr CV3 . . . . . . .77 A5
Iliffe Ho LE10 . . . . .31 B7
Illshaw CV8 . . . . .112 A6
Illshaw Heath Rd B90,
    B94 . . . . .70 D2
Ilmer Cl CV21 . . . . .83 C4
Ilmington CE Prim Sch
    CV36 . . . . .136 A6
Ilmington Cl Coventry CV3 .77 B5
    Hatton CV35 . . . . .114 C6
Ilmington Rd
    Ilmington CV36,CV37 . . . .136 D7
    Tredington CV36 . . . . .136 E6
Ilminster Cl LE10 . . . . .32 B7
Imogen Gdns CV34 . . . . . .109 E3
Imperial Rise B46 . . . . .23 E2
Inca Cl CV3 . . . . .78 F8
Inchbrook Rd CV8 . . . . .93 C7
Inchford Ave CV34 . . . . . .104 F1
Inchford Cl CV11 . . . . .29 F1
Infantry Pl B75 . . . . .13 A6
Ingle Ct CV31 . . . . .109 E7
Ingleton Cl CV11 . . . . .30 A2
Inglewood Cl CV32 . . . . . .106 A3
Ingon La CV37 . . . . .121 B5
Ingram Cl CV36 . . . . .140 E5
Ingram Pit La B77 . . . . .4 A3
Ingram Rd CV5 . . . . .76 D8
Innage Cl CV31 . . . . .110 B8
Innage Park Small Ind Units
    CV9 . . . . .12 B1
Innage Terr CV9 . . . . .18 B4
Innage The B47 . . . . .69 A6
Innis Rd CV5 . . . . .76 E8
Innisfree House Sch B47 . .69 C4
Innsworth Dr B35 . . . . .22 A4
Instone Rd CV6 . . . . .49 A1
Inveraray Cl CV8 . . . . .93 C4
Inverlea Cl GL55 . . . . .135 B6
Inverness Cl CV5 . . . . .60 A4
Invicta Rd CV3 . . . . .78 F8
Ipsley Fst Sch B98 . . . . . .102 C4
Ipswich Wlk B37 . . . . .33 B2
Irelands La B94,B95 . . . . .113 D7
Ireton Cl CV4 . . . . .59 C1

Iris Cl LE10 . . . . .31 E5
Ironmonger Row CV1 . . . .151 B3
Ironstone Hollow OX15 . .142 E4
Irving Rd CV1 . . . . .61 C2
Isambard Dr CV6 . . . . .49 F5
Isis Gr B36 . . . . .33 A8
Islington Cres CV9 . . . . . . .10 B1
Ivanhoe Ave CV11 . . . . . . .29 E1
Ivor Rd Atherstone CV9 . . .18 C4
    Coventry CV6 . . . . .49 F2
Ivy Cl CV13 . . . . .21 B4
Ivy Farm La CV4 . . . . .76 D6
Ivy Gr CV10 . . . . .28 D6
Ivy La Ettington CV37 . . . .131 A3
    Harbury CV33 . . . . .123 F6
    Mollington OX17 . . . . .134 A2
    Shutford OX15 . . . . .139 A3
Ivy Lodge Cl B37 . . . . .44 A7
Ivy Way B90 . . . . .70 A6
Ivybridge Rd CV3 . . . . .78 A8
Ivycroft Rd B79 . . . . .5 C2
Ivyhouse Wlk B77 . . . . .9 C3
Izod's Cl GL55 . . . . .135 A1

J

Jack Cade Way CV34 . . . .109 E4
Jack O'Watton Bsns Pk
    B46 . . . . .23 D3
JackThomson Croft
    WR11 . . . . .127 F6
Jackdaw Dr B36 . . . . .33 A8
Jacker's Rd CV2 . . . . .50 B4
Jacklin Dr CV3 . . . . .77 C4
Jacknell Rd LE10 . . . . .30 D8
Jackson Cl
    Hampton Magna CV35 . . . .114 F3
    Keresley CV7 . . . . .49 A7
Jackson Gr CV8 . . . . .93 C4
Jackson La CV47 . . . . .125 C7
Jackson Rd Coventry CV6 . .49 D1
    Rugby CV21 . . . . .84 A1
Jackson Wlk B35 . . . . .22 A2
Jacksons Mdw B50 . . . . . .148 B3
Jacksons Orch CV37 . . . . .129 B3
Jackwood Gn CV12 . . . . . . .49 C8
Jacob Dr CV4 . . . . .76 D6
Jacobean La B93 . . . . .56 B1
Jacox Cres CV8 . . . . .93 C5
Jacquard Cl CV7 . . . . .77 B4
Jacquard Ho 3 CV1 . . . . . .61 E4
Jade Cl CV1 . . . . .151 D4
James Ct 14 Rugby CV21 . .83 A2
    Warwick CV34 . . . . .108 F7
James Dawson Dr CV5 . . . .59 B8
James Diskin Ct CV11 . . . .29 E2
James Galloway Cl CV3 . . .78 E7
James Green Rd CV4 . . . . .59 F2
James Ho CV2 . . . . .62 C8
James St Arley CV7 . . . . . . .37 A4
    Nuneaton CV11 . . . . .29 A5
    Rugby CV21 . . . . .83 A2
James Watt Cl NN11 . . . . .117 F2
Jamescroft CV3 . . . . .78 C6
Jameson Ct 22 GL56 . . . . .140 A3
Jaques Cl B46 . . . . .23 B2
Jardine Cres CV4 . . . . .59 F2
Jasmine Gr Coventry CV3 . .78 C8
    Royal Leamington Spa
    CV32 . . . . .106 A2
Jasmine Rd B77 . . . . .4 A2
Javelin Ho B35 . . . . .22 C3
Jays Cl B98 . . . . .112 A6
Jean St CV9 . . . . .11 B1
Jedburgh Gr CV3 . . . . .77 A4
Jeff's Cl OX15 . . . . .137 F2
Jeffrey Cl CV12 . . . . .49 D8
Jeffrey Woods Cross CV1 .61 F4
Jeffs Cl CV35 . . . . .138 B6
Jeliff St CV4 . . . . .59 E3
Jenkins Ave CV5 . . . . .59 F4
Jenkins Rd CV21 . . . . .84 A1
Jenner St CV1 . . . . .151 C4
Jenton Rd CV31 . . . . .110 B6
Jephcott Cl B49 . . . . .143 B2
Jephcott Ho 2 CV1 . . . . . .61 E3
Jephson Cl CV2 . . . . .50 C4
Jephson Pl 3 CV31 . . . . . .110 B7
Jersey Croft B36 . . . . .33 B6
Jervis Rd B77 . . . . .9 F7
Jesmond Rd CV1 . . . . .61 F4
Jesson Rd B75 . . . . .13 A5
Jill La B96 . . . . .103 A1
Jim Forrest Cl 4 CV3 . . . . .78 F8
Joan of Arc Ho CV3 . . . . . .77 E6
Joan Ward St CV3 . . . . .61 E1
Joan's Cl CV31 . . . . .110 C6
Joanna Dr CV3 . . . . .77 C3
Job's La CV4 . . . . .60 A2
Jodrell St CV11 . . . . .29 B6
Joe O'Brien Cl CV3 . . . . . .78 C6
Joe Williams Cl 7 CV3 . . . .78 F8
John Grace St CV3 . . . . . . .77 D8
John Gulson Prim Sch
    CV1 . . . . .61 D5
John Knight Rd CV12 . . . . .39 B5
John McGuire Cres CV3 . . .78 E7
John Nash Sq CV8 . . . . . . .92 F3
John Nichols St LE10 . . . . .31 B7
John O'Gaunt Rd CV8 . . . .92 E3
John Rous Ave CV4 . . . . . .76 B7
John Shelton Com Prim Sch
    CV6 . . . . .49 D4
John Shelton Dr CV6 . . . . .49 D4
John Simpson Cl CV8 . . . . .80 A2

John Sinclair Ho CV1 . . . .151 B4
John St Bedworth CV12 . . .39 A2
    Nuneaton, Coton CV11 . . . .29 C2
    Nuneaton, Stockingford
    CV10 . . . . .28 E3
    Royal Leamington Spa
    CV32 . . . . .109 F8
    Stratford-u-A CV37 . . . . . .145 A2
John Taylor Way CV35 . . .123 E8
John Thwaites Cl CV22 . . .83 A1
John Tofts Ho CV1 . . . . . .151 B4
John's Cl LE10 . . . . .31 D5
Johndory B77 . . . . .9 B3
Johns Cl B80 . . . . .103 B2
Johns Ave CV22 . . . . .82 C1
Johnson Ph B95 . . . . .113 B5
Johnson Rd
    Bedworth CV12 . . . . .39 C3
    Coventry CV6 . . . . .62 A8
Johnson St CV9 . . . . .10 B1
Jolyffe Park Rd CV37 . . . .145 A2
Jon Baker Ct LE10 . . . . . . .31 E8
Jonathan Rd CV2 . . . . .62 F8
Jones Rd CV7 . . . . .39 A1
Jones Wood Cl B76 . . . . . .22 A2
Jonkel Ave B77 . . . . .9 A3
Jordan Cl CV8 . . . . .93 B2
Jordan Well CV1 . . . . .151 C2
Jordans Cl B97 . . . . .102 B3
JordansThe CV5 . . . . .60 C4
Joseph Cash Prim Sch
    CV6 . . . . .61 C7
Joseph Creighton Cl CV3 .78 E7
Joseph Halpin Ho 3
    CV1 . . . . .151 C4
Joseph Latham Ho 3
    CV2 . . . . .50 B1
Joseph Luckman Rd
    CV12 . . . . .39 A3
Joseph Way CV37 . . . . . . .144 C3
Jourdain Pk CV34 . . . . . . .109 F3
Joyce Pool CV34 . . . . .108 E7
Joyce Way CV22 . . . . .99 A4
Jubilee Ave
    Lower Shuckburgh NN11 . .116 E1
    Redditch B97 . . . . .102 A3
Jubilee Cl
    Bidford-on-A B50 . . . . . . .148 C3
    Chipping Campden GL55 . .135 A2
Jubilee Cres CV6 . . . . .61 B7
Jubilee Ct B78 . . . . .15 B3
Jubilee St CV21 . . . . .82 C2
Jubilee Terr CV12 . . . . .39 B4
Judd Cl CV12 . . . . .38 F3
Judds La CV6 . . . . .49 E4
Judge Cl CV23 . . . . .82 A3
Judith Way CV22 . . . . .99 A4
Juggins La B94 . . . . .86 B7
Julian Cl CV2 . . . . .62 F8
Juliet Cl CV11 . . . . .30 A1
Juliet Dr
    Royal Leamington Spa
    CV34 . . . . .109 F3
    Rugby CV22 . . . . .99 B3
Julius Dr B46 . . . . .23 F1
Junction One Ret Pk
    CV21 . . . . .83 A3
Junction St CV1 . . . . .151 A2
Junewood Cl CV21 . . . . . . .83 B4
Juniper B77 . . . . .4 A2
Juniper Cl CV12 . . . . .38 E2
Juniper Dr Coventry CV5 . .59 F5
    Sutton Coldfield B76 . . . . . .22 A7
Juno Dr CV31 . . . . .109 F5
Jury St CV34 . . . . .108 E6
Justice Cl CV31 . . . . .110 A4
Justins Ave CV37 . . . . . . .144 C3

K

Kalfs Dr CV22 . . . . .99 A4
Kanzan Rd CV2 . . . . .50 B4
Kareen Gr CV3 . . . . .79 C7
Karen Cl CV10 . . . . .28 E7
Karlingford Cl CV5 . . . . . . .76 D8
Kathleen Ave CV12 . . . . . . .38 D1
Katrine Cl CV10 . . . . .28 C5
Kay Cl CV21 . . . . .83 B4
Kaysbrook Dr CV23 . . . . . .97 A3
Keats Cl CV10 . . . . .28 A4
Keats Ho B97 . . . . .102 B4
Keats Rd Coventry CV2 . . . .62 D2
    Stratford-u-A CV37 . . . . . .145 A1
Keble Ho B37 . . . . .33 A2
Keble Rd GL56 . . . . .140 A2
Kebull Gn CV4 . . . . .75 E8
Kecroft Rd Coventry CV2 . .62 D2
Keeling Rd CV8 . . . . .93 B5
Keenan Dr CV12 . . . . .38 D1
Keepers Cl B46 . . . . .34 A2
Keepers Wlk CV12 . . . . . . .38 E1
Keetley Cl CV36 . . . . .149 C2
Kegworth Cl CV6 . . . . .50 A4
Keir Cl CV32 . . . . .106 A2
Kele Rd CV4 . . . . .76 A7
Kelmscote Rd CV6 . . . . . . .60 F8
Kelsey Cl CV11 . . . . .29 E3
Kelsey La CV7 . . . . .74 B5
Kelsey's Cl CV8 . . . . .79 F3
Kelsull Croft B37 . . . . .33 A2
Kelvin Ave CV2 . . . . .62 D8
Kelvin Rd CV32 . . . . .106 C5
Kelway CV3 . . . . .63 A2
Kem St CV11 . . . . .29 E2
Kemble Dr B35 . . . . .22 A3
Kemerton Way B90 . . . . . .70 F6

Kemp Cl CV34 . . . . .109 A7
Kempley Ave CV2 . . . . .62 C2
Kemps Green Rd
    Balsall Common CV7 . . . . . .74 B6
    Tanworth-in-A B94 . . . . . . .88 A1
Kempsey Cl B98 . . . . .103 A4
Kempsford Cl B98 . . . . . . .102 C3
Kempton Cl CV37 . . . . . . .129 F8
Kempton Cres CV32 . . . . .106 C4
Kempton Dr B77 . . . . .9 B2
Kenal Ave Coleshill B46 . . .33 F7
Kendal Ave Coleshill B46 . .33 F7
    Royal Leamington Spa
    CV32 . . . . .105 C2
Kendal Cl Nuneaton CV11 . .30 A6
    Redditch B98 . . . . .112 A6
Kendal Rise CV5 . . . . .60 C4
Kendall Ave CV37 . . . . . . .145 A2
Kendrine Montessori Sch
    CV5 . . . . .77 A8
Kendron Ave CV6 . . . . .60 E6
Kendrick Cl CV6 . . . . .50 A4
Kenelm Ct CV3 . . . . .78 C5
Kenihurst Rd OX15 . . . . . .138 F5
Kenilcourt CV8 . . . . .92 D6
Kenilworth Castle* CV8 . .102 B3
Kenilworth Cl CV13 . . . . . .77 C8
Kenilworth Dr CV11 . . . . . .29 B3
Kenilworth Hall Mews
    CV8 . . . . .92 F5
Kenilworth Rd
    Balsall Common CV7,CV8 . .74 D4
    Coventry CV3 . . . . .76 E3
    Cubbington CV32 . . . . . . .106 C6
    Hampton-in-A B92 . . . . . . .57 E5
    Kenilworth CV8 . . . . .93 C8
    Knowle B93 . . . . .72 E5
    Lighthorne Heath CV33 . . .123 D2
    Meriden CV7 . . . . .45 D1
    Royal Leamington Spa
    CV32 . . . . .105 E5
Kenilworth Sch CV8 . . . . .93 C5
Kenilworth Sch Castle Hall
    Sixth Form CV8 . . . . . . .92 F2
Kenilworth St 16 CV32 . . .105 F1
Kenilworth Way OX16 . . .139 F3
Kennan Ave CV31 . . . . . . .109 F6
Kennedy Dr CV22 . . . . .82 B1
Kennedy Sq 8 CV32 . . . . .106 A1
Kennel La CV9 . . . . .19 A4
Kenning Cl CV47 . . . . .115 C4
Kenpas Highway CV3 . . . . .77 A5
Kenrick Croft B35 . . . . .22 A2
Kensington Ct
    Coventry CV5 . . . . .61 A1
    Nuneaton CV10 . . . . .28 C6
Kensington Rd CV5 . . . . . . .61 A1
Kent Cl CV3 . . . . .77 E6
Kent Rd CV47 . . . . .132 F5
KentThe CV21 . . . . .84 A1
Kenthurst Cl CV5 . . . . .59 C4
Kentmere Cl CV2 . . . . .50 E2
Kents La CV37 . . . . .131 A4
Kenway B47 . . . . .69 A7
Kenwyn Gn CV7 . . . . .50 B8
Kepler Gr B90 . . . . .22 B1
Keppel St CV1 . . . . .61 E5
Keresley Brook Rd CV6 . . .49 A2
Keresley Cl CV6 . . . . .49 A2
Keresley Grange Prim Sch
    CV6 . . . . .48 F1
Keresley Green Rd CV6 . . .48 F1
Keresley Newland Prim Sch
    CV7 . . . . .48 F7
Keresley Rd CV6 . . . . .61 A8
Kerria Ctr B77 . . . . .4 A2
Kerria Rd B77 . . . . .4 A2
Kerrls Way CV3 . . . . .63 A1
Kerry's Ho 4 CV1 . . . . .61 B2
Kerswell Dr B90 . . . . .71 A5
Kestral Rd B35 . . . . .22 C2
Kestrel B77 . . . . .10 A3
Kestrel Cl Hinckley LE10 . . .31 F6
    Stratford-u-A CV37 . . . . . .145 A3
Kestrel Croft 2 CV3 . . . . . .78 F8
Keswick Cl CV11 . . . . .30 A6
Keswick Dr CV21 . . . . .83 B4
Keswick Gn CV32 . . . . . . .105 D1
Keswick Wlk CV2 . . . . .62 F4
Kettlebrook Rd B90 . . . . . .71 C6
Kettlewell Cl CV34 . . . . . .104 E1
Kevilok Sr CV3 . . . . .77 D6
Kew Cl CV8 . . . . .93 C5
Kew Ho CV4 . . . . .59 F3
Kew Rd CV21 . . . . .83 A2
Keys Dr CV22 . . . . .82 B1
Keys Hill CV9 . . . . .3 A1
Keys La CV47 . . . . .125 F4
Keyte Rd CV36 . . . . .136 B6
Keytes Acre GL55 . . . . . . .135 E3
Keytes La CV35 . . . . .122 B7
Kidlers La CV35 . . . . .131 D2
Kidderminster Rd B93 . . . .72 A4
Kielder Cl CV35 . . . . .22 E2
Kilbury Court Gdns*
    GL55 . . . . .135 C6
Kilburn Dr CV5 . . . . .60 F3
Kilby Gn LE10 . . . . .32 A6
Kilbye Cl B77 . . . . .9 C3
Kilbye St CV11 . . . . .29 D2
Kilderkin Ct CV1 . . . . .151 C1
Kildwick Way 5 CV34 . . . .104 E1

Killworth Rd CV21 ....**101** A4
Kiln Cl Nuneaton CV10 ....**28** E3
  Royal Leamington Spa
  CV32 ....**106** A1
  Studley B80 ....**103** B2
Kiln La B90 ....**70** A5
Kiln Way Polesworth B78 ...**4** C1
  Shilton CV7 ....**51** E7
Kilnsey Gr CV34 ....**104** E1
Kilsby Gr B91 ....**71** C8
Kilsby La CV21 ....**101** B4
Kilsby Rd CV23 ....**101** B1
Kilworth Ho **7** CV32 .....**105** F1
Kimbell Cl CV47 ....**124** B1
Kimberley B77 ....**9** C4
Kimberley Cl CV5 ....**59** F4
Kimberley Rd
  Baginton CV8 ....**77** F2
  Bedworth CV12 ....**39** C4
  Rugby CV21 ....**83** A2
Kimberley Wlk B76 ....**22** D6
Kimble Cl CV5 ....**60** B4
Kimmond Ct **17** CV32 .....**105** F1
Kinchford Cl B91 ....**71** B8
Kineton CE Prim Sch
  CV35 ....**132** B6
Kineton High Sch CV35 ..**132** C6
Kineton La B94 ....**71** A1
Kineton Rd Coventry CV2 ..**62** C6
  Kenilworth CV8 ....**93** C4
  Southam CV47 ....**147** A2
  Wellesbourne CV35 ....**146** C1
Kineton Road Ind Est
  CV47 ....**147** A2
King Edward Rd
  Coventry CV1 ....**61** F4
  Nuneaton CV11 ....**29** D4
  Rugby CV21 ....**83** A2
King Edward VI Coll
  CV11 ....**29** D4
King Edward VI Sch
  CV37 ....**145** A1
King George's Ave
  Bedworth CV12 ....**39** B5
  Coventry CV6 ....**49** F2
King George's Ct CV23 ...**82** A3
King George's Way LE10 ..**31** B7
King Henry VIII Sch
  CV3 ....**151** A1
King John's La CV35 .....**132** E2
King John's Rd CV35 .....**132** B6
King Richard St CV2 ......**61** F3
King St Bedworth CV12 ....**39** C2
  Royal Leamington Spa
  CV32 ....**106** A1
  Rugby CV21 ....**83** A2
King William St CV1 ......**61** E4
King's Ct CV11 ....**29** B4
King's High Sch for Girls The
  CV34 ....**108** E7
King's Hill La CV8 ....**77** B2
King's La Broom B50 .....**148** A3
  Newton Regis B79 ....**2** B3
  Norton WR11 ....**127** B2
  Snitterfield CV37 ....**121** B6
  Stratford-u-A CV37 .....**144** C4
Kingcomb La GL55 ....**135** A2
Kingfield Rd CV1,CV6 ....**61** D7
Kingfisher B77 ....**10** A3
Kingfisher Ave CV10 ......**28** C5
Kingfisher Dr B36 ....**33** A8
Kingfisher Prim Sch B36 ..**33** A8
Kingfisher Way B49 ......**143** A3
Kingham Cl B98 ....**112** A6
Kingham Hill Sch OX7 ....**150** A1
Kingland Dr CV32 ....**105** C1
Kingsley Ave B49 ....**143** B3
Kings Ave CV9 ....**18** C4
Kings Coughton La B49 ..**143** A3
Kings Gdns CV12 ....**39** C2
Kings Gr CV2 ....**62** B3
Kings Mdw CV10 ....**28** C3
Kings Newnham La CV23 ..**80** A4
Kings Newnham Rd CV23 ..**81** A1
Kings Park Dr CV3 ....**63** B1
Kingsbridge Rd CV10 .....**29** D6
Kingsbrook Dr B91 ....**71** B8
Kingsbury Bsns Pk B76 ...**22** C6
Kingsbury Cl B76 ....**22** D5
Kingsbury Comp Sch
  B78 ....**15** B3
Kingsbury Inf Sch B78 ....**15** B3
Kingsbury Jun Sch B78 ...**15** B3
Kingsbury Rd
  Coventry CV6 ....**60** E5
  Curdworth B76 ....**23** B7
  Kingsbury B76 ....**15** A1
  Minworth B76 ....**22** D5
  Sutton Coldfield B35,B76 ..**22** B5
Kingsbury Water Park Visitor
  Ctr* B76 ....**15** A3
Kingsbury Water Pk*
  B76 ....**15** A3
Kingscote Gr CV3 ....**77** A4
Kingscote Rd B93 ....**71** E2
Kingsfield Ind Est CV1 ...**61** C6
Kingsford Cl B36 ....**22** D1
Kingsgate Ho B37 ....**33** A2
Kingsholm Cl CV3 ....**63** B1
Kingsland Ave CV5 ....**60** F2
Kingsland Dr B93 ....**71** E4
Kingsleigh Dr B36 ....**22** B1
Kingsley Ave CV21 ....**83** C1
Kingsley Coll B98 ....**103** B3
Kingsley Cres CV12 ....**40** B3
Kingsley Ct CV3 ....**79** D6
Kingsley Orch CV21 ....**83** C1
Kingsley Prep Sch B93 ....**72** A4
Kingsley Rd **11** CV33 ...**122** F8
Kingsley Sch The CV32 ...**105** F1
Kingsley Terr CV2 ....**62** E8
Kingsley Wlk CV2 ....**62** F7
Kingsmead Mews CV3 ......**78** D6
Kingston La CV35 ....**113** E3
Kingston Mews CV31 ......**110** C6
Kingston Rd CV5 ....**60** F2
Kingsway Coventry CV2 ...**62** A3
  Kingsbury B78 ....**15** B3
  Lighthorne Heath CV33 ....**123** D2
  Nuneaton CV11 ....**29** B4
  Royal Leamington Spa
  CV31 ....**109** F6
  Rugby CV22 ....**83** A1
Kingsway Com Prim Sch
  CV31 ....**109** F6
Kingsway Ho CV12 ....**39** C2
Kingswood Ave CV7 ....**48** B8
Kingswood Cl
  Coventry CV6 ....**49** D1
  Lapworth B94 ....**89** E5
Kingswood Cotts B94 .....**89** D3
Kingswood Gdns CV10 ....**28** B4
Kingswood Rd CV10 ....**28** B4
Kington Rise CV35 ....**113** E2
Kinman Way CV21 ....**83** B3
Kinross Cl CV10 ....**28** F2
Kinross Rd CV32 ....**106** B4
Kinross Way LE10 ....**21** C1
Kinsall Gn B77 ....**10** B3
Kinsham Dr B91 ....**71** B8
Kintyre The CV2 ....**63** B7
Kinver Cl CV2 ....**50** E1
Kinver Croft B76 ....**22** A8
Kinwalsey La CV7 ....**46** F6
Kinwarton Dovecote*
  B49 ....**143** B3
Kinwarton Farm Rd B49 .**143** B3
Kinwarton Rd B49 ....**143** B2
Kinwarton Workshops
  B49 ....**143** B3
Kipling Ave CV34 ....**108** C4
Kipling Cl CV10 ....**28** A5
Kipling Rd Coventry CV6 ..**61** A6
  Stratford-u-A CV37 .....**130** A8
Kirby Ave CV34 ....**104** F1
Kirby Cl Brandon CV8 .....**79** F5
  Coventry CV1 ....**61** D6
Kirby Cnr CV4 ....**76** B6
Kirby Corner Rd CV4 .....**76** B6
Kirby La CV7 ....**52** C3
Kirby Rd CV5 ....**60** F2
Kirigushi Rd CV35 ....**132** E5
Kirkby Cl CV21 ....**83** C1
Kirkby Rd CV21 ....**83** C1
Kirkdale Ave CV6 ....**49** D3
Kirkland Way B78 ....**8** A4
Kirkstone CV21 ....**83** B4
Kirkstone Rd CV12 ....**39** A2
Kirkstone Wlk CV11 ....**30** A6
Kirkwall CV47 ....**147** A2
Kirtland Cl CV9 ....**3** A1
Kirton Cl Coventry CV6 ...**48** F1
  Whitnash CV31 ....**110** B3
Kissing Tree La CV37 ....**121** D3
Kitchener Rd
  Coventry CV6 ....**61** E8
  Long Marston CV37 ......**129** C2
Kitebrook Cl B90 ....**71** A7
Kites Cl CV34 ....**104** D2
Kites Nest La CV35 ......**114** E8
Kittermaster Rd CV7 .....**46** C1
Kitwood Ave B78 ....**10** C3
Kixley La B93 ....**72** C6
Klevedon Cl CV11 ....**30** A1
Knebley Cres CV10 ....**29** C1
Knibbs Sh Ctr The CV34 .**108** E7
Knight Ave CV1 ....**61** E1
Knight Ct B75 ....**13** C5
Knightcote Dr
  Royal Leamington Spa
  CV32 ....**109** E8
  Solihull B91 ....**71** B8
Knightley Cl CV32 ....**106** E5
Knightlow Ave CV3 ....**78** C6
Knightlow CE Prim Sch
  CV23 ....**96** C4
Knightlow Cl CV8 ....**93** C3
Knightlow Way CV33 ....**123** F6
Knights Cl LE10 ....**31** D4
Knights Ct LE10 ....**30** E8
Knights La CV37 ....**145** C2
Knights Templar Way
  CV4 ....**60** A1
Knightsbridge Ave CV12 ..**39** C4
Knob Hill CV23 ....**96** C3
Knoll Croft
  Cheswick Green B90 ......**70** D4
  Coventry CV3 ....**77** C6
Knoll Dr Coventry CV3 ...**77** C6
  Warwick CV34 ....**104** E1
Knottesford Cl B80 ......**103** B2
Knowlands Rd B90 ....**71** A7
Knowle CE Prim Sch B93 .**72** C6
Knowle Hill Hurley CV9 ..**16** B2
  Kenilworth CV8 ....**93** C6
Knowle Rd B92 ....**56** E2
Knowle Wood Rd B93 .....**72** B3
Knowles Ave CV10 ....**28** C4
Knox Cres CV11 ....**29** F8
Kranji Rd CV47 ....**132** F5
Kurtus B77 ....**9** B3
Kwikform Bldg CV6 ....**49** E4
Kyetts Cnr OX17 ....**134** C1
Kynner Way CV3 ....**79** B8
Kyter La B36 ....**22** B1

L

Laburnam Ave
  Coventry CV6 ....**60** F5
  Kenilworth CV8 ....**93** A4
Laburnum Cl
  Bedworth CV12 ....**38** E2
  Hollywood B47 ....**69** A5
  Kingsbury B78 ....**15** B3
Laburnum Dr
  Sutton Coldfield B76 ......**13** A3
  Whitnash CV31 ....**110** B3
Laburnum Gr
  Nuneaton CV10 ....**28** D6
  Rugby CV22 ....**99** C4
  Warwick CV34 ....**105** B1
Lacell Cl CV34 ....**104** E1
Ladbroke By-Pass
  CV47 ....**124** D5
Ladbroke Hall CV47 .....**124** D5
Ladbroke Pk CV34 ....**104** E1
Ladbroke Rd CV47 ....**124** B4
Ladbrook Cl B98 ....**102** C4
Ladbrook Rd CV5 ....**60** A4
Lady Byron La
  Knowle, Copt Heath B93 ...**56** A1
  Knowle, Tilehouse Green
  B93 ....**71** F8
Lady Grey Ave CV34 .....**109** E3
Lady Katherine Leveson CE
  Sch B93 ....**73** B5
Lady La Coventry CV6 .....**49** F4
  Earlswood B90,B94 ....**70** B3
  Kenilworth CV8 ....**92** F4
Lady Warwick Ave CV12 ..**39** D2
Ladycroft CV32 ....**106** E5
Ladyfields Way CV6 ......**49** B4
Ladygrove Cl B98 ....**103** A4
Ladymead Dr CV6 ....**49** B2
Ladysmock CV23 ....**83** B4
Laertes Gr CV34 ....**109** F2
Laggan Cl CV10 ....**28** C5
Lair The B78 ....**10** C4
Lake View Rd CV5 ....**60** F4
Lakeland Dr B77 ....**10** A4
Lakeland Ho CV34 ....**109** A7
Lakes Halt The B94 ......**86** F8
Lakeside CV12 ....**39** A2
Lakeside B90 ....**70** F7
Lakin Ct CV34 ....**108** F8
Lakin Dr CV47 ....**124** A4
Lakin Ho CV34 ....**108** F8
Lakin Rd CV34 ....**108** F8
Lamb St CV1 ....**151** B3
Lambert Cl B50 ....**148** B3
Lambert Ct Barford CV35 .**122** A7
  Warwick CV34 ....**108** D6
Lambert Sch CV37 ....**145** A3
Lambeth Cl
  Birmingham B37 ....**33** B4
  Coventry CV2 ....**62** E7
Lambourn Cres CV31 .....**110** C6
Lambourne Cl
  Bidford-on-A B50 ....**148** B3
  Coventry CV5 ....**60** A4
Lamerton Cl CV2 ....**62** C6
Lamintone Dr CV32 ......**105** D2
Lammas Croft CV31 ......**110** A3
Lammas Ct
  Warwick CV34 ....**108** D6
  Wolston CV8 ....**80** A2
Lammas Ho **6** CV6 ......**61** A4
Lammas Rd CV6 ....**60** F4
Lammas Wlk CV34 ....**108** D7
Lamorna Cl CV11 ....**29** F4
Lamp La CV7 ....**36** C3
Lampitts Gn OX15 ....**139** D4
Lamprey B77 ....**9** B3
Lancaster Cl
  Atherstone CV9 ....**12** C1
  Wellesbourne CV35 ....**146** B1
Lancaster Dr B35 ....**22** B2
Lancaster Pl CV8 ....**92** E2
Lancaster Rd
  Hinckley LE10 ....**31** D8
  Rugby CV21 ....**83** A2
Lance Cl LE10 ....**31** D5
Lanchester Dr OX16 .....**139** F4
Lanchester Rd CV6 ....**61** B6
Lanchester Way
  Birmingham B36 ....**22** F1
  Daventry NN11 ....**117** F2
Lancia Cl CV6 ....**50** B4
Lancing Rd CV12 ....**40** C2
Land La B37 ....**44** E7
Landor Ho CV32 ....**110** A2
Landor Rd Knowle B93 ....**72** A6
  Redditch B98 ....**103** A4
  Warwick CV34 ....**108** D8
Landrail Cl B36 ....**33** A8
Landsdowne Pl CV21 ......**83** B1
Landseer Cl CV31 ....**84** A1
Lane Cl OX15 ....**139** D6
Lane Croft B76 ....**22** A8
Lane The
  Burmington CV36 ....**137** A1
  Little Compton GL56 ......**141** A6
Laneside CV3 ....**78** E6
Lanfear Ct LE10 ....**31** C7
Langbank Ave CV3 ....**78** D7
Langbay Ct CV2 ....**62** F6
Langcliffe Ave CV32 .....**104** F1
Langcomb Rd B90 ....**70** A8
Langdale Ave CV6 ....**49** D3
Langdale Cl
  Royal Leamington Spa
  CV32 ....**106** D3
  Rugby CV21 ....**83** B4
Langdale Ct B77 ....**4** A3
Langdale Dr CV11 ....**30** A6
Langdale Rd LE10 ....**31** A8
Langfield Rd B93 ....**72** A7
Langlands The CV35 ....**121** F4
Langley Croft CV4 ....**60** A2
Langley Dr B35 ....**22** A1
Langley Hall Dr B75 .....**13** B5
Langley Hall Rd B75 .....**13** B5
Langley Heath Dr B76 ....**13** A3
Langley Rd
  Claverdon CV35 ....**113** E3
  Whitnash CV31 ....**110** A4
Langley Specl Sch B75 ...**13** A6
Langley Wlk B37 ....**33** D2
Langloge Rd CV6 ....**49** B2
Langnor Rd CV2 ....**62** C6
Langton Cl
  Birmingham B36 ....**33** B6
  Coventry CV3 ....**78** F8
Langton Rd CV21,CV22 ...**83** C1
Langwood Cl CV4 ....**76** B8
Lankets The CV47 ....**133** D7
Lansbury Cl CV2 ....**62** E7
Lansdowne Cir CV32 ....**106** A1
Lansdowne Cl CV12 ......**39** A3
Lansdowne Cres
  8 Royal Leamington Spa
  CV32 ....**106** A1
  Studley B80 ....**103** B2
  Tamworth B77 ....**9** B4
Lansdowne Rd
  2 Royal Leamington Spa
  CV32 ....**106** A1
  Studley B80 ....**103** B2
Lansdowne St
  Coventry CV2 ....**61** F3
  Royal Leamington Spa
  CV32 ....**106** A1
Lant Cl CV4 ....**75** B7
Lapping Dr B92 ....**57** B7
Lapworth CE Prim Sch
  B94 ....**89** D3
Lapworth Cl B98 ....**102** C4
Lapworth Oaks B94 ....**89** D3
Lapworth Rd CV2 ....**50** B4
Lapworth St B94 ....**89** D4
Larch Cl Alcester B49 ...**143** A3
  Rugby CV22 ....**82** A1
  Stratford-u-A CV37 .....**145** A2
Larch Croft B37 ....**33** B2
Larch Gr CV34 ....**105** A1
Larch Tree Ave CV4 ......**60** A2
Larches The
  Bedworth CV7 ....**49** F3
  Mappleborough Green
  B80 ....**112** A6
Larchfields CV8 ....**80** A2
Larchwood Rd CV7 ....**39** B1
Larkfield Way CV5 ....**60** A6
Larkin Cl CV12 ....**40** B3
Larkin Gr CV2 ....**62** E8
Larkspur Rugby CV23 .....**83** B4
  Tamworth B77 ....**9** B2
Larkspur Ct CV12 ....**49** C8
Latham Rd CV5 ....**61** A2
Latimer Cl CV8 ....**92** F2
Latimer Rd B79 ....**22** A7
Latymer Cl B76 ....**22** A7
Lauderdale Ave CV6 ......**49** D3
Lauderdale Cl CV23 ......**82** A3
Launce Gr CV34 ....**109** F2
Launceston Dr CV11 ......**29** F4
Laundry Cotts CV35 ......**90** E4
Laurel Ave B79 ....**11** A4
Laurel Cl CV2 ....**50** E2
Laurel Ct CV5 ....**60** F1
Laurel Dr Nuneaton CV10 .**28** A7
  Stockton CV47 ....**147** C4
Laurel Fields LE17 ....**43** C3
Laurel Gdns CV22 ....**99** C4
Laurels Cres CV7 ....**74** C6
Laurels The
  Bedworth CV12 ....**38** E2
  Kingsbury B78 ....**15** B4
Lavender Ave CV6 ....**60** F5
Lavender Cl CV23 ....**83** C4
Lavender Hall La CV7 ....**58** C2
Lavenham Cl CV11 ....**40** C8
Lawford Cl CV3 ....**62** E1
Lawford Heath Ind Est
  CV23 ....**98** B4
Lawford Heath La CV23 ..**98** B3
Lawford La CV22 ....**82** A1
Lawford Rd
  Royal Leamington Spa
  CV31 ....**110** B5
  Rugby CV21,CV22,CV23 ...**82** C2
Lawley Cl CV4 ....**60** A2
Lawns The Bedworth CV12 .**38** C2
  Hinckley LE10 ....**31** E8
Lawnsdale Cl B46 ....**23** F7
Lawnswood Hinckley LE10 .**31** A8
  Sutton Coldfield B76 ......**22** A8
Lawrence Ave B79 ....**11** A4
Lawrence Gdns CV8 ....**93** A6
Lawrence Mackie Gdns
  CV35 ....**146** C2
Lawrence Rd
  Bedworth CV7 ....**50** A8
  Rugby CV21 ....**83** B2
Lawrence Saunders Rd
  CV6 ....**61** B5
Lawrence Sheriff Sch
  CV21 ....**83** A1
Lawrence Sherriff St
  CV22 ....**83** A1
Lawson Ave CV37 ....**145** C2
Lawton Cl LE10 ....**30** F8
Laxford Cl LE10 ....**21** C1
Laxton Way OX17 ....**139** F5
Lay Gdns CV31 ....**110** E5
Le Hanche Cl CV7 ....**49** A7
Lea Cl Alcester B49 .....**143** B3
  Stratford-u-A CV37 .....**144** A2
Lea Cres CV21 ....**82** B3
Lea Croft Rd B97 ....**102** B3
Lea Green La B47 ....**69** C5
Lea Wlk CV8 ....**79** B1
Leacrest Rd CV6 ....**49** A2
Leaf Ct CV3 ....**77** D4
Leaf La Coventry CV3 ....**77** D4
Leaf's Ct CV3 ....**77** F6
Leafield Cl CV2 ....**62** F8
Leagh Cl CV8 ....**93** B7
Lealholme Ct CV5 ....**76** D6
Leam Cl CV11 ....**29** F1
Leam Gn CV4 ....**76** D5
Leam Rd
  Lighthorne Heath CV33 ...**123** D2
  Royal Leamington Spa
  CV31 ....**109** D7
Leam St CV31 ....**110** B7
Leam Terr CV31 ....**110** B7
Leam The NN11 ....**117** F1
Leamington Hastings CE Inf
  Sch CV23 ....**116** B6
Leamington Hastings Rd
  CV23 ....**115** F7
Leamington Rd
  Coventry CV3 ....**77** C6
  Kenilworth CV8 ....**93** B2
  Long Itchington CV47 ....**115** C4
  Princethorpe CV23 ....**96** B1
  Ryton-on-D CV8 ....**96** A4
  Southam CV47 ....**124** C8
Leamington Spa Art Gallery
  & Mus* CV32 ....**109** F8
Lear Gr CV34 ....**109** E4
Leas Cl CV12 ....**39** A3
Leasowe's Ave CV3 ....**76** F4
Leasows The
  Chipping Campden GL55 .**135** A1
  Mickleton GL55 ....**135** C6
Leather St CV47 ....**115** D4
Leathermill La CV10 .....**19** B2
Leaward Cl CV10 ....**28** E2
Ledbrook Rd CV32 ......**106** E5
Ledbury Rd CV31 ....**110** C6
Ledbury Way B76 ....**22** A8
Ledwell B90 ....**70** A5
Lee Cl CV34 ....**104** E2
Lee Rd Hollywood B47 ....**69** A7
  Royal Leamington Spa
  CV31 ....**109** E6
Lee The CV5 ....**60** C4
Leeder Cl CV6 ....**49** C2
Leeming Cl CV4 ....**76** C6
Leicester Cres CV9 ......**12** C1
Leicester Cswy CV1 .....**61** D5
Leicester Ct CV12 ....**40** C2
Leicester La
  Cubbington CV32 ....**94** E1
  Royal Leamington Spa
  CV32 ....**106** C6
Leicester Rd
  Bedworth CV7 ....**39** B4
  Nuneaton CV11 ....**29** D5
  Rugby CV21 ....**83** A4
  Shilton CV7 ....**51** F6
Leicester Row **1** CV1 ..**151** B4
Leicester St
  Bedworth CV12 ....**39** B3
  Bulkington CV12 ....**40** C2
  Royal Leamington Spa
  CV32 ....**106** A1
Leigh Ave CV3 ....**77** C3
Leigh CE Prim Sch CV4 ..**75** D8
Leigh Cres CV47 ....**115** D3
Leigh Rd Rugby CV21 .....**82** C4
  Sutton Coldfield B75 ......**13** B5
Leigh St **4** CV1 ....**61** E4
Leighton Cl Coventry CV4 .**76** D2
  Royal Leamington Spa
  CV32 ....**106** C4
Leisure Wlk B77 ....**9** C3
Lennon Cl CV21 ....**101** B4
Lennox Cl CV3 ....**78** E6
Lenton's La CV2 ....**50** E4
Leofric St CV6 ....**61** A5
Leonard Parkins Ho
  CV12 ....**40** D2
Leontes Mdws CV34 ....**109** F1
Leopold Rd CV1 ....**61** F4
Lesingham Dr CV4 ....**59** E1
Lestock Cl CV22 ....**82** B1
Letchlade Cl CV2 ....**62** C8
Level The OX15 ....**138** F5
Leven Cl LE10 ....**31** A8
Leven Croft B76 ....**22** A7
Leven Way CV2 ....**63** A8
Lever Rd CV21 ....**84** A1
Leveson Cres CV7 ....**74** A6
Levett Rd B77 ....**4** A3

Levy Cl CV21 .....82 C2
Lewis Cl CV9 .....18 C3
Lewis Rd Coventry CV1 .....61 D5
  Radford Semele CV31 .....110 F5
Lexington St CV11 .....29 B5
Leyburn Cl Coventry CV6 .....49 E2
  Nuneaton CV11 .....30 A2
  ◆ Warwick CV34 .....104 F1
Leycester Cl CV33 .....123 E7
Leycester Ct CV34 .....108 E6
Leycester Pl ⑱ CV34 .....108 E6
Leycester Rd CV8 .....93 A2
Leyes La CV8 .....93 C5
Leyes The CV23 .....68 A1
Leyfields Cres CV34 .....108 D4
Leyland Rd
  Bulkington CV12 .....40 B2
  Coventry CV5 .....60 D4
  Nuneaton CV11 .....29 E1
Leyland Specl Sch CV11 .....29 E1
Leymere Cl CV7 .....46 C1
Leys Cl Northend CV47 .....133 B7
  Wroxton OX15 .....139 D4
Leyside CV3 .....78 E5
Leysmill Cl LE10 .....31 E1
Libbards Gate ④ B91 .....71 C8
Libbards Way B91 .....71 B8
Liberty Rd B77 .....9 C3
Liberty Way CV11 .....29 F3
Library Cl LE10 .....32 A5
Library Rd CV4 .....76 B5
Lichen Gn CV4 .....76 D5
Lichfield Cl Arley CV7 .....37 A4
  Nuneaton CV11 .....30 A7
Lichfield Cotts B78 .....15 B3
Lichfield Rd Coventry CV3 .....77 D8
  Water Orton B46,B76 .....23 D4
  Wishaw B76,B78 .....14 B3
Lichfield St B78 .....9 A4
Liecester Rd LE10 .....41 C3
Lilford Way CV3 .....79 A7
Light Hall Sch B90 .....70 B8
Light La CV1 .....151 B4
Lighthorne Heath Prim Sch
  CV33 .....123 C2
Lighthorne Rd CV35 .....132 B6
Lightoak Cl B97 .....102 B3
Lightwood Cl B93 .....72 B8
Lilac Ave CV6 .....60 F5
Lilac Cl LE10 .....31 E6
Lilac Dr CV22 .....82 A1
Lilac Gr CV34 .....105 A1
Lilac Rd CV12 .....39 D5
Lilacvale Way CV4 .....76 D5
Lilbourne Rd CV23 .....84 B3
Lilley Cl CV6 .....49 C2
Lilley Green Rd B48 .....85 D5
Lillington Ave CV32 .....105 F2
Lillington Cl
  Royal Leamington Spa
  CV32 .....106 A3
  Sutton Coldfield B75 .....13 A4
Lillington Prim Sch
  CV32 .....106 B3
Lillington Rd
  Coventry CV2 .....50 D1
  Royal Leamington Spa
  CV32 .....106 A3
  Solihull B90 .....70 B8
Limbrick Ave CV4 .....60 A1
Limbrick Wood Prim Sch
  CV4 .....59 F3
Lime Ave CV32 .....106 A4
Lime Cl B47 .....69 A5
Lime Gr
  Birmingham, Chelsley Wood
  B37 .....33 B1
  Coventry CV4 .....60 B2
  Hurley CV9 .....16 A2
  Kenilworth CV8 .....93 A4
  Nuneaton CV10 .....28 C5
Lime Kiln B78 .....11 A4
Lime Rd CV47 .....147 A3
Lime Tree Ave
  Coventry CV4 .....60 A2
  Rugby CV22 .....99 A4
Limekiln La B94 .....70 D1
Limes Ave CV37 .....144 B1
Limes Coppice CV10 .....27 C4
Limes The Bedworth CV12 .....38 E2
  Tiddington CV37 .....145 C2
Limestone Hall La CV23 .....81 A2
Linaker Rd CV3 .....78 C5
Lincoln Ave CV10 .....28 B7
Lincoln Cl Warwick CV34 .....104 E1
  Wellesbourne CV35 .....146 B1
Lincoln Ct CV32 .....110 A8
Lincoln Gr B37 .....33 A1
Lincoln St CV1 .....151 C4
Lincroft Cres CV5 .....60 E4
Lindale CV21 .....83 B4
Linden Ave CV35 .....146 C2
Linden Cl CV34 .....104 E2
Linden Lea CV12 .....39 B3
Lindera B77 .....4 A2
Lindfield The CV3 .....78 C8
Lindhurst Dr B94 .....88 C6
Lindisfarne Dr CV8 .....93 C4

Lindley Rd Bedworth CV12 .....38 D2
Lindley St CV3 .....62 B2
Lindridge Cl B98 .....112 A6
Lindridge Dr B76 .....22 D6
Lindridge Rd B75,B76 .....13 B6
Lindsay Wlk CV47 .....132 F7
Lindsey Cres CV8 .....93 A1
Lineholt Cl B98 .....103 A3
Linen St CV34 .....108 D6
Linford Wlk CV2 .....50 F1
Lingard Rd B75 .....13 A5
Lingfield Cres CV37 .....129 F8
Lingfield Ct CV6 .....50 B4
Lingwood Dr CV10 .....28 F3
Links Rd CV6 .....61 B8
Linkway CV31 .....109 E6
Linley Rd CV47 .....147 A3
Linnell Rd CV21 .....83 C1
Linnet Cl CV3 .....78 D5
Linstock Way CV6 .....50 B4
Linthouse Wlk B77 .....9 C3
Lintly B77 .....10 A4
Linwood Dr CV2 .....50 F1
Lion Fields Ave CV5 .....60 B6
Liskeard Cl CV11 .....30 A5
Liskeard Rd CV35 .....132 D3
Lisle Ct ④ CV31 .....110 A6
Lisle Gdns ④ CV33 .....122 F8
Lismore Croft CV2 .....63 B7
Lister Rd CV9 .....12 C1
Lister St CV11 .....29 D3
Little Acre B97 .....102 B3
Little Back La NN11 .....126 B5
Little Brum CV9 .....11 B1
Little Church St
  ■ Coventry CV1 .....151 C4
  Rugby CV21 .....83 A2
Little Cryfield CV4 .....76 C2
Little Duke St CV11 .....29 C4
Little Elborow St CV21 .....83 A2
Little Farm CV3 .....78 D5
Little Field CV2 .....62 A5
Little Forge Rd B98 .....103 B4
Little Gr CV22 .....83 B1
Little Heath Ind Est CV6 .....50 A2
Little Heath Prim Sch
  CV6 .....49 F1
Little Lawford La CV23 .....82 A4
Little London La CV23 .....68 A1
Little Park St CV1 .....151 C2
Little Pennington St ⑤ 82 C2
Little Pittern CV35 .....132 B6
Little Pk CV47 .....147 A2
Little South St CV1 .....61 E3
Little Woods B97 .....102 C3
Littlemead Rd B90 .....69 E8
Littleshaw Croft B47 .....69 C4
Littleshaw La B47 .....69 C4
Littlethorpe CV3 .....78 D6
Littleton Cl
  Kenilworth CV8 .....93 A7
  Sutton Coldfield B76 .....13 A1
Littleton Croft ⑤ B91 .....71 C8
Littletons CE Fst Sch The
  WR11 .....127 F1
Littlewood Cl ② B91 .....71 B8
Littlewood Gn B80 .....103 B2
Littleworth
  Chipping Campden GL55 .....135 A2
  Henley-in-A B95 .....113 B4
Litton B77 .....4 B1
Liveridge Cl B93 .....71 F6
Liveridge Hill B95 .....113 A2
Livery St CV32 .....109 F8
Livingstone Ave CV23 .....81 C2
Livingstone Rd CV6 .....61 E7
Liza Ct CV21 .....83 B4
Llewellyn Rd CV31 .....110 A6
Lloyd Cl
  Hampton Magna CV35 .....114 F3
  Norton WR11 .....127 C2
  Nuneaton CV11 .....29 D2
Lloyd Cres CV2 .....62 E3
Lloyd Rd CV21 .....83 A2
Loach Dr CV2 .....50 B4
Lobelia Cl LE10 .....31 E5
Lochmore Cl LE10 .....31 A8
Lochmore Dr LE10 .....31 A8
Lochmore Way LE10 .....31 A8
Lochsong Cl B77 .....9 B2
Lock Cl CV37 .....145 A2
Lock La CV34 .....108 D8
Locke Cl CV6 .....49 A1
Lockhart Cl CV8 .....93 A4
Lockheed Cl ⑪ CV31 .....109 F5
Lockhurst La CV6 .....61 D7
Locking Croft B35 .....22 B3
Locks The
  Royal Leamington Spa
  CV31 .....109 D7
  Rugby CV21 .....84 A1
Loder Cl CV4 .....59 F3
Lodge Cl Atherstone CV9 .....19 A3
  Hinckley LE10 .....32 A5
Lodge Cres CV34 .....108 D6
Lodge Croft B93 .....72 B6
Lodge Green La CV7 .....46 F2
Lodge Green La N CV7 .....46 E3
Lodge Rd Coventry CV3 .....62 B1
  Knowle B93 .....72 B6
  Rugby CV21 .....83 A2
  Stratford-u-A CV37 .....144 C2
Logan Rd CV2 .....62 E7
Lole Cl CV6 .....50 A4
Lollard Croft CV3 .....77 D8
Lomita Cres B77 .....9 B4

Lomond Cl LE10 .....31 B8
Lomond Way CV10 .....28 C5
Lomsey Cl CV4 .....60 A1
London End NN11 .....134 E8
London Rd
  Coventry, Cheylesmore CV3 .....77 E7
  Coventry, Willenhall CV3 .....78 B5
  Hinckley LE10 .....31 F6
  Middleton B75,B78 .....13 D7
  Moreton-in-M GL56 .....140 B3
  Ryton-on-D CV8 .....79 B1
  Shipston-on-S CV36 .....149 C2
  Sutton Coldfield B75 .....7 A2
  Willoughby CV23 .....117 C6
London Road Terr GL56 .....140 B3
Long Brook La CV7,CV8 .....73 E5
Long Close Ave CV5 .....60 A6
Long Close Wlk ■ B35 .....22 A3
Long Furlong CV22 .....100 A4
Long Hyde Rd WR11 .....127 F1
Long Itchington CE Prim Sch
  CV47 .....115 E3
Long La CV5,CV7 .....48 D2
Long Lawford Prim Sch
  CV23 .....82 A3
Long Leys Croft B46 .....23 B2
Long Leys Ct B46 .....23 B2
Long Marston Rd
  Mickleton CV37,GL55 .....135 B8
  Pebworth CV37 .....128 F2
  Welford on A CV37 .....129 B5
Long Shoot The CV11 .....30 C6
Long St Atherstone CV9 .....18 B4
  Bulkington CV12 .....40 A2
  Dordon B78 .....11 A3
Longborough CE Prim Sch .....
Longbridge B897 .....102 A3
Longcroft Cl B35 .....22 A2
Longdon Cl B98 .....103 A4
Longdon Croft B93 .....72 A8
Longdon Rd B93 .....72 A6
Longdown La CV23 .....117 D7
Longfellow Ave CV34 .....108 C4
Longfellow Rd CV6 .....61 C3
Longfield No CV6 .....62 A8
Longfield Rd CV31 .....110 B6
Longford Cl
  Bidford-on-A B50 .....148 C3
  Dorridge B93 .....72 B3
Longford Park Prim Sch
  CV6 .....50 A3
Longford Rd
  Bedworth CV7 .....50 A6
  Coventry CV6 .....50 A4
Longford Sq CV6 .....50 A4
Longhope Cl B98 .....112 A6
Longleat Dr B90 .....70 E5
Longleat Gr ⑰ CV31 .....110 C6
Longley Ave B76 .....22 D5
Longrood Rd CV22 .....99 B3
Longstone Cl B90 .....71 B6
Longville Ct CV3 .....78 A6
Longwood Cl CV4 .....75 F6
Lonscale Dr CV3 .....77 B5
Lonsdale Rd CV32 .....106 B4
Lord Lytton Ave CV2 .....62 D2
Lord St CV5 .....60 F2
Lords La B80 .....103 C1
Lorenzo Cl CV3 .....78 D6
Lossiemouth Rd LE10 .....21 C1
Lotherdale B77 .....4 C1
Loudon Ave CV6 .....61 A5
Loudon Gate CV11 .....29 F1
Loughshaw B77 .....4 B1
Louisa Ward Cl CV23 .....115 C7
Love La LE10 .....32 A6
Love Lyne B97 .....102 A3
Loveday Cl CV12 .....38 E1
Loveday Dr CV32 .....105 E2
Lovelace Ave B91 .....71 D8
Lovell Cl CV7 .....50 A8
Lovell Rd CV12 .....49 A3
Loverock Cres CV21 .....83 C1
Lovetts Cl LE10 .....30 F8
Low Rd WR11 .....127 A6
Lowbrook La B90 .....69 D4
Lowdham B77 .....4 B1
Lowe Rd CV6 .....49 A2
Lower Ave CV31 .....109 F7
Lower Cape CV34 .....108 D8
Lower Cladswell La
  B49 .....118 C5
Lower Eastern Green La
  CV5 .....59 F4
Lower End Bubbenhall CV8 .....95 B3
  Salford OX7 .....150 C2
  Shutford OX15 .....139 A3
Lower Farm La OX17 .....133 F2
Lower Ford St CV1 .....151 D3
Lower Grinsty La B97 .....102 A4
Lower High St GL55 .....135 A2
Lower Hillmorton Rd
  CV21 .....83 B1
Lower Holyhead Rd
  CV1 .....151 A3
Lower House La CV9 .....11 A2
Lower Ladyes Hills CV8 .....93 A6
Lower Leam St CV31 .....110 B7
Lower Prec CV1 .....151 B3
Lower Rd CV7 .....51 C6
Lower St Rugby CV21 .....101 A4
  Willoughby CV23 .....117 B6
Lower Villiers St ■
  CV32 .....106 A1
Lowes Ave CV34 .....104 E1
Lowes La CV35 .....146 B1
Loweswater Cl CV11 .....30 A6
Loweswater Rd CV3 .....62 E1

Lowforce B77 .....4 B1
Lowry Cl CV12 .....39 A4
Lowther St CV2 .....61 F4
Loxley CE Com Prim Sch
  CV35 .....130 F7
Loxley Cl Coventry CV2 .....50 D2
  Wellesbourne CV35 .....146 B1
Loxley Ct CV2 .....50 D2
Loxley Fields CV35 .....130 F7
Loxley Rd Alveston CV37 .....121 D1
  Stratford-u-A CV37 .....145 B1
Loxley Way CV32 .....106 A2
Lucas Ct
  Royal Leamington Spa
  CV32 .....109 D8
  Rugby CV21 .....83 A2
Lucas Ho CV32 .....105 F2
Lucas Rd LE10 .....31 D6
Luce Cl B35 .....22 B4
Lucerne Cl CV2 .....50 C3
Lucian Cl CV2 .....63 B7
Luddington Rd CV37 .....129 E8
Ludford Cl Ansley CV10 .....27 A2
  Stratford-u-A CV37 .....144 B2
Ludford Rd CV10 .....28 C6
Ludgate Cl B46 .....23 B3
Ludlow Cl B37 .....33 C2
Ludlow Dr OX16 .....139 F4
Ludlow Rd CV5 .....61 A2
Ludlow's La CV5 .....114 C7
Ludworth Ave B37 .....44 B8
Luff Cl CV3 .....78 B8
Lugtrout La B91 .....56 A6
Lulworth Pk CV8 .....93 C6
Lumley Gr B37 .....33 D2
Lumsden Cl CV2 .....62 F8
Lunar Cl CV4 .....76 D5
Lundy View B36 .....33 B6
Lunn Ave CV8 .....92 E3
Lunn Poly Ho ⑧ CV22 .....105 F1
Lunt The ■ CV8 .....77 E3
Lupin Cl LE10 .....31 D5
Lupton Ave CV3 .....77 C7
Luscombe Rd CV2 .....62 E8
Luther Way CV5 .....59 F4
Lutterworth Rd
  Brinklow CV23 .....64 C2
  Churchover CV23 .....67 B3
  Coventry CV2 .....62 E8
  Hinckley LE10 .....32 C3
  Nuneaton CV11 .....40 C8
  Pailton CV23 .....54 B1
  Shawell LE17 .....68 B3
  Wolvey LE10 .....41 C3
Luxor La CV5 .....59 B8
Lychgate Cl LE10 .....32 A5
Lychgate La LE10 .....32 C5
Lydd Croft B35 .....22 B4
Lydford Cl CV2 .....62 C7
Lydgate Ct Bedworth CV12 .....39 A4
  Nuneaton CV11 .....29 C3
Lydgate Rd CV6 .....61 B5
Lydstep Gr CV31 .....110 C7
Lye Green Rd CV35 .....113 F4
Lyecroft Ave B37 .....33 D2
Lymesy St CV3 .....77 D7
Lymington Cl CV6 .....61 D8
Lymington Dr CV6 .....50 B6
Lymore Croft CV2 .....63 A8
Lynbrook Cl B47 .....69 A7
Lynbrook Rd CV5 .....76 D8
Lynch The Nuneaton CV11 .....29 D2
  Polesworth B78 .....4 C1
Lynchgate Ct CV4 .....76 C6
Lynchgate Ho CV4 .....76 C6
Lynchgate Rd CV4 .....76 C6
Lyndale ■ B77 .....9 C3
Lyndale Cl CV5 .....60 C3
Lyndale Rd CV5 .....60 C3
Lyndhurst Cl Coventry CV6 .....50 B6
  Hinckley LE10 .....32 A6
Lyndhurst Croft CV5 .....59 C4
Lyndhurst Rd CV21 .....83 C1
Lyndon Ct CV32 .....109 E8
Lyndon Ho B77 .....2 A2
Lyneham Gdns B76 .....22 B6
Lyng Cl CV5 .....60 A4
Lyng Hall Sch CV2 .....62 C6
Lynmouth Cl CV11 .....29 E5
Lynmouth Rd CV2 .....50 E2
Lynton Cl CV34 .....104 E1
Lynton Rd CV6 .....49 F1
Lynwood Wlk ⑫ CV31 .....110 C6
Lysander Cl CV35 .....146 B1
Lysander Ct CV37 .....145 A3
Lyster Cl CV34 .....108 B8
Lythall Cl CV31 .....110 F5
Lythalls La CV6 .....49 E2
Lythalls Lane Ind Est CV6 .....49 E1
Lytham B77 .....22 B6
Lytham Cl B76 .....22 B6
Lytham Rd CV22 .....82 C1
Lyttelton Rd CV34 .....108 E8
Lyttleton Cl CV3 .....63 A1

M

M40 Distribution Pk
  CV35 .....146 A1
Macadam Cl NN11 .....117 F3
Macaulay Rd
  Coventry CV2 .....62 D4
  Rugby CV22 .....99 C4
Macbeth App CV34 .....109 D4
Macbeth Cl CV22 .....99 C3
Macdonald Rd CV2 .....62 D3

Macefield Cl CV2 .....50 D2
Mackenzie Cl CV5 .....60 A7
Mackley Way CV33 .....123 E6
Madam's Hill Rd B90 .....70 D7
Madden Pl CV22 .....82 B1
Madeira Croft CV5 .....60 E2
Madrona B77 .....4 A2
Maffey Ct CV22 .....83 A1
Magdalen Cl CV37 .....129 D2
Magdalen Rd CV23 .....117 C6
Magna Pk LE17 .....55 B3
Magnet La CV22 .....99 B4
Magnolia B77 .....4 A2
Magnolia Cl CV3 .....77 B5
Magnus B77 .....2 A2
Magpie Ho CV5 .....59 D5
Magpie La CV7 .....73 E6
Maguire Ind Est CV4 .....75 F8
Magyar Cres CV11 .....40 A8
Maidavale Cres CV3 .....77 C4
Maidenhair Dr CV23 .....83 B4
Maidenhead Cl CV37 .....145 A2
Maidenhead Rd CV37 .....145 A2
Maidwell Dr B90 .....70 E8
Main Rd Ansty CV7 .....51 D3
  Austrey CV9 .....3 A1
  Baxterley CV9 .....17 A4
  Binton CV37 .....120 A1
  Broughton OX15 .....139 E1
  Claybrooke Magna LE17 .....43 C3
  Kilsby CV23 .....126 E1
  Lower Quinton CV37 .....129 E2
  Meriden CV7 .....58 D8
  Newton Regis B79 .....2 B1
Main St Aston le W NN11 .....134 F5
  Badby NN11 .....126 F5
  Birdingbury CV23 .....115 F7
  Bourton on D CV23 .....97 C1
  Burmington CV36 .....141 A8
  Church Lench WR11 .....127 A6
  Claydon OX17 .....133 A6
  Cleeve Prior WR11 .....128 A4
  Clifton u D CV23 .....83 C3
  Easenhall CV23 .....65 C2
  Frankton CV23 .....97 B1
  Grandborough CV23 .....116 F5
  Hanwell OX17 .....139 F6
  Harborough Magna CV23 .....66 A2
  Higham on t H CV13 .....21 A2
  Long Compton CV36,OX7 .....141 C3
  Long Lawford CV23 .....82 A3
  Mollington OX17 .....134 A2
  Monks Kirby CV23 .....53 C2
  Newton CV23 .....68 A1
  North Newington OX15 .....139 D2
  Norton Lindsey CV35 .....114 C2
  Offenham WR11 .....127 D1
  Orton-on-t-H CV9 .....6 B2
  Oxhill CV35 .....137 F8
  Rugby CV22 .....99 B4
  Rugby, Newbold on Avon
    CV21 .....82 B4
  Shawell LE17 .....68 B3
  Sibford Gower OX15 .....142 D8
  South Littleton WR11 .....127 F1
  Stoke Golding CV13 .....21 B4
  Stretton u F CV23 .....98 C2
  Thurlaston CV23 .....98 C2
  Tiddington CV37 .....145 C2
  Tysoe CV35 .....138 B7
  Willey CV23 .....54 C3
  Willoughby CV23 .....117 C6
  Withybrook CV7 .....52 C3
  Wolston CV8 .....80 A2
  Wroxton OX15 .....139 D4
Makepeace Ave CV34 .....104 F1
Malam Cl CV4 .....60 A1
Maldens The CV36 .....149 C3
Malham Cl CV11 .....30 A1
Malham Rd Tamworth B77 .....4 B1
  Warwick CV34 .....104 F1
Malins The CV34 .....109 B6
Mallaby Cl B90 .....70 A8
Mallard Ave CV10 .....28 C6
Mallard Cl CV37 .....144 B3
Mallard Dr LE10 .....31 A7
Mallard Rd B80 .....103 C2
Mallender Dr B93 .....71 F6
Mallerin Croft CV10 .....28 B5
Mallory Dr CV34 .....108 D7
Mallory Rd
  Bishops Tachbrook CV33 .....122 E8
  Lighthorne Heath CV33 .....123 D2
Mallory Way CV6 .....49 E4
Mallow Cl CV23 .....83 B4
Mallow Way CV10 .....28 C6
Malmesbury Rd CV6 .....49 A3
Malt House Cl
  Broom B50 .....148 B4
  Harvington WR11 .....127 B7
Malt House La
  Church Lench WR11 .....127 A6
  Northend CV47 .....133 B7
Malthouse Cl Ansley CV10 .....27 A2
Malthouse La
  Earlswood B94 .....86 E7
  Kenilworth CV8 .....92 E6
  Long Compton CV36 .....141 C3
Malthouse Row B37 .....44 A8
Maltings Ct ② CV37 .....144 C2
Maltings The
  Nuneaton CV11 .....29 E5
  Royal Leamington Spa
  CV32 .....105 F2

Maltings The continued
 Studley B80 ....103 B2
Maltmill La B49 ....143 B2
Malvern Ave
 Nuneaton CV10 ....28 B3
 Rugby CV22 ....83 B1
Malvern Dr B76 ....22 A8
Malvern Ho CV5 ....59 D4
Malvern Rd
 Balsall Common CV7 .....74 C6
 Coventry CV5 ....60 F4
 Redditch B97 ....102 B4
Manby Rd B35 ....22 A4
Mancetter Rd
 Atherstone CV9 ....19 A3
 Nuneaton CV10 ....28 D7
Manchester St ◢ GL56 ..140 A3
Mandarin Cl CE10 ....31 A6
Mander Gr CV34 ....108 C4
Manderley Cl CV5 ....59 C5
Mandrake Cl CV6 ....49 D4
Manfield Ave CV2 ....63 A7
Mann's Cl CV8 ....96 A4
Manning Wlk ◢ CV21 ....83 A2
Mannings Cl OX15 ....142 D8
Manor Barns CV36 ....136 B6
Manor Cl
 Charwelton NN11 ......126 D2
 Grendon CV9 ....11 A1
 Hinckley LE10 ....31 C5
Manor Court Ave CV11 ...29 B5
Manor Court Mews CV11 .29 A5
Manor Court Rd CV11 ....29 A5
Manor Ct
 Cleeve Prior WR11 ....128 A4
 Dorridge B93 ....71 F2
 Ettington CV37 ....131 A3
 Fenny Compton CV47 ..133 D7
 Kenilworth CV8 ....93 A6
 Royal Leamington Spa
 CV31 ....109 F7
Manor Dr
 Stretton on D CV23 .....96 C3
 Ullenhall B80 ....112 D4
 Wilmcote CV37 ....120 C4
Manor Est CV8 ....79 F3
Manor Farm WR11 ....127 F1
Manor Farm Cl CV23 ....101 B1
Manor Farm Cotts CV37 .129 C7
Manor Farm Craft Ctr*
 B94 ....69 F2
Manor Farm Rd CV36 ...136 F6
Manor Gn CV37 ....145 B1
Manor Hall Mews CV3 ....78 D6
Manor House Cl
 Aston Flamville LE10 ...32 C6
 Rugby CV21 ....82 B4
Manor House Dr CV1 ....151 B2
Manor House La
 Astwood Bank B96 .....102 C2
 Water Orton B46 ....23 B3
Manor La Claverdon CV35 114 A4
 Clifton u D CV23 ....84 A3
 Ettington CV37 ....131 A3
 Honiley CV8,CV35 ....91 A5
 Kineton CV35 ....132 B5
 Shipston-on-S CV36 ...149 C3
 Wroxall CV35 ....90 E4
Manor Mews B80 ....103 C2
Manor Orch
 Harbury CV33 ....123 E6
 Honiley CV35 ....139 D6
Manor Park Com Sch
 CV11 ....29 A5
Manor Park Prim Sch
 CV3 ....77 D7
Manor Park Rd CV11 .....29 A5
Manor Pk Claydon OX17 .134 B5
 Harvington WR11 ......127 D3
Manor Prim Sch B78 ......8 C3
Manor Rd Atherstone CV9 .18 C3
 Bishops Itchington CV47 124 A4
 Claybrooke Magna LE17 .43 B3
 Coventry CV1 ....151 B1
 Dorridge B93 ....71 F3
 Harbury CV33 ....123 F6
 Kenilworth CV8 ....92 F6
 Loxley CV35 ....130 F7
 Royal Leamington Spa
 CV32 ....106 B3
 Rugby CV21 ....83 A2
 South Littleton WR11 ..127 F1
 Staverton NN11 ....126 D8
 Stockton CV47 ....147 C4
 Stratford-u-A CV37 ....145 B1
 Studley B80 ....103 C2
 Wythall B47 ....69 A3
Manor Rd Ind Est CV9 ..18 C4
Manor Terr CV10 ....93 A6
Manor View CV9 ....79 F3
Manor Way LE10 ....31 D5
Mansard Ct B46 ....34 A4
Manse Cl CV7 ....39 A1
Manse Gdns B80 ....103 C2
Mansel St CV6 ....61 E8
Mansell Rd B97 ....102 B4
Mansell St CV37 ....144 C2
Mansfield Ho B37 ....33 B3
Mansion Ho The CV35 ..132 B5
Mansion St ◢ LE10 .....31 D8
Mansions Cl CV47 ....124 A4
Mansley Bsns Ctr The
 CV37 ....144 B3
Manston Dr CV35 ....146 B1
Manta Rd B77 ....9 B3

Mantilla Dr CV3 ....77 B5
Manton Croft B93 ....71 E3
Mantua CV37 ....145 A2
Maple Ave CV7 ....39 B1
Maple Cl LE10 ....31 E5
Maple Dr B78 ....15 B4
Maple Gr Rugby CV21 ....83 A2
 Stratford-u-A CV37 ....144 C3
 Warwick CV34 ....105 A1
Maple Leaf Dr B37 ....44 B8
Maple Rd Nuneaton CV10 .28 E5
 Royal Leamington Spa
 CV31 ....109 F6
Maple Rise B77 ....4 A2
Maple Wlk ◢ B37 ....33 B2
Maplebeck Cl CV5 ....61 A3
Maples The CV10 ....38 E2
Mapleton Rd CV6 ....60 F8
Maplewood B76 ....22 A8
Mapperley Cl CV2 ....63 A8
Mappleborough Green CE
 Prim Sch B98 ....112 A5
Marble Alley B80 ....103 C2
March Ct CV22 ....83 A1
March Rd
 Mollington OX17 ....133 F2
 Warmington OX17 .....133 E2
March Way CV3 ....78 D7
Marchant Rd LE10 ....31 C8
Marchfont Cl CV11 ....30 A1
Marcos Dr B36 ....22 F1
Marcroft Pl CV31 ....110 D6
Mardol Cl CV2 ....62 D7
Marfield Cl B76 ....22 A6
Margaret Ave CV12 ......39 B3
Margaret Cl CV33 ....123 F6
Margaret Rd CV9 ....18 C4
Margeson Cl CV2 ....62 E2
Margetts Cl CV8 ....92 F4
Marie Brock Cl CV4 ......60 B1
Marie Cl CV9 ....19 A4
Marie Corelli Sch CV37 .144 B2
Marigold Dr LE10 ....31 E5
Marina Cl CV4 ....75 E7
Marion Rd CV6 ....61 D7
Mark Antony Dr CV34 ...109 D4
Market Cnr Baginton CV8 .77 F2
 ◢ Royal Leamington Spa
 CV31 ....109 F6
Market End Cl CV12 ......38 C2
Market Hill CV47 ....147 A2
Market Mall ◢ CV21 ......83 A2
Market Pl Alcester B49 ..143 A2
 Hinckley LE10 ....31 D8
 Nuneaton CV11 ....29 C4
 Rugby CV21 ....83 A2
 Shipston-on-S CV36 ...149 C3
 Warwick CV34 ....108 E6
Market Sq CV35 ....132 B6
Market St Atherstone CV9 .18 B4
 Polesworth B78 ....5 A1
 Rugby CV21 ....83 A2
 Warwick CV34 ....108 D6
Market Way CV1 ....151 B2
Markham Dr CV31 ....110 B5
Markham La CV6 ....108 E6
Marks Mews ◢ CV34 ....108 E6
Marlborough Ct B75 .....13 A6
Marlborough Dr CV31 ...110 D5
Marlborough Rd
 Coventry CV2 ....62 A3
 Nuneaton CV11 ....29 B3
 Rugby CV22 ....99 C4
Marlborough Way B77 ....9 C4
Marlcroft CV3 ....78 F7
Marlcroft B50 ....148 B3
Marlene Croft B37 ....33 C1
Marler Rd CV4 ....75 F7
Marlin B77 ....9 B3
Marlissa Dr CV6 ....49 E2
Marloes Wlk CV31 ......110 C6
Marlow Cl CV5 ....60 B4
Marlow Rd CV9 ....16 B3
Marlowe Cl
 Banbury OX16 ....139 F3
 Nuneaton CV10 ....27 C3
Marlston Wlk CV5 ....60 B4
Marlwood Cl CV6 ....49 F4
Marne Cl CV34 ....109 A8
Marner Cres CV6 ....61 B5
Marner Rd Bedworth CV12 39 A3
 Nuneaton CV10 ....29 B1
Marnhull Cl CV2 ....62 F4
Marram Cl CV47 ....144 C2
Marrick B77 ....4 B1
Marriners La CV5 ....60 B6
Marriott Rd
 Bedworth CV12 ....38 D2
 Coventry CV6 ....61 A4
Marsett B77 ....10 B4
Marsh Cl WR11 ....127 D4
Marsh La GL56 ....140 A3
Marsh Ho CV2 ....63 A7
Marsh La
 Bradnock's Marsh B92 ..57 D5
 Curdworth B76 ....23 D5
 Hampton-in-A B92 .....57 B6
 Water Orton B46 ....23 C3
Marsh Rd CV37 ....120 B5
Marshall Ave CV36 .....149 C4
Marshall Lake Rd B90 ...70 D8
Marshall Rd CV7 ....49 F8
Marshalls Cl OX15 ......138 F5
Marsham Cl CV34 ....109 B8
Marshbrook Cl CV2 ......50 E3
Marshdale Ave CV6 ......49 E3
Marshfield B90 ....70 B5

Marshfield Dr CV4 ....76 D2
Marston Ave CV33 ......123 D2
Marston Cl CV32 ....106 B2
Marston Dr B37 ....33 A3
Marston Green Jun & Inf
 Schs B37 ....44 A7
Marston Hill CV47 ......125 F4
Marston La
 Bedworth CV12 ....39 D5
 Nuneaton CV11 ....39 E8
 Wishaw B76 ....14 E1
Marten Cl CV35 ....108 A7
Marton Cl Coventry CV5 .59 E4
 Stratford-u-A CV37 ....145 A3
Martin La CV22 ....99 B4
Martindale Rd CV7 ......50 C8
Martinique Sq CV34 ....108 D6
Martins Dr CV9 ....12 C1
Martins Rd CV12 ....38 E1
Martlesham Sq B35 .....22 A4
Martley Cl B98 ....103 A4
Martley Croft B91 ....71 B8
Marton Rd
 Birdingbury CV23 ......115 E7
 Long Itchington CV47 ..115 D5
Martyrs' Cl The CV37 ....77 D8
Marwood Cl CV11 ....39 E7
Mary Arden's Ho*
 CV37 ....120 C5
Mary Herbert St CV3 ....77 D7
Mary Slessor St CV3 ....78 F7
Marystow Cl CV5 ....60 B8
Marywell Cl LE10 ....21 C1
Masefield Ave CV34 ....108 C4
Masefield Rd CV37 .....145 A1
Maseley Cl CV37 ....129 C2
Mason Ave CV32 ....106 C3
Mason Cl
 Bidford-on-A B50 ......148 C3
 Redditch B97 ....102 B4
Mason Ct LE10 ....31 B8
Mason La B94 ....69 F1
Mason Rd Coventry CV6 .49 F1
 Redditch B97 ....102 B4
Masons Cl CV37 ....120 C5
Masons Rd CV37 ....144 B2
Masons Way CV37 ....144 B2
Masser Rd CV6 ....49 D4
Massey Sham Ave GL56 .140 C3
Master's Yd CV23 ....115 F7
Mastery Ave CV31 ....110 A4
Mathe Croft CV31 ......110 C5
Matlock Cl CV21 ....83 B4
Matlock Rd CV1 ....61 D3
Matterson Rd CV6 ....61 A5
Matthews Cl CV37 ......145 A2
Maud Rd B46 ....23 D3
Maudslay Rd CV5 ....60 E2
Maureen Cl CV4 ....59 C1
Maurice Mead Ct ◢
 CV31 ....110 A6
Mavor Dr CV12 ....38 D1
Mawby's La DE12 ....3 C4
Mawnan Cl CV7 ....50 B8
Max Rd CV6 ....60 F5
Maxstoke Cl Meriden CV7 46 B1
 Tamworth B77 ....9 B2
Maxstoke Croft B90 .....70 C8
Maxstoke Ct B46 ....34 A2
Maxstoke Gdns CV31 ...109 F6
Maxstoke La Coleshill B46 34 A3
 Meriden CV7 ....46 B2
May Farm Cl B47 ....69 A6
May La Ebrington GL55 .135 E2
 Hollywood B47 ....69 A7
Mayama Rd B78 ....8 C4
Maybird Ctr CV37 ......144 C2
Maybridge Dr B91 ....71 B8
Maybrook Ind Est CV37 144 C2
Maybrook Rd
 Stratford-u-A CV37 ....144 C2
 Sutton Coldfield B76 ..22 A5
Maycock Rd CV6 ....61 D7
Mayfair Dr
 Drayton Bassett B78 ...9 A4
 Nuneaton CV10 ....27 C2
Mayfield B77 ....10 B4
Mayfield Ave CV37 .....145 A2
Mayfield Cl
 Bedworth CV12 ....39 B3
 ◢ Royal Leamington Spa
 CV31 ....110 C6
Mayfield Dr CV7 ....74 B6
Mayfield Rd
 Henley-in-A B95 ....113 A5
 Kenilworth CV8 ....93 C4
Mayfield Rd Coventry CV5 61 A1
 Nuneaton CV11 ....29 B2
 Southam CV47 ....147 A3
Mayflower Dr CV2 ....62 E2
Mayhurst Cl B47 ....69 C6
Mayhurst Rd B47 ....69 B6
Maynard Ave
 Bedworth CV12 ....49 D8
 Warwick CV34 ....108 B2
Mayne Cl CV35 ....114 F3
Mayo Dr CV8 ....92 F3
Mayo Rd CV36 ....149 C4
Mayou's Croft CV6 ....72 B8
Maypole La CV9 ....11 B1
Maypole Rd B79 ....5 C2
Mayswood Rd B95 ......113 A3
Maythorn Ave B76 ....22 A6
Maythorn Gr ◢ B91 .....71 B8
Maytree Cl B37 ....33 A1

Mc Kinnell Cres CV21 ...83 C1
McDonnell Dr CV6 ....49 F6
McMahon Rd CV12 ....49 E8
Mead Cl ◢ GL56 ....140 A3
Mead The OX17 ....133 F2
Meadfoot Rd CV3 ....78 E6
Meadow Cl Ansty CV7 ...51 D3
 Hockley Heath B94 .....88 C6
 Kingsbury B78 ....15 B3
 Lighthorne CV35 ......123 B4
 Royal Leamington Spa
 CV32 ....106 C4
 Stratford-u-A CV37 ....144 B2
 Stretton on D CV23 ....97 A3
 Wolvey LE10 ....41 B2
Meadow Croft Arley CV7 .26 C1
 Wythall B47 ....69 A3
Meadow Crofts CV47 ...124 B5
Meadow Ct CV11 ....29 C3
Meadow Dr
 Hampton-in-A B92 .....57 B7
 Hinckley LE10 ....32 A7
Meadow Gdns CV9 ......12 B2
Meadow Green Prim Sch
 B47 ....69 A3
Meadow Ho ◢ CV1 ......61 B2
Meadow La B94 ....89 D3
Meadow Pleck La B90 ...70 A6
Meadow Rd Alcester B49 143 A3
 Coventry CV6 ....49 B4
 Henley-in-A B95 ....113 B4
 Hurley CV9 ....28 A8
 Nuneaton CV10 ....28 D6
 Rugby CV21 ....82 C3
 Southam CV47 ....147 A3
 Warwick CV34 ....109 A7
 Wolston CV8 ....80 A2
 Wythall B47 ....69 A3
Meadow Rise
 Balsall Common CV7 ...74 C7
 Ullenhall B95 ....112 C6
Meadow St
 Atherstone CV9 ....18 B4
 Coventry CV1 ....151 A2
 Nuneaton CV11 ....29 B5
Meadow Sweet Rd
 CV37 ....144 C3
Meadow View WR11 ....127 F6
Meadow Way
 Fenny Compton CV47 ..133 E7
 Harborough Magna CV23 66 A2
Meadowcroft Cl CV4 .....75 F8
Meadows Sch The CV4 ..59 E3
Meadows The
 Bidford-on-A B50 ......148 B3
 Hinckley LE10 ....32 A7
 Leek Wootton CV35 ....105 A7
Meadowside CV11 ....40 B8
Meadowsweet CV23 .....83 B4
Meadow Way The CV8 ...92 B3
Meadway N CV2 ....62 B6
Meadway The
 Hinckley LE10 ....31 F7
 Redditch B97 ....102 B4
Mearse La B94 ....112 B5
Medhurst Cl CV22 ......100 B3
Medina Rd CV6 ....49 E1
Medland Ave CV3 ....76 F5
Medley Gr CV31 ....109 F3
Meer End Rd CV8 ....74 D1
Meer St CV37 ....145 A2
Meerhill Ave B90 ....71 A6
Meeting House La CV7 ...74 C6
Meeting La B49 ....143 B2
Meir Rd B98 ....103 B4
Melbourne Cl CV11 ......39 E8
Melbourne Ct ◢ CV12 ..38 F2
Melbourne Rd CV5 ......61 A2
Meldrum Ct CV47 ......132 F7
Meldrum Rd CV10 ....28 B6
Melfort Cl Coventry CV3 ..62 F2
 Nuneaton CV10 ....28 C5
Melksham Sq B35 ....22 A4
Mellish Ct CV22 ....82 C1
Mellish Rd CV22 ....82 C1
Mellor Rd CV21 ....101 A4
Mellowdew Rd CV2 ......62 C7
Mellowship Rd CV5 ......59 D5
Mellwaters B77 ....10 B4
Melnberby B77 ....10 B4
Melrose Ave CV12 ......49 D8
Melrose Cl LE10 ....31 B8
Melton Rd CV32 ....106 B4
Melville Cl Bedworth CV7 50 A8
Melville Rd CV1 ....61 A3
Memorial Rd CV47 .....133 D7
Menai Wlk B37 ....33 B4
Mendip Dr CV10 ....28 B3
Mendip Way B77 ....4 B1
Menin Rd CV3 ....78 B8
Meon Cl CV37 ....129 D1
Meon Rd GL55 ....135 C2
Mercer Ave Coventry CV2 62 A5
 Water Orton B46 ....23 A3
Mercer Ct ◢ CV22 .....100 C4
Mercers Mdw CV7 ....49 A6
Merchants Ct ◢ CV32 ..106 A1
Mercia Ave CV8 ....92 F4
Mercia Ho CV1 ....151 B3
Mercia Way CV34 ......109 B8
Mercot Cl B98 ....103 A4
Mercian Way B77 ....4 A2
Mercot Cl B98 ....103 A3
Mercury Ct B77 ....4 A1
Mere Ave B35 ....22 B3
Mere La LE10 ....42 B2

Meredith Rd CV2 ....62 D2
Merestone Cl CV47 .....147 A3
Merevale Ave
 Hinckley LE10 ....31 C7
 Nuneaton CV11 ....29 A4
Merevale Cl CV11 ....29 A4
Merevale La CV9 ....17 C4
Merevale Rd CV9 ....12 B1
Merevale View CV9 ......18 A3
Merganser B77 ....10 A3
Meriden Bsns Pk CV5 ...59 B8
Meriden CE Prim Sch
 CV7 ....46 C1
Meriden Cl B98 ....112 A6
Meriden Dr B37 ....33 A6
Meriden Hill CV7 ....58 B8
Meriden Rd Berkswell CV7 58 C4
 Fillongley CV7 ....46 B4
 Hampton-in-A B92 .....57 C7
Meriden St CV1 ....61 B3
Merlin Ave CV10 ....28 B6
Merlin Cl Birmingham B35 22 A3
 Rugby CV21,CV23 ......83 B4
 Tamworth B77 ....10 A3
Merrick Ct LE10 ....31 F5
Merrifield Gdns LE10 ...31 E5
Merrington Cl ◢ B91 ....71 C8
Merryfield Rd CV5 ......60 E3
Merryfields Way CV2 ....50 F1
Mersey Rd CV12 ....40 A3
Merstone Specl Sch B37 31 A3
Mertens Dr CV22 ....82 C1
Meryndon Ave CV4 ......76 E5
Meschines St CV3 ....77 D6
Metalloys Ind Est B76 ...22 B5
Metcalfe Cl OX15 ....139 E4
Metchley Croft B90 ......70 F6
Mews Rd CV32 ....109 D8
Mews The Atherstone CV9 18 B4
 Bedworth CV12 ....39 B2
 Kenilworth CV8 ....92 E3
 Rugby CV21 ....84 A1
 Wootton Wawen B95 ..113 B2
Mica Cl B77 ....4 A1
Michael Blanning Gdns
 B93 ....71 E3
Michael Drayton Jun Sch
 CV10 ....28 B8
Michaelmas Rd CV3 ....151 B1
Michel Ho CV1 ....151 C4
Michell Cl CV3 ....78 B8
Mickle Mdw B46 ....23 B3
Mickleborough Rd B77 ...9 B3
Mickleton Dr B90 ....70 B8
Mickleton Rd CV5 ....61 B4
Mickleton Cl B98 ....102 C4
Mickleton Dr CV35 .....114 F5
Mickleton Prim Sch
 GL55 ....135 B6
Mickleton Rd
 Coventry CV5 ....77 A8
 Ilmington CV36 ....136 A7
Middleburg Cl CV11 .....30 A1
Middle Bickenhill La B92 45 A4
Middle Hill OX15 ....142 D4
Middle La
 Nether Whitacre B46 ...24 C3
 Shottesswell OX17 .....138 D1
 Wroxton OX15 ....139 B4
Middle Lock La CV35 ....114 E5
Middle Rd CV33 ....123 D7
Middle Ride CV3 ....78 E5
Middle St Ilmington CV36 136 B6
 Tredington CV37 ....136 E7
Middleborough Rd CV1 .151 A4
Middlecotes CV4 ....60 B1
Middlefield Ave B93 .....72 B4
Middlefield Dr CV3 ....63 B1
Middlefield La CV37 ....130 C1
Middlemarch Bsns Pk
 CV3 ....78 C2
Middlemarch Rd
 Coventry CV6 ....61 C7
 Nuneaton CV10 ....28 A5
Middlemarch Sch CV10 .28 B3
Middlemore Cl B80 .....103 B2
Middlesmoor B77 ....10 B4
Middleton Cl CV35 .....138 B6
Middleton Hall* B78 ....21 C2
Middleton La B78 ....13 F6
Middlemarch Bsns Pk
 CV3 ....78 C2
Middletown
 Moreton Morrell CV35 ..122 F3
 Studley B80 ....103 B1
Middletown La B96 .....103 B3
Midland Air Museum*
 CV3 ....78 B3
Midland Oak Trad Est
 CV6 ....49 C2
Midland Rd Coventry CV6 61 E5
 Nuneaton CV21 ....83 A3
Midland Trad Est CV21 ..83 A3
Midpoint Park Ind Est
 B76 ....22 C5
Milburn B77 ....10 B4
Milburn Hill Rd CV4 ......76 B6
Milby Cl CV11 ....30 A1
Milby Ct CV11 ....30 A7
Milby Prim Sch CV11 ...29 F8
Milcote Cl B98 ....103 A4
Milcote Manor Cotts
 CV37 ....129 C6
Milcote Rd CV37 ....129 C6
Mildmay Cl CV37 ....144 C2
Mile End B94 ....87 A2
Mile La CV1 ....151 C1
Mile Tree La CV2 ....50 F7
Milebush Ave B36 ......22 C1

Mil – New 171

Miles Mdw Coventry CV6 ...50 B1
Newbold-on-S CV37 ...130 E1
Milestone Dr CV22 ...99 C4
Milestone Ho 2 CV1 ...61 B2
Milestone Rd CV37 ...130 B8
Milfoil Cl LE10 ...30 F7
Milford Cl Allesley CV5 ...60 B6
Redditch B97 ...102 B3
Milford Ct CV31 ...110 A8
Milford Gr B90 ...71 C7
Milford St CV10 ...29 B2
Milking La B95 ...113 B4
Mill Bank B46 ...25 B2
Mill Bank Mews CV8 ...93 B6
Mill Cl Braunston NN11 ...117 D5
Broom B50 ...148 A4
Coventry CV2 ...50 B3
Hollywood B47 ...69 A7
Norton Lindsey CV35 ...114 C2
Nuneaton CV11 ...29 F1
Southam CV47 ...147 A3
Wolston CV8 ...79 F3
Mill Cotts B50 ...148 A4
Mill Cres Kineton CV35 ...132 B6
Kingsbury B78 ...15 B2
Southam CV47 ...147 A3
Mill Ct CV36 ...149 C3
Mill End CV8 ...93 A6
Mill Farm Cl CV22 ...99 B2
Mill Field CV37 ...128 F2
Mill Hill CV8 ...77 D3
Mill House Cl CV32 ...109 C8
Mill House Dr CV32 ...109 C8
Mill House Terr CV32 ...109 C8
Mill La Alcester B49 ...143 A1
Aston Cantlow B49,B95 ...119 F6
Atherstone CV9 ...19 A3
Barford CV35 ...122 A7
Bentley Heath B93 ...71 F4
Bramcote CV11 ...40 F8
Broom B50 ...148 A4
Bulkington CV12 ...40 A3
Chipping Warden OX17 ...134 F3
Cleeve Prior WR11 ...128 A4
Clifton u D CV23 ...83 C3
Coventry CV3 ...62 F2
Cubbington CV32 ...106 F5
Drayton OX15 ...139 E4
Earlswood B94 ...86 B8
Fazeley B78 ...9 A4
Fenny Compton CV47 ...133 D7
Fillongley CV7 ...36 B3
Great Alne B49 ...119 E6
Halford CV36 ...136 F8
Harbury CV33 ...123 F7
Kineton CV35 ...132 B6
Lapworth B94 ...89 C4
Lowsonford, Finwood
CV35 ...113 E7
Lowsonford, Turner's Green
CV35 ...113 F8
Mickleton GL55 ...135 B6
Newbold-on-S CV37 ...130 F1
Shrewley CV35 ...114 C6
Stratford-u-A CV37 ...145 A1
Tredington CV36 ...136 F6
Welford on A CV37 ...129 A7
Wolvey LE10 ...41 C3
Wythall B47,B94 ...69 B1
Mill Pleck B80 ...103 C2
Mill Pool La B93 ...89 A8
Mill Race La CV6 ...50 B3
Mill Race View CV9 ...12 B1
Mill Rd
Napton on t H CV47 ...125 C8
Royal Leamington Spa
CV31 ...110 A8
Rugby CV21 ...83 B3
Southam CV47 ...147 A3
Mill Row LE10 ...41 C3
Mill St Bedworth CV12 ...39 B3
Coventry CV1 ...151 A3
Harbury CV33 ...123 E7
Kineton CV35 ...132 B6
Nuneaton CV11 ...29 C4
Royal Leamington Spa
CV31 ...110 A7
Shipston-on-S CV36 ...149 C3
Warwick CV34 ...108 F6
Mill Terr CV12 ...39 B5
Mill Wlk CV11 ...29 C4
Millais Cl CV12 ...39 A4
Millbank CV34 ...105 B1
Millbeck CV21 ...83 B4
Millennium Way CV8 ...79 F3
Miller's Bank B50 ...148 A4
Millers Cl Dunchurch CV22 ...99 A2
Lower Boddington NN11 ...134 E6
Welford on A CV37 ...129 B6
Millers Dale Cl CV21 ...83 B4
Millers Gn LE10 ...31 F6
Millers La Hornton OX15 ...139 B8
Monks Kirby CV23 ...53 B2
Millers Rd CV34 ...108 E8
Millers Wharf B78 ...5 A1
Millfield CV31 ...110 A8
Millfield Cl CV37 ...129 D2
Millfield Prim Sch B78 ...9 A4
Millfields Ave CV21 ...100 C4
Millholme Cl CV47 ...147 B2
Millhouse Ct CV6 ...61 F7
Milliners Ct CV9 ...18 B4
Millison Gr B90 ...71 A7
Mills La OX15 ...139 D4
Millway Dr 1 CV33 ...122 F8
Milner Cl CV12 ...40 D2
Milner Cres CV2 ...50 E1
Milner Dr B79 ...4 C4
Milrose Way CV4 ...75 F8
Milton Ave CV34 ...108 C5
Milton Cl Bedworth CV12 ...39 D1
Bentley Heath B93 ...71 F4
Redditch B97 ...102 B4
Milton Rd B93 ...71 F4
Milton St CV2 ...62 A4
Milverton Cres 1 CV32 ...105 E1
Milverton Cres W 3
CV32 ...105 E1
Milverton Ct CV32 ...109 E8
Milverton Hill CV32 ...109 E8
Milverton House Prep Sch
CV11 ...29 D3
Milverton Lodge 2
CV32 ...105 E1
Milverton Prim Sch
CV32 ...105 E1
Milverton Rd
Coventry CV2 ...50 D2
Knowle B93 ...72 C5
Milverton Terr CV32 ...109 E8
Miners Wlk B78 ...4 C1
Minerva Mews B49 ...143 A2
Minions Cl CV9 ...18 B4
Miniva Dr B76 ...13 A2
Minster Cl
Hampton Magna CV35 ...114 F3
Knowle B93 ...72 B8
Minster Rd CV1 ...61 B3
Minton Rd CV2 ...50 E1
Minworth Ind Pk B76 ...22 B5
Minworth Jun & Inf Sch
B76 ...22 D5
Minworth Rd B46 ...23 A3
Mira Dr CV10 ...20 B2
Miranda Cl CV3 ...78 D7
Miranda Dr CV34 ...109 E2
Mistral Cl LE10 ...31 F8
Mitcheldean Cl B98 ...102 C4
Mitchell Ave CV4 ...76 A7
Mitchell Ho Coventry CV4 ...76 A7
Warwick CV34 ...108 E7
Mitchell Rd CV12 ...39 C2
Mitchison Cl CV23 ...117 E8
Mitford Villas GL56 ...140 A3
Moat Ave CV3 ...76 F5
Moat Cl Bubbenhall CV8 ...95 B3
Thurlaston CV23 ...98 C1
Moat Croft
Birmingham B37 ...33 A2
Sutton Coldfield B76 ...22 B7
Moat Dr B78 ...8 C3
Moat Farm Dr
Bedworth CV12 ...49 C8
Rugby CV21 ...101 A4
Moat Farm La B95 ...112 E6
Moat Gn CV35 ...108 A1
Moat House Ct B80 ...103 C4
Moat House La
Coventry CV4 ...76 C7
Shustoke B46 ...25 A1
Moat La LE10 ...41 C3
Mobbs La OX15 ...142 D4
Mockley Wood Rd B93 ...72 B7
Modbury Cl CV3 ...77 D5
Model Village The
CV47 ...115 D3
Molesworth Ave CV3 ...62 A1
Mollington Gr CV35 ...114 F6
Mollington La OX17 ...133 D2
Mollington Rd
Claydon OX17 ...134 B4
Whitnash CV31 ...110 A3
Momus Bvd CV2 ...62 C2
Moncrieff Dr CV31 ...110 C5
Monk's Croft The CV3 ...77 C7
Monks Cl CV22 ...99 A4
Monks Dr B80 ...103 B2
Monks Field Cl CV4 ...60 A1
Monks Kirby La CV23 ...53 C3
Monks Rd
Binley Woods CV3 ...79 C7
Coventry CV1 ...61 F2
Monks Way CV34 ...108 D6
Monkspath B90 ...71 A6
Monkspath Bsns Pk B90 ...70 F8
Monkspath Cl B90 ...70 D7
Monkspath Hall Rd B90 ...71 B7
Monkspath Jun & Inf Sch
B90 ...71 B6
Monkswood Cres CV2 ...62 D8
Monmouth Cl
Coventry CV5 ...60 B3
Kenilworth CV8 ...92 F6
Monmouth Gdns CV10 ...28 E3
Monnington Ho CV8 ...93 B7
Montague Ho CV37 ...145 A2
Montague Rd Rugby CV22 ...99 B3
Warwick CV34 ...109 A8
Montague's Cnr CV37 ...129 A6
Montalt Rd CV3 ...77 E7
Montana Wlk CV10 ...28 E3
Montfort Rd B46 ...33 F5
Montgomery Ave CV35 ...114 F3
Montgomery Cl
Coventry CV3 ...78 C4
Stratford-u-A CV37 ...144 C1
Montgomery Dr CV22 ...82 B1
Montgomery Rd CV31 ...109 F4
Montilo La CV23 ...66 B3
Montjoy Cl CV3 ...78 D7
Montley B77 ...10 B4
Montpelier Ho CV8 ...92 F5
Montpellier Cl CV3 ...77 C6
Montrose Ave CV32 ...106 B5
Montrose Dr
Birmingham B35 ...22 A4
Montrose Dr *continued*
Nuneaton CV10 ...28 F3
Montrose Rd CV22 ...83 A1
Montsford Cl B93 ...71 F6
Monument Way CV37 ...145 A3
Monwode Lea La B46 ...26 A2
Moor Farm Cl CV23 ...96 C3
Moor La
Tamworth, Amington B79 ...4 A3
Willoughby CV23 ...117 B6
Moor Rd CV10 ...28 A8
Moor St CV5 ...60 F1
Moor The B76 ...22 A8
Moor Wood Farm* CV10 ...18 C1
Moorbrooke CV10 ...28 A7
Moorcroft Cl
Nuneaton CV11 ...30 B1
Redditch B97 ...102 A3
Moorcroft Gdns B97 ...102 A3
Moore Cl
Appleby Magna DE12 ...3 C4
Coventry CV6 ...50 A5
Warwick CV34 ...104 E2
Moore Wlk CV34 ...109 C7
Moorend Ave B37 ...33 B2
Moorfield Ave B93 ...71 F6
Moorfield Rd B49 ...143 A2
Moorfield The CV3 ...78 B8
Moorhill Rd CV31 ...110 A3
Moorhills Croft B90 ...70 B8
Moorings The CV31 ...109 D7
Moorlands Ave CV8 ...92 F3
Moorlands Lodge CV8 ...92 F3
Moorpark Cl CV11 ...40 C8
Moorwood Cres CV10 ...28 A8
Moorwood La
Nuneaton CV10 ...27 C4
Nuneaton CV10 ...28 A7
Morar Cl B35 ...22 C4
Moray Cl LE10 ...31 A8
Mordaunt Rd CV35 ...146 C2
Moreall Mdws CV4 ...76 D3
Moreland Croft B76 ...22 B6
Moreton Cl CV37 ...145 B1
Moreton Morrell La
CV35 ...123 B2
Moreton-in-Marsh District
Hospl GL56 ...140 A3
Moreton-in-Marsh Sta
GL56 ...140 A3
Morfa Gdns CV6 ...60 D5
Morgan Cl Arley CV7 ...36 C4
Banbury OX16 ...139 F4
Norton Lindsey CV35 ...114 C2
Studley B80 ...103 C1
Morgan Gr B36 ...22 F1
Morgans Rd CV5 ...59 C4
Morgrove Ave B93 ...71 F6
Morland Cl CV12 ...40 D2
Morland Rd CV6 ...49 C2
Morningside CV5 ...77 B8
Mornington Ct B46 ...34 A4
Morpeth B77 ...9 B4
Morrell St CV32 ...105 F1
Morris Ave CV2 ...62 D4
Morris Cl CV21 ...82 C3
Morris Croft B36 ...22 F1
Morris Dr Banbury OX16 ...139 F4
Nuneaton CV11 ...29 D1
Whitnash CV31 ...110 B2
Morris Hill B78 ...11 A4
Morris Rd NN11 ...117 F2
Morse Rd CV31 ...110 B3
Morson Cres CV21 ...83 C1
Morston B77 ...9 B2
Mortimer Rd CV8 ...92 F2
Morton Cl CV6 ...49 A1
Morton Gdns CV21 ...83 B1
Morton La B97 ...102 A4
Morton Morrell CE Prim Sch
CV35 ...122 F2
Morton St CV32 ...105 F1
Morville Cl B93 ...71 D3
Mosedale
Moreton-in-M GL56 ...140 B3
Rugby CV21 ...83 B4
Moseley Ave CV6 ...61 A4
Moseley Prim Sch CV6 ...61 A4
Moseley Rd CV8 ...93 B3
Moss Cl CV22 ...82 C1
Moss Gr CV8 ...93 B7
Moss La
Mappleborough Green
B98 ...112 A8
Newbold-on-S CV37 ...130 E1
Moss St 12 CV31 ...110 A7
Mossdale B77 ...10 B4
Mossdale Cl CV6 ...61 B6
Mossdale Cres CV10 ...28 F2
Mossop Ct CV37 ...144 C2
Mosspaul Cl CV32 ...105 D2
Mottistone Cl CV3 ...77 D6
Motts Way B46 ...34 A3
Moultrie Rd CV21,CV22 ...83 A2
Mount Cres CV37 ...144 B2
Mount Dr CV12 ...39 A3
Mount Field Ct CV1 ...151 D4
Mount Gdns CV5 ...77 B8
Mount Nod Prim Sch
CV5 ...60 A3
Mount Nod Way CV5 ...60 B3
Mount Pleasant
Bishops Itchington CV47 ...124 A4
Stockton CV47 ...147 C4
Stratford-u-A CV37 ...144 B2
Tamworth B77 ...9 B4
Mount Pleasant Cl
CV47 ...147 C4
Mount Pleasant Cotts
CV2 ...63 A7
Mount Pleasant La B95 ...112 E6
Mount Pleasant Rd CV12 ...39 A3
Mount Pleasant Terr
CV10 ...28 F6
Mount Rd
Henley-in-A B95 ...113 B4
Hinckley LE10 ...31 D8
Mount St Coventry CV5 ...60 F2
Nuneaton CV11 ...29 B4
Mount Street Pas CV11 ...29 B4
Mount The Coventry CV3 ...77 E8
Curdworth B76 ...23 C6
Mountbatten Ave CV8 ...93 C3
Mountbatten Cl CV37 ...144 B1
Mountford Cl CV35 ...146 C2
Mountford Rise CV35 ...123 B2
Mowbray St CV2 ...61 F3
Mowe Croft B37 ...44 B7
Mows Hill Rd B94,B95 ...113 A8
Moxhull Rd B37 ...33 A5
Moyeady Ave CV22 ...100 C4
Moyle Cres CV5 ...59 D4
Much Park St CV1 ...151 C2
Muirfield B77 ...4 B3
Muirfield Cl CV11 ...40 C8
Mulberry Cl CV32 ...106 A2
Mulberry Ct CV37 ...145 A2
Mulberry Dr 5 CV34 ...108 F8
Mulberry Rd Coventry CV6 ...62 A7
Rugby CV22 ...82 A1
Mulberry St CV37 ...145 A2
Mulberry Tree Ctr The
CV37 ...145 A2
Mulberry Way CV10 ...28 A8
Mull Croft B36 ...33 B7
Mullard Dr CV31 ...110 B3
Mullensgrove Rd B37 ...33 A5
Mulliner St CV6 ...61 F5
Mulliners Cl 2 B37 ...33 D2
Muntz Cres B94 ...88 C6
Murcott Ct CV31 ...110 A3
Murcott Rd E CV31 ...110 A3
Murcott Rd W CV31 ...110 A3
Murray Rd Coventry CV6 ...61 A7
Rugby CV21 ...83 A2
Murrayfield Way CV3 ...63 B1
Murrayian Cl CV21 ...83 A2
Murton B77 ...10 B4
Mus of British Road
Transport* CV1 ...151 B3
Musborough Cl B36 ...22 C1
Museum of Arms & Armour*
CV37 ...145 A1
Myatt Rd WR11 ...127 D1
Myatt's Field WR11 ...127 D4
Myers Rd CV21 ...101 B4
Mylgrove CV3 ...77 D3
Mynors Cres B47 ...69 A6
Myrtle Gr CV5 ...60 F1
Mythe La CV9 ...19 A4
Mythe View CV9 ...12 C1
Myton Cres CV34 ...109 C6
Myton Crofts CV31 ...109 D7
Myton Gdns CV34 ...109 A6
Myton La CV34 ...109 C6
Myton Rd CV31,CV34 ...109 B6
Myton Sch CV34 ...109 B6
Mytton Rd B46 ...22 F3

N

Nailcote Ave CV4 ...75 C8
Nailcote La CV7 ...75 A7
Nailer Cl CV21 ...83 B3
Nailsworth Rd B93 ...71 D2
Nairn Cl CV10 ...29 A2
Napier St CV1 ...61 E3
Naples Rd CV35 ...132 E5
Napton Dr CV32 ...106 A2
Napton Gn CV5 ...60 A3
Napton Rd CV47 ...147 C4
Napton Rise CV47 ...147 B2
Narberth Way CV2 ...62 F8
Nares Cl CV22 ...82 C1
Narrow La
Lowsonford B95,CV35 ...113 F6
Stratford-u-A CV37 ...144 C1
Narrows The 1 LE10 ...31 E8
Naseby Cl CV3 ...78 F8
Naseby Rd CV22 ...83 B1
Nash Croft B37 ...44 B8
Nash's La GL55 ...135 E3
Nashes The CV37 ...129 F7
Nathaniel Newton Inf Sch
CV10 ...28 B8
National Agricultural Ctr*
CV8 ...94 A4
National Distribution Pk
B46 ...24 A3
National Ex Ctr B40 ...44 E4
National Herb Ctr*
OX17 ...133 D1
National Motorcycle Mus
The* B92 ...45 A2
Naul's Mill Ho CV1 ...151 B4
Navigation Way CV6 ...62 A8
Naysmyth Rd NN11 ...117 F3
Neal Ct CV2 ...63 A8
Neale Ave CV5 ...60 A6
Neale Cl CV12 ...40 C1
Neale's Cl CV33 ...123 F7
Nebsworth La CV36 ...135 F5
Needhill Cl B93 ...71 F6
Needle Cl B80 ...103 C2
Needlers End La CV7 ...74 A7
Neilston St 13 CV31 ...110 A7
Nellands Cl CV36 ...136 B6
Nelson Ave CV34 ...109 A8
Nelson Cl CV37 ...131 A4
Nelson La CV34 ...109 A8
Nelson St 7 CV1 ...61 E4
Nelson Way CV22 ...82 B1
Nemesia B77 ...4 A2
Nene Cl CV3 ...78 D7
Nene Side Cl NN11 ...126 F6
Nene Wlk NN11 ...117 F1
Nesfield Gr B92 ...57 B7
Nesscliffe Rd CV47 ...132 F5
Netherfield B98 ...103 A4
Nethermill Rd 1 CV6 ...61 A5
Nethersole CE Prim Sch The
B78 ...5 A1
Nethersole St B78 ...5 A1
Netherwood La B93 ...90 A7
Netting St OX15 ...142 D4
Nevada Way B37 ...33 C1
Nevill Cl CV31 ...109 F6
Neville Ct 5 CV34 ...108 E6
Neville Gr CV34 ...104 F1
Neville Rd
Birmingham, Castle Bromwich
B36 ...22 E1
Solihull B90 ...69 F8
Neville Wlk B35 ...22 A2
New Ash Dr CV5 ...59 F5
New Bldgs CV1 ...151 C3
New Broad St CV37 ...144 C1
New Brook St 3 CV32 ...109 E8
New Century Pk CV3 ...62 C2
New Century Way CV11 ...29 B4
New Cl CV35 ...114 F3
New Cotts CV37 ...144 C1
New End Rd B46 ...35 A2
New Gate Ct CV1 ...151 C2
New Hall Jun & Inf Sch
B75 ...13 A5
New Inn La WR11 ...127 D5
New Leasow B76 ...22 A7
New Mill La B78 ...9 A4
New Park Cotts OX15 ...137 F2
New Place & Nash's Ho
(Mus)* CV37 ...145 A1
New Rd
Alderminster CV37 ...130 D3
Appleby Magna DE12 ...3 C4
Ash Green CV7 ...49 B6
Astwood Bank B96 ...118 C8
Coventry CV6 ...48 F1
Ebrington GL55 ...135 E3
Henley-in-A B95 ...113 A4
Hinckley LE10 ...32 A6
Hollywood B47 ...69 A8
Lowsonford CV35 ...113 E6
7 Moreton-in-M GL56 ...140 A3
Norton Lindsey CV35 ...114 C2
Pebworth CV37 ...128 F1
Ratley OX15 ...133 A2
Shotteswell OX17 ...139 E8
Shuttington B79 ...1 B1
Studley B80 ...103 C2
Tamworth B77 ...9 C4
Temple Grafton B49 ...119 E1
Temple Herdewyke CV47 ...133 A6
Water Orton B46 ...23 B3
New Row B78 ...8 C3
New St
Baddesley Ensor CV9 ...11 B1
Bedworth CV12 ...39 C2
Bulkington CV12 ...40 D2
Cubbington CV32 ...106 E5
Dordon B78 ...11 A3
Fazeley B78 ...9 A4
Kenilworth CV8 ...92 F6
Napton on t H CV47 ...125 C7
Polesworth B78 ...10 C4
Royal Leamington Spa
CV31 ...110 A7
Rugby CV22 ...82 C2
Shipston-on-S CV36 ...149 C3
Stratford-u-A CV37 ...144 C1
Tiddington CV37 ...145 C2
Warwick CV34 ...108 E6
New Union St CV1 ...151 B2
Newall Cl CV23 ...83 C3
Newbold & Tredington CE
Prim Sch
Newbold-on-S CV37 ...130 E1
Tredington CV36 ...136 F6
Newbold Cl
Bentley Heath B93 ...71 F5
Coventry CV3 ...62 F1
Newbold Comyn Pk*
CV32 ...110 D8
Newbold Lawn CV32 ...110 A8
Newbold Pl
Royal Leamington Spa
CV32 ...110 A8
Wellesbourne CV35 ...146 C2
Newbold Quarry Ctry Pk*
CV21 ...82 C3
Newbold Rd Rugby CV21 ...82 C3
Wellesbourne CV35 ...146 C3
Newbold Revel Coll CV23 ...65 B3
Newbold Riverside Prim Sch
CV21 ...82 C3
Newbold St CV32 ...110 A8
Newbold Terr CV32 ...110 A8
Newbold Terr E CV32 ...110 B8
Newborough Cl CV9 ...3 A1
Newburgh Cres CV34 ...108 E8

Newburgh Prim Sch CV34 .....108 C4
Newbury Cl **4** CV31 .....110 C6
Newbury Dr CV37 .....144 C1
Newby Cl CV3 .....77 E6
Newby Gr B37 .....33 B5
Newcastle Croft B35 .....22 C3
Newcombe Cl CV22 .....99 B2
Newcombe Rd CV5 .....61 A1
Newcomen Cl CV12 .....38 D1
Newcomen Rd CV12 .....38 D1
Newdegate Pl CV11 .....29 C4
Newdegate St CV11 .....29 C4
Newdigate Prim Sch CV12 .....38 C1
Newdigate Rd
Bedworth CV12 .....39 A3
Coventry CV6 .....61 F6
Sutton Coldfield B75 .....13 A5
Newent Cl B98 .....112 A6
Newey Ave CV12 .....49 D8
Newey Dr CV8 .....93 A2
Newey Rd CV2 .....62 D4
Newfield Ave CV8 .....93 B3
Newfield Rd CV1 .....61 C5
Newgale Wlk CV31 .....110 C7
Newhall Rd CV2 .....62 D7
Newham Gn CV10 .....28 A7
Newhaven Cl CV6 .....60 E6
Newhouse Croft CV7 .....74 B6
Newing Ct WR11 .....127 D4
Newington Cl CV6 .....60 D6
Newington Rd B37 .....44 B8
Newland Cl B98 .....103 A4
Newland La CV7 .....49 B7
Newland Rd Coventry CV1 .....61 D5
Royal Leamington Spa CV32 .....106 C3
Newland St CV22 .....82 C2
Newlands Cl CV13 .....61 F2
Newlands La B37 .....44 A6
Newlands Rd
Baddesley Ensor CV9 .....11 B1
Bentley Heath B93 .....71 F4
Newlands The B80 .....103 B2
Newlyn Cl CV11 .....29 F4
Newman Cl CV12 .....39 B4
Newmarket Cl
Coventry CV6 .....50 B4
Stratford-u-A CV37 .....129 F8
Newmarsh Rd B76 .....22 B6
Newnham Ho B36 .....33 B5
Newnham La B95 .....120 B7
Newnham Rd
Coventry CV1 .....61 F5
Royal Leamington Spa CV32 .....106 B3
Newport Cl B97 .....102 A3
Newport Dr B49 .....143 A2
Newport Rd CV6 .....49 D1
Newquay Cl CV11 .....29 F5
Newscut La OX17 .....134 C1
Newsholme Cl **1** CV34 .....104 C1
Newstead Ave LE10 .....31 D4
Newstead Cl CV11 .....29 F2
Newstead Dr CV47 .....147 A2
Newstead Way CV3 .....63 B1
Newton Cl Coventry CV2 .....62 F7
Hartshill CV10 .....19 A1
Redditch B98 .....103 A3
Newton La Newton CV23 .....68 A2
Newton Regis B79,CV9 .....2 C1
Seckington B79 .....2 A2
Newton Manor La CV21, CV23 .....83 B4
Newton Rd Hinckley LE10 .....30 E7
Knowle B93 .....72 B7
Newton CV23 .....84 A4
Newton Regis CE Prim Sch B79 .....2 B2
Newtown Bldgs CV12 .....39 B3
Newtown Rd
Bedworth CV12 .....39 A2
Nuneaton CV11 .....29 C5
Nibbits La NN11 .....117 E5
Nicholas Chamberlaine Comp Sch CV12 .....39 D3
Nicholas Cl CV12 .....39 C3
Nicholls St CV2 .....61 F4
Nicholson Cl CV34 .....104 F1
Nickson Rd CV4 .....59 E1
Nightingale B77 .....10 A3
Nightingale Ave B36 .....33 A8
Nightingale Cl
Atherstone CV9 .....12 C1
Great Alne B49 .....119 D6
Nightingale Ct CV31 .....110 B8
Nightingale La
Cleeve Prior WR11 .....128 A4
Coventry CV5 .....76 E7
Nimbus B77 .....9 B2
Nine Days La B98 .....103 A3
Nineacres Dr B37 .....33 A3
Ninefoot La B77 .....9 C4
Ninian Pk B77 .....9 B3
Ninian Way B77 .....9 C3
Niton Rd CV10 .....29 D6
Niven Cl CV5 .....60 A6
No Man's Heath La CV9 .....3 A2
Noble Cl CV34 .....108 D5
Noble Dr CV22 .....99 A4
Nod Rise CV5 .....60 B3
Node Hill Cl B80 .....103 B4

Noel Ct
Chipping Campden GL55 .....135 B2
Redditch B97 .....102 B4
Nolan Cl CV6 .....49 D4
Nook The CV11 .....29 E2
Norcombe Gr B90 .....71 A5
Nordic Drift CV2 .....63 A6
Norfolk Cl LE10 .....31 D4
Norfolk Cres CV10 .....28 E4
Norfolk St Coventry CV1 .....61 B3
Royal Leamington Spa CV32 .....106 A1
Norfolk Terr CV4 .....76 B7
Norluck Ct CV36 .....149 C3
Norman Ashman Coppice CV3 .....79 C7
Norman Ave Coventry CV2 .....50 F1
Nuneaton CV11 .....29 B4
Norman Place Rd CV6 .....60 F7
Norman Rd CV21 .....82 C2
Normandy Mdws CV31 .....110 A2
Normandy Cl CV35 .....108 A7
Normandy Way LE10 .....21 C1
North Ave Bedworth CV12 .....39 D2
Birmingham B40 .....44 F5
Coventry CV2 .....62 A3
North Brook Rd CV6 .....60 D8
North Circular Rd GL56 .....140 C4
North Cl CV47 .....147 E5
Cubbington CV32 .....106 E5
Hinckley LE10 .....31 E6
North Leamington Com Sch & Arts Coll CV32 .....105 F4
North Leamington Com Sch & Arts Coll (Sixth Form) CV32 .....105 F2
North St Atherstone CV9 .....18 C4
Coventry CV2 .....62 B5
Kilsby CV23 .....101 C2
Marton CV23 .....115 C7
Nuneaton CV10 .....28 F3
Rugby CV21 .....83 A2
North View CV7 .....51 A1
North Villiers St CV32 .....106 A1
North Warwickshire & Hinkley Coll
Hinckley LE10 .....31 F8
Nuneaton CV11 .....29 E6
North Warwickshire & Hinkley Coll (Atherstone Coll) CV9 .....18 C4
Northampton La CV22 .....99 B2
Northbourne Dr CV11 .....39 F7
Northcote St **4** CV31 .....110 B7
Northcote Wlk CV9 .....12 B1
Northend Rd CV47 .....133 C7
Northey Rd CV6 .....61 D8
Northfield Rd
Coventry CV1 .....61 F2
Hinckley LE10 .....31 C7
Southam CV47 .....147 A2
Northgate CV34 .....108 E7
Northgate St CV34 .....108 E7
Northlands Prim Sch CV21 .....83 A2
Northolt Dr B35 .....22 B3
Northside Cl B98 .....102 C4
Northumberland Ave Nuneaton CV10 .....29 C2
Northumberland Rd
Coventry CV1 .....61 A3
Royal Leamington Spa CV32 .....105 E2
Northvale Cl CV8 .....93 B6
Northway Birmingham B40 .....44 F5
Royal Leamington Spa CV31 .....110 A5
Rugby CV21 .....83 A2
Norton Curlieu La CV35 .....114 C3
Norton Dr CV34 .....104 E2
Norton Grange CV5 .....60 A6
Norton Green La B93 .....72 C2
Norton Hill CV9 .....3 B1
Norton Hill Dr CV2 .....62 E6
Norton La B47,B90,B94 .....69 E3
Norton Lea CV35 .....114 C2
Norton Leys CV22 .....99 C3
Norton Rd B46 .....33 F8
Norton St CV1 .....151 C3
Norton View GL55 .....135 B6
Nortons Cl CV47 .....133 B7
Norval Cres WR11 .....127 D1
Norwich Cl CV11 .....30 A6
Norwich Dr CV3 .....77 B5
Norwood Gr CV2 .....50 E2
Norwood Ho **1** CV32 .....105 F2
Nova Croft CV5 .....59 C4
Nuffield Ho B36 .....33 A8
Nuffield Rd Coventry CV6 .....62 A7
Hinckley LE10 .....30 E7
Nugent Gr B90 .....70 D3
Nuneaton Borough Football Club CV11 .....29 A4
Nuneaton La CV13 .....20 C1
Nuneaton Mus & Art Gal* CV11 .....29 B3
Nuneaton Rd
Bedworth CV12 .....39 B4
Bulkington CV12 .....40 B4
Fillongley CV7 .....36 C2
Furnace End B46,CV10 .....26 B3
Hartshill CV10 .....19 A1
Nuneaton CV10 .....19 B1
Nuneaton St CV11 .....29 C5
Nunts La CV6 .....49 B4
Nunts Park Ave CV6 .....49 B4

O

Oak Ave CV7 .....26 C1
Oak Cl Baginton CV8 .....77 F2
Bedworth CV12 .....39 C4
Hinckley LE10 .....31 E5
Oak Ct Coventry CV3 .....77 F7
Royal Leamington Spa CV32 .....109 E2
Oak Dr CV10 .....28 A8
Oak Farm Cl B36 .....22 A7
Oak Farm Craft Ctr* B78 .....8 A3
Oak Field Gdns CV9 .....18 C4
Oak La Allesley CV5 .....47 E2
Barston B92 .....57 B1
Oak Leigh CV23 .....123 D2
Oak Rd CV37 .....145 C2
Oak Rise B46 .....33 F5
Oak St CV22 .....83 A1
Oak Tree Ave CV3 .....77 A6
Oak Tree Cl
Bentley Heath B93 .....71 E4
Royal Leamington Spa CV32 .....106 A2
Oak Tree La Cookhill B49 .....118 D5
Hollywood B47 .....69 B6
Sambourne B96 .....103 A1
Oak Tree Rd Coventry CV3 .....79 A7
Harvington WR11 .....127 C4
Oak Trees B47 .....69 A6
Oak Way CV4 .....59 D2
Oakdale Rd CV3 .....79 C7
Oakdene Cl CV35 .....113 F3
Oakdene Cres
Hatton CV35 .....114 C5
Nuneaton CV10 .....29 D7
Oakdene Ct CV37 .....144 C2
Oakenhayes Cres B76 .....22 C5
Oakey Cl CV6 .....49 F4
Oakfield Ho CV3 .....63 A1
Oakfield Jun Sch CV9 .....18 C4
Oakfield Prim Sch CV22 .....82 C1
Oakfield Rd Coventry CV6 .....60 F5
Rugby CV22 .....82 C1
Oakfields Way B91 .....56 B5
Oakford Dr CV5 .....59 F6
Oakhall Dr B93 .....71 F4
Oakham Cl B98 .....103 A3
Oakham Cres CV12 .....40 D2
Oakham La NN11 .....126 D8
Oakham Rd GL56 .....141 A1
Oakington Ho B35 .....22 A2
Oaklands B76 .....23 B5
Oaklands Croft B76 .....22 B7
Oaklands Ct CV8 .....93 A2
Oaklands The
Birmingham B37 .....44 A7
Coventry CV4 .....60 A2
Oaklea Dr CV8 .....93 A3
Oakley CV8 .....73 F1
Oakley Ct CV12 .....38 D1
Oakley Wood Rd CV33 .....122 F7
Oakmoor Rd CV6 .....50 A4
Oakridge Rd CV32 .....106 C4
Oakroyd Cres CV10 .....28 D7
Oaks Pl CV6 .....50 A3
Oaks Prec CV8 .....92 E3
Oaks Rd CV8 .....92 E2
Oaks The Bedworth CV12 .....38 F2
Royal Leamington Spa CV32 .....109 D8
Sutton Coldfield B76,B73 .....13 A3
Oakthorpe Dr B37 .....33 A5
Oakwell Cl CV34 .....104 E2
Oakwood Cl Bearley CV37 .....120 D7
Moreton Morrell CV35 .....122 E3
Oaktree Farm Mobile Homes Pk B94 .....86 B7
Oakwood Cr CV9 .....11 B1
Oakwood Gr CV34 .....105 A1
Oakwood Rd B47 .....69 A6
Oakworth Cl CV2 .....62 F8
Oaston Rd CV11 .....29 D4
Oatlands Cl CV6 .....49 C4
Oban Dr CV10 .....29 A2
Oban Rd Coventry CV6 .....49 F5
Hinckley LE10 .....31 A7
Oberon Cl Nuneaton CV11 .....30 A1
Royal Leamington Spa CV32 .....109 E4
Rugby CV22 .....99 B4
Occupation Rd CV2 .....62 C3
Oddfellows' Terr **2** GL56 .....140 A3
Oddicombe Croft CV3 .....77 D5
Odingsel Dr CV47 .....115 C4

Odstone Dr LE10 .....30 F8
Offa Dr CV8 .....93 A4
Offa Rd CV31 .....110 B5
Offchurch La CV31 .....110 F6
Offchurch Rd CV33 .....124 B6
Offenham CE Fst Sch WR11 .....127 D1
Ogley Dr B75 .....13 A5
Okeford Way CV10 .....29 A1
Okehampton Rd CV3 .....77 E5
Okement Gr CV23 .....82 A3
Olaf Pl CV4 .....108 D7
Oken Rd CV34 .....108 D8
Olaf Pl CV2 .....63 A7
Old Bowling Gn The CV36 .....149 C3
Old Brewery Cl CV36 .....137 A4
Old Budbrooke Rd CV35 .....108 A8
Old Church Rd
Coventry CV5 .....50 A1
Water Orton B46 .....23 B3
Old Courtyard The CV33 .....107 B4
Old Crown Mews CV2 .....50 D5
Old Damson La B92 .....44 A2
Old Dickens Heath Rd B90 .....70 A5
Old Farm Rd B36 .....25 A3
Old Farm Rd CV9 .....18 C3
Old Ford Ave CV47 .....147 A3
Old Forge Bsns Ctr B98 .....103 B4
Old Forge Dr B98 .....103 B4
Old Forge Rd
Fenny Drayton CV13 .....20 A3
Great Rollright OX7 .....142 A2
Old Gated Rd The CV33, CV35 .....123 C4
Old Gram School Mews GL55 .....135 B2
Old Green La CV8 .....73 C1
Old Hall Ct B79 .....2 B2
Old Hedging La B77 .....9 B3
Old Hinckley Rd CV10 .....29 D5
Old Holly La CV9 .....18 C2
Old House La CV7 .....48 A7
Old Kingsbury Rd B76 .....22 C5
Old La B48 .....85 D4
Old Langley Hall B75 .....13 A4
Old Leicester Rd CV21 .....83 A4
Old Manor Cl B78 .....4 B2
Old Manor Gdns GL55 .....135 A6
Old Meeting Yd CV12 .....39 B3
Old Mill Ave CV4 .....76 D5
Old Mill Rd B46 .....33 F7
Old Milverton CV32 .....105 C3
Old Milverton La CV32 .....105 C3
Old Milverton Rd CV32 .....105 C2
Old Orchard The
Birdingbury CV23 .....115 F7
Ettington GL55 .....135 E3
Old Pean's Yd CV12 .....39 A2
Old Rd
Bishops Itchington CV47 .....124 B4
Braunston NN11 .....117 A6
Meriden CV7 .....46 C1
Ratley OX15 .....132 F2
Shipston-on-S CV36 .....149 C3
Southam CV47 .....147 A2
Old Rectory Cl CV33 .....123 B7
Old Rectory Gdn B49 .....143 A2
Old Rectory La CV37 .....130 A6
Old Red Lion Ct CV37 .....145 A1
Old School Cl WR11 .....127 D1
Old School End OX15 .....142 D4
Old School La
Hampton Magna CV35 .....114 F3
Lighthorne CV35 .....123 C2
Wilmcote CV37 .....120 C4
Old School Mews CV32 .....106 B3
Old School Yd The CV36 .....149 C3
Old School Yd The B77 .....4 A3
Old Snitterfield Dr CV37 .....120 E7
Old Sq CV34 .....108 E6
Old Sta Yd CV47 .....141 B1
Old Station Rd B92 .....57 A8
Old Stone Yd CV32 .....105 E1
Old Town
24 Moreton-in-M GL56 .....140 A3
Royal Leamington Spa CV32 .....109 D8
Old Town Mews CV37 .....144 C1
Old Tramway Wlk CV37 .....145 A1
Old Tree La CV35 .....114 C5
Old Vicarage Gdns B80 .....103 C2
Old Walled Gdn The CV35 .....131 E7
Old Warwick Rd
Lapworth B94,CV35 .....89 D3
Rowington CV35 .....114 A7
Royal Leamington Spa CV31 .....110 A6
Old Waste La CV7 .....74 E6
Old Winnings Rd CV7 .....48 F8
Oldany Way CV10 .....28 F2
Oldberrow Cl **4** B90 .....71 A6
Oldborough Dr CV35 .....130 E8
Oldbury Rd Hartshill CV10 .....18 C2
Nuneaton CV10 .....28 A8
Oldbury View CV10 .....18 C2
Oldbutt Rd CV36 .....149 C3
Oldfield Rd CV5 .....60 B3
Oldham Ave CV2 .....62 E4
Oldham Way CV3 .....114 C5
Oldington Gr B91 .....71 B8
Oldwich La E Honiley CV8 .....90 C8
Knowle CV8 .....73 D1
Oldwich La W B93 .....90 C8

Olive Ave CV2 .....62 D5
Oliver St Coventry CV6 .....61 F6
Rugby CV21 .....82 C2
Olivers Lock CV37 .....145 A2
Olivier Way CV2 .....63 B8
Olney Rd CV35 .....132 D3
Olton Ave CV5 .....59 E4
Olton Cl CV11 .....41 A4
Olton Pl CV11 .....28 E4
Olympus Ave CV34 .....109 D5
Olympus Cl CV5 .....59 B8
Omar Rd CV2 .....62 D2
Ombersley Cl B98 .....103 B4
Olaf Pl CV47 .....63 A7
Omega Pl **1** CV21 .....83 A2
Onley La CV22 .....100 B3
Onley Terr CV4 .....76 C7
Onslow Croft CV32 .....109 E3
Openfield Croft B46 .....23 C2
Ophelia Dr CV34 .....109 E3
Oratory Dr CV3 .....78 C6
Orchard Cl Austrey CV9 .....3 A1
Badby NN11 .....126 F6
Bidford-on-A B50 .....148 B2
Bishops Itchington CV47 .....124 B4
Bubbenhall CV8 .....95 B3
Coleshill B46 .....33 F7
Curdworth B76 .....23 B7
Hinckley LE10 .....32 A5
Hurley CV9 .....16 B2
Lower Brailes OX15 .....137 F2
Mickleton GL55 .....135 C7
Nuneaton CV10 .....28 B7
Polesworth B78 .....5 A2
Salford OX7 .....150 C2
Shipston-on-S CV36 .....149 C3
Tamworth B77 .....9 B3
Welford on A CV37 .....129 B6
Witherley CV9 .....19 A4
Wolvey LE10 .....41 B2
Orchard Cres CV3 .....77 E8
Orchard Ct Atherstone CV9 .....18 B4
Coventry CV3 .....63 A1
Lower Quinton CV37 .....129 D2
Orchard Dr Alcester B49 .....143 A2
Coventry CV5 .....59 C4
Orchard Gr
Astwood Bank B96 .....118 C8
Stockton CV47 .....147 C4
Orchard Ho CV6 .....50 A4
Orchard La CV8 .....93 C3
Orchard Meadow Wlk B35 .....22 B3
Orchard Piece OX17 .....134 A2
Orchard Pl
Clifford Chambers CV37 .....129 F7
Harvington WR11 .....127 D4
Redditch B80 .....103 C4
Orchard Rd
Hockley Heath B94 .....88 C6
Hook Norton OX15 .....142 D4
Orchard Ret Pk CV3 .....78 C4
Orchard Rise CV9 .....11 B1
Orchard St Bedworth CV12 .....39 B4
Hinckley LE10 .....31 E8
Nuneaton CV11 .....29 D4
Orchard The
Baxterley CV9 .....17 B4
Lower Quinton CV37 .....129 D2
Marton CV23 .....115 C7
Staverton NN11 .....126 D8
Upper Boddington NN11 .....134 E8
Whatcote CV36 .....137 E7
Orchard View OX17 .....134 C1
Orchard Way
Hollywood B47 .....69 A8
Long Itchington CV47 .....115 C4
Nuneaton CV10 .....28 C6
Rugby CV22 .....99 B4
Southam CV47 .....147 A3
Stratford-u-A CV37 .....144 C1
Stretton on D CV23 .....96 C3
Studley B80 .....103 C1
Orchards The
Astwood Bank B96 .....102 B1
Cheswick Green B90 .....70 D4
Hollywood B47 .....69 A7
Newton CV23 .....84 A4
Orchid Way CV23 .....83 B4
Ordnance Rd CV6 .....61 E5
Orford Cl B35 .....146 C2
Orford Rise CV10 .....27 C2
Oriel Gr GL56 .....140 B3
Oriel Ho B37 .....33 A3
Orion Cres CV2 .....50 E2
Orkney Cl CV10 .....29 A2
Orkney Croft B36 .....33 B7
Orkney Dr B77 .....9 C4
Orlando Cl CV21 .....99 B3
Orlescote Rd CV4 .....76 E6
Orpington Dr CV6 .....49 D4
Orrian Cl CV37 .....144 C3
Orsino Cl CV34 .....109 E2
Orson Leys CV22 .....99 B4
Orton Cl B46 .....23 A3
Orton Hill CV9 .....6 C4
Orton La Austrey CV9 .....6 B3
Orton-on-t-H CV9 .....6 C1
Twycross CV9 .....6 B2
Orton Rd Coventry CV6 .....49 D4
Warton B79 .....5 C2
Orton Way B35 .....22 A2
Orwell Cl Clifton u D CV23 .....84 A3
Nuneaton CV10 .....27 C2
Orwell Ct CV1 .....151 C4
Orwell Rd CV1 .....61 F1
Osbaston Cl CV5 .....59 E4
Osborne Ct CV31 .....110 A4

Osborne Rd CV5 .....77 A8
Oslo Gdns CV2 .....63 A7
Osney Cl OX15 .....142 D4
Osprey B77 .....10 A3
Osprey Cl Coventry CV2 .....63 B6
　Nuneaton CV11 .....40 B8
Ossets Hole La CV35 .....113 E4
Oswald Rd CV32 .....109 D8
Oswald Way CV22 .....82 A2
Oswestry Cl B97 .....102 B4
Oswin Gr CV2 .....62 C4
Othello Ave CV34 .....109 F3
Othello Cl CV22 .....99 B3
Otter Cl B98 .....112 A6
Otters Rest CV31 .....110 C5
Ottery B77 .....10 A3
Our Lady & St Teresa's RC
　Prim Sch CV32 .....106 D5
Our Lady of the Angels RC Inf
　Sch CV11 .....29 C3
Our Lady of the Assumption
　RC Prim Sch CV4 .....59 E1
Our Lady of the Wayside RC
　Prim Sch B90 .....70 C8
Our Lady's RC Prim Sch
　Alcester B49 .....143 A3
　Princethorpe CV23 .....96 B1
Ousterne La CV7 .....36 B2
Outermarch Rd CV6 .....61 C7
Outlands Dr LE10 .....21 C1
Outwood Cl B98 .....102 C4
Outwoods Cl CV9 .....108 B4
Oval Rd CV22 .....100 B4
Over St CV6 .....62 A8
Overbare Cl B94 .....87 A1
Overberry Cl CV2 .....50 D2
Overberry Orch 5 CV23 .....122 E8
Overdale 102 C4
Overdale Rd CV5 .....60 C3
Overell Gr CV32 .....105 D2
Overslade Cres CV6 .....60 E8
Overslade Manor Dr
　CV22 .....99 C4
Oversley Rd B76 .....22 A6
Overstone Rd CV7 .....52 C3
Overton Dr B46 .....23 C3
Overtons Cl CV31 .....110 F5
Overwoods Rd B77 .....10 A3
Owen Cl CV9 .....18 B4
Owen Sq CV9 .....18 B4
Owenford Rd CV6 .....61 C7
Owl End La NN11 .....134 E7
Owl End Way NN11 .....134 E7
Owlets End B50 .....148 C2
Ox Cl CV2 .....62 A6
Ox Leys Rd B75,B76 .....13 D3
Oxendon Way CV3 .....78 E8
Oxford Cl CV11 .....29 D4
Oxford Pl 2 CV32 .....105 F1
Oxford Rd Marton CV23 .....115 D7
　Princethorpe CV8,CV23 .....96 B2
　Ryton-on-D CV8 .....78 F1
Oxford Row 14 CV32 .....105 F1
Oxford St Coventry CV1 .....61 E3
　Moreton-in-M GL56 .....140 A3
　Royal Leamington Spa
　CV32 .....105 F1
　Rugby CV21 .....83 B2
　Southam CV47 .....147 A2
Oxford Way CV35 .....146 A1
Oxhayes Cl CV7 .....74 C6
Oxhey Hill OX17 .....134 B2
Oxhill Bridle Rd CV35 .....131 E3
Oxhill Rd CV35 .....144 B4
Oxley Dr CV3 .....77 C3
Oxstall Cl B76 .....22 D5
Oxway Cl CV36 .....149 C3

P

Packington Ave CV5 .....60 B6
Packington La
　Coleshill B46 .....34 A1
　Little Packington CV7 .....45 C6
　Maxstoke B46 .....35 A1
　White Stitch CV7 .....46 A3
Packington Pl 6 CV31 .....110 A7
Packmore St CV34 .....108 F8
Packmores B90 .....70 A5
Packsaddle Hill CV37 .....145 C4
Packwood Ave CV21 .....101 B4
Packwood Cl
　Bentley Heath B93 .....71 E4
　Nuneaton CV11 .....39 F8
　Royal Leamington Spa
　CV31 .....110 C5
Packwood Cotts B93 .....71 F1
Packwood Gn CV5 .....60 A3
Packwood Ho 7 B94 .....89 A5
Packwood Mews 5
　CV34 .....109 B8
Packwood Rd B94 .....89 A7
Paddiford Pl CV10 .....28 C3
Paddock Cl
　Bidford-on-A B50 .....148 B3
　Napton on the H CV47 .....125 C8
Paddock La Redditch B98 .....102 C4
　Coventry CV1 .....144 C1
Paddock The
　Claybrooke Magna LE17 .....43 C3
　Lower Boddington NN11 .....134 E7
　Newton CV23 .....68 A1
Paddocks Cl
　Polesworth B78 .....4 C1

Paddocks Cl continued
　Wolston CV8 .....80 A2
Paddocks The
　Bulkington CV12 .....40 B3
　Kenilworth CV8 .....93 B5
　Mollington OX17 .....133 F2
　Norton WR11 .....127 B2
　Stretton on D CV23 .....96 C3
　Tamworth B77 .....108 F7
Paddox Cl CV22 .....100 C4
Paddox Prim Sch
　Rugby CV22 .....100 B4
　Rugby CV22 .....100 C4
Padgate Cl B35 .....22 B3
Padmore Cl CV31 .....110 B6
Padstow Cl CV11 .....29 F5
Padstow Rd CV4 .....75 E8
Padua CV37 .....145 A2
Page Rd CV4 .....57 E7
Pages La CV15 .....139 B7
Paget Cl CV8 .....50 B3
Paget's La CV8 .....95 B3
Pailton Cl CV2 .....50 C2
Pailton Rd CV23 .....66 A2
Painswick Cl B98 .....102 C3
Pake's Croft 3 CV6 .....61 A5
Palefield Rd B90 .....70 F6
Palermo Ave CV3 .....77 E6
Pallett Dr CV11 .....29 F7
Palm Tree Ave CV2 .....50 C2
Palmer La CV1 .....151 B3
Palmer Rd CV31 .....110 B4
Palmer's Cl CV21 .....101 A4
Palmers Lane CV35 .....132 B6
Palmerston Rd CV5 .....76 F8
Pampas Cl CV37 .....144 C3
Pancras Cl CV4 .....50 E1
Pandora Rd CV2 .....62 F8
Pangbourne Cl CV11 .....29 F8
Pangbourne Rd CV2 .....62 C8
Pangfield Pk CV5 .....60 C4
Pantolf Pl CV21 .....82 C4
Papenham Gn CV4 .....76 A8
Parade CV32 .....109 F7
Parade The
　Birmingham B37 .....33 A5
　6 Hinckley LE10 .....31 D8
　Nuneaton CV11 .....29 C3
Paradise Ho 4 CV6 .....61 F7
Paradise St
　Coventry CV1 .....151 C1
　Rugby CV21 .....83 B2
　Warwick CV34 .....108 F8
Paradise Way CV2 .....51 B1
Paradise Works CV6 .....61 F7
Paragon Way CV7 .....50 B8
Parbrook Cl CV4 .....75 E8
Parbury B77 .....9 B3
Parisienne Ho CV5 .....60 F2
Park Ave Coleshill B46 .....33 F6
　Coventry CV6 .....49 C3
　Nuneaton CV11 .....29 E3
　Polesworth B78 .....11 A4
　Studley B80 .....103 C2

Park Cl
　Avon Dassett CV47 .....133 C4
　Claverdon CV35 .....113 F3
　Hanwell OX17 .....139 F6
　Hook Norton OX15 .....142 D4
　Kenilworth CV8 .....93 B5
　Wilmcote CV37 .....120 C4
Park Croft B47 .....69 A5
Park Farm CV22 .....82 B1
Park Farm Ind Est B98 .....103 B4
Park Gates CV33 .....11 C4
Park Gr B46 .....23 C2
Park Hall WR11 .....127 E6
Park Hall Cres B36 .....22 C1
Park Hall Sch B36 .....22 E1
Park Hill
　Hook Norton OX15 .....142 D4
　Kenilworth CV8 .....93 B5
　Lower Shuckburgh NN11 .....116 F1
Park Hill Jun Sch CV8 .....93 C5
Park Hill La Allesley CV5 .....60 A6
　Coventry CV5 .....60 A5
Park Hill Prim Sch CV8 .....60 A4
Park La Astley CV10 .....37 B3
　Berkswell CV7 .....58 B2
　Birmingham, Castle Vale
　B35 .....22 C4
　Great Alne B49 .....119 D6
　Harbury CV33 .....123 F6
　Ilmington CV36 .....135 C5
　Lower Shuckburgh NN11 .....116 F1
　North Newington OX15 .....139 E2
　Nuneaton CV10 .....27 C2
　Snitterfield CV37 .....121 C6
　Southam CV47 .....147 A2
Park Lane Prim Sch
　CV10 .....27 C2
Park Paling The CV3 .....77 E7
Park Piece CV35 .....132 B6
Park Rd
　Baddesley Ensor CV9 .....11 A1
　Bedworth CV12 .....39 B2
　Chipping Campden GL55 .....135 A1
　Coleshill B46 .....33 F6
　Coventry CV1 .....151 B1
　Hinckley LE10 .....31 E8

Park Rd continued
　Hook Norton OX15 .....142 D4
　Kenilworth CV8 .....93 B6
　Polesworth B78 .....11 A4
　Royal Leamington Spa
　CV32 .....106 A4
　Rugby CV21 .....83 A2
　Stratford-u-A CV37 .....144 C2
　Tamworth B77 .....9 B3
Park Sq B37 .....44 D8
Park St Coventry CV6 .....61 E7
　Nuneaton CV11 .....29 D3
　Royal Leamington Spa
　CV32 .....105 F1
Park The CV35 .....137 F3
Park View Cookhill B96 .....118 F3
　Coventry CV3 .....62 B2
　Hockley Heath B94 .....88 C6
Park View Cl CV7 .....50 A8
Park Wood La CV4 .....75 D7
Parkend CV21 .....83 D7
Parkers La GL56 .....140 A3
Parkes St CV34 .....108 D7
Parkfield B93 .....72 A1
Parkfield Cres B77 .....9 B4
Parkfield Cl B77 .....9 B4
Parkfield Dr
　Birmingham B36 .....22 C1
　Kenilworth CV8 .....93 B5
Parkfield Rd Coleshill B46 .....33 F6
　Keresley CV7 .....49 A6
　Rugby CV21 .....82 C3
Parkfields CV47 .....147 A2
Parkgate Prim Sch CV6 .....49 B3
Parkgate Rd CV6 .....49 C3
Parkhill Dr CV5 .....60 A5
Parkinson Dr CV9 .....12 C1
Parkland Cl CV6 .....49 C3
Parklands Ave CV32 .....106 C4
Parkside CV1 .....151 C2
Parkside Cl LE10 .....31 E8
Parkstone Rd CV6 .....49 F7
Parkville Cl CV6 .....49 C3
Parkville Highway CV6 .....49 B3
Parkway CV2 .....63 B8
Parkwood Ct CV8 .....93 B5
Parmington Cl B97 .....102 A3
Parmiter Ho CV32 .....105 F2
Parnell Cl CV21 .....82 C2
Parolles Cl CV34 .....109 D6
Parr Cl CV34 .....109 D6
Parrish Cl CV35 .....50 D5
Parry Rd CV2 .....62 C7
Parson St B77 .....9 C4
Parson's La LE10 .....31 F8
Parson's Nook CV2 .....62 A5
Parsonage Cl 3 CV37 .....145 A2
Parsons Cl CV36 .....149 C3
Parsons Hollow B77 .....9 C4
Parsons Rd NN11 .....117 F3
Partridge Cl

Partridge Cl continued
　Charwelton NN11 .....126 D3
Partridge Croft CV6 .....50 A1
Partridge La B97 .....102 A4
Partridge Rd CV37 .....144 B2
Patch La B98 .....102 C3
Paterson Ct B93 .....72 C6
Paterson Dr CV34 .....109 F3
Patricia Cl CV4 .....59 C1
Pattens Rd CV34 .....105 B1
Patterdale CV21 .....83 B8
Patterton Dr B76 .....22 A7
Pattison Cl CV34 .....105 C1
Paul Stacy Ho CV1 .....151 D4
Pauline Ave CV6 .....50 B2
Pavilion The B77 .....4 A2
Pavilion Way CV5 .....60 E4
Paxmead Cl CV6 .....49 A2
Paxton Rd CV6 .....61 A2
Payne's La CV1 .....61 F3
Paynell Cl CV6 .....49 B2
Paynes La CV21 .....82 B2
Payton St CV37 .....145 A2
Peace Wlk B37 .....33 B1
Peacock Ave CV2 .....50 F1
Peacock Ct CV35 .....146 D2
Peacock La CV35 .....138 C7
Peacocks The CV10 .....108 B2
Peake Ave CV11 .....29 E7
Pear Tree Ave
　Kingsbury B78 .....15 B3
　Nuneaton CV10 .....28 E6
Pear Tree Ct
　Chipping Campden GL55 .....135 B1
　4 Coventry CV2 .....50 B2
　Shuttington B79 .....4 C4
Pear Tree Way CV22 .....82 A1
Pearl Hyde Ho 4 CV1 .....151 C4
Pearl Hyde Prim Sch
　CV2 .....63 A5
Pearmans Croft B47 .....69 A6
Pears Cl CV8 .....92 F5
Pearson Ave CV6 .....50 B2
Peart Dr B80 .....103 B2
Peartrees CV47 .....133 B7
Peat Cl CV22 .....82 C1
Pebble Cl B77 .....4 A2
Pebble Island Way
　CV31 .....110 C5
Pebblebrook Way CV12 .....39 C1
Pebworth Ave B90 .....71 B6
Pebworth Cl CV5 .....60 B3
Pebworth Dr CV35 .....114 F6
Pebworth Fst Sch CV37 .....128 F1

Peddimore La B76 .....22 C7
Pedmore Cl B98 .....103 A4
Peel Cl Coventry CV6 .....61 E6
　Drayton Bassett B78 .....8 C3
　Hampton-in-A B92 .....57 B6
Peel La CV6 .....61 E5
Peel Rd CV34 .....108 E8
Peel St CV6 .....61 E6
Pegasus Prim Sch B35 .....22 B3
Pegmill Cl CV3 .....77 F8
Pelham La B49 .....119 C5
Pembridge Rd B93 .....71 E3
Pembroke Cl
　Bedworth CV12 .....38 C1
　1 Warwick CV34 .....108 F8
Pembroke Ct B CV32 .....105 F2
Pembroke Gdns CV35 .....146 B1
Pembroke Way CV11 .....29 D3
Pemdon Rd CV6 .....49 C2
Pembury Ave CV6 .....50 A3
Penarth Gr CV3 .....78 E8
Pencraig Cl CV8 .....93 C5
Penders Cl CV6 .....62 A8
Penderel Ct CV6 .....60 E4
Pendicke Ct CV47 .....147 A2
Pendicke St CV47 .....147 A2
Pendigo Way
　Birmingham B40 .....44 E3
　Birmingham B40 .....44 E4
Pendine Ct 4 CV32 .....109 D8
Pendred Rd CV22 .....82 C2
Pendrell Cl B37 .....33 A3
Penelope Cl CV33 .....123 F6
Penfold Cl 3 CV33 .....122 F8
Penmire Cl CV9 .....11 B2
Penn Ho CV4 .....59 F1
Penn La
　Tanworth-In-A B94 .....86 C4
　Wibtoft LE17 .....43 B1
Pennant Rd LE10 .....31 D5
Pennine Way
　Nuneaton CV10 .....28 B3
　Tamworth B77 .....10 A4
Pennington Mews 4
　.....82 C2
Pennington St 1 CV21 .....82 C2
Penns Cl CV32 .....106 E5
Penns La B46 .....33 F7
Penny Park La CV6 .....49 A3
Pennyford La B95 .....113 B1
Pennymoor Rd B77 .....10 A4
Pennystone Cl CV31 .....110 C6
Penrhyn Cl OX16 .....139 F4
Penrith Cl Coventry CV6 .....49 C2
　Royal Leamington Spa
　CV32 .....105 C2
Penrith Gr B37 .....33 C2
Penrose Cl CV4 .....76 A7
Penryhn Cl CV8 .....93 C5
Penryn Cl CV11 .....30 A4
Pensham Croft B90 .....71 A6
Penshaw Way 2 CV1 .....61 E4
Pentire Cl CV11 .....29 F5
Penzance Way CV11 .....30 A5
Pepper La CV1 .....151 B2
Pepys Cnr CV4 .....59 C2
Perch Ave B37 .....33 A3
Perchfoot Cl CV1 .....151 C1
Percival Dr CV33 .....123 F6
Percival Rd CV22 .....100 D4
Percy Cres CV8 .....92 E2
Percy Rd Kenilworth CV8 .....92 E2
　Warwick CV34 .....108 E8
Percy St Coventry CV1 .....151 A3
　Stratford-u-A CV37 .....145 A2
Percy Terr 5 CV32 .....105 D1
Peregrine Dr CV5 .....60 A5
Perimeter Rd
　Birmingham B40 .....44 D4
　Birmingham B40 .....44 E4
Periwinkle Cotts WR11 .....127 F6
Perkins Cl Hornton OX15 .....139 B8
　Salford Priors WR11 .....127 E6
Perkins Gr CV21 .....83 C1
Permian Cl CV21 .....83 B3
Perry Mill La B95 .....112 E6
Perryfields Cl B98 .....102 C3
Perryford Dr B91 .....71 C8
Perryman Dr B78 .....15 C4
Perrymill La B95 .....112 E6
Pershore Pl CV4 .....76 E6
Perth Rise CV5 .....60 A4
Petard Cl B77 .....9 B4
Peter Hall La CV7,CV23 .....64 A3
Peterbrook Cl B98 .....102 C4
Peterbrook Rd B90 .....69 E8
Peterlee Wlk 8 CV2 .....63 A7
Peters Wlk CV6 .....50 A4
Petitor Cres CV2 .....50 C1
Peto Gr CV34 .....109 F2
Pettiford La B95 .....113 C3
Pettiphers Farm CV37 .....129 A7
Pettifer Cres CV21 .....83 C1
Pettyfields Cl B93 .....72 A5
Peveril Dr CV3 .....77 B5
Peyto Cl CV6 .....49 D3
Pheasant Cl
　Bedworth CV12 .....38 D1
　Stratford-u-A CV37 .....144 B2
Pheasant Croft B36 .....33 A8
Pheasant La B98 .....102 C4
Pheasant Oak CV4 .....59 C2
Philip Cl
　1 Royal Leamington Spa
　CV31 .....109 F6

Philip Ct continued
　10 Rugby CV21 .....83 A2
Philip Docker Ct CV12 .....40 B2
Phillippes Rd 6 CV34 .....104 F1
Phipps Ave CV21 .....83 C1
Phoenix Bsns Pk LE10 .....30 E8
Phoenix Ho CV1 .....151 C4
Phoenix Pk Ind Est CV7 .....50 B2
Phoenix Way CV6 .....49 E3
Piccadilly B78 .....9 C1
Piccadilly Cl B37 .....33 C1
Piccadilly Cres B78 .....9 C1
Pickard Cl CV21 .....83 C4
Pickford Grange La CV5 .....59 C7
Pickford Green La CV5 .....59 C7
Pickford Way CV5 .....60 B6
Picton Croft 6 B37 .....33 D2
Piers Cl CV34 .....108 F8
Pike Cl LE10 .....31 D5
Pike Dr B37 .....33 C3
Pikehorne Croft B36 .....22 D2
Pikers La CV7 .....48 A3
Pilgrims Gate LE10 .....32 A6
Pilgrims La CV23 .....67 C1
Pilkington Rd CV5 .....76 D8
Pill La GL56 .....140 F1
Pilling Cl CV2 .....62 E6
Pimlico La CV37 .....121 D2
Pinbury Croft B37 .....33 B1
Pinchester Cl GL56 .....141 A1
Pinders Ct 8 CV21 .....83 A2
Pinders La CV21 .....83 A2
Pine Cl Stoke Golding CV13 .....21 C4
　Stratford-u-A CV37 .....144 B1
Pine Ct Coventry CV5 .....59 B4
　Royal Leamington Spa
　CV32 .....106 B3
Pine Gr CV21 .....84 A1
Pine Sq B37 .....33 B2
Pine Tree Cres CV47 .....147 B3
Pine Tree Ct CV12 .....39 C4
Pine Tree Rd CV12 .....39 D4
Pineham Ave CV3 .....123 E6
Pinehurst CV32 .....106 E6
Pines The Bedworth CV12 .....38 E2
　Cheswick Green B90 .....70 D2
　Coventry CV4 .....75 D7
Pinewood Ave CV9 .....10 B1
Pinewood Dr CV3 .....79 C7
Pinewood Gr CV5 .....77 B8
Pinfold Gn NN11 .....126 F6
Pinfold St CV21 .....82 C2
Pinfold The B37 .....29 C2
Pink Green La B98 .....112 A8
Pinley Fields CV3 .....78 B8
Pinner's Croft CV2 .....62 A5
Pinnock Pl CV4 .....59 F1
Pinwall La CV9 .....12 C2
Pioneer Ho
　Birmingham B35 .....22 C3
　Coventry CV1 .....151 D4
Pipe La CV9 .....16 B2
Piper's End LE10 .....21 B2
Piper's La CV8 .....93 A5
Pipers La CV10 .....12 B4
Pipers Rd B98 .....103 B4
Pipewell Cl CV22 .....82 B1
Pippin Cl B50 .....148 B2
Pirie Cl CV33 .....123 F6
Pit Hill CV8 .....95 B3
Pittman La B92 .....44 D2
Pittons La CV23 .....101 B1
Pittway Ave CV36 .....149 C3
Pixhall Wlk B35 .....22 B3
Plain Rd The OX15 .....139 A3
Plane Gr B37 .....33 B1
Plank La B46 .....23 A2
Plantagenet Dr CV22 .....99 B2
Plantagenet Pk CV34 .....109 E3
Plantation The OX17 .....134 C1
Planter Cl CV22 .....99 A4
Plants Brook Rd B76 .....22 A6
Plants Hill Cres CV4 .....59 C1
Plato Cl CV34 .....109 E5
Pleasant Way CV32 .....106 A2
Pleck Cl B50 .....148 B2
Pleck The B50 .....148 B2
Plexfield Rd CV22 .....82 A1
Pleydell Cl CV3 .....78 C5
Plomer Cl CV22 .....99 B4
Plott La CV23 .....96 C3
Plough Hill Rd CV10 .....28 A4
Plough La CV47 .....124 A4
Ploughmans Holt CV47 .....147 A3
Plover Cl Alcester B49 .....143 A3
　Stratford-u-A CV37 .....144 B3
Plowden Cl NN11 .....134 F5
Plowman Ct CV22 .....82 B1
Plymouth Cl CV2 .....62 C7
Plymouth Pl CV31 .....110 A7
Poins Cl CV34 .....109 F3
Poitiers Rd CV3 .....77 C6
Polesworth High Sch
　B78 .....10 C4
Polesworth Sta B78 .....5 A2
Polperro Dr CV5 .....60 A5
Pomeroy Cl CV4 .....75 D7
Pond Farm Mews CV35 .....138 E6
Pondthorpe CV3 .....78 E6
Pontrilas Rd CV3 .....132 D4
Pontypool Ave CV3 .....78 F6

Pool Bank St CV11 .... **29** B4
Pool Cl
  Little Compton GL56 .... **140** F1
  Rugby CV22 .... **99** B4
  Welford on A CV37 .... **129** B6
Pool Close Cotts GL56 .. **140** F1
Pool End Cl B93 .... **71** F6
Pool Mdw B76 .... **22** A8
Pool Rd Nuneaton CV10 .. **28** E5
  Studley B80 .... **103** C2
Pool Road Bsns Ctr CV10 **28** F5
Poole Rd CV6 .... **61** A6
Pooley Fields Heritage Ctr***
  B78 .... **8** C2
Pooley La B78 .... **4** C1
Pooley View B78 .... **5** A1
Poolgate CV35 .... **138** B6
Poolhead La
  Earlswood B94 .... **86** C7
  Tanworth-In-A B94 .... **86** E5
Poolside Gdns CV3 .... **77** A5
Pope St CV22 .... **82** D2
Popes La B96 .... **102** C1
Poplar Ave Bedworth CV12 **37** D6
  Birmingham, Coleshill Heath
  B37 .... **44** C8
Poplar Cl Alcester B49 .. **143** B2
  Knightcote CV47 .... **124** B1
Poplar Gr Rugby CV21 .... **83** A2
  Ryton-on-D CV8 .... **79** B1
Poplar Ho CV12 .... **39** D2
Poplar Rd
  Bishops Itchington CV47 .. **124** B4
  Coventry CV6 .... **60** F1
  Dorridge B93 .... **71** F3
  Napton on H CV47 .... **125** C8
Poplar Trees B47 .... **69** A6
Poplars Cl GL55 .... **135** A1
Poplars La B96 .... **102** A1
Poplars The
  Bidford-on-A B50 .... **148** C3
  Nuneaton CV10 .... **28** D3
Poplars Trad Est B80 .... **103** B3
Poppy Dr CV23 .... **83** C4
Poppyfield Ct CV4 .... **76** D3
Porchester Cl CV3 .... **63** A2
Porlock Cl CV3 .... **77** E5
Porter Cl CV4 .... **75** F8
Portia Cl CV11 .... **40** A4
Portia Way CV34 .... **109** E3
Portland Cl ☑ CV32 ...... **109** F8
Portland Dr CV10 .... **28** C4
Portland Pl CV21 .... **83** B1
Portland Pl E CV32 .... **109** F8
Portland Pl W ☑ CV32 .. **109** E8
Portland Rd CV21 .... **83** B1
Portland St CV32 .... **109** F8
Portleys La B78 .... **8** B2
Portmanteau Mews B94 . **88** C6
Portree Ave CV3 .... **62** F2
Portsea Cl CV3 .... **77** D6
Portway Cl Coventry CV4 . **75** E8
  ☑ Royal Leamington Spa
  CV31 .... **110** D6
Porwinkle Ave CV6 .... **62** A6
Poseidon Way CV34 .... **109** F4
Post House Gdns CV23 .. **66** A4
Post Office La
  Lighthorne CV35 .... **123** B2
  Stockton CV47 .... **147** C4
  Witherley CV9 .... **19** A4
Post Office Rd CV9 .... **11** B1
Post Office Wlk B96 ...... **102** C1
Post Office Yd CV23 ...... **64** C2
Postbridge Rd CV3 .... **77** D5
Postle Cl CV23 .... **101** C1
Potters Cl CV23 .... **64** C2
Potters Green Prim Sch
  CV2 .... **50** E2
Potters Green Rd CV2 .... **50** E1
Potters La
  Darlingscott CV36 .... **136** D5
  Polesworth B78 .... **11** A4
Potters Rd CV12 .... **38** E1
Potton Cl CV3 .... **78** E6
Potts Cl CV8 .... **93** C4
Poultney Rd CV6 .... **61** A6
Pound Cl Berkswell CV7 .. **58** D7
  Lapworth B94 .... **89** B3
  Royal Leamington Spa
  CV36 .... **149** C3
Pound Field B95 .... **113** B2
Pound House La
  Tanworth-in-A B94 .... **87** F4
  Tanworth-in-A B94 .... **88** A4
Pound La Badby NN11 ... **126** F6
  Coleshill B46 .... **34** A2
  Furnace End B46 .... **25** A2
  Mickleton GL55 .... **135** B6
  Royal Leamington Spa
  CV32 .... **106** A3
  Sibford Gower OX15 .... **138** D3
Pound The OX15 .... **139** D2
Pound Way CV47 .... **147** B2
Powell Cl CV7 .... **62** A4
Powell Rd CV2 .... **62** A4
Powell Way CV11 .... **29** D3
Powers Ct ☑ CV32 .... **105** F1
Powis Gr CV8 .... **93** C5
Powys Gr OX16 .... **139** F4
Poyser Rd CV10 .... **39** C8
Pratts La B80 .... **112** A4
Prebend The CV47 .... **133** B7
Precinct The CV1 .... **151** B3
Precision Way B49 .... **143** B3

Prentice Cl CV23 .... **82** A3
Prescelly Cl CV10 .... **28** B3
Prescelly Ct CV8 .... **92** F5
Prescott Ave OX16 .... **139** F3
President Kennedy Sch &
  Com Coll CV6 .... **49** B4
Prestbury Ct B98 .... **112** A6
Preston Cl CV4 .... **75** F7
Preston Fields La B95 ... **113** D6
Preston La CV37 .... **130** A4
Prestwick Rd B35 .... **22** B4
Pretorian Way CV21 .... **83** A4
Priam Cir CV34 .... **109** C3
Price Rd CV32 .... **106** E5
Pridmore Rd CV6 .... **61** D7
Priest Meadow Cl B96 .. **102** B1
Priestfield Rd B97 .... **102** C3
Priesthills Rd LE10 .... **31** D8
Primley Ave B77 .... **9** C3
Primrose Cl CV23 .... **83** C4
Primrose Ct GL56 .... **140** A3
Primrose Dr
  Bedworth CV12 .... **38** E1
  Hinckley LE10 .... **31** E5
Primrose Hill CV34 .... **104** E2
Primrose Hill St CV1 ... **151** C4
Primrose La
  Alcester B49 .... **143** B1
  Solihull B90 .... **70** C2
Primsland Cl B90 .... **71** C7
Prince Harry Rd B95 .... **113** B4
Prince Of Wales Rd CV5 . **60** E3
Prince Regent Cl ☑
  CV31 .... **109** F6
Prince William Cl CV6 .... **60** E6
Prince's Ave CV11 .... **29** B3
Prince's Cl CV31 .... **109** D7
Prince's Rd B78 .... **5** A1
Prince's St Nuneaton CV11 **29** C4
  Royal Leamington Spa
  CV32 .... **106** B1
Princes Cl CV3 .... **78** B8
Princes Ct ☑ CV21 .... **83** A2
Princes Dr Coventry CV6 . **50** B1
  Kenilworth CV8 .... **93** B7
Princes Rd CV9 .... **16** B3
Princes St CV21 .... **83** A2
Princess Rd
  Atherstone CV9 .... **18** C4
  Hinckley LE10 .... **31** E8
Princess St CV6 .... **61** F7
Princethorpe Coll CV23 . **96** B2
Princethorpe Way CV3 .. **78** E8
Printers Pl CV37 .... **144** C2
Prior Deram Wlk CV4 .... **76** C7
Priors Cl CV7 .... **74** B6
Priors Ct CV47 .... **125** E4
Priors Field Prim Sch
  CV6 .... **92** D7
Priors Grange WR11 ..... **127** F6
Priors Harnall CV1 .... **151** D4
Priors Marston Rd
  CV47 .... **126** B5
Priors Mdw CV47 .... **147** B2
Priors The CV12 .... **39** C2
Priorsfield Rd
  ☑ Coventry CV6 .... **61** A4
  ☑ Coventry CV6 .... **92** D6
Priorsfield Rd N ☑ CV6 . **61** A4
Priorsfield Rd S ☑ CV6 . **61** A4
Priory Cl Coleshill B46 .... **34** A3
  Lapworth B94 .... **89** B1
Priory Ct Coventry CV5 ... **61** A1
  Nuneaton CV11 .... **29** A4
  Solihull B91 .... **71** B7
  Studley B80 .... **103** C3
Priory Ho CV8 .... **92** F4
Priory La CV35 .... **131** D2
Priory Mews CV34 .... **108** C7
Priory Rd Alcester B49 .. **143** A2
  Kenilworth CV8 .... **93** A4
  Warwick CV34 .... **108** E7
  Wolston CV8 .... **80** A2
Priory Row CV1 .... **151** C3
Priory Sq B80 .... **103** C3
Priory St Coventry CV1 .. **151** C3
  Nuneaton CV11 .... **28** D3
Priory Terr CV31 .... **110** A7
Priory Visitors Ctr*
  CV1 .... **151** C3
Priory Wlk Atherstone CV9 **18** C3
  ☑ Warwick CV34 .... **108** F7
Privet Rd CV2 .... **50** B2
Proffitt Ave CV6 .... **50** A1
Progress Cl CV3 .... **79** A7
Progress Way CV3 .... **79** A8
Projects Dr CV21 .... **83** B3
Prospect Rd CV31 .... **110** A5
Prospect Way
  Daventry NN11 .... **117** F2
  Rugby CV21 .... **83** B3
Prospero Dr CV34 .... **109** E3
Prossers Wlk B46 .... **33** F7
Providence St CV5 .... **76** F8
Provost Williams CE Prim
  Sch CV8 .... **79** A2
Ptarmigan Pl CV11 .... **29** F1
Puckering's La ☑ CV34 . **108** E6
Pudding Bag La CV23 .... **98** C1
Pudlicott La GL55 .... **135** E1
Pughe's Cl LE10 .... **32** A6
Pullman Cl B77 .... **4** A1
Puma Way CV1 .... **151** C1
Pump La CV7 .... **36** B2
Purbrook B77 .... **9** C4

Purcell Ave CV11 .... **40** A7
Purcell Cl CV32 .... **110** A8
Purcell Rd CV6 .... **60** A6
Purefoy Rd CV3 .... **77** D8
Purley Chase La CV9 ...... **18** B2
Purley Way CV9 .... **18** A3
Purlieu La CV8 .... **92** D5
Purnells Way B93 .... **72** A5
Purser Dr CV34 .... **108** B4
Purton Cl B49 .... **143** B3
Purton Mews CV11 .... **110** C6
Purvey Wlk B37 .... **33** B3
Pye Ct CV23 .... **117** B6
Pyeharps Rd LE10 .... **31** E5
Pyt Pk CV5 .... **60** D4
Pytchley Rd CV22 .... **83** B1
Pytman Dr B76 .... **22** A7

Q

Quadrangle The B90 .... **70** E8
Quadrant The
  Coventry CV1 .... **151** B2
  Nuneaton CV11 .... **29** E3
Quail La CV37 .... **144** B2
Quantock Dr CV10 .... **28** B3
Quarry Berry La DE12 ...... **2** C4
Quarry Cl
  Leek Wootton CV35 .... **104** F7
  Rugby CV21 .... **82** C3
Quarry Fields CV35 .... **104** F7
Quarry La Atherstone CV9 **19** A3
  Cleeve Prior WR11 .... **128** A4
  Nuneaton CV11 .... **29** F1
  Rowington Green CV35 ...... **90** C1
Quarry Rd CV8 .... **92** E6
Quarry St CV35 .... **109** C8
Quarry Yd CV10 .... **28** C4
Quarryfield La CV1 .... **151** C1
Quarrywood Gr CV2 .... **62** A4
Queen Eleanors Dr B93 . **72** B8
Queen Elizabeth Rd
  CV10 .... **28** D5
Queen Elizabeth Sch
  CV9 .... **18** C4
Queen Isabel's Ave CV3 . **77** D8
Queen Margaret's Rd
  CV4 .... **76** C8
Queen Mary's Rd
  Bedworth CV12 .... **39** C5
  Coventry CV6 .... **61** F8
Queen Philippa St CV3 .. **77** D6
Queen St
  Astwood Bank B96 .... **102** C1
  Bedworth CV12 .... **39** C2
  Coventry CV1 .... **151** C4
  Cubbington CV32 .... **106** E5
  Hook Norton OX15 .... **142** D4
  Royal Leamington Spa
  CV32 .... **106** A1
  Rugby CV21 .... **83** A2
Queen Victoria Rd
  ☑ Coventry CV1 .... **151** B3
  Coventry CV1 .... **151** B3
Queen Victoria St CV21 .. **83** B2
Queen's Cl CV8 .... **92** F3
Queen's Cres OX15 .... **139** B4
Queen's Rd Nuneaton CV11 **29** F8
Queen's Park Ct ☑ LE10 **31** E8
Queen's Park Flats ☑
  LE10 .... **31** E8
Queen's Park Terr ☑
  LE10 .... **31** E8
Queen's Rd
  Atherstone CV9 .... **18** C4
  Coventry CV1 .... **151** A2
  Hinckley LE10 .... **31** E8
  Kenilworth CV8 .... **92** F3
  Nuneaton CV11 .... **29** F8
Queen's Sq CV34 .... **108** E6
Queen's Ave CV36 .... **149** C3
Queens CE Jun Sch CV11 **29** A4
Queens Cl Harbury CV33 **123** F6
  Shipston-on-S CV36 .... **149** C3
Queens Ct CV11 .... **29** A4
Queens Own Mass Hus
  The* CV34 .... **108** E6
Queens Rd Bretford CV23 **80** C4
  Tredington CV36 .... **136** F6
Queens St CV36 .... **136** F8
Queens Way Dordon B78 **10** C3
  Hurley CV9 .... **16** B2
Queensferry Cl CV22 .... **99** B4
Queensland Ave CV5 .... **60** F2
Queenspark CV11 .... **29** E3
Queensway
  Bidford-on-A B50 .... **148** B3
  Nuneaton CV10 .... **28** E4
  Royal Leamington Spa
  CV31 .... **109** E6
Queensway Trad Est
  CV31 .... **109** E6
Queenswood Ct CV7 .... **48** D4
Quillets Cl CV5 .... **60** C5
Quince B77 .... **4** A2
Quince Tree Sch B77 .... **4** A2
Quiney's Legs CV37 .... **144** B1
Quiney's Rd CV37 .... **144** B1
Quinn Cl CV3 .... **78** B7
Quinney's Ct B50 .... **148** B2
Quinney's La B50 .... **148** B2
Quineys La B98 .... **103** A4
Quinton Flats CV35 ...... **114** C6
Quinton Cl CV35 .... **114** C6
Quinton Grange CV37 ... **129** E1

Quinton Par CV3 .... **77** D7
Quinton Pk CV3 .... **77** D7
Quinton Prim Sch CV37 **129** D2
Quinton Rd CV1 .... **151** C1
Quorndale ☑ B90 .... **70** C8
Quorn Way CV3 .... **78** E7

R

Race Leys Inf Sch CV12 .. **39** B3
Race Leys Jun Sch CV12 **39** B4
Racemeadow Prim Sch
  CV9 .... **12** C1
Racemeadow Rd CV47 .. **147** B2
Rackbourne Cl CV47 ...... **147** B2
Radbourne La CV47 .... **124** E5
Radbrook Way CV31 ...... **110** D6
Radburn Cl GL56 .... **140** B3
Radcliffe Gdns ☑ CV31 **110** A6
Radcliffe Rd CV5 .... **76** F8
Radford Circ ☑ CV6 .... **61** A4
Radford Cl CV9 .... **12** C1
Radford Hall CV31 .... **110** C6
Radford Ho CV6 .... **61** A7
Radford Prim Sch CV6 .... **61** A7
Radford Rd
  Coventry CV1, CV6 .... **61** B5
  Royal Leamington Spa
  CV31 .... **110** C7
Radford Semele CE Prim
  Sch CV31 .... **110** E5
Radley Dr CV10 .... **29** A1
Radnor Cres B37 .... **44** B8
Radnor Dr CV10 .... **28** E2
Radnor Wlk CV2 .... **62** F8
Radway Ind Est B90 .... **70** E7
Radway Rd B90 .... **70** E8
Raglan Cl CV11 .... **29** D4
Raglan Ct ☑ CV1 .... **61** E3
Raglan Gr CV8 .... **93** B3
Raglan St CV1 .... **151** D3
Raglan Way B37 .... **33** D1
Ragley Cl B93 .... **72** B7
Ragley Hall* B96 .... **118** F2
Ragley Mill La B49 .... **143** A2
Ragley Rd WR11 .... **127** D4
Ragley Way CV11 .... **29** F2
Railway Cl B80 .... **103** B2
Railway Cres CV36 .... **149** C4
Railway Mews B49 .... **143** A2
Railway St CV23 .... **82** A2
Railway Terr
  Bedworth CV12 .... **38** A4
  Bedworth CV12 .... **39** C2
  Rugby CV21 .... **83** A2
Rainbow Fields CV36 .... **149** C3
Rainsbrook Ave CV22 ... **100** C4
Rainsbrook Cl CV47 ...... **147** B2
Rainsbrook Dr
  Nuneaton CV11 .... **30** A1
  Solihull B90 .... **70** F6
Rainsbrook Secure Training
  Ctr CV23 .... **100** B3
Rainsbrook Valley Rly*
  CV22 .... **100** B3
Rainscar B77 .... **10** A4
Rainsford Cl CV37 .... **129** F7
Raison Ave CV11 .... **29** F8
Raleigh Rd CV2 .... **62** B2
Ralph Cres B78 .... **5** B3
Ralph Rd CV6 .... **60** F5
Ramp Rd B26 .... **44** C5
Ramsay Cres CV5 .... **60** B7
Ramsay Gn CV35 .... **146** B2
Ramsden Ave CV10 .... **28** C7
Ramsden Cl CV8 .... **28** C7
Ramsden Rd CV9 .... **19** A4
Ramsey Rd CV31 .... **110** B7
Ramshill La B94 .... **112** C7
Ran-tan The B97 .... **102** C3
Ranby Rd CV2 .... **61** F4
Randall Rd CV8 .... **92** F3
Randle Rd CV10 .... **28** B4
Randle St CV6 .... **61** A5
Randolph Cl ☑ CV31 ..... **110** C6
Ranelagh St CV31 .... **110** A6
Ranelagh Terr CV31 ...... **109** F6
Range Meadow Cl CV32 **105** C3
Range Way B78 .... **5** B3
Rangemoor CV3 .... **78** D6
Rangeworthy Cl B97 ..... **102** B4
Rankine Cl CV21 .... **82** B4
Rannoch Cl LE10 .... **31** B8
Rannoch Dr CV10 .... **28** C5
Ransom Rd CV6 .... **61** E8
Ransome Rd CV7 .... **37** A4
Ranulf Croft CV3 .... **77** C7
Ranulf St CV3 .... **77** C7
Raphael Cl CV5 .... **60** C3
Rashwood Cl B94 .... **88** C6
Ratcliffe Cl CV34 .... **28** C4
Ratcliffe La CV9 .... **12** C2
Ratcliffe Rd
  Atherstone CV9 .... **12** C1
  Hinckley LE10 .... **31** F6
  Solihull B91 .... **56** C6
Rathbone Cl Keresley CV7 **49** A6
  Rugby CV21 .... **101** A4
Rathlin Croft B36 .... **33** B6
Ratliffe Rd CV22 .... **99** B4
Rattlecombe Rd OX15 .. **138** C5
Raveloe Dr CV11 .... **39** A8
Raven Cragg Rd CV4 ...... **76** B8
Raven Way CV11 .... **29** F2
Ravenglass CV21 .... **83** B4
Ravensdale Ave CV32 ... **105** C2

Ravensdale Prim Sch
  CV2 .... **62** D4
Ravensdale Rd CV2 .... **62** D3
Ravenshaw La B91 .... **56** A4
Ravenshaw Way B91 .... **56** A3
Ravensholt CV4 .... **76** D6
Ravensthorpe Cl CV3 .... **78** E8
Ravenstone B77 .... **10** A4
Ravenswood Hill B46 ...... **33** F7
Rawlins Croft B35 .... **22** C3
Rawlinson Rd CV32 .... **106** B2
Rawn View CV9 .... **18** C3
Ray Cl CV8 .... **93** C6
Raygill B77 .... **10** A4
Raymond Cl CV6 .... **49** F5
Raynor Cres CV12 .... **38** D1
Raynsford Wlk CV34 ..... **104** D1
Raywoods The CV10 .... **28** F3
Read St CV1 .... **151** C3
Reading Ave CV11 .... **29** F7
Reading Cl CV2 .... **50** B3
Readings The CV47 .... **133** E7
Rebecca Dr CV34 .... **104** E1
Reardon Ct CV34 .... **104** E1
Recreation Rd CV6 .... **50** A3
Rectory Cl Allesley CV5 .... **60** C6
  Barby CV23 .... **101** B1
  Bedworth CV7 .... **39** A1
  Drayton Bassett B78 .... **8** C3
  Harvington WR11 .... **127** D3
  Stockton CV47 .... **147** C4
  Warmington OX17 .... **133** D2
  Whitnash CV31 .... **110** B4
Rectory Dr CV7 .... **39** A1
Rectory Gdns OX15 ...... **139** E4
Rectory La Allesley CV5 .... **60** C6
  Barby CV23 .... **101** B1
  Lower Brailes OX15 .... **137** F2
  Whatcote CV36 .... **137** D7
Rectory Rd Arley CV7 .... **26** C1
  Hook Norton OX15 .... **142** D4
  Sutton Coldfield B75 .... **13** A6
Red Deeps CV11 .... **39** D8
Red Hill CV35 .... **131** B8
Red Hill Cl B80 .... **103** C3
Red Hill Rd B80 .... **103** C3
Red La Ashby Fold CV47 ... **37** C4
  Burton Green CV8 .... **75** C2
  Coventry CV6 .... **61** F5
  Kenilworth CV8 .... **92** D8
Red Lion Cl CV47 .... **147** A3
Red Lion St CV13 .... **134** C1
Red Lodge Dr CV22 .... **99** C4
Red Rd CV35 .... **132** B5
Red Wing Wlk B36 .... **33** A8
Redcap Croft CV6 .... **49** D4
Redcar Cl CV32 .... **106** C4
Redcar Rd CV1 .... **61** E5
Reddicap Heath Rd B75 . **13** A4
Reddings La B46 .... **25** A3
Reddings The B47 .... **69** A5
Redditch Rd B80 .... **103** B3
Redditch Wlk ☑ CV2 ...... **63** A7
Redesdale Ave CV6 .... **60** F5
Redesdale Mews ☑
  GL56 .... **140** A3
Redesdale Pl GL56 .... **140** A2
Redfern Ave CV8 .... **93** B6
Redgrave Cl CV2 .... **63** B8
Redhill Bank CV37 .... **130** B3
Redhill Cl CV35 .... **146** B1
Redhouse Cl B93 .... **71** E4
Redlake B77 .... **9** C4
Redland Cl CV2 .... **50** B8
Redland La CV8 .... **79** A2
Redland Rd CV31 .... **110** B5
Redlands Cres CV37 ...... **144** B2
Redliff Ave B36 .... **22** D1
Redmoor Way B76 .... **22** D6
Redruth Cl Coventry CV6 . **62** A8
  Nuneaton CV11 .... **30** A4
Redthorne Gr CV8 .... **93** B8
Redwing B77 .... **10** A4
Redwing Cl CV37 .... **144** B3
Redwood Croft CV10 .... **29** A1
Redwood Dr B78 .... **15** B4
Reed Sq B35 .... **22** B4
Reeds Pk CV33 .... **111** C1
Rees Dr CV3 .... **77** D4
Reeve Dr CV8 .... **93** A4
Reeves Rd LE10 .... **31** F6
Reg Hadden Ct CV10 .... **28** C3
Regal Cl CV37 .... **144** B2
Regal Ct CV9 .... **18** C4
Regal Rd CV37 .... **144** C2
Regal Road Trad Est
  CV37 .... **144** C2
Regency Arc ☑ CV32 ..... **109** F8
Regency Cl CV10 .... **29** D6
Regency Ct CV11 .... **29** D6
Regency Dr Alcester B49 **143** A3
  Coventry CV3 .... **76** F5
  Kenilworth CV8 .... **92** F3
Regency Ho CV32 .... **110** A8
Regency Mews CV32 ..... **110** A8
Regent Cl ☑ LE10 .... **31** D8
Regent Ct CV32 .... **109** F8
Regent Gr ☑ CV32 .... **109** F8
Regent Pl
  ☑ Royal Leamington Spa
  CV31 .... **110** A7
  Rugby CV21 .... **83** A2
Regent St Bedworth CV12 **39** C4
  Coventry CV1 .... **151** A2
  Hinckley LE10 .... **31** D8
  Nuneaton CV11 .... **29** D4
  Royal Leamington Spa
  CV31 .... **109** F8
Regiment Ct CV6 .... **49** A1

Regina Cres CV2 . . . . .63 A7
Regis Wlk CV2 . . . . .62 F7
Reignier Pl CV34 . . . . .109 F2
Reindeer Rd B78 . . . . .8 C4
Relay Dr B77 . . . . .10 B4
Relton Mews CV6 . . . . .61 F6
Rembrandt Cl CV5 . . . . .60 C3
Remburn Gdns CV34 . . . . .108 F8
Remembrance Rd CV3 . . . . .78 D6
Renfrew Sq B35 . . . . .22 B4
Renfrew Wlk CV4 . . . . .76 A8
Renold Cl CV4 . . . . .38 E1
Renolds Cl CV4 . . . . .64 C1
Renown Ave CV4 . . . . .60 C1
Repington Ave CV9 . . . . . . .12 B1
Repington Rd N B77 . . . . . . .4 A3
Repington Rd B77 . . . . .4 A3
Repington Way B75 . . . . . . .13 B5
Repton Dr CV6 . . . . .50 B2
Reservoir Dr B46 . . . . .24 C1
Reservoir Rd CV21 . . . . .83 B3
Retreat St B96 . . . . .102 C1
Revel CE Prim Sch The
CV23 .53 C1
Rex Cl CV4 . . . . .75 D8
Reynolds Cl CV21 . . . . .84 A1
Reynolds Rd CV12 . . . . .39 A4
Rhoose Croft B35 . . . . .22 B3
Rhyl Rd CV11 . . . . .40 F6
Ribble Cl CV12 . . . . .40 B2
Ribble Rd CV3 . . . . .61 F2
Ribblesdale B77 . . . . .10 A4
Ribbonbrook CV11 . . . . .29 D3
Ribbonfields CV11 . . . . .29 D3
Rich Cl CV34 . . . . .109 B7
Richard Joy Cl CV6 . . . . . . .49 C2
Richard Lee Prim Sch
CV2 . . . . .62 E3
Richards Cl CV8 . . . . .92 F5
Richards Gr CV31 . . . . .110 A5
Richardson Cl CV34 . . . . . .104 F1
Richardson Way CV2 . . . . . .63 B8
Richman Gdns OX16 . . . . . .139 F4
Richmond Cl [6] CV31 . . . . .110 B7
Richmond Ho [2] B37 . . . . .33 C1
Richmond Rd
Atherstone CV9 . . . . .18 B4
Hollywood B47 . . . . .69 C7
Nuneaton CV11 . . . . .29 A4
Rugby CV21 . . . . .83 B1
Richmond St CV2 . . . . .62 A3
Richmond Way [2] B37 . . . .33 C3
Rickard Cl B93 . . . . .71 E6
Rickyard Cl B78 . . . . .5 A1
Rickyard The OX15 . . . . . . .139 A3
Riddell Cl B49 . . . . .143 B2
Riddings Gdns B78 . . . . .11 A4
Riddings Hill CV7 . . . . .74 C8
Riddings La CV9 . . . . .11 B2
Riddings The
Coventry CV5 . . . . .76 E7
Grendon CV9 . . . . .11 B1
Sutton Coldfield B76 . . . . . .22 B8
Riddon Dr LE10 . . . . .31 B8
Ridewell Gr CV31 . . . . .110 A1
Ridge Ct CV5 . . . . .60 A6
Ridge Dr CV21 . . . . .83 B2
Ridge La CV10 . . . . .18 A1
Ridgeley Cl CV34 . . . . .104 E2
Ridgethorpe CV3 . . . . .78 F8
Ridgeway Ave CV3 . . . . .77 C6
Ridgeway Cl B80 . . . . .103 C1
Ridgeway Mid Sch B96 . . . .118 C8
Ridgeway Sch CV34 . . . . . .105 A1
Ridgeway The
Astwood Bank B96 . . . . . . .118 D6
Barby CV23 . . . . .117 F8
Hinckley LE10 . . . . .31 D6
Warwick CV34 . . . . .105 A1
Ridgeway Trad Est B96 . . . .102 C1
Ridgewood Rise B77 . . . . . . .4 A3
Ridgley Rd CV4 . . . . .75 E8
Ridgway The CV37 . . . . . . .120 C3
Ridley La B46 . . . . .25 A3
Ridsdale Cl WR11 . . . . .127 F6
Rigby Cl CV34 . . . . .109 D4
Rigdale Cl CV2 . . . . .62 E2
Riley Cl Daventry NN11 . . . .117 F2
Kenilworth CV8 . . . . .93 D4
Riley Ct CV21 . . . . .83 B2
Riley Dr Banbury OX16 . . . .139 F4
Birmingham B36 . . . . .23 A1
Riley Sq CV2 . . . . .50 B1
Rimell Cl CV37 . . . . .130 E1
Ringway Hill Cross CV1 . . . .151 A3
Ringway Queens CV1 . . . . .151 A2
Ringway Rudge CV1 . . . . . .151 A2
Ringway St Johns CV1 . . . .151 C2
Ringway St Nicholas
CV1 . . . . .151 B3
Ringway St Patricks
CV1 . . . . .151 B1
Ringway Swanswell
CV1 . . . . .151 C3
Ringway Whitefriars
CV1 . . . . .151 C3
Ringwood Highway CV2 . . . .50 E2
Rinhill Gr CV31 . . . . .110 D6
Riplingham [3] CV32 . . . . .105 F2
Ripon Cl CV5 . . . . .60 B8
Risborough Cl CV5 . . . . .60 C3
Risdale Cl CV32 . . . . .105 D2
Rise The B37 . . . . .44 A7
Rising La
Chadwick End B93 . . . . .90 B5
Lapworth B94,B93 . . . . .89 F5
Rising Rd B94 . . . . .89 C5

River Cl Bedworth CV12 . . . .38 F1
Royal Leamington Spa
CV32 . . . . .109 D8
River Ct [3] CV1 . . . . .61 B3
River Dr CV9 . . . . .12 B1
River House Specl Sch
B95 . . . . .113 B4
River Way CV36 . . . . .137 A4
River Wlk CV2 . . . . .50 C2
Riverbank Gdns CV37 . . . .145 A1
Riverford Croft CV4 . . . . . . .76 D4
Rivermead CV11 . . . . .29 A4
Rivermead Ct B50 . . . . . . .148 B2
Rivermead Dr CV37 . . . . . .145 C2
Riversdale [6] CV32 . . . . .109 E8
Riversdale Rd CV9 . . . . .19 A4
Riverside Alcester B49 . . . .143 B2
Studley B80 . . . . .103 C2
Witherley CV9 . . . . .19 A4
Riverside Cl CV3 . . . . .78 A7
Riverside Ct [1] B46 . . . . . .33 F7
Riverside Gdns B95 . . . . . .113 B4
Riverside Ind Est B78 . . . . . .9 A4
Riversleigh Rd CV32 . . . . .105 C1
Riversley Rd CV11 . . . . .29 C3
Ro-Oak Rd CV6 . . . . .60 F5
Roach B77 . . . . .9 B3
Roach Cl B37 . . . . .33 C3
Roanne Ringway CV11 . . . . .29 B4
Robbins Ct [5] CV22 . . . . .100 C4
Robert Cl CV3 . . . . .78 C4
Robert Cramb Ave CV4 . . . .75 F8
Robert Hill Cl CV21 . . . . . . .84 A1
Robert Rd CV7 . . . . .49 F8
Roberts Cl CV23 . . . . .96 C3
Roberts La WR11 . . . . .127 F1
Robertson Cl CV23 . . . . .84 A3
Robey's La B78 . . . . .4 B2
Robin Cl Birmingham B36 . . .33 A8
Tamworth B77 . . . . .9 B4
Robin Hood Rd CV3 . . . . . . .78 C6
Robina Cl CV32 . . . . .106 B2
Robinia B77 . . . . .4 A2
Robins Cl OX7 . . . . .142 A2
Robins Gr CV34 . . . . .108 C4
Robins Way CV10 . . . . .28 A3
Robinson Rd CV12 . . . . .49 D8
Robinson Way LE10 . . . . . . .31 F4
Robinson's Way B76 . . . . . . .22 D5
Robotham Cl CV21 . . . . .82 C3
Rocheberie Way CV22 . . . . .99 C4
Rochester Cl
Nuneaton CV11 . . . . .29 B3
Royal Leamington Spa
CV31 . . . . .109 E7
Solihull B90 . . . . .71 A6
Rochester Rd CV5 . . . . .76 E8
Rochford Cl B76 . . . . .22 A8
Rochford Ct
Royal Leamington Spa
CV31 . . . . .109 E7
Solihull B90 . . . . .71 A6
Rock Cl Coventry CV6 . . . . . .50 B1
Nuneaton CV10 . . . . .27 C2
Rock La CV7 . . . . .48 C7
Rock Mill La CV32 . . . . . . .109 C8
Rocken End CV6 . . . . .61 D8
Rockford Cl B98 . . . . .102 C3
Rockingham Cl B93 . . . . . . .71 D2
Rockingham Dr CV11 . . . . . .39 F7
Rocky La CV8 . . . . .93 D2
Rodborough Rd B93 . . . . . . .71 E3
Rodhouse Cl CV4 . . . . .59 D1
Rodney Cl CV22 . . . . .82 B1
Rodway Dr CV5 . . . . .59 D4
Rodyard Way CV1 . . . . .151 C1
Roe Cl CV34 . . . . .108 F8
Roebuck Pk B49 . . . . .143 A3
Rofs Croft B78 . . . . .5 A1
Rogers La CV37 . . . . .131 A3
Rogers Way CV34 . . . . .108 B4
Rokeby Ct CV22 . . . . .99 C4
Rokeby Inf Sch CV22 . . . . .100 A4
Rokeby Jun Sch CV22 . . . .100 A4
Rokeby St CV21 . . . . .83 B2
Rolan Dr B90 . . . . .69 E8
Roland Ave CV6 . . . . .49 C3
Roland Mount CV6 . . . . .49 C3
Rollason Cl CV6 . . . . .61 C8
Rollason Rd CV6 . . . . .61 B8
Rollason's Yd CV6 . . . . .50 A3
Rolling Stones GL55 . . . . . .135 B2
Rollright Stones * OX7 . . . .141 D1
Rolph Ct GL56 . . . . .140 A2
Roman Cl LE17 . . . . .43 C3
Roman Ct B77 . . . . .9 C4
Roman Pk B46 . . . . .23 F1
Roman Rd CV2 . . . . .62 B3
Roman Row CV36 . . . . .141 F5
Roman Way Alcester B49 . .143 A2
Coleshill B46 . . . . .23 F2
Coventry CV3 . . . . .77 D3
Dordon B78 . . . . .11 A3
Halford CV36 . . . . .136 F8
Rugby CV21 . . . . .83 A4
Southam CV47 . . . . .147 B2
Romeo Arbour CV34 . . . . . .109 E3
Romford Rd CV6 . . . . .49 B2
Romilly Cl B76 . . . . .13 A4
Romney B77 . . . . .9 C4
Romney Rd OX16 . . . . .139 F5
Romsey Ave CV10 . . . . .29 D8
Romsley Rd CV6 . . . . .61 C6
Ronald Gr B36 . . . . .22 D1
Rookery Cl CV13 . . . . .20 A4
Rookery La Coventry CV6 . . .49 B4
Ettington CV37 . . . . .131 A3
Newbold-on-S CV37 . . . . . .130 E1
Preston Bagot B95 . . . . . . .113 E5

Rookery Rd
Birchley Heath CV10 . . . . . .17 C1
Nuneaton CV10 . . . . .27 C3
Rookes Cl [1] CV37 . . . . . .144 C2
Rooks Nest CV23 . . . . .64 C2
Roosevelt Dr CV4 . . . . .59 E2
Rope Way OX15 . . . . .142 D3
Roper Cl CV21 . . . . .101 A4
Ropewalk B49 . . . . .143 A2
Rosaville Cres CV5 . . . . . . .60 A6
Rose Ave Coventry CV6 . . . .60 F5
Henley-in-A B95 . . . . .113 B5
Rose Cottage Flats CV5 . . .59 D5
Rose Croft CV8 . . . . .92 E6
Rose Ct CV7 . . . . .74 B8
Rose Hill CV9 . . . . .18 C4
Rose La
Napton on t H CV47 . . . . . .125 C7
Nuneaton CV11 . . . . .29 C3
Rose Rd B46 . . . . .33 F8
Roseberry Ave CV2 . . . . . . .50 C1
Rosebery Rd B77 . . . . .9 B2
Rosebriars B90 . . . . .69 E7
Rosefield Pl [4] CV32 . . . .109 F8
Rosefield St CV32 . . . . .110 A8
Rosefield Wlk [3] CV32 . . .109 F8
Rosegreen Cl CV3 . . . . .77 C6
Rosehall Cl B98 . . . . .102 C3
Rosehip Dr CV2 . . . . .62 B6
Roseland Rd CV8 . . . . .92 F3
Roselands Ave CV2 . . . . . . .62 D8
Rosemary Cl CV4 . . . . .59 C3
Rosemary Hill CV8 . . . . .92 F5
Rosemary Mews CV8 . . . . . .92 F5
Rosemary Way LE10 . . . . . .31 B7
Rosemount Cl CV2 . . . . .62 E7
Rosemullion Cl CV7 . . . . . . .50 B8
Roses La OX7 . . . . .150 C3
Roseway CV13 . . . . .21 B4
Rosewood CV11 . . . . .29 F1
Rosewood Ave CV22 . . . . .100 A4
Rosewood Cl LE10 . . . . .31 F6
Rosewood Cres CV32 . . . .106 B2
Ross Cl CV5 . . . . .60 A5
Ross Ct CV21 . . . . .83 B2
Ross Way CV11 . . . . .40 B7
Rossendale Way CV10 . . . . .28 E2
Rosslyn Ave CV6 . . . . .60 E6
Rosslyn Rd B76 . . . . .22 A6
Roston Dr LE10 . . . . .31 A8
Rothay B77 . . . . .9 C4
Rother Rd CV6 . . . . .139 F5
Rother St CV37 . . . . .144 C1
Rotherby Gr B37 . . . . .44 B7
Rotherfield Cl CV31 . . . . . .110 B7
Rotherham Rd CV6 . . . . .49 C2
Rotherhams Hill CV9 . . . . . .17 B4
Rotherwick Ct CV36 . . . . . .149 C3
Rothesay Ave CV4 . . . . .60 B2
Rothesay Cl CV10 . . . . .29 A2
Rothley Dr CV21 . . . . .83 C4
Rothwell Rd CV34 . . . . .104 C1
Rough Coppice Wlk B35 . . .22 A2
Rough Farm Ind Est
CV37 . . . . .130 C5
Rough Hill Dr B98 . . . . .102 C3
Rough The B97 . . . . .102 B4
Roughknowles Rd CV4 . . . . .75 D6
Rouncil La CV8 . . . . .104 C8
Round Ave CV23 . . . . .82 A3
Round Cl B90 . . . . .70 A6
Round Close Rd OX15 . . . .142 D4
Round House Rd CV3 . . . . . .78 B8
Round Moor Wlk B35 . . . . . .22 A3
Round Oak Sch The
CV32 . . . . .106 A3
Round St [2] CV21 . . . . . . .82 C2
Roundhill Rd OX17 . . . . . . .134 A2
Rounds Gdns CV21 . . . . . . .82 C2
Rounds Hill CV8 . . . . .92 E2
Rouse La CV35 . . . . .137 F8
Rover Dr B36 . . . . .22 F1
Rover Rd CV1 . . . . .151 B2
Row The CV7 . . . . .51 D3
Rowan Cl
Binley Woods CV3 . . . . .79 D7
Hollywood B47 . . . . .69 B5
Kingsbury B78 . . . . .15 B3
Stratford-u-A CV37 . . . . . .144 C1
Rowan Dr Rugby CV22 . . . . .82 A1
[6] Warwick CV34 . . . . . . .108 F8
Rowan Gdns B78 . . . . .11 A4
Rowan Gr CV2 . . . . .50 E2
Rowan Rd CV10 . . . . .28 C6
Rowan Way
Birmingham, Chelmsley Wood
B37 .33 C1
Nuneaton CV10 . . . . .28 A8
Rowans The
Bedworth CV12 . . . . .38 E2
Harvington WR11 . . . . .127 D4
Rowborough Cl
Astwood Bank B96 . . . . . . .102 C1
Hatton CV35 . . . . .114 F5
Rowbrook Cl B90 . . . . .69 E8
Rowcroft Rd CV2 . . . . .63 A6
Rowington Cl CV6 . . . . .60 D5
Rowington Gn CV35 . . . . . . .89 F1
Rowland Ave
Polesworth B78 . . . . .5 A2
Studley B80 . . . . .103 C2
Rowland Ct CV7 . . . . .26 C1
Rowland St CV21 . . . . .82 C2
Rowland Way CV12 . . . . . . .28 E1
Rowley Cres CV37 . . . . . . .145 A2
Rowley Dr CV3 . . . . .78 B4
Rowley La CV3 . . . . .78 D3

Rowley Rd
Coventry CV3,CV8 . . . . .78 B3
Whitnash CV31 . . . . .110 A2
Rowley's Green La CV6 . . . .49 E4
Rowleys Green Lane Ind Est
CV6 .49 E4
Rowse Cl CV21 . . . . .82 B4
Rowthorn Dr B90 . . . . .71 A6
Roxburgh Croft CV32 . . . . .106 C6
Roxburgh Rd CV11 . . . . .29 E1
Royal Cres CV3 . . . . .78 C5
Royal Ct LE10 . . . . .31 D7
Royal Leamington Spa
Rehabilitation Hospl
CV34 . . . . .109 E4
Royal Oak Ind Est NN11 . . .117 F2
Royal Oak La CV7,CV12 . . . .49 C7
Royal Oak Terr GL55 . . . . .135 A1
Royal Oak Way N NN11 . . .117 F2
Royal Oak Way S NN11 . . .117 F2
Royal Oak Yd CV12 . . . . . . .39 B4
Royal Priors [5] CV32 . . . .109 F8
Royal Shakespeare Theatre *
CV37 . . . . .145 A1
Royston Cl CV3 . . . . .63 A3
Rubens Cl CV5 . . . . .60 C3
Rugbard Rd CV6 . . . . .50 A4
Rulford Cl Alcester B49 . . .143 B3
Hinckley LE10 . . . . .31 D3
Rugby Coll CV21 . . . . .83 B1
Rugby Rd Barby CV23 . . . . .99 B3
Binley Woods CV3 . . . . .79 D8
Brinklow CV23 . . . . .64 C2
Bulkington CV12 . . . . .40 D2
Church Lawford CV23 . . . . .81 B3
Clifton u D CV23 . . . . .83 C3
Cubbington CV32 . . . . .106 C6
Dunchurch CV22 . . . . .99 B2
Easenhall CV23 . . . . .65 C2
Harborough Magna CV23 . . .66 A1
Hinckley LE10 . . . . .31 D6
Kilsby CV21,CV23 . . . . . . .101 C3
Lilbourne CV23 . . . . .84 C3
Long Lawford CV23 . . . . . . .82 A2
Pailton CV23 . . . . .66 A4
Princethorpe CV23 . . . . . . .96 C1
Royal Leamington Spa
CV32 . . . . .105 D1
Shawell LE17 . . . . .68 A4
Stockton CV47 . . . . .115 F3
Rugby Sch CV22 . . . . .83 A1
Rugby Sta CV21 . . . . .83 B2
Ruislip Cl B35 . . . . .22 A4
Rumbush La
Earlswood B90,B94 . . . . . . .69 F3
Solihull B90 . . . . .70 A5
Rumer Cl CV37 . . . . .129 B4
Runcorn Cl
Birmingham B37 . . . . .33 C4
Redditch B98 . . . . .102 C4
Runnymede Gdns CV10 . . . .28 D2
Runnymede Dr CV7 . . . . . . .74 C5
Rupert Brooke Rd CV22 . . . .99 C4
Rupert Kettle Dr CV47 . . . .124 B4
Rupert Rd CV6 . . . . .61 B8
Rush La B77,B78 . . . . .8 D3
Rushbrook La B94 . . . . .86 D3
Rushbrook Rd CV37 . . . . . .145 B1
Rushford Cl B90 . . . . .71 A7
Rushleigh Rd B90 . . . . .69 E8
Rushmoor Cl CV5 . . . . .60 E8
Rushmore St CV31 . . . . . . .110 B7
Rushmore Terr [9] CV31 . .110 B7
Rushock Cl B98 . . . . .103 B4
Rushton Cl CV7 . . . . .74 C7
Rushwick Gr B90 . . . . .71 A6
Ruskin Cl CV6 . . . . .109 F6
Ruskin Cl Coventry CV6 . . . .60 D6
Nuneaton CV10 . . . . .28 A5
Rugby CV22 . . . . .99 C3
Russell Ave CV22 . . . . .99 B2
Russell Cl CV47 . . . . .115 C4
Russell Ct [7] CV31 . . . . .110 A7
Russell St Coventry CV1 . . .151 C4
Royal Leamington Spa
CV32 . . . . .105 F1
Russell St N [2] CV1 . . . . .151 C4
Russell Terr CV31 . . . . .110 A7
Russelsheim Way CV22 . . . .83 A1
Russet Gr CV4 . . . . .76 D3
Rutherford Glen CV11 . . . . .29 F1
Rutherford Way NN11 . . . . .117 F3
Rutherglen Ave CV3 . . . . . . .78 A6
Rutland Ave Hinckley LE10 . .31 C7
Nuneaton CV10 . . . . .28 E4
Rutland Croft [3] CV3 . . . .78 F8
Rydal Av CV11 . . . . .30 A6
Rydal Cl Allesley CV5 . . . . . .60 B8
Hinckley LE10 . . . . .30 F7
Rugby CV21 . . . . .83 B3
Ryde Ave CV10 . . . . .29 D7
Ryder Cl CV35 . . . . .146 B2
Ryder Row CV7 . . . . .37 A4
Ryders Hill Cres CV10 . . . . .28 C7
Rye Cl Banbury OX16 . . . . .139 F5
Stratford-u-A CV37 . . . . . .144 C3
Rye Croft B47 . . . . .69 A6
Rye Fields [6] CV33 . . . . .122 E8
Rye Grass Wlk B35 . . . . . . .22 B3
Rye Hill CV5 . . . . .60 A6
Rye Piece Ringway CV12 . . .39 C3
Ryeclose Croft B37 . . . . . . .33 D3
Ryefield La B76 . . . . .14 B2
Ryegrass La B97 . . . . .102 B3

Reg – St C **175**

Ryelands The CV23 . . . . . . .98 B4
Ryhope Cl CV12 . . . . .38 C1
Ryknild St B49 . . . . .143 A3
Ryland Cl CV31 . . . . .110 C6
Ryland Rd CV35 . . . . .122 B8
Ryland St CV37 . . . . .144 C1
Rylston Ave CV6 . . . . .49 A1
Rylstone Way [4] CV34 . . .104 E1
Ryon Hill CV37 . . . . .145 C4
Ryton B77 . . . . .9 C4
Ryton CV8 . . . . .76 B8
Ryton Organic Gdns *
CV8 .79 E1
Ryton Pools Ctry Pk *
CV8 .95 C3
Ryton Pools Visitor Ctr *
CV8 .95 C3

S

Sabin Cl CV47 . . . . .115 C4
Sabin Dr CV33 . . . . .107 B4
Sackville Cl CV37 . . . . .144 B2
Sackville Ho [4] CV1 . . . . .151 C4
Sackville Ho [1] CV1 . . . . .151 C4
Sacred Heart RC Prim Sch
CV2 .62 A3
Saddington Rd CV3 . . . . . . .78 E8
Saddlebow La CV35,
CV33 . . . . .114 B2
Saddlers Cl LE10 . . . . .31 F6
Saddleton St CV35 . . . . . . .138 C7
Sadler Cl CV37 . . . . .144 C3
Sadler Gdns CV12 . . . . .39 C2
Sadler Rd CV6 . . . . .61 A8
Sadlers Ave CV36 . . . . .149 C3
Sadlers Cl CV36 . . . . .149 C3
Sadlers Mdw B46 . . . . .26 A1
Saddlerswell La B94 . . . . . . .88 B6
Saffron B77 . . . . .4 A2
Saffron Cl CV23 . . . . .83 C4
Saffron Mdw CV37 . . . . . . .144 C1
Saffron Wlk CV37 . . . . .144 C1
Saint's Peter & Paul RC Prim
Sch CV2 . . . . .62 F7
Saintbury Cl CV37 . . . . . . .145 B1
Saintbury Dr B91 . . . . .71 C8
Saints Way CV10 . . . . .29 D5
St Agatha's Rd CV2 . . . . . . .62 A3
St Agnes Cl B80 . . . . .103 B2
St Agnes La CV1 . . . . .151 B3
St Agnes Way CV11 . . . . . . .29 F4
St Albans Cl CV32 . . . . . . .105 C2
St Andrew's CE Inf Sch
CV5 .59 C5
St Andrew's Cres CV37 . . .144 C1
St Andrew's Ct CV21 . . . . . .83 A2
St Andrew's Rd
Coventry CV5 . . . . .76 F8
Royal Leamington Spa
CV32 . . . . .106 B5
St Andrews B77 . . . . .4 A2
St Andrews Benn CE Fst Sch
CV21 . . . . .83 B2
St Andrews Benn CE Prim
Sch CV21 . . . . .83 B2
St Andrews Cres CV22 . . . .100 A4
St Andrews Dr CV11 . . . . . . .30 B1
St Ann's Cl CV31 . . . . .110 C7
St Ann's Rd CV2 . . . . .62 A3
St Anne's RC Prim Sch
Birmingham B37 . . . . .33 A2
Coventry CV3 . . . . .78 C6
Nuneaton CV10 . . . . .28 D7
St Anne's Rd CV22 . . . . . . .82 C1
St Annes Gr B93 . . . . .72 A6
St Anthony's RC Prim Sch
CV31 . . . . .110 C7
St Antony's RC Sch
B37 .33 A5
St Asaphs Ave B80 . . . . . . .103 B2
St Athan Croft B35 . . . . .22 B3
St Augustine's RC Prim Sch
CV6 .61 A7
St Augustine's RC Sch
CV8 .92 E7
St Augustine's RC Sch
B97 . . . . .102 B3
St Augustine's Wlk CV6 . . . .61 A7
St Austell Cl CV11 . . . . .30 A5
St Austell Rd CV2 . . . . .62 E3
St Bartholemew's CE Prim
Sch CV3 . . . . .78 E7
St Benedict's RC High Sch
B49 . . . . .143 B2
St Benedict's RC Prim Sch
Atherstone CV9 . . . . .18 C4
Coventry CV1 . . . . .61 E4
St Benedicts Cl CV9 . . . . . . .18 B4
St Bernards Wlk CV3 . . . . . .78 D6
St Blaise Ave B46 . . . . .23 C2
St Bride's Cl CV31 . . . . . . .110 C6
St Catherine's LE10 . . . . . . .31 F7
St Catherine's Cl CV3 . . . . .78 B8
St Catherine's Cres
CV34 . . . . .109 F3
St Catherine's Lodge [7]
CV6 .61 A4
St Catherine's RC Prim Sch
GL55 . . . . .135 A2
St Chads Mews B94 . . . . . . .89 D3

St Chads Rd
B Bishops Tachbrook
CV33 ....122 E8
Studley B80 ....103 B2
St Christian's Croft CV3 ..77 E8
St Christian's Rd CV3 ....77 E8
St Christopher Prim Sch
CV5 ....60 D4
St Christopher's Cl
CV34 ....108 D8
St Clements Ct CV2 ......62 D8
St Columba's Cl CV11 ...151 B4
St David's Cl CV31 ....110 C7
St David's Ct GL56 ....140 A3
St David's Prim Sch
GL56 ....140 A3
St Davids Orch CV3 ....78 F7
St Davids Way CV10 ....39 A6
St Davids Wlk CV37 ......130 E1
St Denis View CV23 ....66 A4
St Edith's Cl CV23 ....53 C2
St Edith's Gn **B** CV34 ...109 B8
St Edith's Ho **B** CV34 ...109 B8
St Editha's Ct B78 ....5 A1
St Edithas Rd B78 ....11 A4
St Edmonds Rd CV9 ....16 B3
St Edward's RC Prim Sch
B46 ....34 A2
St Edwards Ct GL56 ......140 A2
St Edwin's Cl WR11 ......127 B2
St Elizabeth's RC Prim Sch
CV6 ....61 E7
St Elizabeth's Rd CV6 ....61 E7
St Faith's CE Jun Sch
B49 ....143 B2
St Faith's Rd B49 ....143 B3
St Francis RC Prim Sch
CV12 ....39 C3
St Fremund Way CV31 ...110 C5
St George & St Teresa RC
Prim Sch B93 ....72 A4
St George's Cl
15 Moreton-in-M GL56 ..140 A3
Stratford-u-A CV37 .....144 B2
St George's Rd
Atherstone CV9 ....12 C1
Coventry CV1 ....61 F2
Royal Leamington Spa
CV31 ....109 F6
Solihull B90 ....70 D8
St Georges Ave CV22 .....99 C4
St Georges Way CV10 .....39 B8
St Gerard's (Warwickshire)
Orthopaedic Hospl B46 ..34 A3
St Gerard's RC Prim Sch
B35 ....22 B4
St Giles Jun Sch CV7 .....49 F8
St Giles Rd Coventry CV7 ..49 D6
Gaydon CV35 ....132 E8
St Govan's Cl **2** CV31 ...110 C6
St Gregory's RC Prim Sch
CV2 ....62 D5
St Gregory's RC Prim Sch
CV37 ....145 A2
St Gregory's Rd CV37 ...145 A2
St Helen's Rd CV31 ......110 A5
St Helen's Way CV5 ....60 B8
St Helena Rd B78 ....11 A4
St Ives Rd CV2 ....62 E3
St Ives Way CV11 ....29 F5
St James & Ebrington CE
Prim Sch GL55 ....135 B1
St James CE Jun Sch
CV12 ....40 C2
St James CE Mid Sch
CV12 ....40 C2
St James CE Prim Sch
CV47 ....147 A3
St James Cl WR11 ....127 D3
St James Cres CV47 .....147 A3
St James Ct Coventry CV3 ..78 E6
Moreton-in-M GL56 .....140 A2
St James Gdns CV12 .....40 C2
St James Meadow Rd
CV32 ....105 C2
St James Rd CV47 ....147 A3
St James' Ave CV35 .....146 C2
St James' La CV3 ....78 D6
St James's Cl LE10 ......31 D5
St John Fisher RC Prim Sch
CV2 ....62 D5
St John St CV21 ....83 A2
St John the Baptist RC Prim
Sch B36 ....22 A1
St John the Divine CE Prim
Sch CV3 ....78 C5
St John Vianney RC Prim Sch
CV5 ....60 B3
St John's Ave CV8 ....93 A3
St John's CE Prim Sch
CV5 ....60 C4
St John's Cl
Cherington CV36 ....141 D7
Henley-in-A B95 ....113 A4
St John's Ct **3** CV34 ...108 F7
St John's Flats CV8 ......93 A3
St John's Gn CV23 ....82 A3
St John's Mus* CV34 ...108 F7
St John's Prim Sch CV8 ..92 F2
St John's Rd
Cherington CV36 ....141 D7
Royal Leamington Spa
CV31 ....110 A6
St John's St
Coventry CV1 ....151 C2

St John's St continued
Kenilworth CV8 ....93 A3
St John's Terr **13** CV31 ..110 A6
St Johns CV34 ....108 F7
St Johns Ave CV22 ......100 C4
St Johns Cl Knowle B93 ..72 B6
Stratford-u-A CV37 .....144 C1
St Johns Rd CV10 ....27 C4
St Johns Way B93 ....72 C6
St Joseph's B96 ....118 C8
St Joseph's RC Jun Sch
CV11 ....29 C3
St Joseph's RC Prim Sch
Banbury OX16 ....139 F3
Whitnash CV31 ....110 A4
St Joseph's Sch CV8 .....93 B7
St Jude's Cres CV3 ....78 D7
St Judes Ave B80 ....103 C3
St Laurence Ave CV34 ...108 D5
St Laurence Cl CV35 ...114 A8
St Laurence Way B50 ...148 B3
St Laurence CE Prim Sch
CV47 ....125 C7
St Lawrence Cl
Knowle B93 ....72 B5
Napton on t H CV47 ....125 C8
St Lawrence Rd CV10 ....27 A2
St Lawrence's Rd CV6 ....49 F1
St Leonard's Wlk CV8 ....79 A1
St Leonards Cl
Birmingham B37 ....44 A7
Dordon B78 ....11 A3
St Leonards View B78 ....10 C4
St Luke's Rd CV6 ....49 D3
St Lukes Way CV10 ......28 C4
St Margaret Rd
Coventry CV1 ....61 F2
Stoke Golding CV13 ......21 C4
St Margaret's CE Jun Sch
CV31 ....110 B3
St Margaret's CE Prim Sch
CV31 ....21 B4
St Margaret's Ho CV31 ..110 B4
St Margaret's Rd CV31 ..110 B5
St Marie's RC Inf Sch
CV22 ....83 A1
St Mark's Annexe (Coventry &
Warwickshire Hospl)
CV1 ....151 C4
St Mark's Ave CV22 ......99 B4
St Mark's Cl
Gaydon CV35 ....132 E8
Ullenhall B95 ....112 C6
St Mark's Mews CV32 ...105 E1
St Mark's Rd CV32 ......105 D1
St Marks Cl CV10 ....28 C4
St Martin's LE10 ....31 E6
St Martin's Cl CV37 ....144 C1
St Martin's RC High Sch
CV13 ....21 C4
St Martin's Rd CV8 ......77 D2
St Martins Ave B80 .....103 B2
St Mary St CV1 ....151 C2
St Mary's CE Prim Sch
LE10 ....31 D8
St Mary's Cl
Priors Hardwick CV47 ...125 D3
Southam CV47 ....147 B3
Ullenhall B95 ....112 C6
Warwick CV34 ....108 D8
St Mary's Cres CV31 ....110 B7
St Mary's Ct CV31 ......110 B6
St Mary's Immaculate RC
Prim Sch CV34 ....108 E8
St Mary's La OX7 ....142 F2
St Mary's RC Prim Sch
Aston le W NN11 ....134 C5
Coventry CV2 ....61 F3
Henley-in-A B95 ....113 B4
Southam CV47 ....147 B2
Studley B80 ....103 C2
St Mary's Rd
Alcester B49 ....143 B2
Atherstone CV9 ....18 C4
Fillongley CV7 ....36 C2
Hinckley LE10 ....31 D8
Nuneaton CV11 ....29 B5
Royal Leamington Spa
CV31 ....110 B7
Stratford-u-A CV37 .....145 A2
St Mary's Terr CV31 ....110 B7
St Marys Acre CV37 .....108 B4
St Marys Gr B79 ....2 B2
St Matthew's Bloxam CE Prim
Sch CV22 ....82 C1
St Matthews Cl WR11 ...127 E6
St Matthews St **7** CV21 ..83 A2
St Mawgen **2** B35 .....22 C4
St Michael's CE Prim Sch
CV12 ....39 D3
St Michael's Arley CV7 ...37 A4
Bishops Itchington CV47 ..124 A4
Claverdon CV35 ....113 F3
Lutterworth LE17 ......127 F1
Weston u W CV33 ....107 B4
St Michael's Cres CV47 ..147 C4
St Michael's Dr DE12 ....3 C4
St Michael's Hospl
CV34 ....108 D8
St Michael's Rd
Claverdon CV35 ....113 F3
Coventry CV2 ....62 A3
Warwick CV34 ....108 D8
St Michael's Way CV10 ..28 C4
St Michaels Cl
Atherstone CV9 ....12 C1

St Michaels Cl continued
Ufton CV33 ....111 C1
Wood End CV9 ....10 B1
St Milburgh Cl WR11 ....127 D1
St Nicholas Ave CV8 .....92 F3
St Nicholas CE Prim Sch
CV8 ....92 F5
St Nicholas Church St
CV34 ....108 F6
St Nicholas Cl
Alcester B49 ....143 B2
Austrey CV9 ....3 A1
Coventry CV1 ....61 C5
St Nicholas Ct
3 Coventry, Edgwick CV6 ..61 F7
Coventry, Radford CV6 ...61 B6
Nuneaton CV10 ....27 B2
Southam CV47 ....147 B3
St Nicholas Rd
Henley-in-A B95 ....113 B4
Radford Semele CV31 ...110 F5
St Nicholas St CV1 .....151 B4
St Nicholas Terr CV31 ..110 E5
St Nicholas Wlk B75 .....23 B6
St Nicolas CE Prim Sch
CV11 ....29 B4
St Nicolas Park Dr CV11 ..29 F7
St Nicolas Rd CV11 ......29 D4
St Osburg's RC Prim Sch
CV1 ....151 A3
St Osburg's Rd CV2 ......62 A3
St Oswalds CE Prim Sch
CV2 ....82 B2
St Patrick's CE Prim Sch
B94 ....70 C2
St Patrick's Rd
Birmingham B37 ....33 C2
Coventry CV1 ....151 B1
St Patrick's Rd CV1 ....151 B1
St Patricks RC Prim Sch
CV31 ....109 F6
St Paul's CE Prim Sch
Nuneaton CV10 ....28 C3
Royal Leamington Spa
CV32 ....106 B1
St Paul's Cl CV34 ......108 D6
St Paul's Cres **5** B46 ...33 F7
St Paul's Ct B77 ....9 B2
St Paul's Rd Coventry CV6 ..61 F6
Nuneaton CV10 ....28 D3
St Paul's Sq **4** CV32 ..106 A1
St Paul's Terr CV34 ....108 D6
St Pauls Ct
Moreton-in-M GL56 .....140 A2
Water Orton B46 ....23 B3
St Peter's Ave CV9 ....19 A4
St Peter's Cl
Redditch B97 ....102 C3
Water Orton B46 ....23 B2
Witherley CV9 ....19 A4
St Peter's Ct CV1 ....151 D4
St Peter's Dr CV10 ......27 C2
St Peter's Pl B78 ....15 B3
St Peter's RC Prim Sch
CV32 ....109 F8
St Peter's Rd
Atherstone CV9 ....19 A4
Kineton CV35 ....132 B6
St Swithin's Dr CV37 ...129 D2
St Thomas Cl CV10 ......28 C3
St Thomas More RC Fst Sch
B98 ....103 A4
St Thomas More RC Prim Sch
CV1 ....77 D5
St Thomas More RC Sch
CV10 ....29 A3
St Thomas' Rd CV6 ......50 A3
St Thomas's Cl CV10 ....61 B2
St Thomas's Ho **17** CV1 ..61 B2
St Wulstan Way CV47 ...147 B3
Salcombe Cl Coventry CV3 ..78 D6
Nuneaton CV11 ....29 F5
Salem Rd LE10 ....31 F5
Salford Cl Coventry CV2 ..62 A5
Redditch B98 ....103 A3
Salford Priors CE Prim Sch
WR11 ....127 F6
Salford Rd B50 ....148 B2
Salisbury Ave CV3 ....77 C6
Salisbury Cl CV32 ....79 F3
Salisbury Dr
Nuneaton CV10 ....28 B7
Water Orton B46 ....23 C3
Salisbury Rd LE10 ......32 B3
Salt La CV1 ....151 B2
Saltash Way B94 ....70 C2
Salters La B95 ....120 C7
Saltisford CV34 ....108 D7
Saltisford Gdns CV34 ...108 C8
Salts La B78 ....8 C3
Sam Gault Cl CV3 ....78 E7
Sambourne La
Astwood Bank B96 .....102 C1
Coughton B49,B96 ......118 E7
Sambourne B96 ....103 A1
Sambourne Pk B96 .....118 D8
Sammons Way CV4 ....59 D1
Sampson Cl CV2 ....62 C8
Samuel Hayward Ho **8**
CV2 ....50 B1

Samuel Vale Ho CV1 .....151 B4
Sanby Cl CV32 ....39 A4
Sanctus Dr CV37 ....144 C1
Sanctus Rd CV37 ....144 C1
Sanctus St CV37 ....144 C1
Sand Barn La CV37 .....121 D6
Sanda Croft B36 ....33 B6
Sandbarn Cl B90 ....70 F6
Sandel Cl CV37 ....144 C2
Sanders Cl Warwickshire CV9 ..12 C1
Braunston NN11 ....117 D5
Sanders Ct CV8 ....93 B4
Sanders Rd Bedworth CV6 ..50 B6
Salford Priors WR11 ....127 F6
Sandfield Cl B90 ....70 B8
Sandfield La CV37 ....130 E1
Sandfield Rd CV37 .....144 C1
Sandfine Rd OX15 ......139 D1
Sandford Cl CV2 ....50 E3
Sandford Gn OX16 ......139 F4
Sandford Way CV22 .....99 B2
Sandgate Cres CV2 ......62 E2
Sandhills Cres B91 ......71 B8
Sandhurst Gr CV6 ....61 B5
Sandilands Cl CV2 ......62 E4
Sandon Rd CV11 ....29 B5
Sandown Ave CV6 ....49 F2
Sandown Cl
Royal Leamington Spa
CV32 ....106 C4
Stratford-u-A CV37 .....144 B1
Sandown Rd CV21 ....83 B2
Sandpiper B77 ....10 A3
Sandpiper Cl
Newton CV23 ....67 B1
Stratford-u-A CV37 .....144 B3
Sandpiper Rd CV2 ....50 B3
Sandpits Cl Curdworth B76 ..23 B6
Tysoe CV35 ....138 B6
Sandpits La CV6 ....48 F2
Sandpits Rd CV35 ......138 B7
Sandpits The CV10 ......40 C2
Sandringham Cl CV7 .....75 C5
Sandringham Ct CV10 ...28 F6
Sandwick Cl CV3 ....78 D6
Sandy La Blackdown CV32 ..105 F6
Coventry CV1 ....61 C5
Furnace End B46 ....25 C2
Marton CV23 ....115 D7
Monks Kirby CV23 ....53 C2
Newton Regis B79 ....2 B3
Royal Leamington Spa
CV32 ....105 D4
Rugby CV21 ....82 C2
Sandy Lane Bsns Pk CV1 ..61 C5
Sandy Way Barford CV35 ..122 B7
Tamworth B77 ....4 A2
Sandy Way La B78 ....11 B4
Sandythorpe CV3 ....78 F6
Sankey Gr GL56 ....140 A2
Santos Cl CV3 ....78 F8
Sapcote Gr CV2 ....50 B4
Sapcote Rd LE10 ....32 B7
Saplings The B76 ....22 A8
Sapphire Dr CV31 ......109 F5
Sapphire Gate CV2 ......62 C4
Saracen Dr
Balsall Common CV7 .....73 C6
Sutton Coldfield B75 ...13 A6
Sargeaunt St CV31 .....110 B6
Sark Dr B36 ....33 B6
Satchwell Ct **13** CV32 ..109 F8
Satchwell Wlk **14** CV32 ..109 F8
Saumar Way CV34 ......109 C6
Saunders Ave CV12 ......39 B2
Saunders Ho **13** CV32 ..105 F2
Saunton Cl CV5 ....60 B8
Saunton Rd CV22 ....82 C1
Savages Cl CV33 ....122 F8
Savernake Rd CV35 .....132 C4
Saville Gr CV8 ....93 C5
Sawbridge Rd CV23 ....116 F5
Saxon Cl
Binley Woods CV3 ......79 D7
Polesworth B78 ....4 C1
Rugby CV22 ....99 A4
Stratford-u-A CV37 .....145 B1
Studley B80 ....103 C3
Tamworth B77 ....9 C3
Saxon Ct B50 ....148 B2
Saxon Mdws CV32 ....105 B2
Saxon Rd CV2 ....62 B4
Saxon Wood Rd B90 .....70 D5
Saxonfields B50 ....148 B2
Scafell Cl CV3 ....83 B4
Scafell Cl CV5 ....60 A4
Scammerton B77 ....10 A4
Scar Bank CV34 ....104 E1
Scarborough Way CV4 ...75 F7
Scarman Rd CV4 ....76 B5
Schofield Rd B37 ....33 A6
Scholars Cl CV12 ....144 C2
Scholars La CV37 ......144 C1
Scholfield Rd CV7 ....49 A6
School Ave WR11 ......127 F6
School Bell Mews CV8 ...94 B6
School Cl Birmingham B37 ..33 A6
Braunston NN11 ....117 E5
Coventry CV1 ....61 F2
Great Alne B49 ....119 D6
Hinckley LE10 ....32 A6
Long Compton CV36 ....141 C3
School Cotts CV35 ....90 F3
School Croft CV5 ....91 C2
School Dr B47 ....69 A3
School Fields B78 ....10 C4
School Hill
Mollington OX17 ....133 F2

School Hill continued
Napton on t H CV47 ....125 C8
Nuneaton CV10 ....28 A8
Offchurch CV33 ....111 A4
Wootton Wawen B95 ...113 A3
School House La CV2 .....63 A6
School La Badby NN11 ...126 F6
Bearley CV37 ....120 E7
Bedworth CV7 ....49 F7
Kenilworth CV8 ....92 F5
Ladbroke CV47 ....124 D5
Lea Marston B76 ....24 A4
Lower Brailes OX15 ....137 F2
North Newington OX15 ..139 E2
Nuneaton CV10 ....27 C3
Priors Marston CV47 ...125 D4
Radford Semele CV31 ...110 E5
Shustoke B79 ....4 C4
South Littleton WR11 ..127 F1
Stretton on D CV23 .....96 C3
Tamworth B77 ....9 B3
Tiddington CV37 ....145 C2
Warmington OX17 ....133 D2
Weston u W CV33 ....107 C3
Wolvey LE10 ....41 C2
Wroxall CV35 ....90 E4
School Rd Alcester B49 ..143 A2
Bulkington CV12 ....40 C2
Great Alne B49 ....119 D6
Henley-in-A B95 ....113 B4
Hockley Heath B94 ......88 B7
Pebworth CV37 ....128 F1
Salford Priors WR11 ...127 F6
Snitterfield CV37 ......121 B6
Wellesbourne CV35 ....146 C2
School St
Church Lawford CV23 ...81 A3
Churchover CV23 ....67 B3
Dunchurch CV22 ....99 B2
Long Lawford CV23 .....82 A2
Rugby CV21 ....84 A1
Southam CV47 ....147 B2
Stockton CV47 ....147 C4
Stretton CV8 ....80 A8
School Wlk CV11 ....29 E2
Scotchill The CV6 ....49 A1
Scotland End OX15 .....142 D4
Scots Cl CV22 ....99 B4
Scots La CV6 ....60 F6
Scott Ave CV10 ....29 D8
Scott Cl B50 ....148 B3
Scott Rd Kenilworth CV8 ..92 E2
Redditch B97 ....102 B4
Royal Leamington Spa
CV31 ....110 B6
Seabroke Ave CV22 ......82 C2
Seafield La B48 ....85 E4
Seaford Cl CV6 ....50 B4
Seagrave Rd CV1 ......151 D1
Sealand Dr CV12 ....39 A4
Sear Hills Cl CV7 ....74 B6
Seathwaite CV21 ....83 B4
Seaton B77 ....9 C4
Seaton Cl Hinckley LE10 ..32 B7
Nuneaton CV11 ....29 F5
Sebastian Cl CV3 ....78 B5
Second Ave CV3 ....62 C1
Second Exhibition Ave
B40 ....44 D4
Sedgemere Gr CV7 ....74 C5
Sedgemoor Rd CV3 ....78 B5
Sedlescombe Lodge
CV22 ....99 C4
Sedlescombe Pk CV22 ...99 C4
Seed Field Croft CV3 ....77 E7
Seekings The CV31 .....110 B3
Seeney La B76 ....15 A1
Seeswood Cl CV10 ....28 C2
Sefton Rd Coventry CV4 ..76 E6
Seggs La B49 ....143 A2
Segrave Cl CV35 ....132 B6
Selborne Rd CV22 ....99 B4
Selby Way CV10 ....28 B5
Selina Dix Ho CV1 ......151 C4
Selsdon Cl B47 ....69 C5
Selsey Cl CV3 ....78 C4
Selside CV21 ....83 B4
Selworthy Rd CV6 ....49 E3
Selwyn Cl CV35 ....146 B2
Selwyn Ho B37 ....33 D3
Semele Cl CV31 ....110 E5
Seneschal Rd CV3 ....77 E7
Sennen Cl CV11 ....30 A5
Sentry Way B75 ....13 A6
Sephton Dr CV6 ....50 C6
Servite Ho **2** Coleshill B46 ..33 F7
Kenilworth CV8 ....92 F3
Sett The CV35 ....137 F8
Seven Acre Cl **4** CV33 ..122 E8
Seven Meadows Rd
CV37 ....144 C1
Seven Stars Ind Est CV3 ..78 A7
Severn Ave LE10 ....31 A8
Severn Cl CV32 ....106 C3
Severn Rd Bulkington CV12 ..40 A3
Coventry CV1 ....61 F1
Sevincott Cl CV37 .....144 B2
Sevington Cl B91 ....71 C8
Sewall Ct CV6 ....62 A8
Sewall Highway CV2 ....62 A8
Seymour Cl Coventry CV3 ..78 C5
Hampton Magna CV35 ..114 F3
Seymour Gate GL55 ....135 B2
Seymour Gr CV34 ......109 D6
Seymour Ho CV10 ....77 C8
Seymour Rd
Alcester B49 ....143 B3

Seymour Rd continued
Nuneaton CV11 ....29 D3
Rugby CV21 ....83 B3
Stratford-u-A CV37 ....144 B1
Shackleton Dr LE10 ....31 E4
Shackleton Way LE17 ......55 B3
Shadow Brook La B92 ......56 E7
Shadowbrook Rd CV6 ......61 A5
Shaft La CV7 ....47 A4
Shaftesbury Ave CV7 ......49 A7
Shaftesbury Rd CV5 ....76 F8
Shakells Cl B97 ....102 C2
Shakers La CV47 ....115 C5
Shakesfield Cl CV36 ......136 F6
Shakespeare Ave
  Bedworth CV12 ....39 D2
  Warwick CV34 ....108 C4
Shakespeare Ct CV37 ....145 A2
Shakespeare Ctr Mus The*
  CV37 ....145 A2
Shakespeare Dr CV11 .....30 A1
Shakespeare Gdns CV22 ..99 C4
Shakespeare La WR11 ...127 D3
Shakespeare Rd B90 ......70 D8
Shakespeare St
  Coventry CV2 ....62 B8
  Stratford-u-A CV37 ......145 A2
Shakespeare's Grave*
  CV37 ....145 A1
Shakespeares Birthplace
  Mus* CV37 ....145 A2
Shakleton Rd CV5 ....61 A2
Shanes Castle Rd CV35 ..132 D3
Shanklin Dr CV10 ....29 D6
Shanklin Rd CV3 ....78 B4
Shannon B77 ....9 C4
Shap Fell CV21 ....83 B4
Sharnford Rd LE10 ....32 F6
Sharp Cl CV6 ....49 C2
Sharpe Cl CV34 ....108 E8
Sharpe St B77 ....4 A3
Sharpless Rd LE10 ....31 F7
Sharpley Ct CV2 ....63 A8
Sharratt Rd CV12 ....39 A2
Sharry La CV37 ....129 C1
Shaw's La CV35 ....114 C8
Shawberry Ave B35 ....22 B4
Shawbury La B46 ....35 B4
Shawe Village B46 ....35 C3
Shawe Ave CV10 ....29 C7
Shawell Rd LE17 ....68 B4
Shawfield B47 ....69 A5
Shawhurst Croft B47 ....69 A7
Shawhurst Gdns B47 ....69 B7
Shawhurst La B47 ....69 A6
Shearings The OX15 ......142 D4
Sheen Ho CV2 ....62 D8
Sheep Dip La CV23 ....96 C1
Sheep St
  Chipping Campden GL55 ..135 A1
  Rugby CV21 ....83 A2
  Shipston-on-S CV36 ....149 C3
  Stratford-u-A CV37 ......145 A1
Sheepclose Dr B37 ....33 A3
Sheepcote Cl CV32 ....106 A1
Sheepy La CV9 ....6 C2
Sheepy Rd Atherstone CV9 ..12 B1
  Atherstone, Pinwall CV9 ....12 C3
Shefford Rd CV35 ....132 D3
Shelbourne Rd CV37 .....144 A2
Sheldon Gr CV34 ....104 F2
Sheldon Rd B98 ....103 A4
Sheldrake Cl CV3 ....63 A1
Shelfield Cl Coventry CV5 ..60 B3
  Hockley Heath B94 ....88 C6
Shelley Ave CV34 ....108 C4
Shelley Cl Bedworth CV12 ..39 D1
  Redditch B97 ....102 B4
Shelley Rd Coventry CV2 ..62 C3
  Stratford-u-A CV37 ......144 B1
Shelton Cl CV3 ....78 F8
Shelly Cres B90 ....71 B6
Shelly La B90 ....71 B6
Shelton Sq CV1 ....151 B2
Shelton St B77 ....9 C4
Shenick Gr B93 ....71 F4
Shenington CE Prim Sch
  OX15 ....138 F5
Shenstone Ave CV22 ....83 C1
Shenstone Dr CV7 ....74 A6
Shenton Cl CV13 ....21 C4
Shepherds Hill CV47 .....147 B2
Shepherd Cl Coventry CV4 ..59 F3
  Long Itchington CV47 ...115 D3
Shepherd Pl CV35 ....132 B5
Shepherd St CV23 ....115 C7
Shepherds Cl OX15 ....142 D8
Shepperston Bsns Pk
  CV11 ....29 C1
Shepperton Ct CV11 ....29 C1
Shepperton St CV11 ....29 C2
Sheppey Dr B36 ....33 B5
Sherard Croft B36 ....33 B6
Sherborne Cl B46 ....34 A2
Sherborne Rd LE10 ....32 B7
Sherbourne Ave CV10 ......28 B4
Sherbourne Cres CV5 ......60 E4
Sherbourne Ct CV1 ....151 B1
Sherbourne Fields Sch
  CV6 ....60 D5
Sherbourne St CV1 ....61 A2
Sherbrooke Ave B77 ....9 C1
Sherdmore Croft B90 ......70 F6
Sheridan Cl CV22 ....99 C4
Sheridan Dr CV10 ....27 C3
Sheriden Wlk B35 ....22 A3
Sheriff Ave CV4 ....76 B7
Sheriff Rd CV21 ....83 B2

Sheriffs Orch CV1 ....151 B2
Sheringham Cl CV11 ....29 F2
Sherington Ave CV5 ....60 C4
Sherlock Rd CV5 ....60 D3
Sherwell Dr B49 ....143 A2
Sherwood Dr CV11 ....30 B1
Sherwood Jones Cl CV6 ...61 B6
Sherwood Rd CV13 ....21 C4
Sherwood Wlk CV22 ....106 C4
Shetland Ave B77 ....9 C4
Shetland Cl CV5 ....60 A4
Shetland Dr CV10 ....28 B7
Shetland Wlk B36 ....33 B6
Shevlock Way CV6 ....62 A6
Shillingstone Cl CV2 ....63 A4
Shillingstone Dr
  Nuneaton CV10 ....28 F1
  Nuneaton CV10 ....29 A1
Shilton Cl B90 ....70 F6
Shilton Ind Est CV7 ....51 E7
Shilton La
  Barnacle CV2,CV7 ....51 B4
  Bulkington CV12 ....40 D1
  Coventry CV2 ....50 F3
Shilton St CV7 ....51 D8
Shinehill La WR11 ....128 A1
Shipston High Sch
  CV36 ....149 C3
Shipston Rd
  Aldermister CV37 ....130 B5
  Coventry CV2 ....62 C6
  Long Compton CV36,OX7 ..141 C4
  Tysoe CV35 ....138 B6
Shipton-on-Stour Prim Sch
  CV36 ....149 C3
Shire Cl CV6 ....50 B1
Shirebrook Cl CV2 ....50 D2
Shires Gate Ret Pk
  CV31 ....109 E6
Shires Gate Trad Est
  CV31 ....109 E6
Shires Ret Pk CV34 ....109 D6
Shires The CV23 ....81 A3
Shirland Rd B37 ....33 A1
Shirlett Cl CV2 ....50 B4
Shirley La CV7 ....59 A5
Shirley Rd CV2 ....63 A7
Shirley Trad Est B90 ....70 F8
Shirleydale B B90 ....70 C8
Shirrall Dr B75,B78 ....7 C2
Shopping Ctr The CV31 ..110 B5
Shopping Prec The
  CV34 ....105 A1
Shorncliffe Rd CV6 ....60 E6
Short Acres OX15 ....132 C6
Short La CV47 ....115 C4
Short St Coventry CV1 ....151 C2
  Nuneaton CV10 ....28 D4
Shortfield Cl CV7 ....74 B7
Shortland Cl B93 ....72 A7
Shortlands CV7 ....49 D6
Shortley Rd CV3 ....77 F8
Shortwoods The B78 ....11 A3
Shottery CV37 ....144 B1
Shottery Cl CV5 ....60 B3
Shottery Rd CV37 ....144 C1
Shottery St Andrew's CE Prim
  Sch CV37 ....144 B1
Shotteswell Rd B90 ....70 B8
Shoulderway La CV36 ....149 C1
Showell La CV7 ....47 A1
Shrewley Comm CV35 ....114 B6
Shrubberies The CV4 ....76 E4
Shrubland St CV31 ....110 A6
Shrubland Street Com Prim
  Sch CV31 ....110 A6
Shuckburgh Cres
  Bourton on D CV23 ....97 C1
  Rugby CV22 ....100 B4
Shuckburgh Gr 4 CV32 ..106 A2
Shuckburgh Rd
  Napton on t H CV47 .....125 C8
  Priors Marston CV47 ....125 E4
Shulman's Wlk CV2 ....62 D7
Shultern La CV4 ....76 D6
Shuna Croft CV2 ....63 B7
Shustoke CE Prim Sch
  B46 ....35 A1
Shustoke Resr* B46 ....24 C2
Shutford Rd
  North Newington OX15 ..139 D2
  Shutford OX15 ....139 B1
Shutt La B94 ....70 B1
Shuttington Rd B79 ....4 A3
Shuttle St CV6 ....62 B8
Shuttleworth Rd CV23 .....83 C3
Shylock Gr CV34 ....109 E2
Sibford Gower Prim Sch
  OX15 ....142 D8
Sibford Rd
  Hook Norton OX15 ....142 D4
  Shutford OX15 ....138 F2
Sibford Sch OX15 ....142 D8
Sibree Rd CV3 ....78 B4
Sibton Cl CV2 ....50 C1
Sidbury Gr B93 ....71 E3
Sidbury Rd CV6 ....61 C6
Siddaway Ho CV21 ....83 B4
Siddeley Ave
  Coventry CV3 ....62 B1
  Kenilworth CV8 ....92 D3
Siddeley Way WN11 ......117 F2
Sidelands Rd CV37 ....144 B2
Sidenhill Cl B90 ....70 B8
Sidings The CV21 ....83 A2
Sidmouth Cl Coventry CV2 ..62 C7
  Nuneaton CV11 ....29 F5
Sidney Rd CV22 ....100 B4

Sidney Stringer Com Tech
  Coll CV1 ....151 C3
Signal Hayes Rd B76 ....13 A2
Signal Rd CV36 ....149 C4
Signal Wlk B77 ....4 A1
Silica Rd B77 ....4 A1
Silken Ct CV11 ....29 B4
Silksby St CV3 ....77 D8
Silver Birch Ave CV12 ......38 E2
Silver Birch Dr B47 ....69 B6
Silver Link Rd B37 ....4 A1
Silver St Coventry CV1 ....151 B3
  Newton CV23 ....68 A1
  Wroxton OX15 ....139 D4
Silver Trees Dr CV12 ....40 B4
Silver Wlk CV10 ....28 F3
Silverbirch Cl CV10 ....28 A7
Silverdale Cl CV2 ....50 B4
Silverstone Dr CV6 ....49 F5
Silverton Rd CV6 ....61 F7
Simmonds Way CV9 ....12 B1
Simmons Cl B78 ....8 A1
Simmons Ct CV35 ....146 B2
Simms La B47 ....69 A5
Simon Cl CV11 ....29 D2
Simon Ct CV7 ....50 A8
Simon Stone St CV6 ....61 F8
Simpkins Cl CV33 ....107 B4
Simpson Rd CV36 ....149 C3
Sinclair Ave CV36 ....149 C3
Sinclair Ave OX16 ....139 F4
Sinclair Dr CV6 ....50 C6
Singer Cl CV6 ....62 B8
Singer Croft B36 ....22 F1
Sir Frank Whittle Bsns Ctr
  CV21 ....83 B3
Sir Frank Whittle Prim Sch
  CV2 ....76 C8
Sir Henry Parkes Rd CV5 ..76 D7
Sir John Moore CE Prim Sch
  DE12 ....3 C2
Sir Thomas White's Rd
  CV5 ....60 F2
Sir William Lyons Rd
  CV4 ....76 C6
Sir Winston Churchill Pl
  CV3 ....79 C7
Siskin Cl CV23 ....78 C4
Siskin Parkway E CV3 ......78 C1
Siskin Parkway W CV3 .....78 C1
Sitwell Ave CV47 ....115 D3
Sixteen Acres La B50 .....148 C1
Skelwith Rise CV11 ....30 A6
Sketchley Hall Gdns
  LE10 ....31 C5
Sketchley Hill Prim Sch
  LE10 ....31 D5
Sketchley La LE10 ....31 C5
Sketchley La Ind Est
  LE10 ....31 B5
Sketchley Manor La
  LE10 ....31 D5
Sketchley Mdws LE10 .....31 C4
Sketchley Meadows Bsns Pk
  LE10 ....31 C4
Sketchley Old Village
  LE10 ....31 C5
Sketchley Rd LE10 ....31 E5
Skiddaw CV21 ....83 B4
Skidmore Ave B77 ....9 B3
Skipton Cl CV11 ....30 A6
Skipton Gdns CV2 ....62 B6
Skipton Lodge CV2 ....62 B6
Skipwith Cl CV3 ....64 B2
Skipworth Rd CV3 ....63 A1
Sky Blue Way CV1 ....61 E3
Skydome The CV1 ....151 A2
Skye Cl Birmingham B36 ..33 B6
  Nuneaton CV10 ....28 F2
Slack's Ave CV9 ....18 B4
Slade Cl B76 ....13 A1
Slade La CV37 ....40 C8
Slade Rd Rugby CV21,CV22 ..83 B1
  Sutton Coldfield B75 ....7 A2
Sladen Cl CV37 ....130 E6
Sleath's Yd CV12 ....39 A2
Sledmere Cl CV2 ....50 B3
Sleets Yd CV12 ....39 A2
Smalley Pl CV8 ....92 F4
Small Brook Bsns Ctr
  B50 ....148 C3
Small Ho B76 ....86 E6
Smarts La CV35 ....138 B6
Smarts Rd CV12 ....38 F1
Smeaton La CV23 ....64 C3
Smercote Cl CV12 ....38 D1
Smite Cl CV23 ....53 C2

Smith St Bedworth CV12 ..38 E1
  Coventry CV6 ....61 F5
  2 Royal Leamington Spa
  CV31 ....109 F7
  Warwick CV34 ....108 F7
  Wood End CV9 ....10 B1
Smith's La CV37 ....121 B6
Smith's Way B49 ....143 B3
Smithford Way CV1 ....151 B3
Smiths Cl B50 ....148 C3
Smiths La B93 ....71 E7
Smiths Orch CV21 ....83 B2
Smiths Way B46 ....23 A3
Smiths Wood Sch B36 ......33 A6
Smithy La
  Aston Flamville LE9 ....32 C8
  Church Lawford CV23 .....81 B3
  Tamworth B77 ....9 C4
Smithy Rd CV9 ....17 B3
Smythe Gr CV34 ....104 E1
Snape Rd CV2 ....62 F5
Snarestone Rd DE12 ....3 C4
Sniterfield La CV37 ....121 C7
Sniterfield Rd CV37 ....114 C1
Sniterfield Prim Sch
  CV37 ....121 B6
Snitterfield Rd CV37 ......120 E7
Snitterfield St CV35 ....121 F4
Snowdon Cl CV10 ....28 B3
Snowdrop Cl CV12 ....38 E1
Snowford Hill CV33 ....
Snowshill Cl CV11 ....39 F8
Snuff La OX17 ....139 E8
Soar Way LE10 ....31 A8
Soden Cl CV3 ....78 D6
Soden's Ave CV8 ....79 A1
Solent Dr CV2 ....50 F1
Solihull Coll Chelmsley
  Campus B37 ....33 C4
Solihull Parkway B37 ......44 E8
Solihull Rd B92 ....56 E6
Solihull Ret Pk B90 ....70 C8
Solway Cl CV31 ....110 C6
Somerby Dr B91 ....71 A8
Somerly Cl CV3 ....78 F8
Somers Pl 4 CV32 ....109 E8
Somers Rd Keresley CV7 ..48 D6
  Meriden CV7 ....45 F1
  Rugby CV22 ....82 B2
Somerset Dr CV10 ....28 E4
Somerset Rd CV1 ....61 C5
Somerton Dr B37 ....44 B7
Somerville Ho CV37 ....33 B3
Somerville Rd CV2 ....62 C4
Soot La OX17 ....133 D2
Sopwith Croft B35 ....22 A2
Sorbus B37 ....4 A2
Sorrel B77 ....4 A4
Sorrel Cl CV4 ....75 E8
Sorrel Dr Kingsbury B78 ..15 B4
  Rugby CV23 ....83 B4
Sorrell Pl CV10 ....39 D8
Sorrell Rd CV10 ....39 D8
South Ave CV2 ....62 A2
South Car Park Rd B40 ....44 E3
South Cl NN11 ....117 F5
South Dr B46 ....33 E6
South End OX7 ....142 A2
South Green Dr CV37 ....144 B2
South Par CV33 ....123 F6
South St CV33 ....84 A3
South Ridge CV5 ....60 B4
South St Atherstone CV9 ..18 B4
  Coventry CV1 ....62 E3
  Rugby CV21 ....83 B2
South Terr CV31 ....110 B3
South View Kingsbury B78 ..15 B2
  Warwick CV35 ....108 A6
South View Rd
  Long Lawford CV23 ....81 C2
  Royal Leamington Spa
  CV32 ....106 C5
South Way B40 ....44 F3
Southam Cl CV4 ....75 E7
Southam Coll CV47 ....147 A3
Southam Cres CV33 ....123 D2
Southam Dr CV47 ....147 A1
Southam Prim Sch
  CV47 ....147 A3
Southam Rd
  Dunchurch CV22 ....99 A1
  Kineton CV35 ....132 B6
  Ladbroke CV47 ....124 D6
  Long Itchington CV47 ...115 D3
  Mollington OX17 ....134 A2
  Priors Marston CV47 ....125 E4
  Southam CV33,CV47 ....123 A4
  Ufton CV31,CV33 ....115 A1
  Ufton, Radford Hill CV33,
  CV47 ....111 B2
Southam St CV35 ....132 B6
Southbank Ct CV8 ....92 F4
Southbank Rd
  Coventry CV6 ....60 E5
  Kenilworth CV8 ....92 F4
Southboro Terr 1
  CV31 ....110 A6
Southbrook Rd CV22 ......83 A1
Southcott Way CV2 ....50 F1
Southern La CV37 ....145 A1
Southey Cl B91 ....71 B8
Southey Rd CV22 ....99 C4
Southfield Cl CV10 ....29 D5

Southfield Dr CV8 ....93 A6
Southfield Rd
  Hinckley LE10 ....31 E7
  Rugby CV22 ....83 B1
  Southam CV47 ....147 A1
Southfields CV32 ....106 A3
Southfields Cl B46 ....34 A2
Southfields Prim Sch
  CV1 ....61 E3
Southlands
  Atherstone CV9 ....18 C4
  2 Royal Leamington Spa
  CV31 ....110 B7
Southlea Ave CV31 ....109 E6
Southlea Cl CV31 ....109 E6
Southleigh Ave CV5 ....76 F7
Southmead Gdns B80 ....103 C2
Southport Cl CV3 ....78 B5
Southrop Rd OX15 ....142 D3
Southway CV31 ....110 A5
Sovereign Cl CV8 ....92 F1
Sovereign Ct CV47 ....147 A2
Sovereign Rd CV5 ....61 A2
Sovereign Row CV5 ....61 A2
Sowe Valley Prim Sch
  CV3 ....78 D7
Spa View CV31 ....110 B4
Sparkbrook St CV1 ....61 F3
Sparkbrook Workshops
  CV1 ....61 F3
Sparrow Cock La B93 ....73 C1
Sparrowdale Specl Sch
  CV9 ....11 B2
Sparta Cl CV21 ....83 A3
Spartan Cl CV34 ....109 E4
Speedway La CV8 ....79 F7
Speedwell Dr CV7 ....74 A6
Speedwell La CV9 ....11 A1
Speedwell Rd CV23 ....83 C4
Speenham Dr CV8 ....83 C1
Spencer Ave CV5 ....61 A1
Spencer Rd CV5 ....151 A1
Spencer St CV31 ....109 F7
Spencer Yd CV31 ....109 F7
Spencer's La CV7 ....58 E1
Spennall Barn B49 ....103 C1
Spernal La
  Great Alne B80 ....119 C2
  Studley B80 ....112 A1
Sperrin Cl CV12 ....40 B2
Spetchley B78 ....10 C4
Spicer Pl CV22 ....82 B1
Spiers Cl B93 ....72 A6
Spiers Ct B50 ....148 B3
Spilsbury Cl CV32 ....105 E2
Spilsbury Croft B91 ....71 A8
Spindle La B90 ....70 A6
Spindle St CV1 ....61 D6
Spindles The LE10 ....31 F5
Spinners Bridge CV36 ....149 C3
Spinney Cl Arley CV7 ......36 C4
  Coventry CV3 ....79 F7
Spinney Dr B90 ....69 A4
Spinney La CV10 ....28 C4
Spinney Rd LE10 ....31 C6
Spinney The
  Banbury NN11 ....117 E5
  Coventry CV4 ....105 A1
Spinney La CV10 ....28 C4
Spinneyfield CV37 ....19 A4
Bishops Itchington CV47 ..124 B4
  Coventry CV4 ....76 D3
Long Lawford CV23 ....82 A3
Royal Leamington Spa
  CV32 ....105 D1
Spitfire Way 1 B35 ....22 A2
Spon End CV1,CV5 ....61 A3
Spon Gate Ho CV1 ....61 A2
Spon Gate Prim Sch CV1 ..61 A3
Spon La CV9 ....11 C3
Spon St CV1 ....151 A3
Spottiswood Cl CV22 ......99 A4
Spring Cl 8 Coventry CV1 ..61 E3
  Ettington CV37 ....131 A3
Spring Coppice Dr B93 ....72 A3
Spring Ct CV8 ....
Spring Hill Arley CV7 ....36 C4
  Bubbenhall CV8 ....95 B3
  Combrook CV35 ....131 F7
Spring Hill Rd CV10 ....28 C6
Spring La
  Combrook CV35 ....131 E6
  Hockley Heath B94 ....88 C5
  Lapworth B94 ....88 D3
  Radford Semele CV31 ..110 E5
  Spring Pool CV34 ....108 E6
Spring Rd Barnacle CV7 ....51 B8
  Coventry CV6 ....49 F1
  Combrook CV35 ....131 F7
Spring St CV21 ....83 A2
Springbrook La B94 ....87 A7
Springdale Ct CV11 ....29 C3
Springfield Cl OX17 ....139 F6
Springfield Cres CV47 ....149 C3
  Bedworth CV12 ....39 B2
Springfield Ct B15 ....13 C5
Springfield Gr CV47 ......147 A3

Springfield House Speci Sch
B93 ....73 A5
Springfield Pl CV1 ...151 C4
Springfield Rd
Coventry CV1 ....151 C4
Hinckley LE10 ....31 D7
Nuneaton CV11 ....29 E2
Shipston-on-S CV36 ...149 C2
Sutton Coldfield B75,B76 ...13 A4
Tamworth B77 ....9 B4
Springfields B46 ....33 F5
Springfields Rd B49 ...143 A3
Springhill CV10 ....28 A8
Springhill Ind Pk CV7 ...36 C4
Springs Cres CV47 ...147 A3
Springside B98 ....103 B4
Springwell Rd CV31 ...110 D6
Spruce B77 ....4 A2
Spruce Ct 4 CV31 ...109 F5
Spruce Rd 6 CV2 ...50 B2
Squadron Cl B35 ....22 C4
Square La CV7 ....37 A1
Square The
Clifford Chambers CV37 ...129 F7
Coventry CV2 ....63 A7
Dunchurch CV22 ....99 B2
Ettington CV37 ....131 A3
Fazeley B78 ....9 A4
Kenilworth CV8 ....92 F4
Long Itchington CV47 ...115 D4
Nuneaton CV11 ....29 E2
Stockton CV47 ....147 C4
Swalcliffe OX15 ....142 F8
Tysoe CV35 ....138 B7
Wolvey LE10 ....41 B2
Wootton Wawen B95 ...113 A3
Squire Pl CV47 ....133 D7
Squires Croft
Coventry CV2 ....50 F1
Sutton Coldfield B76 ...13 A2
Squires Gate Wlk 1 B35 ...22 A3
Squires Gn LE10 ....31 F6
Squires Rd CV23 ....96 C3
Squires Way CV4 ....76 D6
Squirhill Pl 2 CV31 ...110 B7
Squirrel Hollow B76 ...13 A2
Sring La CV8 ....93 A5
Stable Wlk CV11 ....29 F2
Stableford Cl B97 ....102 B4
Stables The Berkswell CV7 ...58 C4
Hinckley LE10 ....31 D5
Royal Leamington Spa
CV32 ....105 C1
Stacey Ct CV22 ....99 B3
Stadium Cl CV6 ....49 D2
Stafford Cl CV12 ....40 C2
Stafford St CV9 ....18 B4
Staines Cl CV11 ....29 F7
Stainforth Cl CV11 ....30 A2
Stainsby Croft B90 ....71 B5
Staircase La CV5 ....60 C7
Stamford Ave CV3 ....77 C6
Stamford Gdns CV32 ...105 E1
Stanbrook Rd B90 ....71 A5
Stand St CV34 ....108 D5
Standard Ave CV4 ....60 B1
Standedge B77 ....10 A4
Standish Cl CV2 ....62 E2
Standlake Mews 14
CV31 ....110 C6
Stanford Cl B97 ....102 A3
Stanier Ave CV1 ....61 B4
Stanley Cl CV31 ....110 C7
Stanley Rd Atherstone CV9 ...18 B4
Coventry CV5 ....76 F8
Nuneaton CV11 ....29 A5
Rugby CV21,CV22 ....83 C1
Stannells Cl CV37 ...129 E8
Stansfield Gr CV8 ....93 B5
Stanton Bridge Prim Sch
CV6 ....61 F6
Stanton Rd CV31 ....110 C6
Stanton Wlk CV34 ...104 D1
Stanway Rd CV5 ....77 A8
Stapenhall Rd B90 ....71 A5
Staple Hill Ho CV35 ...122 D2
Stapledon Gn CV47 ...132 F7
Staples Cl CV12 ....40 C3
Stapleton Cl Studley B80 ...103 B2
Sutton Coldfield B76 ...22 B6
Stapleton Dr B37 ....33 A4
Stapleton La CV13 ....21 C4
Stapleton Rd B80 ....103 B2
Star Cnr CV23 ....101 B1
Star Ind Pk CV2 ....62 F5
Star La CV35 ....114 A4
Starbold Cres B93 ....72 B5
Starbold Ct B93 ....72 A6
Starbold Rd CV47 ...124 A4
Starcross Cl CV2 ....62 C7
Stare Gn CV4 ....76 D5
Stareton Cl CV4 ....76 F6
Starkey Croft B37 ....33 D2
Starley Cl CV3 ....79 A7
Starley Pk CV7 ....50 B8
Starley Rd CV1 ....151 A2
Starley Way B37 ....44 C6
Starmer Pl CV35 ....114 D6
Startin Cl CV7 ....49 F7
Station App Dorridge B93 ...71 F2
Royal Leamington Spa
CV31 ....109 F7
Station Ave Coventry CV4 ...75 D8
Warwick CV34 ....108 F8
Station Bldgs B46 ....23 B3

Station Dr B94 ....69 D1
Station La B94 ....89 D3
Station Link Rd B26 ...44 D4
Station Rd Alcester B49 ...143 A2
Arley CV7 ....36 B4
Balsall Common CV7 ...74 B7
Birmingham, Marston Green
B37 ....44 A8
Bishops Itchington CV47 ...124 A4
Chipping Campden GL55 ...135 C2
Claverdon CV35 ....114 A3
Clifton u D CV23 ....83 C3
Coleshill B46 ....23 F1
Cropredy OX17 ....134 C1
Fenny Compton CV47 ...133 E7
Hampton-in-A B92 ....57 B7
Harvington WR11 ....127 D3
Hatton CV35 ....114 C5
Henley-in-A B95 ....113 A5
Higham on t H CV13 ...20 C2
Hinckley LE10 ....31 D8
Hook Norton OX15 ...142 E4
Kenilworth CV8 ....92 F4
Knowle B93 ....72 B4
Lapworth B94 ....89 D4
Long Marston CV37 ...129 C2
8 Moreton-in-M GL56 ...140 A3
Polesworth B78 ....3 A2
Salford Priors WR11 ...127 F6
Shipston-on-S CV36 ...149 C3
Shustoke B46 ....24 B2
Stockton CV47 ....116 A3
Stoke Golding CV13 ...21 B4
Stratford-u-A CV37 ...144 C2
Studley B80 ....103 B2
Warwick CV34 ....108 F7
Wilmcote CV37 ....120 C5
Wythall B47 ....69 A3
Station Sq CV1 ....151 B1
Station St E CV6 ....61 E7
Station St W CV6 ....61 F7
Station Street W Bsns Pk
CV6 ....61 D7
Staunton Rd CV31 ...110 A5
Staveley Way CV21 ...83 B3
Staverton CE Prim Sch
NN11 ....126 E8
Staverton Cl CV5 ....60 A3
Staverton Leys CV22 ...100 A4
Staverton Rd NN11 ...126 F8
Staverton Sports Ctr
NN11 ....117 F1
Steeds Cl CV35 ....122 A7
Steele St CV22 ....82 C2
Steels La CV36 ....141 D7
Steeping Rd CV23 ...82 A3
Steeplefield Rd CV6 ...61 A5
Steeples The CV23 ...116 A5
Stephen Way NN11 ...126 F8
Stella Croft B37 ....33 C2
Stennels Cl CV6 ....60 F8
Stephen St CV21 ....82 C2
Stephens Rd B76 ....13 A4
Stephenson Cl
Daventry NN11 ....117 F2
CV32 ....105 C1
Stephenson Ct CV21 ...101 C1
Stephenson Dr B37 ...33 B2
Stephenson Rd
Bedworth CV7 ....50 C7
Hinckley LE10 ....30 E7
Stepney Rd CV2 ....62 A4
Steppes Piece B50 ...148 B3
Stepping Stones B50 ...148 B3
Stepping Stones Rd CV5 ...60 F4
Sterling Pk LE10 ....30 C8
Sterling Way CV11 ....39 B8
Stevenage Wlk 2 CV2 ...63 A7
Stevens Ho CV1 ....151 C4
Stevenson Rd CV6 ....61 A8
Stewart Cl CV4 ....60 D2
Stewart Ct CV37 ....37 A4
Stewart St CV11 ....29 C3
Stidfall Gr CV31 ....110 D6
Stileman Cl CV37 ...129 D2
Stiper's Hill B78 ....5 A1
Stirling Ave CV32 ...106 B6
Stirling Cl CV3 ....78 F8
Stirling Ct OX16 ....139 F3
Stirling Rd B90 ....70 E8
Stivichall Croft CV3 ...77 B6
Stivichall Prim Sch CV3 ...77 A6
Stocking La OX15 ....138 B5
Stocking Mdw CV23 ...53 C2
Stockingford Inf & Jun Sch
CV10 ....28 D3
Stockley Rd CV6 ....50 C6
Stocks Ct CV22 ....99 B4
Stocks La CV23 ....98 C2
Stockton Cl
Birmingham B76 ....22 C5
Knowle B93 ....72 B4
Stockton Gr 2 CV32 ...106 A2
Stockton Prim Sch
CV47 ....147 C4
Stockton Rd
Coventry CV1 ....151 D4
Long Itchington CV47 ...115 E3
Stockwell La NN11 ...126 B5
Stockwells GL56 ....140 A3
Stoke Gn CV3 ....62 A2
Stoke Heath Prim Sch
CV2 ....62 A6
Stoke La

Stoke continued
Stoke Golding, Wykin LE10 ...21 C2
Stoke Park Com Coll
CV2 ....62 B4
Stoke Park Mews CV2 ...62 A3
Stoke Prim Sch CV2 ...62 A4
Stoke Rd
Fenny Drayton CV13 ...20 C4
Stoke Golding CV13 ...21 C3
Stoke Row CV2 ....62 A4
Stokesay Cl CV11 ....29 B3
Stone Ave B75 ....13 A5
Stone Bridge LE10 ....32 C5
Stone Cross B46 ....23 B3
Stone Ct OX7 ....142 A2
Stone Mdw CV7 ....49 A6
Stone Pits Mdw CV37 ...120 C5
Stoneacre Cl CV4 ....59 B1
Stonebridge Highway
CV3 ....77 E4
Stonebridge Trad Est
CV3 ....78 B4
Stonebrook Way CV6 ...49 E3
Stonebury Ave CV5 ....59 E4
Stonefield Cl CV2 ....63 A8
Stonehall Rd CV22 ....99 A4
Stonehaven Dr CV3 ....77 C3
Stonehill Croft B90 ...70 F6
Stonehill Wlk B77 ....9 C3
Stonehills CV21 ....83 B4
Stonehouse Cl CV32 ...106 D5
Stonehouse La CV3 ...78 C4
Stoneleigh Ave CV8 ...93 A6
Stoneleigh Cl
Hartshill CV10 ....19 A1
Redditch B98 ....102 C3
Stoneleigh Ct CV11 ....29 C3
Stoneleigh Deer Park Bsns
Village CV8 ....94 D4
Stoneleigh Gdns CV11 ...29 C3
Stoneleigh Rd
Blackdown CV32 ...106 A7
Coventry CV4 ....76 E2
Kenilworth CV8 ....93 A6
Stoneleigh CV8 ....94 B3
Stonely Rd CV13 ....21 B3
Stonepits La B97 ....102 B2
Stoneton Cl CV47 ....147 B2
Stoneton Cres CV7 ...74 A6
Stoneway NN11 ...126 F5
Stoneway Gr CV31 ...110 D6
Stonewell Cres CV11 ...40 B8
Stoney Cl CV3 ....79 A7
Stoney La CV35 ....114 C6
Stoney Rd
Coventry CV1,CV3 ...151 B1
Nuneaton CV10,CV11 ...29 B6
Stoney Stanton Rd
CV1,CV6 ....61 E5
Stoneydelph Prim Sch
B77 ....4 A1
Stoneymoor Dr B36 ...22 D1
Stoneywood Rd CV2 ...62 F6
Stonleigh Ave CV5 ...76 F7
Stonydelph La B77 ...10 A4
Stornoway Rd B35 ....22 B4
Storrage La B48 ....85 A3
Stour B77 ....10 A3
Stour Ct CV36 ....149 C3
Stour View CV36 ....137 A8
Stourton CV37 ....72 B7
Stow Rd GL56 ....140 A2
Stowe Dr CV47 ....147 A2
Stowe Pl CV4 ....59 C1
Strachey Ave CV32 ...105 E2
Straight Mile CV23 ...98 A2
Stratford Ave CV9 ...18 B4
Stratford Butterfly Farm*
CV37 ....145 A1
Stratford Coll CV37 ...144 C2
Stratford Rd
Alcester B49 ....143 B2
Bidford-on-A B50 ...128 D7
Dorridge B94 ....71 B3
Drayton OX15,OX16 ...139 E4
Hampton Lucy CV35&CV37 ...121 E4
Harvington WR11 ...127 D3
Henley-in-A B95 ....113 A3
Illmington CV36 ....136 B7
Henley-in-A B95 ....113 D2
Loxley CV35 ....130 F8
Mickleton GL55 ....135 B7
Newbold-on-S CV37 ...130 E1
Shenington OX15 ....138 F7
Shipston-on-S CV36 ...149 C3
Solihull B90 ....70 D7
Tanworth-in-A, Hockley Heath
B94 ....88 C5
Temple Grafton B49 ...128 A2
Warwick CV34 ....108 C3
Wellesbourne CV35 ...146 A2
Wroxton OX15 ....139 B5
Stratford St Coventry CV2 ...62 A4
Nuneaton CV11 ....29 B3
Stratford-upon-Avon Gram
Sch For Girls CV37 ...144 B1
Stratford-upon-Avon High
Sch CV37 ....144 C2
Stratford-upon-Avon Hospl
CV37 ....144 C2

Stratford-upon-Avon Prim
Sch CV37 ....144 C1
Stratford-upon-Avon
Racecourse CV37 ...129 E8
Stratford-upon-Avon Shire
Horse Ctr* CV37 ...129 F7
Stratford-upon-Avon Sta
CV37 ....144 C2
Strath Cl CV21 ....101 A4
Strathearn Rd CV32 ...105 E1
Strathmore Ave CV1 ...61 E1
Strathmore Rd LE10 ...31 A7
Strawberry Fields CV7 ...46 B1
Strawberry Wlk CV2 ...50 D2
Streamside Cl CV5 ....60 A8
Stretton Ave CV3 ....78 C6
Stretton Cl LE10 ....31 D6
Stretton Cres CV31 ...110 B5
Stretton Ct Hinckley LE10 ...31 D3
Rugby CV21 ....83 B4
Stretton Rd
Nuneaton CV10 ....29 A3
Solihull B90 ....70 B8
Wolston CV8 ....80 A1
Strutt Rd LE10 ....32 A5
Stuart Cl CV34 ....108 D5
Stuart Ct Coventry CV6 ...62 A8
Royal Leamington Spa
CV32 ....105 E1
Stuart Gdns CV47 ...132 F7
Stubbs Cl CV12 ....39 A4
Stubbs Gr CV2 ....62 B5
Stud Farm Cl OX17 ...134 F1
Studland Ave CV21 ...83 C1
Studland Gn CV2 ....63 A4
Studley Coll Inf Sch
B80 ....103 C2
Studley High Sch B80 ...103 C2
Studley Rd B98 ....103 A4
Studley St Mary's CE Jun Sch
B80 ....103 C2
Sturley Cl CV8 ....93 B6
Sturminster Cl CV2 ...63 A4
Styles Cl
Hampton Magna CV35 ...114 F4
Royal Leamington Spa
CV31 ....110 A7
Styvechale Ave CV5 ...77 A8
Sudbury Cl CV32 ...106 C3
Sudeley B77 ....9 B4
Sudeley Rd CV10 ....39 C8
Suffolk Cl Bedworth CV12 ...39 A3
Coventry CV5 ....60 B3
Nuneaton CV10 ....28 E3
Suffolk St CV32 ....106 A1
Sugarswell La OX15 ...138 D7
Sulgrave Cl CV2 ....62 E7
Sullivan Ct CV6 ....62 B7
Sullivan Rd CV6 ....62 B7
Sumburgh Croft B35 ...22 A3
Summer La B76 ....22 D6
Summerhouse Cl B97 ...102 A3
Summerton Rd CV31 ...110 A5
Sumner Cl CV35 ...114 F3
Sumner Rd B46 ....34 A3
Sun Rising Hill OX15 ...132 D1
Sun St CV21 ....83 B2
Sunart Way CV10 ....28 C5
Sunbeam Cl
Birmingham B36 ....22 F1
Rugby CV21 ....83 B2
Sunbridge Terr CV21 ...83 B2
Sunbury Rd CV3 ....78 C6
Suncliffe Dr CV8 ....93 A2
Sunderland Pl CV35 ...146 B1
Sundew St CV2 ....50 D2
Sundorne Cl CV5 ....60 A4
Sunningdale B77 ....4 B3
Sunningdale Ave
Coventry CV6 ....49 D2
Kenilworth CV8 ....93 B4
Sunningdale Cl CV11 ...30 A1
Sunningdale Ct CV10 ...39 A4
Sunnybank Ave CV3 ...78 B5
Sunnydale Cres LE10 ...31 A7
Sunnydale Rd LE10 ...30 F7
Sunnyhill LE10 ....31 F6
Sunnyhill S LE10 ....31 F6
Sunnyside B95 ....119 F7
Sunnyside Cl
Balsall Common CV7 ...74 C7
Coventry CV5 ....60 F3
Sunnyside Ct CV10 ....28 F3
Sunnyside La CV7 ....74 C7
Sunset Cl CV9 ....12 B1
Sunset Dr CV37 ....129 C8
Sunshine Cl CV8 ....93 A2
Sunway Gr CV3 ....77 B6
Surrey Cl Hinckley LE10 ...31 E4
Nuneaton CV10 ....28 E3
Surrey Ct CV34 ....108 E8
Sussex Cl CV10 ....28 E3
Sussex Ct CV34 ....108 E8
Sussex Rd CV5 ....60 F4
Sutcliffe Ave CV37 ...130 D3
Sutcliffe Dr CV33 ...122 F8
Sutherland Ave CV5 ...60 A4
Sutherland Cl CV34 ...104 C1
Sutherland Dr CV12 ...39 A4
Sutton Ave CV5 ....59 C4
Sutton Cl NN11 ....134 F6
Sutton Ho CV22 ....82 B1
Sutton La OX15 ....137 E1
Sutton Pk CV10 ....28 B7
Sutton Rd B78 ....8 A4
Sutton Sq B76 ....22 E6
Sutton Stop CV6 ....50 B5

Swadling St CV31 ....109 F6
Swain Crofts CV31 ...110 B6
Swains Gn LE10 ....31 F6
Swalcliffe Park Sch Trust
OX15 ....142 F8
Swale Rd B76 ....13 A1
Swaledale CV4 ....76 D6
Swallow Ave B36 ...33 A8
Swallow Cl CV37 ...145 A3
Swallow Ct CV12 ....49 C8
Swallow Dr CV6 ....49 C1
Swallowdean Rd CV6 ...60 E8
Swallows Ind Est The
B90 ....70 E8
Swallows' Mdw B90 ...70 D8
Swan Cl GL56 ....140 A3
Swan Ct CV37 ....145 A1
Swan La CV2 ....61 F4
Swan St Alcester B49 ...143 A2
Royal Leamington Spa
CV32 ....106 A1
Warwick CV34 ....108 E6
Swan's Nest CV37 ...145 A1
Swancroft Rd CV2 ....62 A5
Swanfold CV37 ....120 C5
Swans Cl CV37 ....120 C5
Swanswell St CV1 ...151 C4
Swanswood Gr 3 B37 ...33 C3
Sweet Knowle Farm Cotts
CV37 ....130 A2
Swerford Rd OX15,OX7 ...142 D3
Swift Cl Birmingham B36 ...33 A8
Kenilworth CV8 ....93 A2
Swift Point CV21 ....66 C1
Swift Rd CV37 ....145 A3
Swift Valley Ind Est CV21 ...82 C4
Swift's Cnr CV3 ....77 E8
Swillington Rd CV6 ...61 B5
Swinburne Ave CV2 ...62 D2
Swinburne Cl CV10 ...28 A5
Swinburne Rd B97 ...102 B4
Swindale B77 ....10 A4
Swindale Croft CV3 ...78 F8
Swinford Rd Shawell LE17 ...68 B3
Shawell LE17 ....68 C4
Swiss Lodge Dr B78 ...8 C4
Sycamore B77 ....9 C4
Sycamore Ave B78 ....11 A4
Sycamore Cl
Hinckley LE10 ....31 E5
Sibford Gower OX15 ...142 D8
Stockton CV47 ....147 C4
Stratford-u-A CV37 ...144 C3
Wellesbourne CV35 ...146 C2
Sycamore Cres Arley CV7 ...37 A4
Birmingham B37 ....44 A8
Sycamore Ct Allesley CV5 ...59 F7
Kineton CV35 ....132 B5
Sycamore Dr B47 ....69 B6
Sycamore Gr Rugby CV21 ...83 A2
Southam CV47 ....147 A3
Warwick CV34 ....105 A1
Sycamore Rd
Coventry CV2 ....50 B2
Kingsbury B78 ....15 B4
Nuneaton CV10 ....28 D6
Sycamores The CV12 ...38 E2
Sydenham Dr CV31 ...110 B6
Sydenham Ind Est CV31 ...110 B6
Sydenham Prim Sch
CV31 ....110 C6
Sydnall Fields CV6 ...49 F4
Sydnall Rd CV6 ....49 F4
Sydney Ct 3 CV12 ...38 F2
Sykesmoor B77 ....10 A4
Sylvan Dr CV3 ....76 F6
Synkere Cl CV7 ....49 A6
Sywell Leys CV22 ...99 C3

T

Table Oak La CV8 ....74 B1
Tachbrook Cl CV2 ....50 C2
Tachbrook Link CV34 ...109 E4
Tachbrook Park Dr
CV34 ....109 E5
Tachbrook Rd CV31 ...109 F4
Tachbrook St CV31 ...110 A6
Tackford Cl B36 ....22 D1
Tackford Rd CV6 ....62 A8
Tackley Cl B90 ....70 B8
Tailor's La CV37 ....129 D1
Tainters Hill CV8 ....92 F4
Talbot Cl CV10 ....116 F4
Royal Leamington Spa
CV32 ....106 A1
Talbot Rd CV9 ....12 B1
Talisman Cl CV8 ....92 F3
Talisman Sq CV8 ....92 F4
Talland Ave CV6 ....62 A6
Tallants Cl CV6 ....62 A8
Tallants Rd CV6 ....62 A8
Talton Cl B90 ....71 A5
Tamar Cl CV12 ....38 C2
Tamar Dr B76 ....22 B7
Tamar Rd Bullington CV12 ...82 B2
Tamworth B77 ....10 A3
Tame Bank B78 ....15 B3
Tame Cl B77 ....9 A4
Tame Valley Bsns Ctr B77 ...9 C4
Tame Valley Ind Est B77 ...9 C4
Tame Way LE10 ....31 A8

Tameside Dr B35 .... 22 A1
Tamworth Bsns Ctr B77 .... 4 A2
Tamworth Bsns Pk B77 .... 4 A2
Tamworth Rd Corley CV7 .... 37 A1
  Fillongley CV7 .... 36 B3
  Keresley CV6,CV7 .... 48 D5
  Kingsbury B78 .... 15 B4
  Polesworth B78 .... 4 C1
  Sutton Coldfield B75 .... 7 A1
  Tamworth B77 .... 8 A3
  Wood End CV9 .... 10 B1
Tamworth Rd (Amington) B77 .... 4 A3
Tamworth Rd (Dosthill) B77 .... 9 B3
Tancred Cl CV31 .... 109 F5
Tandra Cl CV34 .... 109 D3
Tangmere Dr B35 .... 22 A2
Tanhill B77 .... 10 A4
Tankards Hill GL56,GL55 .... 136 B1
Tanners Ctyd CV34 .... 108 D5
Tanners Green La B47,B94 .... 69 B2
Tanners' La CV4,CV7 .... 59 B1
Tannery Cl CV9 .... 18 C4
Tannery Cl CV8 .... 92 F4
Tannery The CV36 .... 149 C3
Tanser Ct CV22 .... 99 B2
Tansley Cl B93 .... 71 F4
Tanwood Cl
  Redditch B97 .... 102 A3
  Solihull B91 .... 71 B8
Tanworth La
  Henley-in-A B95 .... 113 A7
  Redditch B98 .... 112 B8
  Solihull B90 .... 70 C5
Tanworth-in-Arden CE Prim Sch B94 .... 87 A2
Tanyard Cl CV4 .... 59 D1
Tapcon Way CV2 .... 62 F5
Tappinger Gr CV8 .... 93 C5
Tapster La B94 .... 88 F2
Tara Ct CV2 .... 62 B4
Tarlington Rd CV6 .... 60 E6
Tarn Cl CV12 .... 39 A2
Tarquin Cl CV3 .... 78 D7
Tarragon Cl CV2 .... 50 D1
Tarrant B77 .... 9 C4
Tarrant Wlk CV2 .... 63 A5
Tatchbrook Ct 5 CV31 .... 109 F6
Tatnall Gr CV34 .... 108 E8
Tattle Bank CV47 .... 147 A2
Taunton Way CV6 .... 49 A2
Tavern La CV3 .... 144 B1
Taverners La CV9 .... 18 B4
Tavistock Ct CV32 .... 105 F1
Tavistock Way CV11 .... 29 E5
Tavistock Wlk CV2 .... 62 C2
Tay Croft B37 .... 33 C4
Tay Rd CV6 .... 61 B6
Taylor Ave CV32 .... 106 B2
Taylor Cl CV8 .... 93 B6
Taylor Ct CV34 .... 108 D7
Tea Gdn The CV12 .... 49 E8
Teachers Cl CV6 .... 61 A5
Teal Bsns Ctr LE10 .... 30 D7
Teal Cl CV37 .... 144 B3
Teal Rd LE10 .... 31 A6
Teal Rd B80 .... 103 C2
Teasel Cl CV23 .... 83 B4
Ted Pitts La CV5 .... 48 B2
Teign B77 .... 10 A3
Telegraph St CV36 .... 149 C3
Telephone Rd CV3 .... 62 C2
Telfer Rd CV6 .... 61 B7
Telford Ave CV32 .... 106 B5
Telford Rd CV7 .... 36 A1
TelfordInf & Jun Sch CV32 .... 106 C5
Templar Ave CV4 .... 60 A1
Templar Ct CV11 .... 29 C3
Templars Prim Sch CV4 .... 60 A1
Templars The CV34 .... 108 F5
Templars' Fields CV4 .... 76 B7
Temple Ave CV7 .... 73 F6
Temple Ct Coleshill B46 .... 23 F1
  Rugby CV22 .... 83 B1
Temple End CV33 .... 123 E6
Temple Gr CV34 .... 108 D5
Temple Grafton CE Prim Sch B49 .... 119 E1
Temple Herdewyke Prim Sch CV47 .... 133 A7
Temple Hill LE10 .... 41 C3
Temple La B93 .... 73 A4
Temple Rd B93 .... 72 A3
Temple St CV21,CV22 .... 83 B1
Temple Way B46 .... 23 F1
Templeton Cl B93 .... 72 A3
Ten Acres B49 .... 143 B2
Tenby Cl CV12 .... 38 C1
Tenby Ct CV32 .... 109 E8
Teneriffe Rd CV6 .... 49 F1
Tenlons Rd CV10 .... 28 E2
Tennant Cl CV21,CV22 .... 83 C1
Tennant St CV11 .... 29 E3
Tennyson Ave Rugby CV22 .... 99 C4
  Warwick CV34 .... 108 C4
Tennyson Cl CV8 .... 93 C4
Tennyson Rd
  Coventry CV2 .... 62 C3
  Redditch B97 .... 102 B4
  Stratford-u-A CV37 .... 130 A8
Ternhill Ho 4 B35 .... 22 A2
Terrace Rd CV9 .... 18 B4
Terrace The CV35 .... 122 F2
Terrett Ct CV37 .... 145 A1
Terry Ave CV32 .... 105 C1

Terry Rd CV1 .... 61 F1
Tewkesbury Dr CV12 .... 39 C3
Thackeray Cl
  Lower Quinton CV37 .... 129 D2
  Nuneaton CV10 .... 28 A4
  Rugby CV22 .... 99 C4
Thackhall St CV2 .... 61 F4
Thame Cl B80 .... 103 C2
Thames Cl CV12 .... 40 A3
Thames Rd NN11 .... 117 F1
Thamley Rd CV6 .... 61 A4
Thatchers Cl CV15 .... 138 D3
Thatchings The CV22 .... 99 B2
Theatre Ct CV34 .... 108 D6
Theatre St CV34 .... 108 D6
Thebes Cl CV5 .... 59 B8
Theddingworth Cl CV3 .... 78 E8
Thickthorn Cl CV8 .... 93 B2
Thickthorn Mews CV8 .... 93 B2
Thickthorn Orchs CV8 .... 93 B2
Thimble End Rd B76 .... 13 A1
Thimbler Rd CV4 .... 76 C7
Third Exhibition Ave B40 .... 44 D4
Thirlestane Cl CV8 .... 93 C6
Thirlmere CV21 .... 83 B4
Thirlmere Ave CV11 .... 29 F6
Thirlmere Cl CV4 .... 59 E3
Thirlmere Rd
  Bedworth CV12 .... 39 A2
  Hinckley LE10 .... 31 A7
Thirsk Rd CV3 .... 77 C5
Thistle Way CV23 .... 83 B4
Thistlewood Gr B93 .... 90 B6
Thistley Field E CV6 .... 61 A7
Thistley Field N CV6 .... 61 A7
Thistley Field S CV6 .... 60 F6
Thistley Field W CV6 .... 60 F6
Thomas Jolyffe Prim Sch CV37 .... 145 A3
Thomas King Ho 6 CV1 .... 61 E4
Thomas Landsdail St CV3 .... 77 D8
Thomas Lane St CV6 .... 50 A1
Thomas Naul Croft CV4 .... 59 F3
Thomas Sharp St CV4 .... 76 A7
Thomas St Bedworth CV12 .... 39 A2
  Royal Leamington Spa CV32 .... 106 A1
Thomas Way CV23 .... 82 A3
Thomas Wlk B35 .... 22 B3
Thompson's Rd CV7 .... 48 F6
Thomson Cl CV21 .... 83 A3
Thorn Cl CV21 .... 83 B3
Thorn Stile Cl CV32 .... 106 E6
Thorn Way CV47 .... 115 D4
Thornbury Rise OX16 .... 139 F3
Thornby Ave
  Kenilworth CV8 .... 93 B3
  Solihull B91 .... 71 A8
Thorncliffe Cl B97 .... 102 A3
Thorncliffe Way CV10 .... 27 C4
Thorney Rd CV2 .... 62 B6
Thornfield Ave CV13 .... 21 C4
Thornfield Way LE10 .... 31 E8
Thorngrove Ave 7 B91 .... 71 C8
Thornhill Dr CV11 .... 40 C8
Thornhill Rd CV1 .... 61 D5
Thornley Cl CV31 .... 110 C5
Thornley Gr B76 .... 22 C6
Thorns Com Inf Sch CV8 .... 93 A3
Thornton Cl Coventry CV5 .... 59 C4
  Warwick CV34 .... 104 F1
Thornton Rd B90 .... 70 F6
Thorntons La CV47 .... 125 C7
Thorntons Way CV10 .... 28 A3
Thornycroft Rd LE10 .... 31 E8
Thorpe Rd OX17 .... 134 F1
Threadneedle St CV1 .... 61 D6
Three Acres La B90 .... 69 F6
Three Cocks La WR11 .... 127 D2
Three Corner Cl B90 .... 69 E8
Three Cornered Cl CV32 .... 106 E6
Three Oaks Rd B47 .... 69 B4
Three Pots Rd LE10 .... 31 E4
Three Shires Jct CV6 .... 49 E1
Three Spires Ave CV6 .... 60 F5
Three Spires Ind Est CV6 .... 50 A5
Three Spires Sch CV6 .... 60 B6
Throckmorton Cl CV35 .... 114 C8
Throckmorton Rd
  Bidford-on-A B50 .... 148 C3
  Redditch B98 .... 103 A4
Thurlestone Rd CV6 .... 60 F8
Thurne CV21 .... 82 B2
Thurnmill Rd CV23 .... 82 B2
Thursfield Rd CV32 .... 106 B3
Tibberton Cl B91 .... 71 A8
Tibbetts Cl B49 .... 143 B2
Tibbits Ct 8 CV34 .... 108 E6
Tiber Cl CV5 .... 59 F4
Tiber Way CV6 .... 82 C4
Tiberius Cl B46 .... 23 F1
Tidbury Cl B97 .... 102 B3
Tidbury Green Sch B90 .... 69 E4
Tiddington Cl B36 .... 22 E1
Tiddington Ct CV37 .... 145 C2
Tiddington Rd CV37 .... 145 B2
Tidmarsh Cl CV7 .... 63 A1
Tidmarsh Cl CV7 .... 74 A6
Tidmarsh Rd CV35 .... 114 F5
Tidmington Cl CV36 .... 149 C4
Tile Gr B37 .... 33 A5
Tile Hill La
  Coventry, Allesley CV4,CV5 .... 60 D2
  Coventry, Tile Hill CV4 .... 60 B1
Tile Hill Sta CV4 .... 75 D8

Tile Hill Wood Sch & Language Coll CV4 .... 59 D2
Tilehouse Green La B93 .... 71 F6
Tilehouse La B90 .... 69 E6
Tilehurst Dr CV4 .... 59 D1
Tilemans La CV36 .... 149 C4
Tilesford Cl B90 .... 71 A6
Tilewood Ave CV5 .... 59 F4
Tilia Rd B77 .... 4 A3
Tilton Rd LE10 .... 31 E6
Timber Ct CV22 .... 83 A1
Timberlake Cl B90 .... 71 B6
Timon View CV34 .... 109 E3
Timothy Gr CV4 .... 60 B1
Timothy's Bridge Rd CV37 .... 144 B2
Timsa Rd CV35 .... 132 E5
Tink-A-Tank CV34 .... 108 E6
Tinker's Cl GL56 .... 140 A3
Tinkers Green Rd B77 .... 10 A3
Tinkers La Earlswood B94 .... 87 E7
  Lapworth B94 .... 88 E1
  Mollington OX17 .... 133 F2
Tintagel Cl CV3 .... 78 D5
Tintagel Gr CV8 .... 93 B4
Tintagel Way CV11 .... 30 A5
Tintern Way CV12 .... 39 C3
Tipper's Hill La CV7 .... 36 C3
Tippett Cl CV11 .... 40 A7
Tipping's Hill B97 .... 102 B3
Tisdale Rise CV8 .... 93 B6
Titan Bsns Ctr CV34 .... 109 E4
Tithe La OX15 .... 142 D4
Tithe Barn Cl CV35 .... 114 F4
Tithe Barn La B94 .... 87 C6
Tithe Cl CV13 .... 21 B3
Tithe Ct NN11 .... 127 F2
Titheway WR11 .... 127 F2
Tithings The OX15 .... 142 F8
Tiverton Dr CV11 .... 29 F5
Tiverton Gr CV2 .... 62 D5
Tiverton Rd CV2 .... 62 D5
Tiverton Sch CV2 .... 62 D5
Tiveycourt Rd CV6 .... 50 A3
Tocil Croft CV4 .... 76 C6
Todenham Way CV36 .... 114 F6
Toft Hill CV23 .... 99 A1
Tokchong Rd CV35 .... 132 E5
Toler Rd CV11 .... 29 B5
Toll Gate Cl CV47 .... 144 A2
Toll Gate Rd CV47 .... 147 A3
Tollard Cl CV2 .... 62 F5
Tolson Ave B78 .... 9 A4
Tolson Cl B77 .... 9 C3
Tom Brown St CV21 .... 83 B2
Tom Ellis Ct CV7 .... 50 A8
Tom Henderson Cl CV3 .... 78 F7
Tom Hill B94 .... 87 B3
Tom Ward Cl CV3 .... 78 E7
Tom Williams Way B77 .... 9 A4
Tomkinson Rd CV10 .... 28 F4
Tomlinson Rd B36 .... 22 D1
Tommy's Turn La OX15 .... 137 E1
Tompson Cl NN11 .... 117 E5
Toms Town La B80 .... 103 C2
Tomson Ave CV6 .... 61 B4
Tomwell Cl CV47 .... 147 A3
Tonbridge Rd CV3 .... 78 A6
Top Rd CV7,CV12 .... 51 B7
Top St Appleby Magna DE12 .... 3 C4
  Northend CV47 .... 133 B7
Topcliffe Sch B35 .... 22 A3
Topp's Dr CV12 .... 38 E1
Topp's Heath CV12 .... 38 E1
Torbay Rd CV5 .... 60 C4
Torcastle Cl CV6 .... 61 F7
Torcross Ave CV2 .... 62 C6
Torpoint Cl CV2 .... 62 C6
Torrance Rd CV21 .... 82 C2
Torridge B77 .... 10 A3
Torrington Ave CV4 .... 75 E8
Torside B77 .... 10 A3
Torwood Cl CV4 .... 75 F6
Torwoods B77 .... 148 C3
Touchstone Rd CV35 .... 109 F2
Tove Ct CV23 .... 82 A3
Towbury Cl B98 .... 102 C3
Tower Cl
  Bidford-on-A B50 .... 148 C3
  Stratford-u-A CV37 .... 145 A3
Tower Croft
  Bidford-on-A B50 .... 148 C3
  Birmingham B37 .... 33 B4
Tower Hill B50 .... 148 C2
Tower Rd Bedworth CV12 .... 39 B2
  Rugby CV22 .... 83 B1
Tower St Coventry CV1 .... 151 A3
  16 Royal Leamington Spa CV31 .... 110 A7
Tower View Cres CV10 .... 28 B3
Towers Cl CV8 .... 92 F2
Town Fields Cl CV5 .... 60 B7
Town Ground CV35 .... 131 F5
Town Yd CV23 .... 64 C2
Townesend Cl CV34 .... 104 F1
Townhill OX15 .... 142 D4
Townsend Cl
  Binton CV37 .... 120 A1
  Newton Regis B79 .... 2 B2
Townsend Croft CV3 .... 77 C7
Townsend Dr CV11 .... 40 A6
Townsend La
  Long Lawford CV23 .... 82 A2
  Upper Boddington NN11 .... 134 E8
Townsend Rd
  Coventry CV3 .... 77 C8
  Rugby CV21 .... 83 B3
  Tiddington CV37 .... 145 C2

Townsends Cl CV11 .... 31 A1
Trafalgar Ct B50 .... 148 B2
Trafalgar Ho 3 CV1 .... 61 B2
Trafford Cl CV9 .... 12 B1
Trafford Dr CV10 .... 28 C6
Trafford Lodge 4 CV31 .... 110 B7
Traitor's Ford La OX15, CV36,OX7 .... 142 B6
Trajan Hill B46 .... 23 F1
Travellers Way B37 .... 33 D3
Tredington Cl B98 .... 103 A4
Tredington Pk CV35 .... 114 F6
Tredington Rd CV5 .... 59 A4
Treedale Cl CV4 .... 75 D8
Trefoil B77 .... 4 A3
Treforest Rd CV3 .... 78 C8
Tregaron CV37 .... 145 A2
Tregorrick Rd CV7 .... 50 A8
Tregullan Rd CV7 .... 50 B8
Treherne Cl B93 .... 72 A5
Treherne Rd CV6 .... 60 F7
Trelawney Rd CV7 .... 50 A7
Tremaine Way CV7 .... 36 C4
Tremelling Way CV7 .... 36 C4
Trenance Rd CV7 .... 50 A8
Trench La B49 .... 143 C2
Treneere Rd CV7 .... 50 B8
Trensale Ave CV6 .... 60 F4
Trent Rd Birmingham B26 .... 44 C4
  Bulkington CV12 .... 40 A2
  Hinckley LE10 .... 31 A8
  Nuneaton CV11 .... 29 D5
Trent Wlk NN11 .... 117 F1
Trentham Cl CV11 .... 39 F8
Trentham Gdns CV8 .... 93 C5
Trentham Rd
  Coventry CV1 .... 61 F4
  Hartshill CV10 .... 19 A1
Tresillian Rd CV7 .... 50 B8
Tressel Croft CV34 .... 109 E2
Trevelyan Cl
  Claverdon CV35 .... 113 F3
  Stratford-u-A CV37 .... 144 B2
Trevelyan Cres CV37 .... 144 B2
Trevelyan Ho 1 B37 .... 33 C1
Treviscoe Cl CV7 .... 50 A7
Trevor Cl CV4 .... 75 D8
Trevor White Dr CV22 .... 83 A1
Trevose Ave CV7 .... 50 B8
Trewint Cl CV7 .... 50 A8
Triangle The CV5 .... 60 B4
Tribune Trad Est CV21 .... 83 A3
Trident Bsns Pk CV11 .... 29 D3
Trimpley Cl B93 .... 71 F3
Trinculo Gr CV34 .... 109 F2
Trinity Churchyard CV1 .... 151 B3
Trinity Ct Banbury OX16 .... 139 F4
  Stratford-u-A CV37 .... 145 A1
Trinity Ho B78 .... 5 C2
Trinity Ct Hinckley LE10 .... 31 C8
  Rugby CV21 .... 83 A2
Trinity La CV1 .... 151 B3
Trinity RC Sch The CV34 .... 109 C6
Trinity RC Tech Coll CV32 .... 105 D2
Trinity Rd B78 .... 15 C4
Trinity St Coventry CV1 .... 151 B3
  Royal Leamington Spa CV32 .... 105 F1
  Stratford-u-A CV37 .... 145 A1
Trinity Vicarage Rd LE10 .... 31 C8
Trinity Wlk CV11 .... 29 E3
Triton Pk CV21 .... 82 C4
Triumph Cl CV2 .... 62 E3
Triumph Wlk B36 .... 23 A1
Troon CV23 .... 82 A3
Troon Way LE10 .... 31 D4
Trossachs Rd CV5 .... 59 F3
Troubridge Wlk CV22 .... 82 B1
Troughton Cres CV6 .... 61 A5
Troutbeck Ave CV32 .... 105 C2
Troutbeck Rd CV5 .... 59 F3
Troy Ind Est B96 .... 103 A2
Troyes Cl CV3 .... 77 E7
Trueman Cl CV34 .... 108 E8
Truemans Heath La B47, B90 .... 69 C7
Truggist La CV7 .... 74 E8
Trundalls La B90 .... 70 A5
Truro Cl CV11 .... 29 F5
Truro Wlk B37 .... 33 B2
Trussell Way CV22 .... 99 A4
Trust Cotts B49 .... 118 D8
Trusteel Hos CV23 .... 67 B3
Tryan Rd CV10 .... 28 C4
Tuckwell Cl CV47 .... 147 C4
Tudman Cl B76 .... 22 A7
Tudor Ave CV5 .... 59 F4
Tudor Cl CV37 .... 74 A6
Tudor Cres CV9 .... 12 B1
Tudor Ct Coventry CV7 .... 49 F7
  Stratford-u-A CV37 .... 144 C2
  Warwick CV34 .... 108 F6
Tudor La CV47 .... 147 A2
Tudor Rd CV10 .... 28 C6
Tue The WR11 .... 127 C6
Tulip Tree Ave CV8 .... 93 B5
Tulip Tree Ct CV8 .... 93 B5
Tulip Wlk B37 .... 44 C8
Tulliver Cl CV12 .... 39 B3
Tulliver Rd CV10 .... 28 C6
Tulliver St CV6 .... 61 B5
Tunnel Rd CV10 .... 27 B7
Turchil Rd CV22 .... 99 A4
Turchill Dr B76 .... 22 B8
Turlands Cl CV2 .... 63 A7
Turnberry B77 .... 4 B3
Turnberry Dr CV11 .... 40 C8
Turner Cl Bedworth CV12 .... 39 C2

Turner Cl continued
  Rugby CV21 .... 101 A4
  Warwick CV34 .... 108 B8
Turner Rd CV5 .... 60 D3
Turnhouse Rd B35 .... 22 B4
Turnpike Cl
  Balsall Common CV7 .... 74 B7
  18 Moreton-in-M GL56 .... 140 A3
Turnpike Dr B46 .... 23 C2
Turnstone Cl CV23 .... 83 B4
Turpin Ct CV31 .... 109 F6
Turpin Ho CV21 .... 83 B4
Turton Way CV8 .... 93 C4
Turville Cl LE10 .... 31 F5
Tutbury B77 .... 9 B4
Tutbury Ave CV4 .... 76 E6
Tutehill B77 .... 10 A4
Tutnall Dr B94 .... 88 B6
Tuttle Hill CV10 .... 28 F6
Tuttle Hill Ind Est CV10 .... 28 C7
Twenty One Oaks CV9 .... 17 C3
Twickenham Way CV3 .... 63 B1
Two Gates Com Prim Sch B77 .... 9 B4
Two Gates Ind Est B77 .... 9 B4
Twycross La CV9 .... 6 E1
Twycross Rd LE10 .... 31 F6
Twycross Wlk CV34 .... 104 D1
Twycross Zoo* CV9 .... 6 E3
Twyford City Ctr* WR11 .... 127 C1
Tybalt Cl Coventry CV3 .... 78 C5
  Royal Leamington Spa CV34 .... 109 D4
Tyler St CV37 .... 145 A2
Tylers Gr B90 .... 70 F6
Tylney Cl CV3 .... 63 B2
Tyne Cl B37 .... 33 C4
Tyne Rd NN11 .... 126 F8
Tynemouth Cl CV2 .... 50 D5
Tynward Cl CV3 .... 77 B5
Tysoe CE Prim Sch CV35 .... 138 C7
Tysoe Cl B94 .... 88 C6
Tysoe Croft CV3 .... 78 F8
Tysoe Rd Kineton CV35 .... 132 B4
  Oxhill CV35 .... 137 F8
Tyte End OX7 .... 142 A2
Tythe Barn Cotts WR11 .... 127 B2
Tythebarn La B90 .... 69 F6
Tything Rd B49 .... 143 B3

U

Ufton Croft CV5 .... 60 A3
Ufton Cross Rds CV33 .... 124 A8
Ufton Fields CV33 .... 123 F8
Ufton Hill CV33 .... 111 C1
Ullapool Cl B97 .... 102 B3
Ullenhall La B95 .... 112 D6
Ullenhall Rd Knowle B93 .... 72 A6
  Ullenhall B95 .... 112 E5
Ullenhall St B95 .... 112 E6
Ullswater B77 .... 10 A4
Ullswater Ave
  Nuneaton CV11 .... 29 F6
  Royal Leamington Spa CV32 .... 105 C2
Ullswater Rd
  Bedworth CV12 .... 39 A2
  Coventry CV3 .... 62 E1
Ulverscroft Rd CV3 .... 77 D7
Ulverston CV21 .... 83 B4
Umberslade Children's Farm* B94 .... 87 C2
Umberslade Rd
  Earlswood B94 .... 87 C1
  Tamworth-In-A B94 .... 87 E3
Underhill Cl Coventry CV3 .... 77 D3
  Redditch B98 .... 102 C3
Underpass The B40 .... 44 E4
Underwood Cl B97 .... 102 A4
Unicorn Ave CV5 .... 59 E4
Unicorn La CV5 .... 59 F4
Union Bldgs CV1 .... 151 B2
Union Pl CV6 .... 49 F4
Union Rd CV32 .... 105 F1
Union St Rugby CV22 .... 83 A1
  Stratford-u-A CV37 .... 145 A2
Unity Ho CV1 .... 151 C4
Univ of Birmingham (The Shakespeare Inst) CV37 .... 144 C1
Univ of Warick (Gibbet Hill) CV4 .... 76 C4
Univ of Warwick CV4 .... 76 C4
Univ of Warwick (Westwood) CV4 .... 76 B6
Univ of Warwick Science Pk CV4 .... 76 B6
University Farm 10 GL56 .... 140 A3
University Rd CV4 .... 76 C5
Upavon Cl B35 .... 22 A4
Uplands CV2 .... 62 A5
Upleadon Cl B97 .... 102 A3
Upper Abbey St CV11 .... 29 B4
Upper Cape CV34 .... 108 D8
Upper Crossgate Rd B98 .... 103 A4
Upper Eastern Green La CV5 .... 59 E5
Upper Farm Mdw CV35 .... 123 E1
Upper Grove St 8 CV32 .... 105 F1

Upper Hill St
Coventry CV1 ....151 A3
Royal Leamington Spa
CV32 ....106 A1
Upper Holly Wlk CV32 .106 A1
Upper Ladyes Hills CV8 .93 A6
Upper Pk CV3 ....78 D6
Upper Ride CV3 ....78 D5
Upper Rosemary Hill CV8 .92 E5
Upper Spon St CV1 .....61 B2
Upper Spring La CV8 ...92 F7
Upper Well St CV1 .....151 B3
Upper York St CV1 .....61 B2
Upperfield Way CV3 ....63 A1
Upton Dr CV11 ....39 F8
Upton Ho* OX15 ....138 E8
Upton La CV13 ....21 A4
Upton Rd CV22 ....82 B2
Utrillo Cl CV5 ....60 C3
Uxbridge Ave CV3 ......62 C2

V

Valanders La CV36 ....136 B6
Vale Cl CV21 ....101 A4
Vale The CV3 ....78 C8
Vale View CV10 ....28 E4
Valencia Croft B35 ....22 B4
Valentine Cl CV37 ....129 F8
Valiant Cl LE10 ....31 E4
Vallet Ave B49 ....143 A3
Valletta Way CV35 ....146 B1
Valley Cl B97 ....102 A3
Valley Dr
Harborough Magna CV21 .67 A1
Rugby CV21 ....83 A4
Valley La Lapworth B94 .89 E7
Tamworth B77 ....9 C4
Valley Rd Coventry CV2 .62 A6
Earlswood B94 ....70 A1
Nuneaton CV10 ....27 C2
Radford Semele CV31 ..110 E4
Royal Leamington Spa
CV32 ....106 C3
Valley The CV31 ....110 E4
Van Dyke Cl CV5 ....60 C3
Vanguard B77 ....9 B3
Vanguard Ave CV5 .....60 C1
Vanguard Rd B26 ......44 C4
Vardon Dr CV3 ....77 D4
Vauxhall Cl 4 CV1 ....61 E3
Vauxhall Cres B36 ....22 F1
Vauxhall La B49 ......119 D1
Vauxhall St CV1 ......61 E3
Vaynor Dr B97 ....102 B4
Vaynor Fst Sch The B97 .102 B4
Veasey Cl CV11 ....29 E3
Vecqueray St CV1 .....61 E2
Ventnor Cl CV2 ....62 E3
Ventnor St CV10 ....29 D6
Venture Ct LE10 ....30 E8
Verbena Cl CV2 ....50 B1
Verden Ave CV34 .....108 A4
Verdon Pl CV35 ....122 B8
Verdun Cl CV31 ....110 B2
Vere Rd CV21 ....83 C1
Vermont Gr CV31 .....110 C6
Verney Cl
Butlers Marston CV35 .131 F4
Lighthorne CV35 ......123 B2
Verney Dr CV37 ....144 C3
Verney Gdns CV37 ....144 C3
Verney Rd CV33 ......123 C3
Vernon Ave CV22 ......100 C4
Vernon Cl 5 Coventry CV1 .61 E2
Royal Leamington Spa
CV32 ....105 C3
Vernon Ct 9 CV1 ......61 E4
Vernons Ct CV10 ......28 F4
Vernons La CV10,CV11 .28 F4
Verona CV37 ....145 A2
Verona Cl CV11 ....30 A1
Vesey Cl B46 ....23 B2
Vicarage Cl
Atherstone CV9 ....18 C4
Dordon B78 ....10 B3
Vicarage Cotts GL55 ..135 B2
Vicarage Field CV34 ..108 B6
Vicarage Gdns OX17 ..134 C1
Vicarage Hill
Badby NN11 ....126 F5
Clifton u D CV21,CV23 .83 C3
Middleton B78 ....8 A1
Tanworth-In-A B94 .....86 F3
Vicarage La Coventry CV7 .49 D7
Dunchurch CV22 ....99 B2
Harbury CV33 ....123 F6
Long Compton CV36 ...141 C3
Priors Marston CV47 ..125 F4
Warwick CV35 ....108 A1
Water Orton B46 ....23 B2
Vicarage Rd
Cheswick Green B90,B94 .70 C3
Flecknoe CV23 ....117 B2
Napton on t H CV47 ..125 C8
Royal Leamington Spa
CV32 ....106 B3
Rugby CV22 ....82 C2
Stoneleigh CV8 ....94 B6
Tanworth-in-A B94 .....86 F1
Vicarage Rise 8 CV33 .122 F8
Vicarage St CV11 ......29 C4
Victor Hodges Ho CV47 .147 A2
Victoria Ave CV21 .....82 C2

Victoria Bsns Ctr 11
CV31 ....110 A7
Victoria Cl CV37 ......145 A2
Victoria Ct CV5 ....60 D4
Victoria Dr B78 ....9 A4
Victoria Mews
Coventry CV3 ....62 E2
Warwick CV34 ....108 D7
Victoria Rd
Atherstone CV9 ....18 C3
Bidford-on-A B50 .....148 B3
Hinckley LE10 ....31 F5
Nuneaton CV10 ....28 B8
Royal Leamington Spa
CV31 ....109 E8
Victoria St Coventry CV1 .151 D4
Nuneaton CV11 ....29 C4
Royal Leamington Spa
CV31 ....109 E8
Rugby CV21 ....82 C2
Warwick CV34 ....108 D7
Victoria Terr
Royal Leamington Spa
CV31 ....109 F7
Stockton CV47 ....147 C4
Victoria Way B50 ....148 B3
Victory Rd CV6 ....49 E1
Victory Terr B78 ......9 A4
Vienna Ho CV5 ....60 E2
Viking B77 ....9 B4
Viking Rd B26 ....44 C3
Villa Cl LE10 ....31 E4
Villa Cl CV12 ....40 C2
Villa Cres CV12 ....40 C1
Villa Rd CV6 ....61 B6
Village Hall Yd CV47 .115 D4
Village Mews CV22 ....99 B4
Village Rd OX17 .....133 D2
Village St WR11 .....127 D4
Villebon Way CV31 ...110 A2
Villiers Rd CV8 ....93 B5
Villiers St Coventry CV2 .62 A3
Nuneaton CV11 ....29 B3
Royal Leamington Spa
CV32 ....106 A1
Vincent Ave CV37 ....145 A2
Vincent Ct CV37 .....145 A2
Vincent St Coventry CV1 .61 B2
Royal Leamington Spa
CV32 ....106 A1
Vincent Wyles Ho CV2 .62 E3
Vine Ct CV34 ....108 F8
Vine La CV34 ....108 F8
Vine St CV1 ....151 C3
Vinecote Rd CV6 ......49 F4
Vinery Ct CV37 ....144 C1
Vineyard The LE17 ....43 C3
Violet Cl Coventry CV2 .50 B2
Rugby CV23 ....83 C4
Virginia Pl CV10 ......28 E3
Virginia Rd CV1 ......61 E3
Viscount Cl
Birmingham B35 ....22 A2
Royal Leamington Spa
CV31 ....109 F6
Vittle Dr CV34 ....108 D7
Vodena Ct 5 CV32 ...105 E1
Vogue Cl CV1 ....151 D3
Vulcan Ho B35 ....22 C3
Vulcan Way LE17 ......55 B4

W

Wackrill Dr CV32 ....106 C3
Wadburn B90 ....70 A5
Wade Ave CV3 ....77 B5
Wade Gr CV34 ....104 E2
Wade La CV33 ....123 D2
Wadebridge Dr CV11 ..29 F5
Wadham Ho B37 ....33 D3
Wadleys Cl B50 ......148 B3
Waggoner's La B78 ....7 C4
Waggoners Cl CV8 .....95 B3
Wagstaffe Cl CV33 ...123 E6
Wain Cl B49 ....143 B3
Wainbody Ave N CV3 ..77 A4
Wainbody Ave S CV3 ..76 F5
Wainbody Wood Sch
CV4 ....76 D2
Wainrigg B77 ....10 A4
Wake Gr CV34 ....108 B5
Wakefield Gr B46 .....33 B3
Wakeford Rd CV10 ....18 A2
Wakehurst Cl CV11 ....39 F8
Wakelin Rd B90 ....70 B7
Walcot Gn B93 ....72 A2
Walcote Cl LE10 ......30 F8
Waldron Ct CV37 .....145 A2
Walford Gr CV34 .....104 F1
Walford Pl CV22 .....100 C4
Walkers Orch CV8 ....94 B6
Walkers Rd CV37 ....145 A3
Walkers Way
Bedworth CV12 ....38 F1
Coleshill B46 ....34 A3
Kenilworth CV8 ....92 F3
Walkwood CE Mid Sch
B97 ....102 B4
Walkwood Cres B97 ..102 B3
Walkwood Rd B97 ....102 B3
Wall Ave B46 ....33 F5
Wall Hill Rd CV5,CV7 .48 B2
Wallace Ho CV34 .....108 D7
Wallace Rd CV6 ....61 A8
Waller Cl CV35 ......104 F7

Waller St CV32 ......106 A2
Wallingford Ave CV11 ..29 F7
Wallsgrove Cl CV32 ..106 B3
Wallwin Ct CV34 .....108 D6
Walmer Way B37 ......33 C3
Walmley Ash La B76 ..22 C6
Walmley Ash Rd B76 ..22 C7
Walmley Jun & Inf Schs
B76 ....22 A7
Walnut Cl Birmingham B37 .33 B1
Braunston NN11 ......117 E5
Harvington WR11 ....127 D3
Nuneaton, Camp Hill CV10 .28 C6
Nuneaton, Hartshill CV10 .28 A8
Walnut Croft CV9 .....17 B4
Walnut Dr CV32 ......106 B3
Walnut Gdns OX17 ...134 B5
Walnut St CV2 ....50 B2
Walnut Tree Cl CV8 ...93 A3
Walnut Way CV22 .....82 A1
Walsal End La B92 ....56 F3
Walsall St CV4 ....76 D7
Walsgrave CE Prim Sch
CV2 ....63 A6
Walsgrave Gdns 5 CV2 .63 A7
Walsgrave Hospl CV2 .62 F5
Walsgrave Rd CV2 ....62 D3
Walsgrave Ret Pk CV2 .63 B7
Walsh La CV7 ....46 E2
Walsingham Dr CV10 ..39 A7
Walter Scott Rd CV12 .39 C1
Waltham Cres CV10 ...28 B5
Walton Cl Coventry CV3 .78 E7
Nuneaton CV11 ....40 A7
Walton Fields CV35 ..132 C5
Walton Rd
Hampton Lucy CV35 ..121 F4
Wellesbourne CV35 ..146 C1
Walton W ay CV35 ...146 B1
Wandsbeck B77 ....9 C4
Wanley Rd CV3 ....77 D6
Wansfell Ct CV4 ......76 A7
Wantage Rd B46 ......23 E1
Wappenbury Cl CV2 ...50 C2
Wappenbury Rd CV2 ..50 D2
Wapping La B98 ......112 A7
Ward Gr CV34 ....109 C7
Warden Rd CV6 ....61 A6
Wardens Ave The CV5 ..60 B6
Wardens The CV8 .....93 C5
Wardour Dr B37 ....33 C2
Ware Orch CV23 .....101 B1
Ware Rd CV23 ....101 B1
Wareham Gn CV3 .....78 E5
Waring Way CV22 ....100 A4
Warings Green Rd B94 .70 D1
Warkworth Cl OX16 ..139 F4
Warmington Cl CV3 ...78 E8
Warmington Gr CV34 .108 B8
Warmington Rd B47 ..69 A6
Warmwell Cl CV2 .....62 F4
Warneford Mews 9
CV31 ....110 A6
Warneford Pl 10 GL56 .140 A3
Warner Cl CV34 ......104 D1
Warner Row 2 CV6 ....61 F7
Warren Cl
Royal Leamington Spa
CV32 ....106 A3
Rypton-on-D CV8 ......79 A1
Warren Dr B93 ....72 A3
Warren Field CV9 .....79 A1
Warren Gn CV4 ....75 F7
Warren Rd CV22 ....83 B1
Warrington Cl B76 ....13 A1
Warton Cl CV8 ....93 C4
Warton La Austrey CV9 ..3 A1
Orton-on-t-H CV9 ......6 B2
Warton St CV37 ......145 A2
Warton Nethersole's CE Prim
Sch B79 ....5 C2
Warwick Ave CV5 .....77 A8
Warwick By-Pass
Warwick, Hampton Magna
CV34,CV35 ....108 A5
Warwick, Heathcote CV34 .109 A1
Warwick Castle* CV34 .108 E6
Warwick Cl B80 ......103 B2
Warwick Cres CV37 ..144 C1
Warwick Ct
5 Birmingham, Chelmsley Wood
B37 ....33 D2
Coventry CV3 ....151 B1
Stratford-u-A CV37 ..145 A2
Warwick Dr CV9 ......12 B1
Warwick Gdns CV10 ..28 E4
Warwick Gn CV12 .....40 C1
Warwick Highway
Mappleborough Green
B80 ....112 A5
Redditch B98 ....102 C4
Warwick Hospl CV34 .108 E8
Warwick House Ind Pk
CV47 ....147 A1
Warwick La CV1 ......151 B2
Warwick Mews CV37 .145 A2
Warwick New Rd CV32 .109 C7
Warwick Parkway CV35 .108 A7
Warwick Pl
Royal Leamington Spa
CV32 ....105 E1
Shipston-on-S CV36 ..149 C3
Southam CV47 ....147 A2
Warwick Rd
Chadwick End B93 .....90 A7
Coventry CV3 ....151 B1
Ettington CV37 ......131 A4
Hanwell OX16,OX17 ..139 F5

Warwick Rd continued
Henley-in-A B95 .....113 C4
Kenilworth CV8 ....93 A1
Kineton CV35 ....132 B6
Knowle B93 ....72 D3
Leek Wootton CV35 ..104 F7
Norton Lindsey CV35 .114 C2
Sherbourne CV35 ....121 E7
Snitterfield CV37 ....121 C5
Southam CV47 ....147 A2
Stratford-u-A CV37 ..145 B3
Upper Boddington NN11 .134 E8
Wellesbourne CV35 ..146 B2
Wolston CV8 ....80 A2
Warwick Row CV1 ....151 B2
Warwick Sch CV34 ...109 A6
Warwick St Coventry CV5 ..60 F1
Royal Leamington Spa
CV32 ....105 F1
Rugby CV21 ....83 A1
Southam CV47 ....147 A2
Warwick Sta CV34 ...109 B7
Warwick Tech Pk CV34 .109 B5
Warwick Terr CV32 ..105 E1
Warwicks The CV35 ..114 F3
Warwickshire Coll
CV32 ....109 D8
Warwickshire Coll (Moreton
Morrell Ctr) CV35 ..122 E2
Warwickshire Coll of Ag
CV11 ....29 E6
Warwickshire Mus*
CV34 ....108 E6
Warwickshire Nuffield Hospl
The CV32 ....105 E5
Wasdale Cl CV32 .....105 C2
Washbourne Rd CV31 .110 A2
Washbrook La CV5 ....48 A1
Washbrook Pl CV36 ..136 B6
Washford Dr B98 .....103 B4
Washford Ind Est B98 .103 C4
Washford La B98 .....103 B4
Wasperton Cl 8 CV35 .78 F8
Wasperton La CV35 ..122 C7
Waste La
Baddesley Ensor CV9 ..11 C1
Balsall Common CV7 ..74 F5
Coventry CV6 ....48 F1
Watch Cl CV1 ....151 A3
Watchbury Cl B36 ....22 C1
Watchmaker Ct CV1 ..151 A2
Watcombe Rd CV2 ....62 E8
Water Orton La B76 ..22 E4
Water Orton Prim Sch
B46 ....23 B2
Water Orton Rd B36 ..22 E1
Water Orton Sta B46 ..23 A3
Watercall Ave CV3 ....77 C6
Waterdale B90 ....70 A5
Waterfall Cl CV7 ......46 C1
Waterfield Gdns CV31 .110 C7
Waterfield Way LE10 ..31 C5
Watergall Ct CV47 ..147 B2
Waterloo Ave B37 ....33 B4
Waterloo Cl
Stratford-u-A CV37 ..130 B8
Wellesbourne CV35 ..146 B1
Waterloo Cres B50 ..148 C3
Waterloo Ct CV34 ...109 A8
Waterloo Dr CV37 ...145 B1
Waterloo Ind Est
Bidford-on-A B50 ....148 C3
Birmingham B37 ......33 B5
Waterloo Pl 8 CV32 .105 F1
Waterloo Rd
Bidford-on-A B50 ....148 C3
Hinckley LE10 ....31 D8
Waterloo St
8 Coventry CV1 ....61 E4
Royal Leamington Spa
CV31 ....110 B7
Waterman Rd CV6 .....61 F6
Watersbridge Gdns CV10 .29 C1
Waterside Coventry CV6 ..50 C6
Polesworth B78 ....5 A1
Royal Leamington Spa
CV31 ....109 D7
Stratford-u-A CV37 ..145 A1
Waterside B24 ....22 A5
Waterside Ct CV31 ..110 B6
Waterside Dr CV21 ...83 B3
Watersmeet Gr CV2 ..62 B6
Watersmeet Ho B78 ..9 A4
Watersmeet Rd CV2 ..62 B6
Waterson Croft B37 ..33 D3
Watery La
Cheswick Green B90 ..70 D4
Corley CV7 ....47 D5
Coventry CV6 ....49 A4
Hook Norton OX15 ..142 D4
Keresley CV7 ....48 F4
Kineton CV35 ....132 C7
Knowle B93 ....72 E4
Pillerton Hersey CV35 .131 E3
Portway B48 ....85 D2
Shipston-on-S CV36 ..149 C3
Shustoke B46 ....24 B1
Ullenhall B95 ....112 E6
Warwick CV35 ....108 A1
Wathen Rd
Royal Leamington Spa
CV32 ....106 A2
Warwick CV34 ....108 E8
Watling Cl LE10 ......31 C4
Watling Cres CV23 ...68 B1
Watling Ct CV11 ......29 A1
Watling Dr LE10 ......31 C4

Watling Rd CV8 ....93 B6
Watling St Atherstone CV9 .19 A4
Dordon B77,B78 ....10 B3
Hinckley CV11,LE10 ..30 C8
Watson Cl 3 CV34 ...104 E1
Watson Rd CV5 ....60 D2
Watson Way CV7 ......74 C8
Wattisham Sq B35 ....22 A4
Watton Gn B35 ....22 A3
Watton La B46 ....23 D2
Watton's La CV47 ...147 A2
Watts La CV21 ....101 A4
Watts Rd B80 ....103 C1
Waugh Cl B37 ....33 B2
Wavebeck Ct CV23 ....82 A3
Waveley Rd CV1 ......61 A3
Wavendon Cl CV2 ....50 F1
Waveney Cl LE10 .....31 A8
Waveney Rd 9 C4
Waveney Cl LE10 .....31 A8
Waverre Ct CV21 .....83 B4
Waverley Ave CV11 ...29 F1
Waverley Rd
Kenilworth CV8 ....93 A4
Royal Leamington Spa
CV31 ....110 B6
Rugby CV21 ....84 A1
Waverley Sq CV11 ....29 F1
Waverton Ave B79 .....5 C2
Waverton Mews 15
CV31 ....110 C6
Wavytree Cl CV34 ...108 D7
Wawersmere Rd B95 .113 A2
Wayside B37 ....44 A8
Weale Gr CV34 ....104 F2
Weatheroak Rd B49 .143 B2
Weaver Ave B76 ......13 A1
Weaver Dr CV23 ......82 B2
Weavers Cl Redditch B97 .102 B2
Shipston-on-S CV36 ..149 C3
Weavers Cotts CV36 .141 C3
Weavers Hill B97 ....102 B2
Weavers Row OX15 ..139 A3
Weavers Wlk CV6 .....50 A4
Webb Dr CV23 ....83 B4
Webb Ellis Bsns Pk CV21 .83 A2
Webb Ellis Rd CV22 ..82 C1
Webb St CV10 ....28 D3
Webster Ave CV8 ......93 B5
Webster Steet CV6 ...61 E7
Webster Way B76 .....22 B8
Weddington Ctry Wlk*
Higham on t H CV10 ..20 B1
* Nuneaton CV10 .....29 B8
Weddington La CV10 ..20 C2
Weddington Prim Sch
CV10 ....29 D7
Weddington Rd CV10 .29 C7
Weddington Terr CV10 .29 D5
Wedge-Woods CV5 ...76 F8
Wedgewood Cl CV2 ..62 E8
Wedgewood Ho B37 ..33 B4
Wedgnock Gn CV34 ..108 D8
Wedgnock Ind Est CV34 .104 C1
Wedgnock La CV34 ..104 C1
Wedon Cl CV4 ....75 E7
Weigh Bridge Ct GL55 .135 B2
Weilerswist Dr CV31 ..109 F4
Welbeck Ave LE10 ....31 D4
Welcombe Ct CV37 ...145 B1
Welcombe Ctr CV37 ..18 C4
Welcombe Hills Ctry Pk (Nat
Res)* CV37 ....145 A4
Welcombe Rd CV37 ..145 A2
Welcome St CV9 ......18 C4
Welford Cl B98 ......103 C3
Welford Dr CV35 ....114 E6
Welford Pl CV6 ....61 D7
Welford Rd
Bidford-on-A B50,CV37 .128 D6
Long Marston CV37 ..129 B4
Rugby CV21 ....83 B2
Tamworth B77 ....9 C4
Welford-on-Avon Prim Sch
CV37 ....129 A6
Welgarth Ave CV6 .....48 F1
Welham Croft B90 .....71 A6
Well Bank OX15 .....142 D4
Well Cl B97 ....102 C3
Well La Shenington OX15 .138 F5
Staverton NN11 ......126 D8
Tanworth-In-A B94 .....87 A1
Well Spring Cl CV9 ...18 C4
Well St CV1 ....151 B3
Welland Cl
Long Lawford CV23 ...82 B3
Water Orton B46 ......23 B2
Welland Rd CV1 ....61 F1
Welland Way B76 ......22 A7
Wellesbourne CE Prim Sch
CV35 ....146 C2
Wellesbourne Dr CV37 .144 C1
Wellesbourne Rd
Alveston CV37 ....121 D3
Barford CV35 ....122 B7
Coventry CV5 ....60 A3
Lighthorne CV35 ....123 B2
Loxley CV35 ....130 F8
Wellesbourne Water Mill*
CV35 ....146 C1
Wellesford Cl CV35 ..146 C3
Wellington Cl CV35 ..146 B1
Wellington Dr CV37 ..145 A1
Wellington Gdns 1 CV1 .61 B2
Wellington Parkway
LE17 ....55 B3
Wellington Rd
Moreton-in-M GL56 ..140 B3

Wellington Rd *continued*
Royal Leamington Spa
CV32 ....106 C2
Wellington St CV1 .....151 D4
Wellington Terr GL56 ...140 B3
Wellington Way **2** B35 ...22 A3
Wellmeadow Gr B92 ......57 A7
Wells Cl CV10 ....27 C2
Wells Ct CV3 ....77 F7
Wells St CV21 ....83 A2
Wells Wlk B37 ....33 A1
Welsh Cl CV34 ....104 E2
Welsh Rd
Aston le W NN11 ......134 F6
Bascote CV47 ....115 B2
Coventry CV2 ....62 B4
Cubbington CV33 .....106 F2
Lower Boddington NN11 .134 E7
Napton on t H CV47 ...125 C5
Offchurch CV33 ....111 C4
Welsh Rd E CV47 ......147 B1
Welsh Rd W CV47 .....147 A3
Welton Cl B76 ....13 A2
Welton Pl CV22 ....100 E2
Welton Rd
Braunston NN11 ......117 C5
Warwick CV34 ....104 D1
Wembrook Cl CV11 .....D9 D2
Wembrook Ho CV11 .....29 E2
Wembrook Prim Sch
CV11 ....29 C2
Wendiburgh St CV4 .....76 B7
Wendover Rise CV5 .....60 C4
Wenlock Way CV10 ......28 B3
Wensum Cl LE10 ....31 B8
Wentworth Dr
Coventry CV4 ....49 B4
Nuneaton CV11 ....30 A1
Wentworth Rd
Royal Leamington Spa
CV31 ....110 D6
Rugby CV22 ....82 C1
Wesley Rd CV21 ....101 A4
Wessenden B77 ....30 A4
Wessex Cl CV12 ....39 A4
Wessex St B79 ....4 C4
Wessons Rd B50 ......148 C3
West Ave Bedworth CV12 .39 D2
Coventry CV2 ....62 A2
Keresley CV7 ....49 A5
West Cl LE10 ....31 D7
West End
Cleeve Prior WR11 ...128 A4
Hornton OX15 ....139 B7
West End Ct CV34 .....108 D6
West Green Dr CV34 ...144 A2
West Leyes CV21 ....83 A2
West of St Laurence
CV35 ....114 A8
West Orchards Sh Ctr
CV1 ....151 B3
West Park Cl CV37 ....144 A2
West Ridge CV5 ....60 A5
West Rock CV34 ....108 C4
West Side WR11 ....128 A2
West Side Bsns Ctr CV4 .75 F8
West St Coventry CV1 ...61 E3
Long Lawford CV23 .....82 A2
3 Royal Leamington Spa
CV31 ....110 A7
Shipston-on-S CV36 ...149 C3
Stutford OX15 ....139 A3
Stratford-u-A CV37 ...144 C1
Warwick CV34 ....108 D5
West View Rd
Royal Leamington Spa
CV32 ....106 C5
Rugby CV22 ....82 C1
Westbourne Gr CV22 ...82 C1
Westbrook Ct CV5 ......60 A4
Westbury Ct Coventry CV2 .62 A3
Warwick CV34 ....109 A7
Westbury Rd
Coventry CV5 ....60 D5
Nuneaton CV10 ....28 D3
Westcliff Dr CV34 ....104 E2
Westcliffe Dr CV3 .....77 B5
Westcotes CV4 ....60 B1
Westend Terr GL55 ...135 A2
Western Hill Cl B93 ...71 F6
Western Dr LE17 ....43 C3
Western Hill Cl B96 ..102 C1
Western Rd CV37 ......144 C2
Western Road Ind Est
CV37 ....144 C2
Westfield Barns CV47 .125 E4
Westfield Cl Dorridge B93 .71 F2
Nuneaton CV10 ....29 D5
Stratford-u-A CV37 ...144 C3
Westfield Cres CV35 ..146 B2
Westfield Ct LE10 .....31 C7
Westfield Ho B36 ......33 A7
Westfield Jun & Inf Schs
LE10 ....31 B7
Westfield Rd
Hinckley LE10 ....31 B7
Rugby CV22 ....82 C1
Southam CV47 ....147 A2
Westgate Cl CV34 ....108 D6
Westgate Ho **11** CV34 .108 E6
Westgate Prim Sch
CV34 ....108 D6
Westgate Rd CV21 .....83 C1
Westgrove Ave **3** B90 .71 A6
Westgrove Terr **1**
CV32 ....109 D8
Westham Ho B37 ....33 B4
Westham La CV35 .....122 A7

Westhill Rd
Blackdown CV32 ......106 A6
Coventry CV6 ....60 F6
Westholme Rd B50 ...148 B3
Westlea Rd CV31 ......109 E6
Westleigh Ave CV5 .....76 F7
Westmead Ave B80 ...103 C2
Westmede Ctr CV5 .....60 C4
Westminster Dr
Hinckley LE10 ....31 F4
Nuneaton CV10 ....28 B7
Westminster Rd CV1 ..151 A1
Westmorland Ave CV10 .28 E4
Westmorland Rd CV2 ...62 F4
Weston Cl Dorridge B93 .72 A2
Dunchurch CV22 ....99 B2
3 Royal Leamington Spa
CV31 ....110 C6
Warwick CV34 ....108 F7
Weston Ct
Long Compton CV36 ...141 D3
Rugby CV21 ....83 B2
Weston Hall Stables
CV12 ....40 A3
Weston La
Bubbenhall CV8,CV33 ..95 A2
Bulkington CV12 ....40 A3
Weston St CV1 ....151 C4
Westonbirt Cl CV8 .....93 C6
Westway CV21 ....83 A2
Westwood Bsns Pk CV4 .75 F6
Westwood Cl CV10 .....28 E3
Westwood Cres CV9 ...18 B4
Westwood Heath Rd CV4 .75 E6
Westwood Rd
Atherstone CV9 ....18 B4
Coventry CV5 ....61 A1
Rugby CV22 ....100 C4
Westwood Way CV4 ....76 A6
Wetherby Way CV21 ..144 C1
Wetherell Way CV21 ...83 B4
Wexford Rd CV2 ....50 D1
Weymouth Cl CV3 ......78 D5
Whaley's Croft CV6 ....61 B8
Wharf Ind Est The CV23 .65 A4
Wharf La B94 ....88 D4
Wharf Lodge CV31 ...109 D7
Wharf Rd Coventry CV6 ..61 F5
Stratford-u-A CV37 ...144 C2
Wharf St CV34 ....109 A8
Wharf The CV37 ......120 C5
Wharrage Rd B49 ....143 B2
Wharrington Cl B98 ..103 A4
Wharrington Hill B98 .103 A4
Wharcote Rd CV35 ...137 F8
Whateley Ct CV11 ......29 B4
Whateley Hall Cl B93 ..72 C7
Whateley Hall Rd B93 ..72 B7
Whateley La B77,B78 ...9 C2
Whateley Villas CV9 ....10 A1
Whateley's Dr CV8 .....93 A5
Wheat St CV11 ....29 D4
Wheatcroft Dr B37 .....33 D3
Wheate Croft CV4 ......59 F2
Wheaten Cl B37 ....33 D3
Wheatfield Cl B36 .....33 A7
Wheatfield Ct GL55 ..135 B6
Wheatfield Rd CV22 ...82 B1
Wheathill Cl CV32 ....105 E2
Wheatley Grange B46 ..33 F6
Wheatmoor Rd B75 ....13 A6
Wheatsheaf La B94 ...113 C8
Wheelbarrow La CV35 .114 A3
Wheeler Cl CV35 ....90 B7
Wheeley Moor Rd B37 ..33 A5
Wheelwright Ct **3**
CV37 ....144 C2
Wheelwright La CV6,CV7 .49 C4
Wheelwright Lane Prim Sch
CV7 ....49 B5
Wheler Rd CV3 ....78 A7
Whernside CV21 ....83 B4
Whetstone Dr CV21 ....83 C4
Whichcote Ave CV7 ....46 C1
Whiley Cl CV23 ....83 C4
Whimbrel Cl CV23 .....83 B4
Whitacre Rd Knowle B93 .72 B7
Nuneaton CV11 ....29 E4
3 Royal Leamington Spa
CV32 ....106 A2
Whitacre Rd Ind Est
CV11 ....29 E4
Whitaker Rd CV5 ....60 C3
Whitburn Rd CV12 .....38 C1
Whitchurch Cl B98 ...102 C3
Whitchurch Way CV4 ...75 F8
White Beam Rd B37 ....44 D8
White Friars La CV1 ..151 C2
White Friars St CV1 ..151 C2
White Hart La CV33 ..124 B6
White Horse Hill CV37 .121 B6
White House Hill B95 .120 B7
White Rose Ho **4** CV32 .105 F2
White St CV1 ....151 C3
Whitebeam Cl CV4 .....59 D1
Whitefield Cl CV4 .....75 D6
Whitehall Cl CV10 .....19 A1
Whitehall Rd CV21 .....83 A1
Whitehead
Kenilworth CV8 ....93 C7
Minworth B76 ....22 D6
Wellesbourne CV35 ...146 C2
Whitehead Gr CV7 .....74 B7
Whitehorn Dr CV32 ...106 B2
Whitehorse Cl CV6 .....50 B6
Whitehouse Cres CV10 .28 D3
Whitehouse Rd B78 ....11 A3
Whitelaw Cres CV5 ....60 C6

Whitemoor Dr B90 .....71 A7
Whitemoor Hill Rd B96 .118 D8
Whitemoor Rd CV8 ....93 B5
Whitemoors Cl CV13 ...21 C4
Whitemoors Rd CV13 ..21 C4
Whitepits La B48 ......85 F4
Whitepump Ce B89 ...112 C7
Whites Row CV8 ....93 A3
Whiteside Cl CV3 ......78 F8
Whiteslade Cl B93 .....72 A7
Whitestitch La CV7 .....46 C3
Whitestone Inf Sch CV11 .40 A8
Whitestone Rd CV11 ...40 B7
Whiteway OX17 ....133 F2
Whitfield Cl CV37 ....145 C2
Whitford Dr B90 ....71 C7
Whiting B77 ....9 B4
Whitley Abbey Com Sch
CV3 ....77 F5
Whitley Abbey Prim Sch
CV3 ....78 A6
Whitley Ct CV3 ....77 F7
Whitley Rd B95 ....113 B4
Whitley Village CV3 ...77 F7
Whitlocks End Halt B90 .69 E7
Whitmore Park Prim Sch
CV6 ....49 A1
Whitmore Park Rd CV6 .49 D3
Whitmore Rd CV31 ...110 A3
Whitnash Cl CV7 ....74 A6
Whitnash Dr CV3 ....62 D5
Whitnash Rd CV31 ....110 A4
Whitnash Rd CV31 ....110 B4
Whittington La CV34 ..109 B8
Whittington St CV1 ....12 A1
Whittle Cl Coventry CV3 .78 F8
Daventry NN11 ....117 F3
Rugby CV22 ....99 B4
Whittle Ct **9** CV32 ...106 A1
Whittle Rd LE10 ....30 E7
Whittleford Gr B36 .....22 C1
Whittleford Rd CV10 ...28 C4
Whittons Cl OX15 .....142 D4
Whitwell Dr B90 ....71 A6
Whitworth Ave
Coventry CV3 ....62 B1
Hinckley LE10 ....30 D7
Whitworth Cl CV35 ...146 B1
Whoberley Ave CV5 ....60 D2
Whoberley Hall Prim Sch
CV5 ....60 C3
Wickham Cl CV6 ....49 C2
Wickham Ct CV6 ......106 B3
Wickham Rd B80 .....103 C2
Wickmans Dr CV4 ......59 C2
Wiclif Way CV10 ....28 B3
Widdecombe Cl CV2 ...62 D7
Widdrington Rd CV1 ...61 C5
Widney Cl B93 ....71 F5
Widney La B91 ....71 A8
Widney Manor Rd B91 ..71 D7
Widney Manor Sta B91 .71 C7
Widney Rd B93 ....71 F5
Wigford Rd B77 ....9 B3
Wiggins Hill Rd B76 ...23 A7
Wight Croft B36 ....33 B6
Wigston Hill CV9 ......17 B3
Wigston Rd Coventry CV2 .50 F1
Rugby CV21 ....84 A1
Wike La B96 ....118 E8
Wilcox Cl CV47 ....124 A4
Wilcox Leys CV35 ....122 F2
Wild Goose La B98 ...103 B4
Wildcroft Rd CV5 ......60 A4
Wildey Rd CV12 ....38 D2
Wildmoor Cl CV2 ......50 B4
Wilford Gr B76 ....22 B6
Wiles Way B98 ....148 B3
Wilkins Cl CV35 ....122 A7
Wilkinson Way B46 ....25 A1
Willday Dr CV9 ....12 B1
Willenhall La CV3 .....78 F7
Willenhall Wood Prim Sch
CV3 ....78 C6
Willes Ct **3** CV31 ...110 B7
Willes Rd CV31,CV32 .110 A8
Willes Terr CV31 .....110 B8
Willett Gdns CV35 ...146 B2
William Arnold Cl CV2 .62 A4
William Batchelor Ho
CV1 ....151 B4
William Beesley Cres
CV11 ....40 E6
William Bree Rd CV5 ...59 C5
William Bristow Rd CV3 .77 E7
William Cl OX16 ......139 F4
William Cree Cl CV8 ...79 F3
William Groubb Cl CV3 .78 D7
William Iliffe St LE10 ..31 B7
William Malcolm Ho CV2 .62 E3
William McCool Cl CV3 .78 F7
William McKee Cl CV3 ..78 E7
William Morris Cty Prim Sch
CV10 ....139 F4
William Sheriden Ho
CV2 ....62 E3
William St Bedworth CV12 .39 D2
Nuneaton CV11 ....29 E3
Royal Leamington Spa
CV32 ....110 A8
Rugby CV21 ....83 A2
William Tarver Cl CV34 .109 A7
William Thomson Ho **2**
CV1 ....151 D4
Williams Rd CV31 ....110 E4

Willicote Pastures
CV37 ....129 D4
Willington St CV11 ....29 B5
Willis Croft B79 ....5 C2
Willis Gr CV12 ....39 C3
Willoughby Ave CV8 ...92 E3
Willoughby Cl
Alcester B49 ....143 A3
Coventry CV3 ....78 E8
Willoughby Pl CV22 ..100 B4
Willow Bank CV37 ....129 A7
Willow Bank Rd B93 ...71 F6
Willow Brook Rd CV8 ..80 A2
Willow Cl Alcester B49 .143 A1
Bedworth CV12 ....39 B5
Hinckley LE10 ....31 E5
Kingsbury B78 ....15 B4
Nuneaton CV10 ....28 A7
Whitnash CV31 ......110 B2
Willow Ctyd CV7 ....62 D7
Willow Dr
Cheswick Green B90 ...70 D4
Wellesbourne CV35 ...146 C2
Willow End GL56 ....141 A1
Willow Gdns CV47 ...147 A2
Willow Gr CV4 ....60 B2
Willow Gr CV4 ....32 B1
Willow Lea CV22 ......83 B1
Willow Meer CV8 ....93 B5
Willow Park Ind Est
CV13 ....21 B4
Willow Rd CV10 ....28 F5
Willow Sheets Mdw
CV32 ....106 E6
Willow Tree Gdns CV21 .101 A4
Willow Way
Birmingham B37 ....33 B1
Studley B49 ....103 C1
Willowbank Rd LE10 ...31 C7
Willowdale LE10 ....32 C7
Willowfields Rd CV11 ..30 A1
Willowherb Cl **5** CV3 .78 F8
Willowherb Way CV10 .29 C4
Willows CE Prim Sch The
CV37 ....144 C1
Willows Dr N CV37 ...144 C2
Willows The
Atherstone CV9 ....12 C1
Bedworth CV12 ....38 E2
Hollywood B47 ....69 A6
Stratford-u-A CV37 ...144 C1
Wilmcote CE Prim Sch
CV37 ....120 C4
Wilmcote Gn CV5 ......60 A3
Wilmcote La B95 .....120 A3
Wilmcote Sta CV37 ..120 C5
Wilmhurst Rd CV34 ..108 C8
Wilmot Ave B46 ....33 F6
Wilmot Cl CV7 ....74 B8
Wilncote High Sch CV1 .110 B5
Wilnecote High Sch B77 ..9 C4
Wilnecote Sta B77 .....9 C4
Wilson Cl CV22 ....82 B1
Wilson Dr B75 ....13 A5
Wilson Gn CV3 ....62 F1
Wilson Gr CV8 ....93 C4
Wilson's La CV6 ....49 F6
Wilsons La CV7 ....50 A6
Wilsons Rd B93 ....72 C6
Wilton Rd CV7 ....74 B5
Wiltshire Cl
Bedworth CV12 ....39 A3
Coventry CV5 ....60 B3
Wimborne Dr CV2 ......63 A8
Wimborne Dr CV10 ....28 B5
Wimborne Rd B76 .....13 A4
Wimpstone La CV37 ..130 B4
Winceby Pl CV4 ....59 D1
Winchat Cl CV3 ....62 F1
Winchcombe Rd B49 .143 B2
Winchelsea Cl OX16 .139 F5
Winchester Ave CV10 ..29 C7
Winchester Ct CV22 ...99 B2
Winchester Dr
Birmingham B37 ....33 A2
Hinckley LE10 ....32 B7
Winchester St CV1 ....61 E3
Wincott Cl CV37 .....145 B1
Windermere B77 ....10 A4
Windermere Ave
Coventry, Binley CV3 ...62 E1
Coventry, Upper Eastern Green
CV5 ....59 E4
Nuneaton CV11 ....29 F2
Windermere Cl CV21 ..83 B4
Windermere Dr CV32 .105 D2
Winderton Ave CV35 .114 E5
Winding House La CV6 ..50 A4
Windmill Ave **4** B46 ...33 F7
Windmill Cl
Ilmington CV36 ......136 B6
Kenilworth CV8 ....93 A6
Warton B79 ....5 C2
Windmill Croft CV32 ..106 A6
Windmill Cres CV6 .....50 A3
Windmill Dr CV32 ....102 B3
Windmill Gdns
Redditch B97 ....102 A3
Nuneaton CV11 ......126 E8
Windmill Hill
Bidford-on-A B50 ....128 E8
Royal Leamington Spa
CV32 ....106 D5
Windmill Hill The CV5 ..60 A7
Windmill Ind Est CV5 ..59 F7
Windmill La Astley CV10 .37 C3

Windmill La *continued*
Austrey CV9 ....3 A1
Balsall Common CV7 ...74 B4
Baxterley CV9 ....17 B3
Corley CV7 ....9 D2
Dorridge B93 ....71 F1
Dunchurch CV22 ....99 A2
Ladbroke CV47 ....124 D6
Ladbroke CV47 ....124 E5
Staverton NN11 ......126 E8
Tamworth-in-A B94 ...89 A8
Windmill Rd
Atherstone CV9 ....12 B1
Bedworth CV7 ....50 A8
Coventry CV5 ....50 A3
Nuneaton CV10 ....28 D7
Royal Leamington Spa
CV31 ....109 F5
Windmill Way
Southam CV47 ....147 A3
Tysoe CV35 ....138 B6
Windridge Cl CV3 .....78 C6
Windrush Cl B97 .....102 B3
Windrush Dr LE10 .....31 A8
Windrush Rd B47 ......69 B7
Windrush Way CV23 ...82 A3
Windsor Ct Coventry CV4 .60 B2
Hinckley LE10 ....32 A5
Nuneaton CV10 ....28 E6
3 Royal Leamington Spa
CV32 ....109 F8
Windsor Gdns CV10 ...28 E4
Windsor Pl **6** CV32 .105 F1
Windsor Rd B78 ....5 A2
Windsor St CV21 ......61 B2
Hinckley LE10 ....32 A5
Nuneaton CV11 ....29 B4
Royal Leamington Spa
CV32 ....109 F8
Stratford-u-A CV37 ..144 C2
Windward Way B36 .....33 B6
Windy Arbor Jun & Inf Sch
B37 ....33 D2
Windy Arbour CV8 .....93 B4
Windyridge Rd B76 ....22 A6
Winfield Rd CV11 ......29 B5
Winfield St CV21 ......83 B2
Wingfield Rd B46 ......33 F5
Wingfield Way CV6 ....49 A2
Wingrave Cl CV5 ....60 A6
Winifred Ave CV5 ......61 A1
Winnallthorpe CV3 ....78 E6
Winsford Ave CV5 .....60 B4
Winsford Cl CV7 ......74 A6
Winslow Cl CV5 ....60 C4
Winsham Wlk CV3 .....77 D3
Winslow Cl Coventry CV5 .60 B3
Royal Leamington Spa
CV32 ....105 C1
Winslow Ho **1** CV1 ...61 B2
Winspear Cl CV7 ......46 B1
Winster Ave B93 ....71 E4
Winster Cl CV7 ....49 A7
Winston Ave CV2 ......62 D8
Winston Cl Coventry CV2 .62 D8
Stratford-u-A CV37 ..144 B1
Winterdene CV7 ....74 B7
Winterton Rd CV12 ....40 C2
Winthorpe Dr B91 .....71 C8
Winton Gr B76 ....22 A6
Winwick Pl CV22 ......99 B4
Winyates Rd CV33 ...123 D2
Wise Gr Rugby CV21 ...83 C1
Warwick CV34 ....104 E2
Wise St CV31 ....109 F7
Wise Terr CV31 ......109 F7
Wishaw Cl B98 ....103 A4
Wishaw La Curdworth B76 .23 A7
Middleton B78 ....14 C6
Minworth B76 ....22 E7
Wisley Gr CV8 ....93 C5
Wistaria Cl CV2 ....50 B2
Witham The NN11 ....117 F1
Witherley CE Prim Sch
CV9 ....19 A4
Witherley Rd
Atherstone CV9 ....18 C4
Witherley CV9 ....19 A3
Withington Gr B93 .....71 E4
Withy Hill Rd B75 .....13 B8
Withybrook Cl CV2 ....50 D2
Withybrook La CV7 ....51 F5
Withybrook Rd
Bulkington CV12 ....40 D2
Shilton CV7 ....51 D8
Withycombe Dr CV10 .139 F3
Witnell Rd CV6 ....61 C6
Wixford Rd B49,B50 ..119 B1
Woburn Cl CV31 ......110 C6
Woburn Dr CV10 ....28 B4
Woburn Gr CV8 ....93 D6
Wolds End Cl GL55 ...135 B2
Wolds La LE10 ....41 C2
Wolfe Rd CV4 ....75 F8
Wolford Rd GL56 .....140 D6
Wolfe End CV2 ....50 B7
Wollacombe Dr CV6 ...139 F3
Wolsey Cl CV3 ....99 B3
Wolsey Rd CV36 ......23 A1
Wolston Bsns Pk CV8 ..80 A2
Wolston La CV8 ....79 E2
Wolston St Margaret's CE
Prim Sch CV8 ....80 A2

Wolverton Prim Sch
CV35 ....114 B2
Wolverton Rd
Birmingham, Marston Green
B37 ....44 B7
Coventry CV5 ....60 A3
Norton Lindsey CV35 ......114 C2
Snitterfield CV37 ....121 B7
Wolvey CE Prim Sch
LE10 ....41 B2
Wolvey CE Prim Sch (annexe)
CV7 ....51 E5
Wolvey Rd
Bulkington CV12 ....40 E2
Hinckley LE10 ....31 E4
Wood Cl B46 ....33 F7
Wood Croft B47 ....69 B6
Wood Ct CV2 ....62 D7
Wood End La
Fillongley CV7 ....37 A2
Tanworth-In-A B94 ....86 F5
Wood End Prim Sch
Coventry CV2 ....50 D1
Wood End CV9 ....10 B1
Wood End Sta B94 ....86 F4
Wood Hill Rise CV6 ......49 D2
Wood La Arley CV7 ....26 B1
Aston Cantlow B49,B95 ....119 F5
Astwood Bank B96 ....118 C6
Birmingham, Marston Green
B37 ....44 A8
Cherington CV36 ....141 D7
Earlswood B94 ....69 E1
Hampton-in-A B92 ....56 F2
Higham on t H CV13 ....20 C2
Nuneaton CV10 ....28 A8
Shilton CV7 ....51 D5
Wood St Bedworth CV12 ...39 B5
Nuneaton CV10 ....28 F4
Royal Leamington Spa
CV32 ....110 A8
Rugby CV21 ....83 A2
Southam CV47 ....147 A2
Stratford-u-A CV37 ....145 A1
Wood End CV9 ....10 B1
Wood Terr B96 ....118 D8
Woodbank LE10 ....32 A7
Woodberrow La B97 ......102 B3
Woodberry Dr B76 ....13 A2
Woodbine Cotts ⛓
CV32 ....109 E8
Woodbine St ⛓ CV32 ....109 E8
Woodbine Wlk B37 ....33 D2
Woodbridge Ct CV21 ......83 A2
Woodbridge Pk CV9 ......16 B2
Woodbrook Ho ⛓ B37 .....33 B2
Woodburn Cl CV5 ....60 B4
Woodbury Cl B97 ....102 A3
Woodby La LE17 ....55 C4
Woodchester Rd B93 ......71 E2
Woodclose Ave CV6 ....60 F6
Woodclose Rd B37 ....33 A3
Woodcock Cl B94 ....86 E3
Woodcot Park Dr CV37 ...120 B5
Woodcote Ave
Kenilworth CV8 ....92 D6
Nuneaton CV11 ....29 F8

Woodcote Dr
Dorridge B93 ....72 B2
Leek Wootton CV35 ....104 F7
Woodcote La CV8,CV35 ...104 F7
Woodcote Rd
Royal Leamington Spa
CV32 ....105 F3
Warwick CV34 ....108 F8
Woodcraft Cl CV4 ....60 A2
Woodend Croft CV4 ....75 E8
Woodfield Rd
Coventry CV5 ....76 E8
Hinckley LE10 ....31 C6
Woodford Cl
Ash Green CV7 ....49 D5
Nuneaton CV10 ....28 D4
Woodford La CV9,CV10 ....19 B2
Woodgate Rd LE10 ....32 A8
Woodgreen Cl B97 ....102 A4
Woodhall Cl CV11 ....30 A2
Woodhams Rd CV3 ....78 C3
Woodhouse Cl CV3 ....78 E8
Woodhouse High Sch B77 ..4 A2
Woodhouse La B77 ....4 A3
Woodhouse St CV34 ......108 D6
Woodington Rd B75 ....13 B5
Woodland Ave
Claybrooke Magna LE17 ....43 C3
Coventry CV5 ....76 F7
Hinckley LE10 ....32 A7
Woodland Rd
Kenilworth CV8 ....93 B7
Tamworth B77 ....4 A2
Woodland Way B78 ....10 C4
Woodlands Ave B46 ......23 B2
Woodlands Cl B78 ....11 A3
Woodlands Ct
Binley Woods CV3 ....79 D7
Coventry CV5 ....77 A8
Woodlands Farm Rd B24 ..22 A4
Woodlands Inf Sch B90 ...70 B8
Woodlands Jun & Inf Sch
B36 ....33 B6
Woodlands La
Bedworth CV12 ....38 E4
Solihull B90 ....70 B8
Woodlands Rd
Binley Woods CV3 ....79 D7
Stratford-u-A CV37 ....144 C8
Woodlands Sch The CV5 ...59 D3
Woodlands Terr B78 ......11 A3
Woodlands The
Nuneaton CV10 ....28 A8
Staverton NN11 ....126 D8
Sutton Coldfield B75 .....13 A6
Wood End CV9 ....10 B1
Woodlands Way B37 ....33 D3
Woodleigh Rd CV4 ....75 F5
Woodloes Ave N CV34 ...104 F2
Woodloes Ave S CV34 ...104 F1
Woodloes Inf Sch CV34 ..104 E1
Woodloes Jun Sch
CV34 ....104 E1
Woodloes La CV34,CV35 ..104 F2
Woodloes Rd B90 ....70 B7
Woodman Ct CV37 ....144 C2
Woodmill Mdw CV8 ....93 B6
Woodpecker Gr B36 ....33 A7
Woodridge Ave CV5 ....60 A6

Woodroffe Wlk CV6 ....50 A4
Woodrow Cres B93 ....72 A5
Woodrow Ctr B98 ....103 A4
Woodrow Dr B98 ....103 A3
Woodrow Fst Sch B98 ...103 A4
Woodrow N B98 ....103 A4
Woodrow S B98 ....103 A4
Woodrow Wlk B98 ....103 A4
Woodrush Dr B47 ....69 A5
Woodrush High Sch The
B47 ....69 A6
Woods Piece
Coventry CV7 ....49 A6
Keresley CV7 ....48 F6
Woodshires Rd CV6 ....49 F5
Woodsia Cl CV23 ....83 B4
Woodside Arley CV7 ......26 B1
Grendon CV9 ....11 B1
Woodside Ave N CV3 ......76 F6
Woodside Ave S CV3 ......76 F5
Woodside Bsns Pk CV21 ..83 A2
Woodside Cl CV9 ....10 B1
Woodside Cres B93 ....72 B4
Woodside Pk CV21 ....83 A3
Woodstock Cl LE10 ....32 A5
Woodstock Cres B93 .....71 F3
Woodstock Rd
Coventry CV3 ....77 D7
Nuneaton CV11 ....29 E1
Woodston Gr B91 ....71 C8
Woodville Rd CV34 ......108 E8
Woodward Cl CV31 ....110 A2
Woodward Ct CV37 ....121 B6
Woodway CV35 ....114 F3
Woodway Ave CV35 ....114 F3
Woodway Cl CV2 ....62 F8
Woodway La
Claybrooke Parva LE17 ....43 B2
Coventry CV2 ....50 F1
**Woodway Park Sch & Com
Coll** CV2 ....50 F1
Woodway Rd OX15 ....142 D8
Woodway Wlk CV2 ....62 E8
Woolaston Rd B98 ....103 B4
Woolgrove St CV6 ....50 A3
Wooll St ⛓ CV21 ....83 A2
Woolpack The ⛓
CV34 ....108 E6
Woolpack Way CV9 ....18 B4
Woolscott Rd CV23 ......117 B6
Woolwich Rd CV11 ....40 F6
Wootton Cl CV37 ....145 B1
Wootton Ct Coventry CV2 .62 D7
⛓ Royal Leamington Spa
CV32 ....105 F2
Wootton Green La CV7 ....74 A8
Wootton Hall B95 ....113 B2
Wootton La CV7 ....57 E1
Wootton St CV12 ....39 D3
Wootton Wawen CE Prim Sch
B95 ....113 A2
Wootton Wawen Sta
B95 ....113 A2
Worcester Cl CV5 ....60 B7
Worcester Cl CV6 ....50 B4
Worcester Ho B36 ....33 A8
Worcester Pl CV36 ......149 A3
Worcester Rd CV8 ....93 B3
Worcester St CV21 ....83 A2
Worcester Wlk B37 ....33 A1

Wordsworth Ave
Redditch B97 ....102 B4
Warwick CV34 ....108 D5
Wordsworth Dr CV8 ....93 C4
Wordsworth Rd
Bedworth CV12 ....39 D1
Coventry CV2 ....62 C4
Rugby CV22 ....99 C3
Workhouse La LE10 ....32 A4
Works Rd B26 ....44 A3
**World of Shakespeare
(Mus)*** CV37 ....145 A1
Worsdell Cl CV1 ....61 B4
Worsfold Cl CV5 ....60 A7
Worthy Down Wlk B35 ....22 B3
Wr Twr La CV8 ....92 F6
Wren Cl DE12 ....3 C4
Wren St CV2 ....61 F3
Wren's Nest Cl B90 ....70 A5
Wrenbury Dr CV6 ....50 A4
Wright Cl B78 ....15 B3
Wright St CV1 ....61 E4
Wrigsham St CV3 ....77 D8
Wroxall Dr CV3 ....78 D5
Wroxton CE Prim Sch
OX15 ....139 D4
Wroxton Coll OX15 ......139 D4
Wroxton Ct OX15 ....139 D4
Wyatt Cl CV12 ....39 B3
Wyatt Ho CV2 ....62 D7
Wyatt Rd B75 ....13 B5
Wych Elm Dr ⛓ CV31 ....109 F5
Wych-Elm Cl CV22 ....82 A1
Wychbold Cl B97 ....102 A3
Wychbury B76 ....13 A1
Wychwood Ave
Coventry CV3 ....77 C3
Knowle B93 ....72 B8
Wychwood Cl ⛓ CV33 ...122 F8
Wychwood Dr B97 ....102 B3
Wycliffe Gr CV2 ....62 B5
Wycliffe Rd W CV2 ....62 C5
Wye Cl Bulkington CV12 ...40 B2
Hinckley LE10 ....31 A8
Royal Leamington Spa
CV32 ....106 C3
Sutton Coldfield B76 .....22 A7
Wyke Rd CV2 ....62 D7
Wykeham Ho CV21 ....83 B4
Wykeley Rd CV2 ....62 C4
Wyken Ave CV2 ....62 D5
Wyken Cl B93 ....71 E2
Wyken Croft CV2 ....62 D6
Wyken Croft Nature Pk*
CV2 ....62 D6
Wyken Croft Prim Sch
CV2 ....62 E5
Wyken Grange Rd CV2 ....62 C5
Wyken Way CV2 ....62 B5
Wykham La OX15,OX16 ...139 F1
Wykin La CV13 ....21 C3
Wyld Ct CV5 ....60 B5
Wyley Rd CV6 ....61 B5
Wynbrook Gr B90 ....71 A6
Wyncote Cl CV8 ....93 A4
Wyndshiels B46 ....34 A3
Wynter Rd CV22 ....82 B2
Wyre La CV37 ....129 B3
Wythall Sta B47 ....69 C4
Wythburn Way CV21 ......83 B4

Wythwood Gr B47 ....69 C6
Wythwood Rd B47 ....69 C6
Wyver Cres CV2 ....62 C3
Wyvern Cl CV35 ....146 B1

Yardley Chase Rd CV35 ..13?
Yardley Cl CV34 ....104?
Yardley St CV1 ....61 ?
Yarmouth Gn CV4 ....75 ?
Yarn Cl B47 ....69 A?
Yarningale Cl B98 ....102 C3
Yarningale La CV35 ......113 E5
Yarningale Rd CV3 ....78 D5
Yarningdale ⛓ B90 ....70 C8
Yarranton Cl CV37 ......144 C3
Yarrow Cl CV23 ....83 B4
Yates Ave CV21 ....82 C3
Yatesbury Ave B35 ....22 A3
Yelverton Rd CV6 ....61 D8
Yeomanry Cl ⛓ CV34 ....108 F7
Yew Cl CV3 ....62 C1
Yew Tree Cl B94 ....89 D3
Yew Tree Ct Austrey CV9 ..3 A1
⛓ Royal Leamington Spa
CV31 ....109 F5
Yew Tree Gdns B95 ......113 A4
Yew Tree Hill CV23 ......64 C2
Yew Tree La B94 ....113 D8
Yew Trees The B95 ......113 B4
Yew Wlk B37 ....33 B2
Yewdale Cres CV2 ....50 E1
Yewdale Ct CV2 ....50 F1
Yews The CV12 ....38 E2
York Ave Atherstone CV9 ..12 C1
Bedworth CV12 ....39 D2
York Cl Coventry CV3 .....78 C5
Studley B80 ....103 B2
York Rd CV31 ....109 F8
York St Coventry CV1 .....61 B2
Nuneaton CV11 ....29 A4
Rugby CV21 ....82 C2
Yorkminster Dr B37 ......33 D3
Yorksand Rd B78 ....8 C4
Young Cl CV34 ....108 B5
Yule Rd CV2 ....62 D5
Yvonne Rd B97 ....102 B4

Z

Zorrina Cl CV10 ....28 B5